FORTEVIOT

A PICTISH AND SCOTTISH
ROYAL CENTRE

FORTEVIOT

A PICTISH AND SCOTTISH ROYAL CENTRE

NICK AITCHISON

TEMPUS

For Blane

First published 2006

Tempus Publishing Limited
The Mill, Brimscombe Port,
Stroud, Gloucestershire, GL5 2QG
www.tempus-publishing.com

British Library Cataloguing in Publication Data.
A catalogue record for this book is available from the British Library.

ISBN 0 7524 3599 X

Typesetting and origination by Tempus Publishing Limited
Printed in Great Britain

CONTENTS

Acknowledgements   7
Introduction   9

PART 1   THE ROYAL CENTRE

1   Pictish and Scottish kings at Forteviot   15
2   Topography and archaeology   31
3   The character and functions of the royal centre   51
4   The church at Forteviot   85
5   Sculpture and metalwork   103

PART 2   THE FORTEVIOT ARCH

6   Introducing the arch   143
7   Imagery and interpretation   163
8   The iconography of the arch   189
9   The arch, architecture and liturgy   209

PART 3   EPILOGUE

10   The fate of the royal centre and its church   243

Appendix: visiting Forteviot and its arch   257
Bibliography   259
Index   283

ACKNOWLEDGEMENTS

The origins of this book lie in my doctoral research on the royal and ecclesiastical centres of early medieval Ireland (published as Aitchison 1994). To me at least, this appeared to offer an approach and parallels that could assist the study and interpretation of early medieval power centres elsewhere and the Pictish and early Scottish royal centre at Forteviot seemed to be a prime candidate. My interest in Forteviot was initially sparked because, while at the University of Glasgow during the 1980s, I was very fortunate to have been a student and colleague of two archaeologists who have done much to advance our understanding of the Picts in general and Forteviot in particular, Professors Leslie Alcock and Stephen Driscoll. I hope that they will forgive my trespass. Although I have not agreed with all their conclusions, I could not have embarked on this project without the firm foundations that their studies have provided. My sincere thanks are due to them both.

The more immediate inspiration for this book lies in the explosion of interest in the study of early medieval sculpture in Scotland that has occurred over the past decade and the wide range of high-quality publications this has generated. Although all have been of use, I must acknowledge a debt to Dr Sally Foster's edited volume on the St Andrews sarcophagus (ed. Foster 1998). While I cannot hope to match the range and standard of scholarship displayed there, her book has provided both inspiration and an exemplary model to aspire to.

This study also draws extensively on a wide range of work by other scholars. I have attempted to acknowledge my debts to them in the references and bibliography. Nevertheless, I accept full responsibility for any errors, idiosyncrasies, interpretations, omissions and opinions offered.

My warmest thanks are due to those who provided practical assistance and advice during the research and fieldwork for this book. I am particularly indebted to Rev. Colin Williamson, Minister of the Stewartry of Strathearn Parish, and members of his family for their patience in arranging access to the Church of St Andrew at Forteviot and for his generous permission to study and photograph the sculptures and hand-bell in his custodianship. I am grateful to Dr Alison Sheridan of the National Museum of Scotland for kindly responding to my obscure queries. I would also like to thank Mr Coulthard, Manager of the Invermay Estate, for permission to visit the Invermay high-cross and Jim Coulthard, of Green of Invermay, for giving so freely of his time to take me to the site. I am grateful to Alison Chartres and Greg Ross, Bursar's Assistant and Archivist respectively, of Strathallan School, Forgandenny, for their helpful responses to my queries. Garry Malcolm, Historic Scotland's Monument Warden at St Serf's Church, Dunning, proved a helpful and knowledgeable guide. I am very grateful to Peter Kemmis Betty for taking on this project in the first place and for his patience and understanding when it failed to appear to deadline. I would also like to thank Laura Perehinec and Tom Sunley at Tempus for seeing this book through publication with great professionalism and patience.

But my greatest debt is to Karen and Blane for their patience throughout the research, fieldwork and writing of this book and for agreeing to base our recent family holidays in Perth. I am also indebted to Karen for doing the driving that enabled me to visit many of the sites referred to in the book, for her skill in negotiating the seemingly impassably muddy farm tracks on the Invermay estate.

INTRODUCTION

Around 1200 years ago, the rolling fields around a Perthshire hamlet were the site of an extensive and impressive royal centre of the Pictish kings and its associated church, cemeteries and ceremonial monuments. Forteviot was one of the most important political centres in northern Britain during the early medieval period. It held this status for several centuries, firstly under the Picts, then in the newly emergent kingdom of Alba, which was forged from the kingdoms of the Picts and the Scots of Dál Riata. Lastly, Forteviot was a royal centre of the medieval kings of Scots before it was abandoned during the twelfth century. No remains of this royal complex are now visible on the surface, although its former grandeur is attested by isolated fragments of evidence.

One item stands out amongst this evidence. This is a magnificent arch, carved from a single block of sandstone and decorated with men and beasts in an enigmatic and unique scene that has eluded interpretation since its discovery over 170 years ago. The Forteviot arch is a masterpiece of early medieval sculpture and provides the most tangible evidence of the royal centre of Forteviot, a direct link with a distant and forgotten past and its inhabitants. This prestigious item of sculpture is indelibly saturated with Dark Age history, its beliefs and characters.

It is difficult to exaggerate the importance of the Forteviot arch. The earliest surviving fragment of a stone church in Scotland and the only known structural component of a Pictish church or royal centre, this arch is unique in several respects and not only among the Picts. There is nothing like it from any of the other Insular nations (the early medieval peoples of Britain and Ireland) or, indeed, from the Continent.

The Forteviot arch has long held a personal fascination for me, linking my interests in the Picts and Scots, kingship, royal sites, architecture and ritual. I included a photograph of the arch in *Scotland's Stone of Destiny* (Aitchison 2000: 54, fig. 15) as a testament to the architectural and artistic richness of a Pictish and early Scottish royal centre. But I was conscious about using a photograph of the arch for largely illustrative purposes, without making any contribution to the study of the building to which it once belonged, the royal centre as a whole, or, above all, the mysterious scene on the arch. Photographs of the arch are used in a similar manner in several other recent studies on early medieval Scotland (e.g. Laing and Laing 1993: 28, fig. 20; Foster 1996: 49, fig. 28; Driscoll 2002: 34). The arch appeared at risk of being used to illustrate any discussion of Pictish or early Scottish kingship or royal sites, but without any genuine understanding of its meaning and devoid of the wider understanding that it could yield. The arch, it seemed to me, deserved better than this. Moreover, there was a strong case, on archaeological, artistic and historical grounds, for bringing Forteviot and its arch to the attention of a wider public. Distinctive and celebrated, but enduringly enigmatic, this eye-catching sculpture merits detailed analysis.

Although Professor Leslie Alcock's 1982 and 1992 papers on Forteviot added greatly to the understanding of the arch, they are limited in scope and have inevitably become dated as renewed interest in early medieval Scotland has advanced our knowledge about many aspects of the Picts and Scots. Moreover, despite Alcock's research, Forteviot is still labelled as enigmatic, even by leading experts on the Picts (e.g. Foster 1996: 48). Despite its unique character and outstanding importance, the arch has not received the study it deserves and, as a result, is not nearly as well known or understood as other masterpieces of Pictish sculpture. The arch merits a fresh and comprehensive study in its own right, but not only because it is of exceptional artistic merit and architectural importance. As the mute witness to the royal centre of Forteviot, its *basilica* and kings, the scene on the arch comprises the single most tangible, graphic and illuminating repository of their history, providing unique insights into wider aspects of Pictish society in general and kingship, royal centres and the Church in particular. Solving the enigma of the meaning of this sculpture presents the potential for making an original contribution to our knowledge of Pictish culture in significant areas that are not illuminated by any of the other scarce sources concerning the Picts. By unlocking the symbolism of this scene, the arch opens up new vistas in our understanding of that most enigmatic of peoples, the Picts, and one of the most obscure periods of Scottish history, the ninth century. The meaning of the arch only emerges slowly and is revealed as a result of detailed and painstaking analysis. This book describes the quest for the meaning of the arch's sculptural scene and its wider cultural significance revealed by those these hard-earned conclusions.

In order to interpret the arch, it is necessary to place it within its broader physical and historical contexts. Part 1 therefore examines the royal centre of Forteviot. This begins by placing Forteviot within its socio-political context, the southern Pictish kingdom of Fortriu, examining its association with Pictish and Scottish kings as well as its appearance in mythology and literature. Chapter 2 focuses on the physical context, the location, topography and placename of Forteviot. Changes in the landscape of Forteviot and the poor survival of archaeological evidence means that greater emphasis must be placed on antiquarian accounts and these are evaluated. Although poorly documented, the character and varied functions of the royal centre, including its status as a monumental focus of royal power and ritual, are investigated in Chapter 3. Chapter 4 looks at the evidence for the early medieval church of Forteviot, re-evaluating a pivotal but poorly understood source and examining the significance of the status of this church as a *basilica*. The physical evidence for the presence of a major early ecclesiastical centre at Forteviot, comprising mostly fragmentary but informative sculpture, is assembled and investigated in Chapter 5.

Despite the paucity of both archaeological and historical evidence for the royal centre and the fragmentary nature of most of the little evidence that does survive, it is still possible to shed new light on many aspects of Forteviot. This provides the context for the study of the Forteviot arch, which forms the focus of Part 2.

Part 2 contains a detailed examination of the arch, its form, sculptured scene, iconography and their wider architectural, liturgical and socio-political implications. Chapter 6 begins by investigating what little is known about the discovery of the arch and provides a brief description before reviewing previous studies. Acknowledging the sculptor himself as the agent of insight and discovery in this investigation, the imagery of the arch and the symbolism of its individual components are examined in Chapter 7. These strands are drawn together in Chapter 8, which presents new interpretations of the iconography and date of the arch. Those interpretations assist the study of the architectural and liturgical contexts of the arch, providing clues about the church the arch belonged to and the rituals celebrated there. The socio-political context of the arch is also considered and its ideological significance identified (Chap. 9).

In Part 3, the concluding chapter examines the fate of the arch, assessing whether the demise of the church it belonged to may be attributed to the ninth-century Scottish reform of the Pictish Church, the Scottish Reformation in the sixteenth century or, more probably, the ravaging of Strathearn by Viking armies in the ninth and tenth centuries. The book concludes with information about visiting Forteviot and its arch.

This book is the first to be devoted not only to the royal centre of Forteviot but also to that most elusive phenomenon of Dark Age Scotland, the 'palace'. In seeking to decipher the meaning of the arch and to explore its setting and wider significance, it draws together fragmentary information from a disparate range of sources: archaeological, architectural, sculptural and textual. Only as a result of detailed analysis and by adopting a fully multi-disciplinary approach can the arch be made to give up its secrets. Nevertheless, this is not intended to be a definitive study of Forteviot, its royal centre, church and sculpture. Although the iconography of the scene on the arch has been solved, many more mysteries about the royal centre and its church remain. Much further research, including field survey and excavation, are required before this will be possible. It is hoped that this book makes a worthwhile contribution to the study of Forteviot and will encourage others into conducting the research required to advance our understanding of Forteviot.

NAMES, DATES AND NOTES

Early medieval personal names are problematical because there is very little consistency of spelling in either primary or secondary sources. This problem is most pronounced with Pictish names because of the rarity of Pictish textual sources. As a result, most Pictish names are recorded in Irish or Gaelic forms in Irish and medieval Scottish documents respectively. Although both Pictish and Scottish names are popularly known by their anglicised versions, the established practice amongst historians is to use original name forms where these are known or can be inferred and this convention is followed here. In order to assist the correlation of different name forms, the original Pictish and Gaelic versions are used here where these can be established or inferred and their anglicised and (for Pictish names) Gaelic equivalents are included in parenthesis where they first appear in the text.

All dates given are AD unless stated otherwise and all dates given for kings are regnal dates.

Harvard-style short references are used throughout, the expansions for which may be found in the Bibliography. These references are intended to provide guidance to both the primary and secondary sources used and to assist those wishing to check source material or pursue their own studies. They are not essential to the understanding of the text and may be ignored by the casual reader.

PART 1

THE ROYAL CENTRE

1

PICTISH AND SCOTTISH KINGS AT FORTEVIOT

This village was rebuilt by John Alexander, First Baron Forteviot of Dupplin in the years 1925-26 and occupies part of the site of the Pictish capital of Fothuir-Tabaicht, a royal residence from the VII to the XII centuries. Here Kenneth I (MacAlpin) died AD 860.

Apart from this inscription (*colour plate 1*), mounted on the facade of a house in the hamlet's only street, there is now little to indicate that Forteviot was once an important royal power centre and ecclesiastical site. Located in the picturesque countryside of lower Strathearn, 6 miles (9km) south-west of Perth, Forteviot was remodelled by the successful Perth whisky distiller and merchant, John Alexander Dewar, first Baron Forteviot (1856-1929). Although unfortunately dismissed by Professor Leslie Alcock (2003: 229) as an 'undistinguished village', Forteviot is not only picturesque but also has an unusual layout for a Scottish settlement. Planned in the style of an English garden 'city' to a design by James Miller, its lawns, hall and bowling green give it a distinctive appearance and its houses are in the Arts and Crafts style (*colour plate 2*). But regardless of the merits of its architecture and planning, Forteviot's appearance masks its origins, antiquity and former importance as a place with royal associations recorded over several centuries during the early Middle Ages.

Of Forteviot's former status as a royal centre, there are now no visible traces on the ground. So how do we know about Forteviot and what can we tell about its form, function and fate, and of the kings who were associated with it? More generally, what does this royal centre tell us about the institution of kingship among the Picts and Scots, its character, powers, rituals and relationships with other institutions, such as the Church? These issues form the context within which the most impressive and significant find from the site to date, the Forteviot arch, its previously enigmatic iconography and wider significance, may be examined. Before considering the evidence for the royal centre and examining its arch, this chapter attempts to trace Forteviot's royal associations and identify the Pictish and Scottish kings who had a royal centre there.

THE KINGDOM OF FORTRIU

Forteviot's origins and status as a royal centre are intimately associated with the Picts. First recorded in 297, the Picts were the indigenous inhabitants of Scotland north of the Forth–Clyde isthmus (Henderson 1967; Laing and Laing 1993; Sutherland 1994; Foster 1996; Carver 1999). Pictland was not a single territorial and political entity for much, or possibly all, of its history. Textual sources reveal a two-fold division of Pictland. Bede (*Historia Ecclesiastica*, III.4; trans. Colgrave 1994: 114), writing in 731, describes how 'the kingdoms of the Northern Picts ... are separated from the southern part of their land by steep and rugged mountains. The Southern Picts ... live on this side of the mountains.' Although Bede does not name the mountains concerned, they are probably the same feature recorded in the death notice of Dub Tholarg, which styles him 'king of the Picts on this side of *Monoth*', in 782 (AU s.a. 781.1). *Monoth* is probably the Pictish name for the mountain range that historians traditionally refer to as the Mounth (Jackson 1955: 149; Broun 2000a: 38). More popularly known as the Grampians, these mountains divide northern Scotland, from Argyll in the south-west almost to the North Sea near Stonehaven, Kincardineshire, in the north-east. This natural barrier marked the boundary between the Northern and Southern Picts (*1*).

The Picts were descended from the indigenous Iron Age population of what is now northern Scotland. They probably represent an amalgamation or coalescence of earlier peoples, perhaps forged in opposition to the periodic Roman campaigns in northern Scotland or that at least emerged from the socio-political turmoil that the Roman presence to the south produced. The indigenous origins and constituent peoples of the Picts are revealed by the Classical historian Ammianus Marcellinus (*Res Gestae*, XXVII, 8, 4; Rivet and Smith 1979: 496-7), who refers to 'the Picti divided into two peoples, the

Dicalydones and the Verturiones.' This is the first and only recorded reference to the Verturiones, although the Dicalydones are presumably linked with the Caledonii, who were first recorded in the late second century (Rivet and Smith 1979: 290-1). The name of the Verturiones is of particular interest because it is cognate with *Fortrenn*, which appears in *rex Fortrenn*, the royal title given to several Pictish kings in the Irish annals. *Fortrenn* is the genitive and only recorded form of a hypothetical nominative singular *Fortriu (Watson 1926: 68-9; Wainwright 1955: 21; Broun 1998a; 2000a: 32). Although the earliest documentary reference to Fortriu is not until 664 (AU s.a. 663.4), its name suggests that the origins of Fortriu as a socio-political entity lay in the Iron Age.

The territory of Fortriu is of uncertain extent, although it can be linked with Strathearn from two different records of the same battle (Skene 1890, vol. 3: 43, n.4; Broun 2000a: 32). The Irish annals record that, in 904, the 'men of Fortriu' (*fir Fortrenn*) defeated the Vikings in a battle which the *Chronicle of the Kings of Alba* places 'in Strathearn' (*Sraith hErín*) (AU s.a. 903.4; ed. and trans. Hudson 1998: 150, 155). In addition, an eleventh-century verse history of Scottish kings known as the *Prophecy of Berchán* (§139; trans. Hudson 1996: 86; on which see Anderson 1973: 141) records that a king was killed 'on the bank of the Earn' by the men of Fortriu. These sources suggest that Fortriu at least included Strathearn, although there is no evidence to equate Fortriu with Strathearn (Duncan 1978: 47).

Historians have traditionally derived their knowledge of the political geography of Pictland from a source known as *De Situ Albanie* ('Concerning the Topography of Alba'). This describes the legendary division of Alba, as Scotland was known during the tenth and eleventh centuries, into seven kingdoms, each comprising two paired districts, and the kingdom comprising Strathearn and Menteith (*Sradeern cum Meneted*) was widely identified with Fortriu (Watson 1926: 108, 113; Chadwick 1949: 38-9; Wainwright 1955: 46-7; Anderson 1973: 140-1, 198-9; Smyth 1984: 69; Hudson 1994a: 9). However, *De Situ Albanie* only survives in two early thirteenth-century versions and is no longer regarded as reliable evidence of political organisation over three centuries earlier (Broun 2000a). Indeed, Fortriu appears to have been more extensive than Strathearn and Menteith and also probably encompassed Angus and Gowrie (O'Rahilly 1946: 371, n.3; Anderson 1973: 140-1, 198-9; Henderson 1996; Broun 2000a: 32-5, 37-40). Moreover, a P-Celtic or Brittonic form of Fortriu, *Werter*, may be identified in the placename *Wertermorum*, which is associated with Dunnottar, Kincardineshire, in an entry recording an invasion of Alba by Athelstan, king of Wessex, in 934 (ed. Anderson 1908: 68 and n.5; on which see Anderson 1973: 174; Broun 2000a: 34, 37-8). This suggests that Fortriu may have extended as far north as the Mounth.

1 Early medieval northern Britain and its inhabitants

There may have been no single kingdom of 'Fortriu' with definable borders but, instead, a flexible polity that expanded over time, from a 'lesser Fortriu' comprising the south-western provincial kingdom of the Picts, to a 'greater Fortriu', with the power of its kings. The kings of Fortriu became the dominant power in Southern Pictland during the seventh century. Reflecting this, the kingship of Fortriu appears to have become synonymous with that of Southern Pictland as a whole and this is probably the sense in which the kings of Fortriu appear in the Irish annals. The earliest recorded king with the title *rex Fortrenn*, 'king of Fortriu' is Bridei son of Bile (Brude mac Bili) (671-92) (AT s.a. 693.2; AU s.a. 692.1; FAI §115 [693]), revealing that this kingship was established by his reign at the latest. The kingship of Fortriu was probably the most powerful in Pictland as a whole, perhaps – at least periodically – extending its power north of the Mounth and westwards over the kingdom of the Scots of Dál Riata in what is now Argyll.

Forteviot's origins as a royal power centre are obscure but are implied by its location in Strathearn, which formed the heartland of the Pictish provincial kingdom of Fortriu. Forteviot was probably one of the principal royal centres of the kings of Fortriu. Tradition maintains that Forteviot was 'the chief residence of the *Pikish* [sic] kings' as early as the seventh century and the ancient 'capital' of Pictland (Pinkerton 1789, vol. 1: 177, see also p. 302). Despite this, there is no documentary evidence to confirm Forteviot's royal associations before the ninth century. This may, however, reflect the poor survival of Pictish sources. That Forteviot was already an established and important focus of royal activity by then suggests that its origins as a royal power centre may be considerably older.

FORTEVIOT'S ROYAL ASSOCIATIONS

The textual evidence varies in nature and origin, but paints a consistent picture of Forteviot as a royal centre for successive kings throughout the ninth century. Although his presence at Forteviot is not recorded, the earliest king whose association with the royal centre may be inferred is Causantín son of Uurguist (Constantine son of Fergus), king of Picts (789-820). Causantín's link with the Forteviot area is apparent from an inscription recording his name on the Dupplin cross (Chap. 5), which formerly stood less than a mile (1.4km) from Forteviot. Their proximity strongly suggests that this high-quality and prestigious monument was closely linked with the royal centre. The inscription probably records the erection of the cross by or under the patronage of Causantín, attesting his personal association with the locality, almost certainly including the nearby royal centre itself. This is supported by the evidence that Causantín's brother, Unuist son of Uurguist, is also associated with Forteviot, implying a dynastic link with the royal centre.

Unuist son of Uurguist is the earliest king to be linked explicitly with Forteviot in textual sources. Recorded in the St Andrews foundation legend as 'Ungus son of Urguist' and 'Hungus son of Forso', these variant names are derived from a combination of their Gaelic and Pictish forms, Oengus son of Fergus and Unuist son of Uurguist respectively. Confusingly, there were two Pictish kings of this name, traditionally referred to as 'Oengus I' (729-61) and 'Oengus II' (820-34). The later Unuist was Causantín's brother.

The identity of the Unuist associated with Forteviot has been the subject of enduring controversy. Central to this debate has been the attribution in the Pictish king lists of the building of a church at Kilrimont, 'Church of the Royal Mount', as St Andrews was known before the twelfth century, to the later Unuist son of Uurguist (Lists D, F, K; ed. Anderson 1973: 266, 273, 287). There has been little consensus about the identity of the Unuist responsible. This debate has been influenced by the existence of an important monastery at Kilrimont during the reign of the earlier Unuist, as revealed by a death record for an abbot of *Cinrighmonai*, another early name for St Andrews, in 747 (AU s.a. 746.10). As a result, the foundation of the church of St Andrews is usually credited to the earlier Unuist. The earlier Unuist has traditionally been regarded as one of the best-documented of Pictish rulers (Woolf 2001a; Anderson 2004a; 2004b: 245), largely because the first half of his reign coincides with the last decades during which annalistic records were kept on Iona. These entries, many recording events in Dál Riata and Pictland, were subsequently incorporated in various Irish annalistic compilations (Smyth 1972; Bannerman 1973: 9-26). A powerful warrior-king who seized the Pictish kingship in 729 after a bloody five-year long civil war between four claimants, Unuist then embarked on a series of campaigns against firstly the Scots of Dál Riata and then the Strathclyde Britons, having first neutralised any potential threat from the Anglian kingdom of Northumbria by entering a treaty relationship with its king, Ceolwulf (Aitchison 2003: 38-9). This Unuist certainly fits the description of 'great king of the Picts' (*magnus rex Pictorum*) given to the Hungus in the St Andrews foundation legend (ed. Skene 1867: 183).

Despite this, several later sources are consistent in recording or implying that the king referred to in the St Andrews foundation legend was the later Unuist. Against their entry for this Unuist, two Gaelicised versions of the Pictish regnal lists, which survive as twelfth-century copies, record that 'He built Kilrimont' (*Kilremont, Kilremonth*) (Lists D, F; ed. Anderson 1973: 266, 273), while another contains the gloss that Kilrimont is 'now [known as] St Andrews' and gives an abridged version of the St Andrews foundation legend (List K; ed. Anderson 1973: 287). In addition, a note in one Pictish regnal list attributes the foundation of the Church of St Andrews to the later Unuist (List Q; ed. Anderson 1973: 98; Anderson 1974a: 7). By itself, this could be attributed to a later scribal error, introduced during the copying and transmission of the texts. But one version of the St Andrews foundation legend refers to a son of Unuist called 'Howonam', who may be identified as the mid-ninth-century king of Picts who was known in Gaelic as Eóganán mac Óengusa and in Pictish as Uuen son of Unuist (?837–39). As the earlier Unuist died in 761 (AClon s.a. 755, 757; AT s.a. 761.4; AU s.a. 760.4; CB s.a. 761), Eóganán's father must have been the later Unuist.

Unuist is also linked with Forteviot, according to the St Andrews foundation legend. The sons of Unuist remained in Forteviot, presumably because they were too young to take up arms, while their father led a military expedition to Argyll (ed. Skene 1867: 185). This implies Forteviot's status as a royal residence sometime between 820 and 834. As Uuen himself held the kingship from probably 837 and was killed in battle in 839 (Chap. 10), the date concerned was probably nearer 820 than 834. Forteviot's royal associations and Unuist's attachment to the place are reinforced by Unuist's foundation of a church at Forteviot (Chap. 4).

Forteviot also appears to have been a royal centre during the reigns of Unuist's successors in the Pictish kingship. Although Uuen son of Unuist is claimed to have been based at Forteviot (Small 1999: 57), there is no evidence to support this. This association may have been inferred from Uuen's death in a battle fought in Fortriu in 839 (Chap. 10) and reflect a common confusion between the placenames Forteviot and Fortriu (Chap. 3). However, the frequency with which early medieval battles were fought at or near royal centres (Aitchison 1994: 59-61, 133-5; 2003: 98–105) suggests that the location of the battle may have been influenced by the proximity of the royal centre. In addition, Uuen's association with Forteviot during his reign may be inferred from his dynastic links with the royal centre.

Uuen's probable successor, Drust son of Wrad (Drest son of Ferat) (?845–?848), is associated with Forteviot in two related texts. What is traditionally believed to have been the final decade of Pictish royal succession is obscure, with a rapid succession of short-lived kings and several inconsistencies between different versions of the Pictish regnal lists (Anderson 1973: 193-5). As a result, there is uncertainty about the dates of several of these kings. However, two regnal lists (Lists D and F; ed. Anderson 1973: 266, 273) record that, after reigning for three years, Drust 'was killed by the Scots at Forteviot or, according to some, at

Scone' (*occisus est apud Fertheviot secundum quosdam Sconam a Scottis*). Although this (presumably later) scribal gloss attests the existence of contradictory traditions concerning the place of Drust's death, Forteviot was almost certainly the original location.

The reference to Scone, Perthshire, reflects the later importance of that site, not only as a royal centre but also as the inauguration place of the medieval kings of Scots and the location of the famous Stone of Destiny (Aitchison 2000: 77-106). This reference was probably inserted when the regnal lists were being copied, probably in the eleventh or twelfth centuries (Alcock and Alcock 1992: 221). More specifically, this gloss refers to one of the most enduring myths of early Scottish history, that of the 'betrayal of Scone', the treacherous massacre of the Pictish nobility by their Scottish guests during a feast, in what is traditionally believed to comprise the decisive moment in the conquest of the Picts by the Scots. This myth may be attributed to a later rationalisation of the disappearance of the Picts, their culture and language, the function of which was to explain how the Scots came to control all the territory between the Forth–Clyde isthmus and the Moray Firth (Anderson 1982: 116-17; Hudson 1991). But although this event is mythical, its original setting at Forteviot is significant nevertheless. It implies Forteviot's perceived status as a Pictish royal centre during the mid-ninth century and this is consistent with the documentary evidence.

The traditional, but still prevalent, interpretation of the mid-ninth century was heavily influenced by this mythology. After the eclipse of Pictish power and the ascendancy of the kings of Dál Riata over Pictland, the Scots under Cináed mac Ailpín (Kenneth mac Alpin, 'Kenneth I') (843-58) were believed to have moved the institutions of Scottish kingship eastwards from Dál Riata, which was then being subjected to periodic attacks by the Vikings, into the Southern Pictish heartland of Fortriu. Forteviot continued to function as a royal centre, attesting both its appropriation by the Scots and its importance to the exercise of royal power in eastern central Scotland during this formative period. But the evidence indicates that Cináed mac Ailpín and his immediate successors were Pictish, not Scottish, kings (Woolf 2001b: 42; forthcoming; Johnston 2004). Cináed is described as king of the Picts (*rex Pictorum*) in contemporary death records in both Irish and Welsh annals (ACamb s.a. [856]; AU s.a. 857.2), as were the four kings who succeeded him, while both Cináed and Alpín are Pictish rather than Gaelic names.

The ninth century saw the culmination of a long period of cultural, linguistic and eventually political integration and assimilation between the Picts and Scots (Smyth 1984: 176-85; Hudson 1994a: 29-33; Bannerman 1999: 75-88; Woolf in prep.), frequently making it difficult to distinguish between Pictish and Scottish kings. Indeed, close dynastic links between the kingships of the Picts and the Scots may have resulted in Dál Riata and Pictland being jointly ruled from the late eighth century (but see Broun 1998b: 76-80). The union of Pictland and Dál Riata appears to have been a more gradual and peaceful process than was traditionally thought. Not until *c*.900 does this appear to have resulted in the emergence of a new political unit, the kingdom of Alba, which stretched from the Forth–Clyde isthmus in the south to the Moray Firth in the north.

The principal source for Scottish history in the period between *c*.850 and *c*.975 is the text known traditionally as the *Scottish Chronicle* or *Old Scottish Chronicle* and, more recently, as the *Chronicle of the Kings of Alba* (ed. Anderson 1973: 240-60; ed. and trans. Hudson 1998: 148-61; for discussion see Anderson 1973; Cowan 1981; Hudson 1998: 129-47; Dumville 2000). The *Chronicle of the Kings of Alba* survives in various manuscript copies, the earliest of which are fourteenth-century transcriptions of twelfth-century versions of an 'original' compiled during the latter half of the tenth century. This was, in turn, a composite text created by combining a regnal list with a set of annals, the entries in which were made contemporaneously or nearly so, that was probably kept in Brechin or Dunkeld (Cowan 1981; Hudson 1998: 133-136; Broun 1999: 97-8).

The *Chronicle of the Kings of Alba* associates its first two kings with Forteviot, implying a continuity in the functions and significance of the royal centre during the mid-ninth century. It records that Cináed mac Ailpín, famous in Scottish tradition as the king who 'conquered' the Picts and forged the new kingdom of Alba or Scotland, died of a tumour 'in the palace at Forteviot (*in palacio Fothiurtabaicht*) on the Tuesday before the Ides of February [8 February]' (ed. and trans. Hudson 1998: 148, 153). The precision of Cináed's obit, which gives both a cause and date of death, is most unusual. The incidental detail recorded not only reflects Cináed's perceived importance as the 'first [king] of the Scots [who] ruled Pictland', as the *Chronicle of the Kings of Alba* distinguishes him (trans. Hudson 1998: 152), but also the familiarity of the *Chronicle's* compilers with the kings whose reigns they recorded. Although preserved in later sources, this argues persuasively for the contemporary, or nearly contemporary, nature of this information, and therefore its reliability. Cináed's death is dated independently from Irish annalistic entries to 858 (ACamb s.a. [856]; AI s.a. [858]; AU s.a. 857.2; FAI, §285 [858]).

In what substituted for a synopsis of his poorly recorded reign, Cináed mac Ailpín appears in early sources to have been as well known for his death at Forteviot as his conquest of the Picts. These events also feature in the stanza about Cináed in the *Prophecy of Berchán* (§124; trans. after Hudson 1996: 84):

Seventeen years, heights of valour,
In the high-kingship of Alba;
After slaughtering Picts, after harassing Vikings,
He dies on the banks of the Earn.

Here, 'the banks of the Earn' is either a poetic reference to Forteviot or reflects subsequent changes in the course of the River Earn, which now flows no closer than half a mile (1km) from Forteviot (Chap. 2).

The presence at Forteviot of Cináed's brother and successor, Domnall mac Ailpín (Donald mac Alpin, 'Donald I') (858-62), is also recorded. According to the *Chronicle of the Kings of Alba*, 'In his [Domnall's] time, in Forteviot, the Gaels with their king made the rights and laws of Áed son of Eochaid' (trans. Hudson 1998: 153) (Chap. 3). The *Prophecy of Berchán* (§139; trans. after Hudson 1996: 86) records that another nineteenth-century king, Giric (878-89), was also associated with Forteviot and may have been killed there:

The strong house is built by him – alas my heart – on the bank of the Earn;
There will be a red stain [i.e. blood] in the house of my chief,
He will fall by the hands of the men of Fortriu.

The references to a 'strong house' and the River Earn have traditionally led to the fortress of Dundurn, in upper Strathearn, being identified as the place of Giric's death (Watson 1926: 227; Hudson 1996: 86, n. 86). Indeed, the regnal lists record his death there (Lists D, F, I; ed. Anderson 1973: 267, 274, 283), although these survive in versions that are no earlier than the twelfth century, later than the *Prophecy of Berchán*. However, there is no explicit mention of a fortification and his death on 'the bank of the Earn' is inconsistent with a hilltop citadel. In contrast, the *Prophecy of Berchán* refers to Forteviot being 'on the bank(s) of the Earn' (above). Moreover, the close dynastic association that existed between the successors of Cináed mac Ailpín and Forteviot reinforces the interpretation that Forteviot is the royal centre referred to.

Although this evidence only amounts to a handful of terse references, Forteviot has recorded associations with more ninth-century Pictish and Scottish, or Picto-Scottish, kings than any other royal centre. This consistency and the nature of the activities recorded – a royal assembly, and the death and killing of kings – reveal that Forteviot was a, and perhaps the, most important centre of royal power among both the later Pictish kings and the early kings of Alba.

Forteviot does not appear in the historical record again until some two centuries later. As a result, the tenth and eleventh centuries are a major lacuna in our knowledge of the status of Forteviot. However, an event that occurred nearby in the mid-tenth century implies Forteviot's continued status as an important royal centre during this period. The *Chronicle of the Kings of Alba* (ed. and trans. Hudson 1998: 151, 159) records that '[A battle was fought] between Dubh and Cuilén *super Dorsum Crup*, in which Dubh had the victory, where Dúnchad, abbot of Dunkeld, and Dubdúin, *satrap* [probably *mormaer*] of Atholl, perished. Dubh was expelled from the kingship and Cuilén held it a short time.' This event may be dated to 965 from its recording in Irish annals (AU s.a. 964.4): 'A battle [was fought] between the men of Alba themselves in which many were killed, including Donnchad, the abbot of Dunkeld.' This battle was fought for the kingship of Alba, while the identities of the combatants and reference to numerous casualties reveals that it was a major encounter. *Dorsum Crup* is identified as Duncrub, only 3 miles (4.8km) south-west of Forteviot (Pinkerton 1729, vol. 2: 186; Chalmers 1848, vol. 1: 391-2; Skene 1867: cxliii; 1876: 367; Watson 1926: 56; Hudson 1994a: 92). Their proximity is most unlikely to be coincidental and provides another example of the close association of early medieval royal centres and battles. Although Forteviot was not the site of this battle, it and its royal occupants were probably Cuilén's target. The attacking force was presumably advancing eastwards along Strathearn towards Forteviot when the king and his army met them in open battle. Indeed, this battle has prompted claims that Dubh was driven from Forteviot (Chalmers 1848, vol. 1: 392) and, by implication, the kingship. There is, however, no historical record of the presence of either Dubh (Duff) (962-6) or Cuilén (Culen) (966-71) at Forteviot itself.

Forteviot's absence from the sources during this period reflects the complete lack of surviving royal charters issued during the reigns of Malcolm III (Malcolm 'Canmore', Mael Coluim mac Donnchada) (1057-93) and his predecessors and their scarcity before the reign of Malcolm IV. The evidence of royal charters does, however, link two kings of Scots, Malcolm IV ('the Maiden') (1153-65) and William I ('the Lion') (1165-1214), with Forteviot in the mid-twelfth century. In 1162x64, Malcolm IV issued a royal charter at Forteviot (*apud Fetherteuiet*) granting to Ralph Frebern and his heirs, in fee and inheritance, Rosyth, Dunduff and the land that belonged to Master Robert the ironsmith beside Nebattle (Masterton in Newbattle), in return for the service of one knight (RRS, vol. 1: 271, no. 256). And, in 1165x71, William I issued a royal charter at Forteviot confirming to Scone Abbey the teind (tithe) of the whole parish of Scone in grain, cheese and catches of fish (RRS, vol. 2: 131, no. 17). The issuing of charters at Forteviot attests its status as a royal power centre.

In further evidence of their association with Forteviot, two charters record the same kings making grants of the church of Forteviot. In 1164, Malcolm IV granted the church of Forteviot, with all its appurtenances which were in the king's gift, to his chaplain, Richard of Stirling, to be held as freely as any church of the king's demesnes in Scotland (RRS, vol. 1: 272, no. 257). And in 1173x77, William I granted the church of Forteviot to Cambuskenneth Abbey, Stirling, after the death of Richard the priest, in exchange for a tenth of the king's pleas and profits of Stirling, Stirlingshire and Callendar (RRS, vol. 2: 228, no. 161). The extent of the dues exchanged appears to reflect the importance and wealth of the church of Forteviot at that time. It is presumably no coincidence that both these kings also issued charters at Forteviot. These records belong to the twilight of Forteviot's status as a royal centre (Chap. 10).

The poorly documented nature, not only of Forteviot but also of Pictland and the Picts in general, means that many more early medieval kings were probably linked with the royal centre than surviving sources record. As a result, our knowledge of Forteviot and its kings is unavoidably episodic, making it impossible to produce a straightforward narrative history of the royal centre. Instead, the fragmentary and terse documentary record leads us to focus on a very small number of particular moments in time at Forteviot, when events of such great importance occurred that they merited recording by early medieval scribes, and the themes they help to illuminate. Nevertheless, Forteviot's recorded associations enable it to be identified as a royal centre of the kings, firstly of the Picts and then of Scots, and a place of great political significance between at least the ninth and mid-twelfth centuries. Thereafter, evidence of Forteviot's royal connections disappears and, with its decline and abandonment, the royal centre slips from the documentary record and into historical obscurity (Chap. 10).

FORTEVIOT IN MYTHOLOGY AND LITERATURE

Myth and legend have filled the void created by the absence of more reliable sources documenting the early history of Forteviot. This mythology is the origin of both medieval and modern traditions claiming the association of several Pictish and Scottish kings with Forteviot. The process of mythologisation is usually thought to have begun with the St Andrews foundation legend, which survives in eleventh-century form. This source refers to the foundation of a church at Forteviot by a king Hungus in the eighth or ninth century.

Although the historical veracity of this source has traditionally been dismissed because of its late date and mythological and ideological content, the St Andrews foundation legend incorporates an earlier historical core concerning Forteviot (Chap. 4).

Some Pictish and early Scottish kings are associated with Forteviot in popular tradition. Their association with the royal centre is plausible, perhaps even likely, given the recorded presence of other Pictish and Scottish kings at Forteviot, although there is no historical evidence to corroborate this. Many of these traditions are no earlier than the nineteenth century and reflect growing antiquarian interest in the royal centre. For example, a Pictish king, Bred, is said to have been slain at 'the seat of his power' at Forteviot in 843 (Chalmers 1848, vol. 1: 333). This presumably concerns Brude son of Wrad (Bred son of Ferat) who appears in the Pictish king lists (Lists A, B, D, F, I, K; ed. Anderson 1973: 249, 263, 266, 273, 281, 287) and ruled in ?842. However, the event recorded is a variant of the mythical conquest of the Picts by the Scots and the confusion about the king involved, with Drust son of Wrad also appearing in this role (above), underlines the mythological nature of this episode.

But the best-known myth relating Forteviot's royal associations belongs to the medieval period. This concerns the ill-fated Duncan (1034-40), who was famously killed by Macbeth, and the daughter of the miller of Forteviot. This episode is first recorded in Andrew of Wyntoun's *Orygynale Cronykil of Scotland* (Book 6, chap. 16; ed. Amours 1906, vol. 4: 256), a metrical history of Scotland composed *c.*1410. It relates how Duncan became separated from his retinue while out hunting and, with night fast approaching, took refuge at the Mill of Forteviot:

> As he past apon a day
> In till his hunting him to play,
> With all his court in cumpany,
> On his gammyn all thochty,
> The still and þe settys set,
> Him self with bow and wiþ brachet,
> Fra slak to slak, oure hill and hicht,
> Travalit all day, to þe myrk nycht
> Partit him fra his cumpany.
> [Than] he wes [will] of his herbry
> Till at the last, he wauerand will,
> Of hapnyng he come to þe myll
> Off Fortevyot.

In an attempt to improve his position, the miller was keen to offer his king every comfort and, as a result, the miller's daughter became pregnant by Duncan. The child born as a result of their union was Malcolm Canmore (Máel Coluim Ceann Mór, 'Malcolm III'), king of Scots (1057-93), according to Wyntoun. Duncan and the miller's daughter became an established element of medieval Scottish mythology, appearing in several later chronicles.

Wyntoun (*c.*1355-1422), prior of St Serf's Island in Loch Leven, drew on earlier sources that no longer survive. These may have been preserved in the now lost *Register* of St Andrews and perhaps included a mid-thirteenth-century chronicle of Scotland to Malcolm Canmore by Veremondus, possibly a monk of St Andrews. However, this colourful episode is uncorroborated by any earlier or historically reliable sources and appears to be more mythological in character. Wyntoun's *Orygynale Cronykil* incorporates many themes drawn from Celtic mythology, including, in this episode, the link between hunting and Otherworldy adventure and magical or mysterious conceptions and births (*coimperta*). The geographical setting of the tale also defies logic. The mill where Duncan sought shelter is presumably identifiable with Milton of Forteviot, one third of a mile (0.6km) north-west of Forteviot. As the tale implies that Duncan was hunting from his royal centre at Forteviot, it is puzzling that he was unable to travel such a short distance, even after dark. An attempt at rationalising this topographical anomaly by claiming that Duncan was based at Scone, not Forteviot (Meldrum 1926: 13), simply reflects Scone's later prominence as a royal centre. Wyntoun's account cannot be accepted at face value.

This episode may be a device to explain Forteviot's traditional association with Malcolm Canmore but could equally have inspired that tradition. This myth presumably gave rise to the tradition that Malcolm's fortified residence was at Forteviot. The earliest recorded reference to this is in the poem *The Muses' Threnodie; or, Mirthful Mournings on the Death of Mr John Gall* by Henry Adamson (1581-1637). Composed around 1620 (Peacock 1849: 610), but not published until 1638, this contains the lines (Adamson 1638: 82):

> Right over to Forteviot, did we hy,
> And there the ruin'd castle did we spy
> Of Malcolme Ken-more.

Malcom Canmore is the king most frequently associated with Forteviot in popular belief. According to 'the constant tradition of the country', Malcolm Canmore 'erected a palace at Forteviot' and 'made the ... ancient metropolis of Scotland ... his principal residence' (Skene 1857: 276), 'favourite residence' ('T' 1772) or 'summer residence' (*Statistical Account* 1797 [1976: 199]). Forteviot's claimed status as Malcolm's 'capital' conflicts with his close association with Dunfermline, Fife. Presumably the location of a fortress (*dùn*), this is where Malcolm and his queen (later saint), Margaret, were married in 1069 or 1070 and where Margaret founded firstly a church and then a Benedictine priory (Duncan 1978: 119, 123; Wilson 1993: 63-6; Fawcett 1990: 4-5; 1994: 26-8; Macquarrie 1997: 215; Fawcett (ed.) 2005). If any royal centre enjoyed a favoured status during Malcolm's reign it was Dunfermline, not Forteviot. However, early medieval kingship was peripatetic, with kings progressing around their kingdoms from one royal centre to another (Chap. 3). The concept of a single royal 'capital' is therefore anachronistic and Malcolm would have had many other royal centres in addition to Dunfermline. Although Forteviot's status as a royal centre of Malcolm III has been doubted (Alcock and Alcock 1992: 221), Forteviot's status as a major royal centre between the ninth and late twelfth centuries strongly suggests that this was a Canmore power centre (Driscoll 1998a: 43, 56, n.40). It is almost inconceivable that Malcolm did not have a royal centre in lower Strathearn, given its strategic significance and agricultural richness, and Forteviot is the most likely candidate by far.

Antiquarian interest during the late eighteenth century (Chap. 2) brought Forteviot to the attention of a wider audience. This resulted in the royal centre featuring, in a minor role, in the mythology that attested an emerging British national consciousness. Published in 1801, *Alfred, an Epic Poem* by Henry James Pye (Book I, lines 11-22; on which see Pratt 2000), poet laureate from 1790 to 1813, opens with the arrival of Alfred the Great at the court of 'Gregor, King of Caledonia' to seek help against the Danes:

> Dark was the night, against Forteviot's tower
> Howl'd the loud blast, and drove the sleety shower;
> In the arch'd hall, with storied drapery hung,
> While sacred bards the song of triumph sung,
> Scotia's hoar monarch, with his peers around,
> The genial board, with social temperance crown'd;
> Beside him sat the leaders of his host,
> Return'd, exulting, from Ierne's coast;
> Where, edged by Justice, his victorious sword
> To Donach's brow the regal wreath restored:
> When, through the portal, with majestic mien,
> A wandering stranger join'd the festive scene.

The tradition that Forteviot was a residence and/or fortification of firstly the Pictish and subsequently the early Scottish kings has a long pedigree. Although the historical veracity of some of the various sources that refer to the royal centre may be questioned, Forteviot clearly had an established reputation as a royal centre by the fifteenth century, even if it was the more salacious episodes that attracted the attention of medieval chroniclers. But Forteviot is the setting of relatively few mythological events, certainly when compared with the more famous Scone. This probably reflects Forteviot's earlier decline, while Scone remained an important royal centre throughout the medieval period and beyond, retaining its prominence because of its status as a royal inauguration place.

Over a millennium after its heyday as a royal centre, Forteviot's royal associations continue to attract controversy. The monarch who is most prominently associated with Forteviot in modern popular tradition is Cináed mac Ailpín, 'Kenneth MacAlpine', famous as the king who led the Scots to victory over the Picts in battle in 843, thereby uniting the two kingdoms, their kingships and peoples. This is popularly regarded as a pivotal event in Scottish history and one that led to the emergence of the medieval kingdom of the Scots. However, the reality is that very little is known about this king and his reign. Indeed, the only place at which Cináed mac Ailpín is recorded in reliable historical sources is Forteviot (above), with the result that Forteviot is popularly perceived to have been his 'royal capital'.

Popular tradition has recently invested Forteviot with a more fundamental significance. Commonly perceived as the 'capital' of Scotland's founding king, Forteviot is now claimed as the 'birthplace of Scotland' on the grounds that 'The decision that formed Scotland took place in Forteviot' (Johnston and Duncan 2005). In recognition of Forteviot's association with Cináed mac Ailpín and its perceived role in the forging of the kingdom of the Scots, in 2005 the Clan MacAlpine Society proposed the erection of a memorial at Forteviot to commemorate this momentous event and important person in Scottish history (Johnston and Duncan 2005). But the proposal was blocked by Lord Forteviot, the owner of the Forteviot estate, reportedly because it would 'bring attention to the area' and presumably attract visitors to his land. Long after it ceased to be a political centre, Forteviot has emerged at the centre of highly political and charged debates concerning national identity, ethnicity, land ownership, access and the commemoration of the past.

2

TOPOGRAPHY AND ARCHAEOLOGY

Forteviot's royal associations between the ninth and twelfth centuries prompt the question: why did this place become such an important power centre? In order to address this, this chapter examines the physical and archaeological setting of the Pictish and Scottish royal centre and church at Forteviot. It firstly considers the location and topography of Forteviot, including the evidence of its placename and antiquarian accounts ranging from the seventeenth to the twentieth century. The implications of these sources for the location, form and interpretation of the royal centre and its church are then reviewed. In the absence of surviving upstanding remains, this chapter also examines the evidence of aerial reconnaissance, some of the archaeological remains at and around Forteviot revealed by this technique and the insights this provides for the character of the royal centre, its function and the activities performed there.

LOCATION AND TOPOGRAPHY

The River Earn is a major watercourse in eastern central Scotland, flowing 46 miles (74km) from Loch Earn in the west to the Firth of Tay in the east (2). Strathearn encompasses the basin of the River Earn and its tributaries and cuts a broad swathe, over 30 miles (48km) long and averaging 8 miles (13km) wide, through southern Perthshire (Foster 1999). The southern limits of Strathearn are defined by the Ochil Hills, which rise to a maximum height of 2365ft (721m),

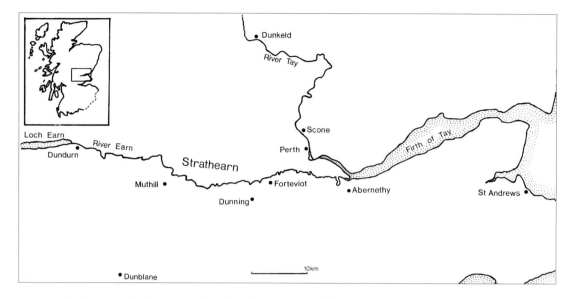

2 Strathearn and adjacent areas, showing places mentioned in the text

while the southern flank of the Highlands form the northern boundary of Strathearn. Strathearn varies considerably in character, from upland moorland pasture in its upper reaches, to rolling terrain and flat and fertile terraces along the valley sides and low-lying floodplains on the valley floor, which widens towards the east. A series of alluvial gravel terraces within Strathearn, including that known as the 'Main Perth Shoreline', were formed as the sea level fell at the end of the last ice age, possibly about 14,000 BP, and during the Flandrian (post-glacial) period (Browne 1980; Cullingford *et al.* 1980).

Lower Strathearn comprises some of the best-quality agricultural land in Scotland (*colour plates 3* and *4*). Its rich and well-drained terraces provide extensive areas of lowland arable land. In terms of modern agricultural capability, this land belongs to Classes 2 and 3, capable of producing high and good yields respectively of cereals and grass (Walker *et al.* 1982). These fertile soils and lush pastures form the economic basis of the rich prehistoric settlement along Strathearn. There is evidence for cereal cultivation in Strathearn as early as the third millennium BC (Caseldine 1983) and the attractiveness of this area to generations of agricultural communities is reflected in its rich and varied archaeological remains.

Forteviot (National Grid Reference NO052175) is located in the midst of the broad, fertile expanse of lower Strathearn, Perthshire, 5.5 miles (9km) south-west of Perth (*3*). Forteviot is situated above the floodplain of the River Earn, where the flat valley floor is about a mile (1.6km) wide and only 36ft (11m) above sea level. It occupies a slight eminence on the edge of an alluvial gravel terrace forming the southern limits of the Strathearn floodplain, on the east bank of the Water of May and half a mile (0.8km) south-south-east of the confluence of the May and the Earn (at NO050184). The May rises high in the Ochil Hills, 6 miles (10km) south-south-west of Forteviot, its course describing a wide arc before flowing into the River Earn 12 miles (20km) downstream. Although little more than a stream for most of the year, the May has gouged a deep trench into the hillside as it descends the north side of the Ochils and, downstream, has cut into the gravel of the Forteviot terrace as it flows northwards from Invermay (Walker 1963: 18). It is on the edge of this prominent and steep-sided scarp carved by the May that Forteviot is located (*colour plate 5*).

Several factors were probably involved in the selection of this site for a royal centre. Forteviot occupies a strategic location in the midst of southern Strathearn and at a nodal point within the landscape. It controls both east–west and north–south communication routes along and across Strathearn by its proximity to the confluence of the River Earn and Water of May, fording places across them and the normal tidal limit on the Earn (NO106195), which is now 4 miles (6.5km) downstream from Forteviot but may have been closer during the early medieval period. Forteviot is also situated within a wider landscape of Pictish royal power. Two other important Pictish royal centres are located in Strathearn: Dundurn (Alcock *et al.* 1990), a fortress besieged by the Scots in 683, 21 miles (34km) west-north-west of Forteviot, and Abernethy, a poorly documented but major ecclesiastical and royal centre (Anderson 1973: 92-6), 8.5 miles (14km) east of Forteviot.

The site of Forteviot itself is well drained but with a plentiful water supply from the nearby Water of May. In marked contrast to the rocky crags and promontories favoured for early medieval fortified sites, the level and extensive Forteviot terrace could have accommodated a sizeable palace complex and enabled events involving substantial numbers of people to be held there (Chap. 3). Although not occupying a location of great natural strength, the steep drop to the Water of May on its western side provides some natural defence and it is from this feature that Forteviot derives its name.

FORTEVIOT: THE PLACENAME

Forteviot's placename has attracted speculation and caused much confusion for over two centuries. Unusually, this is not attributable to the absence of surviving early name forms or the wide variety of medieval name forms recorded for

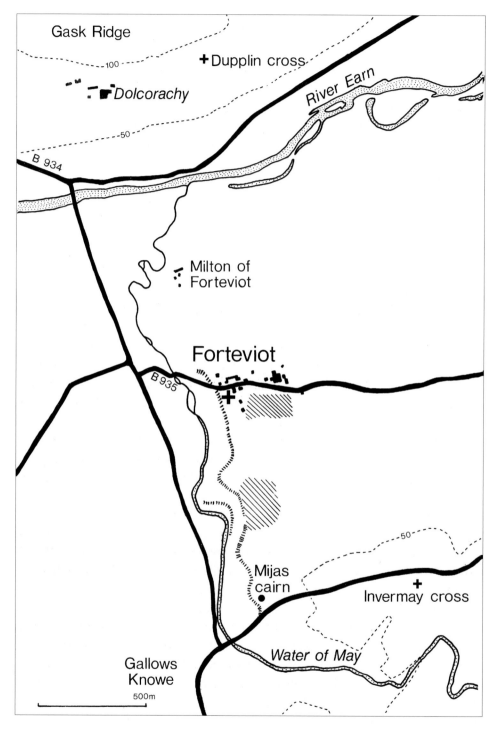

3 Forteviot and its environs, showing places mentioned in the text

Forteviot. The earliest commentators adhered to the fundamental principle of placename studies, that any attempt to elucidate the meaning of a placename should attach greatest weight the earliest surviving or recorded name form. Forteviot is referred to twice in the *Chronicle of the Kings of Alba*, where it is recorded as *Fothuírtabaicht* and *Fochíurthabaichth* (ed. Anderson 1973: 250; ed. Hudson 1998: 148). The name is preserved in more readily recognisable forms in the Scottish regnal lists (Lists D, F, I; ed. Anderson 1973: 266; 273, 282, 288) as *Fertevioth, Fertheviot, Ferteuyoth* and *Fortevioth* as well as the now familiar Forteviot. In addition, a wide range of spellings are recorded in royal charters issued at, or referring to, Forteviot between the mid-twelfth and early fourteenth centuries, including *Ferteuieth, Fetherteuiet, Forteuiet, Forteuyot* and *Fortheuiet* (RRS, vol. 1: 271, 272, nos 256, 257; vol. 2: 131, 138, 228, 259, nos 17, 28, 161, 208; vol. 5: 328, no. 39). These early name forms expose the flawed logic behind the many popular attempts to interpret Forteviot's name.

False etymologies abound. The tendency during the eighteenth and nineteenth centuries to spell the placename 'Fort-teviot' or even 'Fort Teviot' was linked with Forteviot's interpretation as a place of strength (Burton 1867-70, vol. 2: 52, 101). But persistent claims that the placename refers to a fort, such as the 'fort of the birches' (Campbell 1888: 6), have no basis in reality. The fort with which Forteviot was traditionally, but mistakenly, identified is the *Dun Fother* referred to in early medieval sources (Innes 1729; MacPherson 1796: s.v. 'Fother'; Chalmers 1848, vol. 1: 384, n. l; Skene 1857: 275; Stuart 1867: 58; Meldrum 1926: 5, 11). However, *Dun Fother* is the fortress of Dunottar, Kincardineshire (Watson 1926: 68-9; on which see Alcock and Alcock 1992: 267-83). Another traditional misconception equates, or at least links, Forteviot's name with that of the provincial kingdom in which it is located, Fortriu or its dative form, *Fortrenn* (Pinkerton 1789, vol. 1: 302; Chalmers 1848, vol. 1: 296; Skene 1857: 275; Driscoll 1991: 102).

Other misinterpretations of the placename are more prosaic, deriving Forteviot from the nature of its hinterland. These include 'rich land', from British *faethir*, referring to the quality of the surrounding agricultural land (Chalmers 1848, vol. 1: 208, n. r), 'land of the abbey', from *fothuir*, 'land', and *tabaicht*, 'of the abbey' (Johnston 1892: 113; on which see Watson in lit., quoted in Meldrum 1926: 2), and 'sorrel forest', from Irish *fothar, foithre*, 'woodland' (Mackenzie 1931: 170). More bizarrely, the placename was claimed to be derived from *foirthir*, 'farther, remote', and *tabachta*, 'state, condition', allegedly reflecting Forteviot's remoteness from the 'ancient seats of government and power' at Abernethy, Perth and Stirling (*Statistical Account* 1797 [1976: 193]). However, as these places are only 8, 6 and 21 miles (13, 10 and 34km) from Forteviot respectively, this seems implausible.

William Watson, the pioneering scholar of Celtic placenames in Scotland, placed the study of Forteviot's name on a sound etymological basis for the first time. He identified the first part of the placename as being derived from Gaelic *fothair*, 'slope, terraced declivity' (Watson 1926: 510; in lit., quoted in Meldrum 1926: 2), which corresponds exactly with Forteviot's location at the edge of an alluvial terrace. Gaelic *fothair* appears in several Scottish placenames north of the River Forth, usually in its various anglicised forms of *fether, fetter, fodder, fother* or *foyers* (Innes 1729, vol. 1: 77-8; Watson 1926: 509-12).

But the second element of Forteviot's name was of uncertain derivation and its meaning eluded Watson and subsequent scholars. Watson likened it to an Irish placename, *Ráith Tobachta* (Watson 1926: 510), the subject of a lost epic tale, 'The Sacking of the Rath of Tobacht' (*Argain Rátha Tobachta*) (*Book of Leinster*, 190a; eds Best and O'Brien 1965: 836). However, any similarity between *Ráith Tobachta* and the second element of Forteviot's name is coincidental. The second element of Forteviot's name is claimed to be a personal name (Mackay 2000: 37; Ross 2001: 91), 'Torbacht' (Hanks *et al.* 2002: 1037) or 'Tabhach' (Mac an Tàiller 2003: 50-1), although these are otherwise unattested in early medieval Scotland.

The origins and significance of the *tabaicht/thabaichth* element of Forteviot's name are suggested by its similarity to an ancient, complex and widespread group of river names in both Britain and on the Continent. The many British watercourses with names belonging to this group include the Taf, Taff, Tain, Tamar, Tame, Tave, Tavy, Taw, Tawye, Tees, Teifi, Teign, Teith, Teiwi, Tema, Teme, Test, Thame, Thames, Tian, Tweed, Tyne, Tynet and Tywi. The Earn flows into yet another river belonging to this group, the Tay. Moreover, the river name preserved in Forteviot's name is not unique but is identical to that of the River Teviot, Roxburghshire, with which it presumably shares a common origin and meaning. These river names are derived from a common root, Indo-European *⋆ta-, te-*, 'to melt, dissolve, flow' and may mean 'that which expands, spreads', referring to these rivers' tendency to break their banks (Chalmers 1848, vol. 1: 47, nn. 52, 63; Nicolaisen 1976: 190). This is particularly appropriate for the Water of May, which is prone to seasonal torrents and flooding. Forteviot therefore derives its name from its most distinctive physical feature, the steep slope carved into the edge of a terrace by a river formerly known as *Tabaicht/Thabaichth*.

River names are often the most durable of placenames and many are of ancient origin. In keeping with this, the widespread distribution of river names belonging to this group reveals that these are not Pictish but are considerably older. This explains why the river with the closest name form to *Tabaicht/Thabaichth*, the Teviot, is in the Scottish Borders, some distance outside historical Pictland. Although the names of Forteviot and the River Teviot are claimed to be unrelated (Mackay 2000: 37; Ross 2001: 91), they are both derived from a common river name. The linguistic origins of this group of river names is uncertain but may be either Celtic or pre-Celtic Indo-European (Nicolaisen 1976: 190). Nevertheless, many of these names were retained by later populations, explaining their survival. A pre-Pictish name, *Tabaicht/Thabaichth* was probably the river name adopted firstly by the Picts and then inherited by the Scots for the river now known as the Water of May. This newly identified River *Tabaicht/Thabaichth* may therefore be added to those Pictish river names (Nicolaisen 1996: 18-19; 1997: 114-16) derived from earlier name forms.

This leaves a question mark over the origins of the name of the Water of May. May is widely believed to be a name of Celtic origin, although there is no consensus about its meaning. It has been claimed to preserve both an ancient British river name, *Mai* or *My-ai*, meaning 'agitated, troubled' water, referring to the precipitous descent of the upper reaches of the May from the Ochil Hills (Chalmers 1848, vol. 1: 47, n. 52). In contrast to this, it has also been derived from a Celtic word meaning 'failure, ceasing, deficiency, falling short', referring to the May's greatly diminished flow in summer (Breeze 2000). As a Brittonic rather than Gaelic name form located within Pictland, *May* could be of Pictish origin. But without documented early forms of this river name, its antiquity, origins and meaning all remain obscure.

ANTIQUARIAN ACCOUNTS

Forteviot was the focus of antiquarian interest from the early seventeenth century, when substantial ruins of the royal centre still appeared to survive. The earliest reference to upstanding remains at Forteviot is in Henry Adamson's *The Muses' Threnodie* (1638: 82). Referring to 'the ruin'd castle ... / Of Malcolme Kenmore', this contains the couplet:

> These Castles ruines when we did consider,
> We saw that wasting time makes all things wither.

The reliability of this source is supported by the poet's familiarity with the area. Adamson was born and lived in Perth and refers to other archaeological sites in the locality.

The Muses' Threnodie established a tradition that Forteviot and its 'ruinous buildings' were a popular visitor attraction during the reign of Charles I (1625-49) (*Statistical Account* 1797 [1976: 199]; Skene 1857: 278). Unfortunately, no descriptions by any of those early visitors survive. But awareness of the place, its former significance and traditions, survived throughout the eighteenth century. Thomas Innes, for example, described Forteviot as 'another habitation of the Pictish and Scotish [sic] kings' (Innes 1729, vol. 1: 77). Bishop Richard Pococke referred to 'King Malcolm Kenmores Castle at Fort Eveot' in his account of his tour of Scotland in 1760 (Pococke 1887: 257). However, Pococke gave no description of the site and it is unclear if he visited Forteviot or was simply repeating an existing tradition.

The earliest and most informative antiquarian account of Forteviot is a short untitled letter, published in the Edinburgh *Weekly Magazine* in 1772. Signed only 'T', the author was subsequently identified as a Mr Taylor, the schoolmaster at Forteviot (*Statistical Account* 1797 [1976: 199]). 'T''s position probably makes him a reliable source of local knowledge and this is supported by details included in his account. In 1772, Forteviot was considered 'an object of curiosity, perhaps the most antient of any in Strathearn.' The focus of antiquarian interest there was a slight mound known as Haly Hill: 'Hard by the village of Fort-teviot is ... an eminence, commonly called *The Holy Hill*' ('T' 1772), 'a small eminence at the west end of [the village of] Forteviot' and 'near the present church' (*Statistical Account* 1797 [1976: 199]). More precisely, Haly Hill stood 'a little to the north-west of the village, about two hundred yards [182m] from the place where the church now stands' (Brown and Jamieson 1830: 208). From this information, Haly Hill appears to have been a natural mound located on the eastern edge of the scarp overlooking the Water of May.

There is no contemporary evidence for the function of Haly Hill, although several local traditions are recorded. It was reputedly the site of Malcolm Canmore's palace, a castle built by David, Earl of Strathearn, or an abbey or other place of worship ('T' 1772). The presence of a nearby field name, The King's Haugh, was cited in support of the Haly Hill's royal associations. But others were unequivocal: 'Halyhill ... was the summer residence of Malcolm Canmore, and others of the Scottish kings .... the site of a royal residence, first ... of the Pictish, and afterwards of some of the Scottish, kings' (*Statistical Account* 1797 [1976: 199]). Traces of this royal centre were still visible during the late eighteenth century. The editor of a 1774 edition of Adamson's *The Muses' Threnodie* noted that 'The ruins of this [Malcolm Canmore's] palace remain at Forteviot' (Cant 1774, vol. 1: 178, n). In 1830, Sir John Jamieson recorded that 'Some persons yet alive recollect that, about fifty years ago, an acre [0.4ha] of ground was covered with the ruins; and that part of the walls, to the height of from fifteen to twenty feet [4.6-6.1m], was then standing' (Brown and Jamieson 1830: 208). Jamieson, who visited Forteviot before 1790, had himself seen 'a small part of the walls remaining'.

But these terse references appear to contradict 'T''s more detailed account of 1772. 'T' described the remains on Haly Hill as 'a heap of rubbish', referring to the 'present ruined condition' of the structures and how they had been 'raze[d] ... to the foundation'. Other sources used the past tense. Thomas Pennant (1776 [1998: 451]), the antiquarian, naturalist and traveller, visited Forteviot in 1772, describing it as 'once the site of a Pictish palace'. Pennant does not refer to any remains of the royal centre but, in contrast, mentions the nearby traces of Edward Balliol's camp from the Battle of Dupplin Moor in 1332. This suggests that Pennant either did not consider them noteworthy or, more probably, saw none. The *Statistical Account* (1797 [1976: 199]) records that Haly Hill 'was once the site of a royal residence' but that 'nothing now remains of these buildings'. This suggests that references to standing walls on Haly Hill are either exaggerated or relate to an earlier period, and were possibly based on oral traditions dating from when the site was in a better state of preservation.

Nevertheless, 'T' refers to the presence of archaeological deposits on Haly Hill: 'From its present ruined condition, one would be naturally led to imagine that the elements have combined to raze it to the foundation; for the burnt stones and embers, of which it is composed, evidently prove that its destruction has been effected by fire.' Moreover, erosion caused by the Water of May had exposed stratified deposits on one side of Haly Hill. These comprised 'some stratas of black earth, resembling that dug out of graves; and also a great many bones apparently human' ('T' 1772: 332; see also *Statistical Account* 1797 [1976: 199]; Stuart 1856: 17). Although there are cemeteries at Forteviot (Chap. 3), this account need not refer to mortuary deposits. Deposits of dark soil often occur on early medieval occupation sites, including the hillfort and probable royal centre of the Scots of Dál Riata at Dunadd, Argyll (Lane and Campbell 2000: 69-76). Known to soil scientists as anthropic plaggen soils, these deposits develop as a result of intense and/or prolonged human occupation, are characterised by a high organic content and contain midden material. The reference to human bones lacks authority and may have arisen from the misidentification of animal bones, which frequently occur in dark soil deposits, as at Dunadd (Craw 1930: 114; Noddle 2000).

Although antiquarian accounts differ about the state of preservation of the remains at Forteviot, their terse and vague nature indicates that the structures concerned were in such a ruinous condition that their form, function and date were not apparent. It is of interest, therefore, that the earliest antiquarian record of Forteviot, in *The Muses' Threnodie*, also contains the only reference to Malcolm Canmore's castle. This, however, is anachronistic, as the earliest masonry castles in Scotland do not predate the twelfth century, while Malcolm reigned during the eleventh. Moreover, there is no evidence, archaeological or documentary, to support the former presence of a castle at Forteviot. If Malcolm had a fortification at Forteviot it is more likely to have been a motte, a man-made earthen mound that formerly supported a timber castle, although there is no evidence of this.

Nevertheless, there is a persistent tradition that Forteviot was the site of a fortified royal residence. David Smith's poem, *The Emigrant's Farewell to the Banks of the May*, written in Perth sometime between 1820 and 1835 (quoted in Meldrum 1926: 143), refers to Forteviot as a 'fortress and city', although his allusions to the Philistine city of Gaza reflect some poetic licence. MacGibbon and Ross (1897, vol. 3: 623) believed that 'an ancient church ... formerly occupied a site within a rath or stronghold which stood on the Haly Hill'. Their description of the site as a rath, a term more commonly used to refer to Irish ringforts, implies an earthwork fortification, presumably comprising an earthen rampart. In contrast, David Christison, the pioneer of hillfort studies in Scotland, makes no reference to Forteviot in his surveys (Christison 1898; 1900). However, a fort, particularly a poorly preserved one that no longer survived by the time Christison was conducting his fieldwork, could have escaped his attention. Uncertainty whether the royal centre was fortified still continues (Chap. 3).

The Church of St Andrew at Forteviot (NO050174) is located on the edge of the Forteviot scarp a short distance south-east of where Haly Hill once stood (*colour plate 6*). Although the present structure (*colour plates 7 and 8*) dates only from 1778 and was renovated and altered in 1867, it probably occupies the site of the pre-Reformation church consecrated by David de Bernham, Bishop of St Andrews, in 1241 and repaired in 1624 and 1688 (Meldrum 1926: 279; Churches 2002: 314; Forteviot n.d.). It is unclear if this was also the location of the early medieval church or if it occupied Haly Hill. Either way, the location of the church at Forteviot may have moved a short distance over time in response to erosion of the terrace edge by the Water of May. The sculptural assemblage and Celtic hand-bell (Chap. 5) indicate the site of an important early medieval ecclesiastical centre at or near the present church, implying continuity of worship at this location.

The location of the church on Haly Hill may be supported by parallels with other Pictish ecclesiastical sites. Low hills or mounds and terraces near the confluence of rivers were favoured sites for Pictish churches, probably influenced by the location of pagan ritual sites. The impressive steep-sided knoll at St Vigeans, Angus, now crowned by a thirteenth-century church (4), was previously occupied by an early medieval church, as its extensive assemblage of Pictish sculpture reveals (ECMS, vol. 2: 234-42, 267-80, 281; Cruden 1964: 23-8; Henderson and Henderson 2004: *infra*). The mound within the graveyard of St Bride's Church, Kildrummy, Aberdeenshire, may also be an early ecclesiastical site.

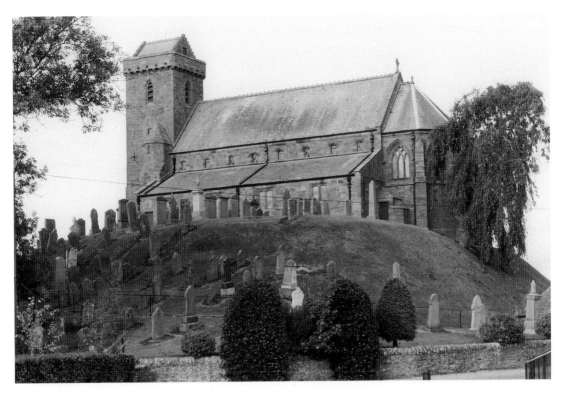

4 The impressive steep-sided knoll at St Vigeans, Angus, now crowned by a medieval church

The placename Haly Hill supports the presence of an early ecclesiastical site at Forteviot. The name appears to mean 'Holy Hill' or may be derived from 'All Hallows' (i.e. All Saints') Hill'. Although Haly Hill is not an ancient name, similar placenames are associated with medieval ecclesiastical sites. For example, Haly Mill, on the River Almond near Buchanty, Perthshire, was recorded as 'Sanct Mavane's mill' in 1542 (Watson 1926: 311). Revealing the association of such placenames with early Christian sites, the long cist cemetery at Hallow Hill, St Andrews, dates to the sixth to ninth centuries (Proudfoot 1996). It has been claimed that 'Hallow' placenames may be deliberate transliterations of earlier placenames and reflect attempts to promote the use of English and weaken any surviving reverence for the site and adherence to ancient, non-conformist Pictish or Culdee liturgy (Proudfoot 1996: 396-7, citing G. W.S. Barrow).

Antiquarian accounts are clearer about the fate of Haly Hill and whatever remains then survived on it. The shifting course of the Water of May was eroding the western scarp of the Forteviot terrace, a problem exacerbated by the periodic torrents that surge down the May from high in the Ochil Hills. The destructive

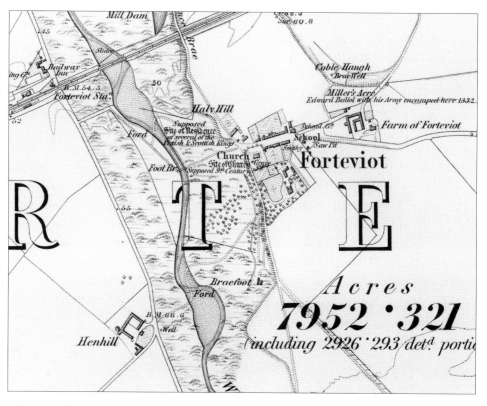

5 Forteviot, as depicted on the first edition Ordnance Survey six-inch map (sheet CIX) of 1866 (detail). *British Library*

character of the May when in spate and the fate of the royal centre are vividly captured in Smith's *The Emigrant's Farewell to the Banks of the May* (quoted in Meldrum 1926: 143):

> Take ancient Forteviot, the theme of my tale,
> In proof that a sandy foundation will fail.
> The May could not surely inundate their town,
> But, roaring beneath, brought everything down;
> Like fiercest invader who everything mars,
> The May ran away with their gates and their bars.
> As Samson took off, in a more remote day,
> The strong gates of Gaza and bore them away,
> So May when it rose, unsuspected in power,
> The fortress and city made bold to devour.

These periodic torrents frequently damaged or destroyed a wooden footbridge over the Water of May at Forteviot and the session books of the Parish of Forteviot record the Parish Session's continuous struggle to raise the funds required to maintain and replace this bridge throughout the eighteenth century (Meldrum 1926: 143-4, 281). In an entry recording that the footbridge was swept away and broken in the Lammas floods of 1739, the Session Books locate it 'bewest the kirk', revealing that this bridge crossed the May a very short distance downstream from Haly Hill. Concerns about the erosion caused by the May peaked in 1768-9, when the river was eroding its east bank to such an extent that it threatened to undercut the churchyard and the parish church itself (Meldrum 1926: 281-3). In response, a channel was cut and its banks revetted to canalise a stretch of the river. These measures were at least partially successful, because both the church and churchyard survived. However, Haly Hill and its ruins were less fortunate, possibly because the work undertaken on the banks of the May below the church may have exacerbated erosion a short distance downstream.

The decades either side of 1800 saw the greatest destruction wrought by the Water of May, threatening not only the remains of the royal centre but also the mound they occupied. In 1772, 'T' recorded that 'the water of May ... continues to sweep away yearly less or more of its [Haly Hill's] remaining ruins'. In 1797, 'the water of Mey [sic], by undermining below, is continually washing away less or more of the rubbish' (*Statistical Account* 1797 [1976: 199]). By that time, 'a great part of the site [Haly Hill]' had been 'carried off by the water of Mey [sic]', leaving 'only a part of the eminence' surviving and Haly Hill 'only about half as big as it was 30 years ago' (*Statistical Account* 1797 [1976: 199]). The destruction of Haly Hill was complete by 1830: 'Every vestige of the ruins, and even of the ground on which they stood, has now disappeared' (Brown and Jamieson 1830: 208; see also Skene 1857: 278; Stuart 1867: 59; Meldrum 1926: 19). There is no trace of any feature that may be identified as Haly Hill in the lithograph by William Brown, published in 1830, which shows the May flowing around the foot of the escarpment immediately below the church (*6*). But the destruction of the site was not solely attributable to the May (Marshall 1880: 103):

> They [the ruins of the palace] were used as a quarry for the building of minor structures as long as they supplied material for that purpose, and the remaining *debris* of them the May has been gradually encroaching on and reducing, mingling it with the rude mass of boulder, granite and other stuff in its channel.

This provides the physical context of the destruction of the remains of the royal centre and the site it occupied, as well as the discovery of the Forteviot arch (Chap. 6).

6 The Water of May is depicted flowing around the foot of the escarpment immediately below St Andrew's Church in this lithograph by William Brown, published in 1830. *Jamieson and Brown*, Select Views of the Royal Palaces of Scotland

The destructive powers of the Water of May when in full spate are well documented. The first railway bridge over the May at Forteviot was carried away in 1852, only six years after its construction, while the first road bridge shared the same fate in 1909, only a decade after it was built (Meldrum 1926: 281). In 1993, the May broke its banks and damaged the railway bridge at Forteviot so severely that the main line between Dunblane and Perth was closed for three months. The May is prone to changing course after breaking its banks. In 1852, the May shifted course 600ft (183m) to the west (Meldrum 1926: 281) to the channel it still occupies, its banks now reinforced with large rocks to prevent it from changing course again. Faint traces of relict river channels are visible in the low-lying area between the foot of the scarp north-west of the parish church and the present river channel.

This is only the latest of many changes in course made by the Water of May over time. The ease with which the May has scoured new courses out of the gravel is revealed by aerial reconnaissance, where the relict channels show as dark, sweeping arcs south-west of Forteviot (7). North of Forteviot, relict river channels at Coble Haugh and Forteviot Haugh suggest that the May once flowed around Forteviot on the west and north before meeting the River Earn at Newmillhaugh, 1 mile (1.5km) downstream from their present confluence. If so, the royal centre occupied a promontory that was all but surrounded by the May (8).

7 Cropmarks of the henge monuments at Forteviot (centre). Traces of relict river channels are visible as sweeping dark bands between the edge of the Forteviot terrace and the present course of the Water of May (left). St Andrews Church is at the top left and the features in *colour plate 9* appear in the field at the top centre. *Crown copyright: Royal Commission on the Ancient and Historical Monuments of Scotland (John Dewar Collection)*

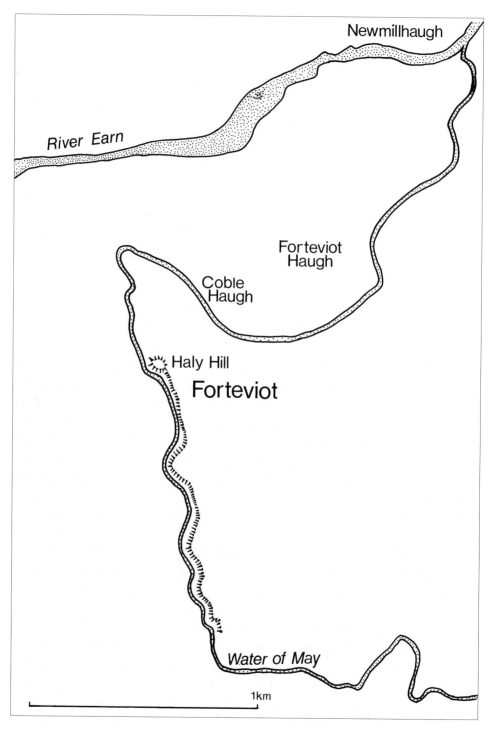

8 Forteviot: a conjectural reconstruction of the topography during the early medieval period

The changing course of the Water of May and the destruction it has wrought have changed the landscape, not only destroying the site of the royal centre but also removing the ground on which it once stood. This has caused some confusion about the former location of Haly Hill. The first edition Ordnance Survey six-inch map (sheet CIX) of 1866 (5) locates Haly Hill but carries the legend 'Supposed Site of the Residence of several of the Pictish & Scottish Kings' in the low-lying area between the scarp and the May, on the edge of the Forteviot terrace north-west of the village. This map also records 'Site of Church – Supposed 9th Century' a short distance to the south-east, on the site of the modern parish church. It is unclear why the Ordnance Surveyors made a distinction between these sites and located them where they did. This map and earlier accounts consistently record that Haly Hill was located north-west of the parish church. This places it in the area where the B935 now ascends the edge of the scarp as it enters the village of Forteviot from the west and, just beyond the road, a waterlogged area at the foot of the escarpment.

Given the limited documentary references to early medieval Forteviot, archaeological evidence potentially provides more information about the character and functions of the royal centre. The only archaeological excavations conducted at Forteviot were directed by Professor Leslie Alcock in 1981 (Alcock and Alcock 1992: 228-30). Recognising 'the primary significance of Haly Hill for any programme of archaeological research' at Forteviot (Alcock and Alcock 1992: 228), Professor and the late Mrs Alcock's objective was to test whether any of the structural remains attributed to the royal centre in the late eighteenth century still survived. These exploratory excavations were very limited in scale and comprised two small trenches located on what the Alcocks believed were the remains of Haly Hill, on the edge of the scarp overlooking the Water of May (3). But the Alcocks' objective and strategy was based on a false premise because it underestimated the extent to which the landscape around Forteviot has changed as a result of erosion of the edge of the Forteviot terrace by the Water of May. Although the Alcocks acknowledged that this was formerly a more pronounced feature, they marked Haly Hill on their map and referred to it in the present tense (Alcock and Alcock 1992: 220, 228), as if it still existed. However, antiquarian accounts state clearly that Haly Hill had disappeared by the early nineteenth century.

Despite this, the Alcocks' excavations comprised a useful, though negative, test to see if any traces of early medieval activity survived on the Forteviot terrace near the former site of Haly Hill. Both trenches revealed no evidence of any activity earlier than the eighteenth century, although it is unclear if this was a result of the limited nature of the excavations and/or of later disturbance of the site. Despite claims that 'the wider archaeological and topographical context [of the Forteviot arch] has been fully explored' (Henderson and Henderson 2004: 209), no early medieval archaeological feature at Forteviot has ever been investigated.

MONUMENTS AND RITUAL AT FORTEVIOT

Despite the disappearance of Haly Hill, significant archaeological remains still survive at Forteviot. Aerial reconnaissance by Professor J.K.S. St Joseph of the Cambridge University Committee for Aerial Photography in 1973-5 and 1977 revealed a complex of prehistoric and early medieval monuments in the landscape around Forteviot (*colour plate 9; 9*), some of which appear to have been associated with the early medieval royal centre (St Joseph 1976: 56-7, pl VIIa; 1978; Alcock 1982: 229-33; 2003: 28; Alcock and Alcock 1992: 230-1, 234-6; Brown 1992). Identified from cropmarks in ripening arable crops, this technique has made the single greatest contribution to our understanding of the royal centre at Forteviot, although it has still to be followed up with the geophysical survey and excavation required to test the interpretation of cropmark features and their dating.

Aerial reconnaissance identified two main concentrations of archaeological features at Forteviot. The first, in fields on the south-east of the village, includes a sub-circular enclosure, linear ditch and rectangular enclosure (*colour plate 9; 9* features 1, 2 and 3), the functions and dates of which are unclear. But the most numerous and interesting features discovered in this area are a scatter of funerary monuments and graves comprising a cemetery that was probably associated with the royal centre (Chap. 3).

The second concentration of archaeological features revealed by aerial reconnaissance lies about one third of a mile (0.5km) south of Forteviot (7, 9). Although no longer visible on the ground, the most striking component of this is a complex of henge monuments (Harding and Lee 1987: 409-11; Darvill 1996: 190-1; Gibson 1998: 71-3, 76-7; 2002: 9-13, 18). This class of monument, which typically comprises an enclosure formed by an earthwork bank and/or timber uprights, was associated with ritual activity and belongs to the late Neolithic or early Bronze Age, *c.*3000-2000 BC (Clare 1986; Harding and Lee 1987; Wainwright 1989; Burl 1991; Harding 2003). The principal structure at Forteviot is a massive palisaded enclosure, sub-circular in plan, its former presence now revealed only by the individual post-holes which would have held substantial timber uprights (*9*, feature F). This enclosure measures approximately 730 x 600ft (265 x 220m) and encloses an area of about 15 acres (6ha). Although unexcavated, the interpretation of this structure as a Neolithic henge monument is supported by the close similarities it shares with excavated palisaded enclosures in Britain and Ireland (Gibson 1998; 2002).

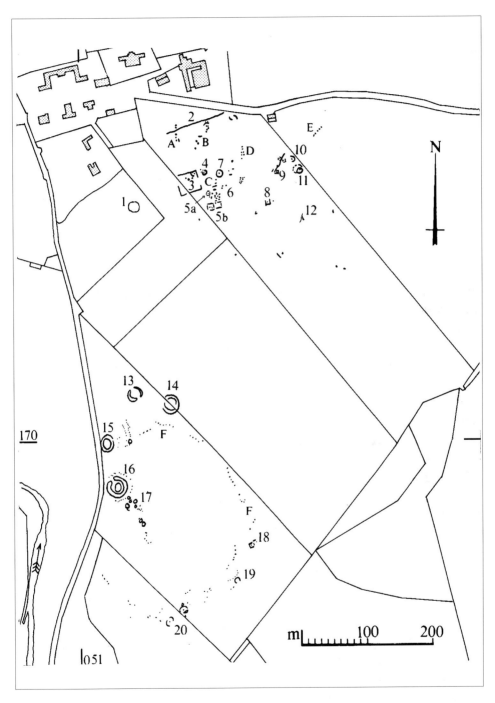

9 Aerial reconnaissance revealed a complex of prehistoric and early medieval monuments in the landscape around Forteviot. This reconnaissance identified two main concentrations of archaeological features at Forteviot

The palisaded enclosure is approached from the north by a short avenue, defined by two rows of post-pits, 20ft (6m) apart and 115ft (35m) long. This suggests that the enclosure was an integral part of a wider ritual landscape, to which it may have been linked by processions. This ritual landscape held another four earthwork enclosures, circular in plan, ranging from about 50-165ft (15-50m) in diameter and each with one or two entrances (9, features 13-16). One of these enclosures lies within its own palisaded enclosure and is also located within the interior of the much larger palisaded enclosure. The other three lie just outside the large enclosure and adjacent to the avenue.

An upstanding monument just to the south of this complex reinforces Forteviot's status as a focus of early prehistoric ritual activity. A large cairn stands in a small wood at Mijas (NO053166), near the edge of the Forteviot terrace overlooking the Water of May and half a mile (0.8km) south of Forteviot. Despite being disturbed and covered with trees, this monument still survives 72ft (22m) in diameter and 4ft 7in (1.4m) high. Although unexcavated, this is probably a funerary monument of the late Neolithic or early Bronze Age, c.2500-1500 BC.

Although the henge monuments at Forteviot no longer survive as upstanding structures, this is a result of their destruction by ploughing, probably reflecting both the cumulative impact of cultivation over several centuries and more intensive farming and mechanised ploughing in recent decades. These henges would have been very different during the early medieval period, impressive structures with a conspicuous monumental presence that dominated the landscape surrounding the royal centre. This remarkable complex of monuments reveals that Forteviot was an important focus of ritual activity around 3000 years before it was a Pictish royal centre. But while there is no evidence of continuous activity at Forteviot during the intervening millennia, the relationship between prehistoric monuments and early medieval royal centre is no coincidence. Instead, these monuments were probably invested with an ideological significance and were the setting of rituals of royalty (Chap. 3).

Aerial reconnaissance provides some tantalising and unique insights into the nature and extent of early activity at Forteviot. The archaeological features detected from the air hint at the richness of Forteviot and provide obvious targets for archaeological investigation.

3

THE CHARACTER AND FUNCTIONS
OF THE ROYAL CENTRE

Sources record the association of several Pictish and early Scottish kings with Forteviot (Chap. 1). But what were these kings doing there? In order to identify the royal activities performed at Forteviot, this chapter examines the character and functions of the royal centre, insofar as they can be inferred from the limited documentary and archaeological evidence available. Unfortunately, the form and appearance of the royal centre remain elusive, given the limited archaeological evidence, although future work will hopefully add to this. Nevertheless, the function, or rather functions, of the royal centre may be identified from the fragmentary evidence. Forteviot was a veritable royal complex, a combination of royal residence or 'palace', church, cemetery, assembly place and focus for ritual activities, as well as a centre for the management of agricultural production and redistribution on an extensive royal estate.

The specialist terms used to describe Forteviot in early medieval sources are of particular interest. Forteviot is referred to as a *palacium* in the *Chronicle of the Kings of Alba* (ed. Hudson 1998: 148) and as an *urbs* in the St Andrews foundation legend (ed. Skene 1867: 185). *Palacium* and *urbs* convey Forteviot's great importance and are of particular significance because only a very small number of places, not only in Pictland but in early medieval northern Britain as a whole, are referred to by these terms. But the significance of Forteviot's status as a *palacium* and *urbs* is not straightforward because of uncertainty surrounding the meaning of these terms, while little detail can be gleaned from analogy with other sites referred to by the same terms.

What did early medieval scribes mean when they described Forteviot as a *palacium* and *urbs*?

ROYAL RESIDENCE

Palacium is an alternative spelling of Latin *palatium*, 'palace'. 'Palace' evokes images of architectural splendour and opulent furnishings associated with buildings intended for the private pursuit of royal pleasure. But relatively modern preconceptions must be set aside to consider the definition and functions of early medieval palaces (Steane 1999: 71–116; 2001: 21–124; Keevill 2000: 12–18). Although their function changed over time, the basic definition of a royal palace is a residence, a place where the king and his court lodged for one or more nights at a time on a reasonably regular basis over a prolonged period.

That Forteviot was a royal residence is supported by its association with several Pictish and Scottish kings between the ninth and twelfth centuries (Chap. 1). In particular, the St Andrews foundation legend records that the sons of the Pictish king, Hungus (Unuist son of Uurguist), remained at Forteviot while their father was away on campaign (ed. Skene 1867: 185). Forteviot's status as a royal residence during the mid-twelfth century is attested by the witnesses to a charter issued by William the Lion at Forteviot in 1162x64, who included the king's mother, Countess Ada, and brother, also William (RRS, vol. 1: 271, no. 256).

Forteviot is traditionally described as a royal 'capital' of the Picts and, later, of Malcolm Canmore. However, Pictish and Scottish kings were not permanently resident or based at a single royal centre. Indeed, there were no such things as 'capitals', single seats of royal government and administration, during the Middle Ages. Instead, peripatetic kingship was the norm and the success of a king's reign depended on his visible presence to his subjects. The king, accompanied by his court and household, comprising royal relatives, nobles, officials, servants and bodyguard, travelled around his kingdom. Rather than residing at single locations, kings probably had several favourite royal centres at which they preferred to engage in certain activities, such as hunting, or where they celebrated the major Christian festivals. This would probably have been done according to a combination of personal preference, logistical factors and traditions inherited from their predecessors. Kings were therefore likely to spend certain times of year at certain royal centres, which corresponds with the practice of an annual progress.

There are no contemporary references to the royal progress in early medieval Scotland, although it is perhaps implied by Hungus' presence at *Chondrochedalvan* after leading a campaign in Argyll and leaving his wife at *Monichi* and his sons at Forteviot (ed. Skene 1867: 185-6). A later chronicle records that Duncan I (1034-40) 'observed the praiseworthy custom of traversing all the provinces of his kingdom once a year to comfort graciously with his presence his own peaceful people' (Bower, book IV, ch. 49; trans. Watt 1989: 421). The royal progress in early medieval Northumbria also provides an analogy for Pictish practices. In 681, Ecgfrith of Northumbria and his queen 'were making their progress through the cities, fortresses and villages (*per civitates et castellas vicosque*) with worldly pomp and daily feasts and rejoicings', according to the *Life of Bishop Wilfrid* by Eddius Stephanus (chap. 39; ed. Colgrave 1927: 78; trans. Webb 1983: 146). Separately, Bede (*Historia Ecclesiastica*, II.16; trans. Sherley-Price 1990: 135) refers to the progress of Edwin of Northumbria (617-33) 'on horseback through city, town and countryside in the company of his thegns'.

The royal progress is implied by the large number of Pictish and Scottish royal centres (on which see Alcock 1981; Foster 1998), where kings would have resided while travelling around their kingdoms and the number and nature of locations where the presence of kings was recorded. Many of these early medieval royal centres occupied naturally-defended locations, usually hilltops or coastal promontories, strengthened with man-made defences. Attesting their fortified character, several sites with royal associations are referred to in Irish and Scottish sources as *dùn*, 'fort, fortress', such as Dundurn, the *Dùn Duirn* of the Irish annals (AU s.a. 682.3), in upper Strathearn (*colour plate 10*) (Alcock *et al.* 1990).

As a result of their siting, space was very restricted within the interiors of most Pictish and Scottish fortified royal centres. In contrast, Forteviot occupied a site of greater utility and flexibility. The Forteviot terrace comprised an open, extensive and gently sloping area that was suitable for many uses, including the construction of sizeable buildings and public activities such as assemblies and ceremonies. However, no traces of buildings belonging to the royal centre have been identified, despite the wide range of features, including timber structures, detectable as cropmarks. This is presumably because their sites were either swept away by the Water of May (Chap. 2) or lie under the modern hamlet of Forteviot, leaving a sizeable area within which structures may lie undetected or have been destroyed. In the absence of any structural evidence, the layout of the royal centre remains unknown, although Anglo-Saxon palace complexes may be instructive. These are sometimes characterised as 'dispersed', implying only informal planning or no planning at all. However, it is clear that the principal buildings of some royal centres, notably Yeavering, Northumberland (Hope-Taylor 1977), are aligned, implying careful planning and reflecting their formal and ceremonial functions (*10*).

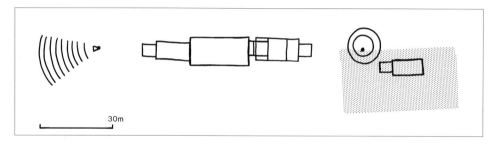

10 The Anglian royal centre at Yeavering, Northumberland: the alignment of the grandstand (left) with the royal halls and cemetery. *After Hope-Taylor 1977*

Although it is unclear what structures formerly stood at the royal centre, its nucleus probably comprised one or more royal halls, supported by various ancillary buildings and a church, of which there is evidence (Chaps 4 and 8). These buildings were probably the setting of many great affairs of state, including councils, feasts and a wide range of royal ceremonies, around which the lives of the kings and his court revolved when in residence. Although it has been claimed that *palacium* refers to a royal hall rather than the overall palace (Cowan 1981: 9; Alcock 1982: 212; but see Alcock and Alcock 1992: 222), the use of *palacium*, in preference to *regia aula*, 'royal hall', is significant. *Palacium* probably refers to the wider palace complex and perhaps to the royal centre as an institution rather than simply a building or group of buildings.

Royal halls were probably an integral component of Pictish royal centres. The hall features prominently in Celtic and Germanic heroic literature as the focus of the royal centre and the scene of equally heroic drinking and feasting, although they also had a domestic function (Alcock 2003: 248-54). Evidence for royal halls in Pictland is limited but two sources imply a similar importance and function. The St Andrews foundation legend refers to two royal halls (ed. Skene 1867: 140, 185), one of which belonged to Findchaem (*Finchem*), queen of Hungus. Findchaem gave to God and St Andrew not only the house (*domus*) at *Monichi* in which she gave birth but also the royal hall (*atrium regale*). The second reference does not belong to the ninth-century core of the legend but a version of *c.*1130, which uses a royal hall (*aula regia*) in St Andrews as a landmark for the site where a gate of the royal centre stood during Hungus' reign. But the most revealing reference to a Pictish royal hall is the *aula regia* of Bridei (Brude) son of Maelchon, king of the Northern Picts. Together with his *domus* (house), this stood in Bridei's royal fortress (*regis munitio*) near the River Ness and provides the setting for St Columba's mission to the Northern Picts (Adomnán, VSC II.33, 35; eds and trans Anderson and Anderson 1991: 142, 143, 146, 147).

Possible timber halls have been identified by aerial reconnaissance at 11 sites in Pictland, all of which occur singly except for at least five hall-like structures at Lathrisk, Fife (Maxwell 1987: 33-4) (*11, 12*). Although interpreted as royal palaces (Sutherland 1994: 67), this seems unlikely, as royal halls would normally be associated with ancillary structures and possibly a defensive enclosure. The interpretation of long, hall-like buildings should be treated with caution. Demonstrating the importance of confirming by excavation the interpretation of features detected from the air, a cropmark site at Balbridie, Aberdeenshire, was interpreted as an early medieval hall but, when excavated, proved to be a Neolithic mortuary house constructed some 3000-4000 years earlier (Hope-Taylor 1980; Reynolds 1980a; 1980b; Ralston and Reynolds 1981; Ralston 1982; Fairweather and Ralston 1993).

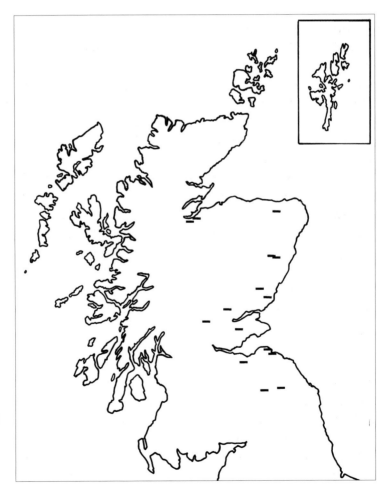

11 Distribution map of hall-like structures identified from aerial reconnaissance in Scotland. *After Maxwell 1987*

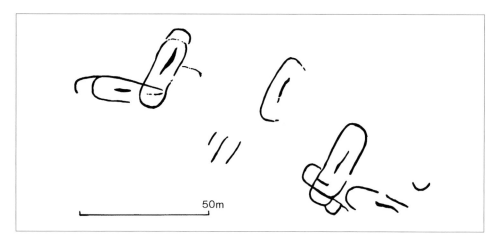

12 A plan of hall-like structures revealed by aerial reconnaissance at Lathrisk, Fife. *After Maxwell 1987*

The closest analogies to Pictish royal halls are probably the buildings of the Anglo-Saxon palace complexes at Yeavering, Cheddar (Somerset), Cowdery Down (Hampshire), Northampton (Northamptonshire), Milfield (Northumberland) (*13*) and Sprouston (Roxburghshire) (*14*) (Hope-Taylor 1977; Rahtz 1979; Millett and James 1983; James *et al.* 1984; Williams *et al.* 1985; Gates and O'Brien 1988; Smith 1991; see also Welch 1992: 17-21, 43-53; Keevill 2000: 19-22; Alcock 2003: 241-8). Despite their timber construction, these halls were substantial and must have been most impressive buildings. At Cheddar, a palace of the West Saxons, the principal building before *c.*930 was an aisleless timber long hall, rectangular in plan but with slightly bowed sides and measuring 78 x 20ft (23 x 6.5m). At Yeavering, a palace of the Anglian kingdom of Northumbria, the seventh-century hall (building A4) was even larger, measuring 83 x 48ft (25.3 x 14.7m) overall (*15*). These are widely believed to have been secular buildings, although those at Cheddar and Northampton have also been interpreted as minster churches (Blair 1996).

A similar structure has been excavated closer to Pictland. Hall A at Doon Hill, Dunbar, East Lothian, measured 75 x 34ft (23 x 10.4m) (Hope-Taylor 1966a; 1980; Reynolds 1980a; Alcock 1988: 5; 2003: 212-17). This may have belonged to an Anglian royal or lordly centre, although a Neolithic date has also been claimed (Smith 1991: 267). Other Anglian halls have been detected by aerial reconnaissance at Milfield and Sprouston (Gates and O'Brien 1988; Smith 1991: 276-80). A characteristic of many halls is the presence of a walled chamber at one or occasionally both ends, either as an integral element of the hall or as a projecting annexe. These were possibly the private chambers of kings.

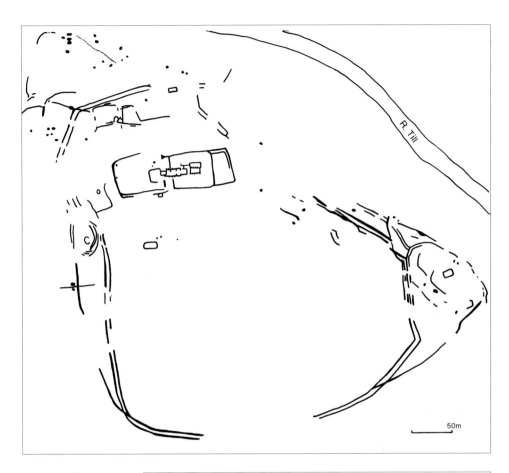

Above: 13 The Anglian royal centre at Milfield, Northumberland. A plan of the features revealed by aerial reconnaissance (detail). *After Gates and O'Brien 1988*

Right: 14 The Anglian royal centre at Sprouston, Roxburghshire. A plan of the Phase III features revealed by aerial reconnaissance. *After Smith 1991*

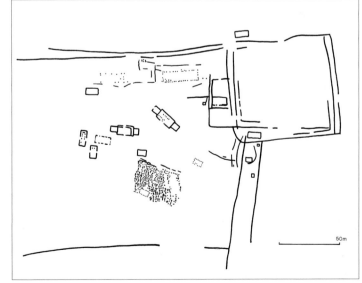

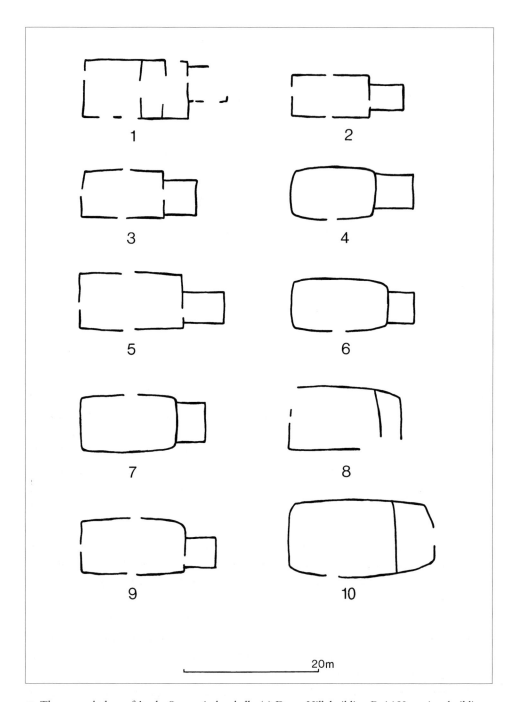

15 The ground plans of Anglo-Saxon timber halls: (1) Doon Hill, building B; (2) Yeavering, building Bb; (3) Yeavering, building A1c; (4) Sprouston, building E1; (5) Yeavering, building C4a; (6) Thirlings, building A; (7) Sprouston, building E2; Whitekirk, building B; (9) Yeavering, building C4b; (10) Whitekirk, building A. *After Smith 1991*

Royal residence implies a high standard of accommodation and this is probably reflected in the scale of construction, the quality of materials and craftsmanship employed and the comfort provided to royal residents. All these factors are apparent at Anglo-Saxon palace sites and may also have been the case at Forteviot. It is currently fashionable to view the royal centre at Forteviot against a Continental background and claim that it was equivalent to, modelled on, or at least ultimately inspired by, the Carolingian and Ottonian palaces at Aachen, Ingelheim and Maastricht (Airlie 1994: 33–6; Foster 1996: 48; Driscoll 2002: 36; Oram 2004: 37). Although the study of Continental palaces may assist the interpretation of Insular royal centres, such comparisons are ambitious (Driscoll 1998a: 47). Forteviot was on a much smaller scale and, with the exception of its church, even its grandest buildings were probably of timber construction. In terms of function, appearance, construction and size, Anglo-Saxon and other Insular royal centres provide more appropriate analogies.

ROYAL OWNERSHIP

Ownership is another defining quality of royal palaces. Residence alone does not identify a palace, as kings must also have resided with their nobles and senior officials, who would have owed obligations of hospitality to their king. Indeed, this was a key element of the relationship between a lord and his king, to whom he also owed dues in the form of food renders that were usually consumed by the king and his retinue when in residence. Palaces, however, were owned by the king. Uniquely among the royal centres of early medieval Scotland, the royal ownership of Forteviot is indicated by the St Andrews foundation legend (ed. Skene 1867: 185), which records that the sons of Hungus granted a tenth of the *urbs* of Forteviot to God and St Andrew for the foundation of a church. This reveals that Hungus' sons had the right to dispose of this royal land and, therefore, that they, or their father, or perhaps the royal dynasty as a whole, owned it. What land they actually gave is unclear. The implication is that Hungus' sons gave a tenth of the royal centre and this is supported by its description as an *urbs* (below). But it may refer to the giving of one tenth of the royal estate of Forteviot, not only for the construction of a church but also to support the foundation and its clergy from the dues and tribute of agricultural produce owed from those lands.

Charters and exchequer rolls confirm Forteviot's status as a royal thanage at a later date. Malcolm IV granted Forteviot's unappropriated parsonage to his chaplain in 1164 and it was subsequently granted to Cambuskenneth Abbey, Stirling, by William I in 1173x77 (RRS, vol. 2: 228, no. 161). William I also granted to Cambuskenneth Abbey four acres of arable land plus one croft and toft, that is, a homestead and the arable land attached to it, from his lands at Forteviot in 1178x88 (RRS, vol. 2: 259, no. 208). Robert I ('The Bruce') granted the lands of *Cardny* and *Dolcorachy* in the thanage of Forteviot to the canons of Inchaffray Abbey, Perthshire, in 1314 (RRS, vol. 5: 327-8, no. 39) and separately gave the 'lands of Fortevioté' to John Trollop (RMS, vol. 1, 541, no. 482; see also 541, no. 464). Forteviot remained in royal ownership until the late fourteenth century. Robert II granted land 'in tenement of Forteviot' in 1372 and gave his illegitimate son James 'all our lands and our mill of Forteviot with its appurtenances' in 1383 (RMS, vol. 1: 139, no. 395, 271, no. 730).

ROYAL GOVERNANCE

Royal centres were essential to the exercise of royal governance. Kings ensured that royal authority was exercised throughout their kingdom by progressing between their royal centres. The presence of the king, accompanied by his retinue of nobles, officials and his warband, would have helped to maintain royal authority and stifle dissent and revolt. In addition, the institutions of kingship enabled royal authority to be enforced through the making of laws and dispensing of justice, as well as the collection and consumption of dues and tribute from subjects. For example, the St Andrews foundation legend describes how Hungus was accompanied by an unspecified number of nobles at his royal centre at *Chondrochedalvan* (ed. Skene 1867: 186), presumably his entourage and/or local lords who gathered at his court there.

The dispensing of justice is emphasised in a later account of the progress of Duncan I (1034-40) (Bower, book IV, ch. 49; trans. Watt 1989: 421):

> When ... King Duncan was making his annual progress through the kingdom
> ... it was his practice to correct abuses unlawfully inflicted on the lower classes
> by the more powerful, to prevent unjust and irregular imposts on the part of his
> officials, to crush the wickedness of brigands and other criminals, who raged
> violently among the people, with a kind of judicious severity, and to calm down
> the internal disputes of his subjects.

Although there is no evidence of the dispensing of justice at Forteviot during the early medieval period, it would be surprising if kings did not preside over courts hearing legal cases there. There is, however, evidence of later judicial activity nearby. Gallows Knowe (NO049162) is a small promontory in the foothills of the Ochil Hills, overlooking the Water of May upstream from, and only 0.8 miles (1.3km) south-south-west of, Forteviot (Driscoll 1991: 102). Medieval execution places in Scotland, revealed by the gallows placename element, are often associated with an early court site, assembly place, administrative or royal centre. Although its placename is probably medieval or later in date, Gallows Knowe may have been used for the dispensing of justice from an earlier period and may have served the nearby royal centre.

The two twelfth-century charters issued at Forteviot attest the exercise of judicial powers at the royal centre. These charters probably reflect the outcome of cases brought before the king to receive his judgement while he was in residence at Forteviot. The exercise of governance at Forteviot is reinforced by the witnesses to the charter issued by William I at Forteviot in 1162x64 (RRS, vol. 1: 271, no. 256), who included both the king's Chancellor, Engelram, and his Constable, Richard de Moreuill', two of the most powerful royal officials.

Another manifestation of royal governance is the exercise of legislative powers and this is recorded at Forteviot as early as the mid-ninth century. During the reign of Domnall mac Ailpín (858-62), 'in Forteviot, the Gaels with their king made the rights and laws [that are called the laws] of the kingship of Áed son of Eochaid' (CKA, ed. Anderson 1973: 250; ed. Hudson 1998: 148; trans. after Anderson 1973: 189; Hudson 1998: 153). The distinction between rights and laws (*iura ac leges*) also occurs in the record of the legislation proclaimed by Causantín mac Áeda (Constantine son of Áed, 'Constantine II') and bishop Cellach 'on the Hill of Belief near the royal city of Scone' in 906 (CKA, trans. after Hudson 1998: 156). On that occasion, Causantín and Cellach 'covenanted to guard the laws and disciplines of the faith and also the rights of the churches and gospels in like manner with the Scots' (trans. Hudson 1998: 156).

These references indicate that *ius*, 'right' or 'law', refers to customary legal rights. The events recorded at Forteviot and Scone are probably the equivalent of the *rechtgae fénechais* described in early Irish law tracts, an ordinance of traditional law chosen by a people and confirmed by their king (*Críth Gablach*; ed. Binchy 1943: 20, ll. 515-16; see also Kelly 1988: 21-2; Hudson 1998: 153, n.12, 156, n.36). Indeed, the traditional character of those rights and laws made at Forteviot by Domnall and the Gaels is confirmed by their attribution to Áed Find mac Echdach (748?-778), king of Dál Riata. This assembly appears to have proclaimed in Pictland the traditional laws of the Scots of Dál Riata (Skene 1876, vol. 1: 323; Anderson 1922, vol. 1: 291). That this was done by 'the Gaels with their king' implies the public proclamation of laws in the presence of the king and before his assembled subjects. This is paralleled in eighth-century Ireland, where ecclesiastical laws had to be proclaimed publicly among the laity and in the presence of the king and senior clerics (*Collectio Canonum Hibernensis*, ed. Wasserschleben 1885: 62, 81; see also Hudson 1998: 156, n. 36). Early medieval political ceremonies were often celebrated on holy days (Schaller 1974) and this particular event may have involved considerable numbers of people gathering at Forteviot.

The participation of 'the Gaels' (*Goídel*) in the proclamation at Forteviot is significant. As a term of collective kinship, denoting the belief in their descent from the eponymous, but mythical, Goídel Glas, *Goídel* emphasises that the Scots were of different ancestry from the Picts. Invoking the identity of the Gaels in the making of these laws has been interpreted as part of the strategy by which the conquering Scots replaced Pictish legal institutions with their own (Hudson 1998: 153, n.12). However, the identification of the descendants of Alpín as Pictish rather than Scottish kings (Chap. 1) weakens this interpretation. Nevertheless, there appears to have been an ethnic dimension to this event, although its nature and significance are unclear. By reissuing the laws of his predecessor in the kingship of Dál Riata, Domnall was proclaiming the ascendancy of his dynasty over Pictland and using the enactment of legislation to entrench his power over Pictland and the Picts.

The proclamation of laws and rights at Forteviot by Domnall and the Gaels was clearly an occasion of major importance for it to merit recording. This is reinforced by its status as one of only two events at Forteviot recorded in the *Chronicle of the Kings of Alba* and the only event in Domnall's reign recorded in any source. Forteviot's role as a place of national assembly, with legislative and presumably judicial functions, underlines its status as a royal power centre and gives an insight into the type of activities underpinning royal governance that were performed there.

RITUALS OF ROYALTY

Another defining quality of royal centres was as foci for the celebration of rituals, particularly those associated with kingship. Indeed, Forteviot may owe its origins as a royal centre to its status as a central meeting place and place of ritual activity. The physical context of ritual is of particular significance and the open and level terrain of the Forteviot terrace was well suited to hosting large, open-air assemblies. In addition to practical factors, ideological and symbolic considerations probably also played an important part in the siting of the royal centre at Forteviot. The setting of rituals within a landscape dominated by prehistoric monuments (Chap. 2) enabled Pictish kings to draw upon the legitimacy conferred by the past. The association of early medieval royal centres and prehistoric monuments is readily paralleled in northern Britain and Ireland (Bradley 1987; 1993: 113-26; 2002: 141-8; Aitchison 1994: 50-130).

Its location within an extensive complex of ritual monuments attests the importance of the physical setting of early medieval kingship and distinguishes Forteviot as a place of special significance, a theatre for rituals of royalty. This may have been one of the functions of the ancient henge monuments (Foster 1998: 20), their substantial banks providing a grandstand for participants to view or participate in a wide range of public occasions, possibly including ceremonial and ritual events, assemblies and legislative and judicial courts. Such events were typically performed in the open air during the early medieval period. Adding to the socio-political significance of these occasions, while the banks of these prehistoric monuments would have formed a convenient area for participants, they also facilitated the deliberate exclusion of those outside. These embanked enclosures may have performed a similar function to the purpose-built wedge-shaped wooden 'grandstand' at Yeavering, which seated an estimated 150 people and latterly up to 320 (Hope-Taylor 1977: 119-24, 241-4; Alcock 2003: 238-40).

But the henge monuments at Forteviot were more than simply convenient stadia. Instead, they attest the relationship between monuments, memory and place. Monuments derive their significance as cultural foci from their status as physical sites that belong simultaneously to both the past and the present. By bridging the gap between past and present and making sense of place, monuments can function as places or markers of communal memory and national identity, providing the foci around which social memory coalesces and histories or mythologies are constructed. It is this interplay between past and present that explains the later reuse of many monuments as sacred sites of re-enactment and commemoration. This gives monuments a potent role in the negotiation of power and identity, providing socio-political élites with a means of controlling the landscape. Relations of social and cultural dominance and dependency are (re)produced within a selective and deliberate landscape created by the dominant culture and by excluding or marginalising subordinate and minority groups.

The juxtaposition of a Neolithic/early Bronze Age ritual complex and an early medieval royal centre is an expression of the power of the past and attests the appropriation of ancient monuments within the landscape by later socio-political élites. Those élites actively manipulated their association with the past to promote their own political aspirations and legitimise a changing social order by creating and emphasising a direct, linear relationship between past and present. This may have been done through the celebration of royal inauguration rituals within the monumental complex, reinforcing the legitimacy of the king and his kingship by projecting him as a descendent of those who were believed to have built the ancestral monuments and of the royal predecessors who were buried in the barrows sited around the enclosure (below). Such associations not only demonstrate that Forteviot was a landscape *of* memory but emphasise the status of landscape *as* memory, incorporating monuments, cemeteries (below) and significant natural features, such as the Forteviot terrace, the Water of May and its confluence with the River Earn. All presumably fostered shared memories of important socio-political or religious events, beliefs and practices or the personalities associated with them.

The status of the Forteviot henges as arenas of ritual activity during the first millennium is confirmed by the presence of several barrows within and around them (below). And, although there is no direct evidence, the promulgation of the rights and laws of Áed son of Eochaid by Domnall mac Ailpín and his subjects may have taken place within one of the henges. This may be paralleled by Anglo-Saxon practices. On succeeding to the kingship of Northumbria in 926, Athelstan, king of Wessex, summoned the rulers of northern and western Britain to an assembly at Eamont Bridge, near Penrith, Westmorland, where 'they confirmed peace with pledges and with oaths ... and they forbade all devil-worship' (ASC, version D, s.a. 926; but see Hudson 1994a: 74-5). The choice of assembly place is significant because Eamont Bridge, like Forteviot, is the location of a complex of henge monuments (Topping 1992).

With the exception of the promulgation of the rights and laws of Áed, no royal ceremonies at Forteviot are recorded. Nevertheless, a wide range of rituals were probably performed there and different rituals may have been celebrated at specialised foci. The henge monuments were not the only location of royal rituals at Forteviot. Reflecting the close relationship that existed between kingship and the Church, the *basilica* at Forteviot (Chap. 4) was presumably the setting of the more overtly Christian rituals of royalty performed within the royal centre. This is where the king and his court, when in residence, would have celebrated the major Christian festivals and venerated the holy relics kept there, particularly on the feast days of the saints concerned. Many of the great affairs of state, including royal weddings and funerals, and possibly the inauguration of kings and ecclesiastical councils, may have been conducted inside the *basilica*. Royal worship was probably more public in early medieval society, reflecting the relative closeness of a king to his people before the extension of the social hierarchy and the consequent distancing of kings from their subjects during the high Middle Ages. As a result, the *basilica* was probably the setting of public rituals, the ecclesiastical equivalent of those open-air legislative assemblies that may have been held within the monumental landscape surrounding the royal centre.

Although unconfirmed, circumstantial evidence points to the possible status of Forteviot as a royal inauguration site. One of the laws of Aed Find may have concerned royal succession (Skene 1876, vol. 1: 323). If so, its proclamation at Forteviot is significant, the setting of the royal inauguration centre symbolically strengthening the legitimacy of these laws. That Pictish kings were inaugurated at Forteviot is also supported by the close parallels that exist between the royal centre and the royal inauguration places of the Scots of Dál Riata at Dunadd and of the medieval kings of the Scots at Scone (Driscoll 1998b; Aitchison 2000: 77-111; Campbell 2003). All three sites occupy symbolic locations, within ritual landscapes dominated by prehistoric monuments, on elevated sites overlooking rivers and near their upper tidal limits. There, 'the king was made ... where the salt waters of the sea (and the powers of death who dwell in it) are finally turned back by the living waters of the river' (Duncan 1978: 115). In addition, Forteviot is near the confluence of the Water of May and the River Earn. Confluences were sacred to the pagan Picts, who may have believed them to be propitious locations for the worship of river deities (Nicolaisen 1996: 17-22; 1997: 117). Many retained a ritual significance after the conversion of the Picts to Christianity, as the number of early ecclesiastical sites with *aber-* placenames (Nicolaisen 1996: 15-23; 1997) and/or located at or near confluences attest.

Forteviot and Scone share another similarity in that the focus of both royal centres appears to have been a mound. Moot Hill at Scone is a large, flat-topped mound, probably the *collis credulitatis*, 'the Hill of Belief', where laws were proclaimed in 906 (above), and the setting of the inauguration of the Scottish kings from at least the thirteenth century (Aitchison 2000: 78-9, 102-5) (*colour plate 11*). Mounds are a recurring feature of royal sites, including assembly and inauguration places, in early medieval Ireland (Aitchison 1994: 96-7, 139-42; Herity 1995; Swift 1996; FitzPatrick 2004a: 41-97; 2004b; Warner 2004: 57-8), indicating their integral role in rituals of royalty. In early medieval Scotland, mounds, whether purpose-built or appropriated prehistoric funerary monuments, were an integral component of the ceremonial apparatus of kingship and lordship (Driscoll 1991: 98-9; 1998c; 2000: 239). Although the form and significance of Haly Hill is unclear, these parallels suggest that it performed a central function in royal activities at Forteviot, perhaps including the setting of royal inauguration rituals. Alternatively, this role could have been performed by the prehistoric monuments at Forteviot (compare Anderson 1973: 203-4).

Another link between Forteviot and Scone has been claimed. Scottish kings were inaugurated on the Stone of Destiny at Scone until it was removed by Edward I of England in 1296. According to some, the Stone was kept at Forteviot during the reigns of the descendants of Cináed mac Ailpín (Meldrum 1926: 11) or even came from Forteviot (Campbell 2003: 58). However, the Stone's geology proves that it originates in the Scone area (Fortey *et al.* 1998; Phillips *et al.* 2003) and there is no evidence that it was kept anywhere else before 1296 (Aitchison 2000: 42-9). As Scone appears to have eclipsed Forteviot's importance as a royal centre after the ninth century (Chap. 10), the role of royal inauguration place may then have been transferred from Forteviot to Scone.

ROYAL BURIAL

Ritual activity at Forteviot is confirmed by the evidence of cropmarks. Although the features revealed need to be tested by excavation, provisional interpretations may be offered on the basis of analogies with excavated sites. Two concentrations of funerary monuments can be identified. The northern cemetery, south-east of Forteviot, includes about a dozen small square or circular enclosures, usually with a feature at their centre (*colour plate 9; 9*, features 4, 5a, 5b, 7, 8, 9, 10, 11). These are the remains of barrows, originally comprising an earthen mound covering a central grave and enclosed within a ditch. With the burial mound now ploughed away, all that remains of these monuments are the grave and enclosing ditch. The southern cemetery comprises about 13 round and square barrows (*9*, features 17-20) located inside and around the perimeter of the large henge monument (Chap. 2). These barrows are evidence that mortuary rituals were celebrated at the royal centre.

Round barrows belong to a class of simple monument that was common during prehistory and into the early medieval period. Square barrows are rarer and have a restricted distribution, confined to East Yorkshire and north-east Scotland. Around 35 sites with square barrows, occurring either singly or in cemeteries, are recorded in Pictland (Maxwell 1983: 31-3; 1987: 34-5; Close-Brooks 1984: 90-1, 94, 110; Ashmore and Maxwell 1996: 49; Murray and Ralston 1997: 376-9) (*16*). As at Forteviot, these often occur with round barrows in small cemeteries. Some of the square barrows display distinctive structural features. Two square barrows in both the northern and southern cemeteries at Forteviot are conjoined, sharing a common enclosing ditch on one side, and their ditches are not continuous but gapped by causeways at the corners (*9*, features 5b, 18).

Excavations at two sites in Angus reveal that square barrows date from the late Iron Age and early medieval period. At Boysack Mills, a square barrow with a continuous enclosing ditch covered an extended inhumation probably dating to the first or second centuries (Murray and Ralston 1997). The mixed composition of the Forteviot cemeteries, once considered unique (Alcock and Alcock 1992: 234), is now paralleled elsewhere in Pictland. At Redcastle, a cemetery

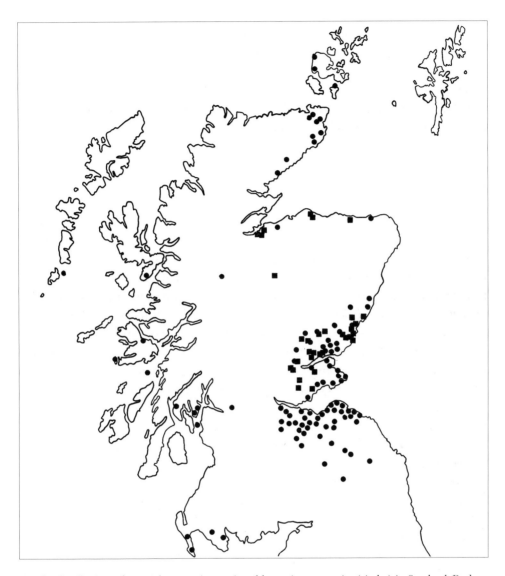

16 The distribution of square barrows (squares) and long cist cemeteries (circles) in Scotland. Both single sites and cemeteries are shown

comprised five square barrows, two round barrows and nine unenclosed graves (Selkirk 1999) (*colour plate 12*). The enclosing ditches of the square barrows had no corners. Radiocarbon dates ranged from the first to eighth centuries, with a concentration in the period 400–700 (Selkirk 1999: 396; Alexander 2000; Alexander and Dunwell 2003), placing them within the period of the historic Picts.

Related funerary monuments occur in northern Scotland. These are round and square cairns, comprising low platforms of stones covering a central long cist and surrounded by a kerb and sometimes a ditch. Although stone-built, a pair of square cairns at Sandwick, Unst, Shetland, and cemeteries of round and square cairns at Garbeg and Whitebridge, Inverness-shire, are otherwise similar to round or square barrows and the ditches enclosing some square cairns also have interrupted corners (Bigelow 1984; Close-Brooks 1984: 97-106; Stevenson 1984; Wedderburn and Grime 1984). Supporting its identification as a Pictish funerary monument, a square cairn at Dunrobin, Sutherland, was associated with a Pictish symbol stone (Close-Brooks 1980a; 1984; see also Ashmore 1980: 352; Gourlay 1984; Morris 1996: 50-3).

The royal centre at Forteviot was located within a monumental landscape of prehistoric enclosures and burial mounds (Chap. 2). The presence of two barrow cemeteries suggests that prehistoric henges were adopted for secondary burials or used as a focal point for early medieval burials. This is common in Anglo-Saxon England (Williams 1998) but is also attested in early medieval Scotland; for example, the 13 orientated burials inserted in the Neolithic henge monument at Strathallan, Perthshire, and radiocarbon dated to between 700 and 820 (Barclay 1983: 145, 148-50, 188). The timber uprights of the palisaded enclosure at Forteviot would have rotted away within decades of its construction. However, the siting of about seven barrows around the perimeter of the henge, including one in its entrance, indicates that an earthwork bank associated with it was still prominent during the early medieval period (Foster 1998: 20). The burials may have been inserted within this bank and the barrows raised from the earthwork. Around another seven barrows are grouped beside the smaller henge within the interior of the palisaded enclosure (9).

Although requiring confirmation by excavation and scientific dating techniques, these barrow cemeteries suggest that Forteviot was the focus of mortuary rituals from the early or mid-first millennium. These barrows, or some of them, may pre-date the founding of a church at Forteviot and attest the status of the site, and perhaps the origins of the royal centre, as a place of pagan ritual activity, focused on the prehistoric henge monuments.

A variety of mortuary rites is attested in early medieval Scotland (Close-Brooks 1984; Alcock, E. 1992) and this is also the case at Forteviot. Two small and compact clusters of short linear features also appear as cropmarks in the same areas as both barrow cemeteries, while several occur singly, scattered across the site (*colour plate 9; 9*, features A, B, C, D, 6, 17) (Alcock and Alcock 1992: 234; Brown 1992: 233). About 6ft (2m) in length, these are arranged in rows and aligned approximately east–west. Their size and context indicate that these are graves holding extended inhumations. They may be either long cist graves, where the sides and sometimes floor of the grave are lined with stone slabs, or simple dug graves, where the grave is dug directly into the soil and is unlined. Long cists, often in cemeteries, occur widely throughout Scotland but are concentrated in Lothian, Fife and Angus (Duncan 1996: 330; Proudfoot 1996: 441-6; Burt 1997) (*16*). Forteviot lies on the edge of this distribution.

The burials and funerary monuments identified from cropmarks at Forteviot probably represent only a small proportion of those surviving beneath the surface. Nevertheless, the range of mortuary rites represented and the association with a prehistoric monumental complex and Pictish royal centre make these cemeteries unique within Pictland. Forteviot provides the only evidence for the cemetery of a Pictish royal centre, a feature found more commonly at Northumbrian royal centres, as at Yeavering and Sprouston (Hope-Taylor 1977; Smith 1991: 280-3). The cemeteries at Forteviot present a unique opportunity, not only for understanding an important function of the royal centre but also for contributing to the study of the royal centre itself and, more widely, of Pictish social organisation.

It is unclear if these cemeteries were used by the inhabitants of Forteviot over a long period or by a wider community over a shorter timespan. Nevertheless, analysis of the cemeteries may enable the size and character of the community represented to be estimated and the relative status of individuals within that community to be assessed. The development and organisation of these cemeteries are probably closely related to the fortunes and function of the royal centre itself. For example, do the different types of burial at Forteviot represent a change in mortuary practices over time and perhaps reflect wider religious and social changes, for example from pagan barrow burials to Christian extended inhumations? Or does this reflect different mortuary rites for different social groups? Despite the apparent absence of buildings, it may still be possible to learn much about both the royal centre and its occupants. This, however, will require extensive excavation and analysis and will be largely dependent on the state of preservation of the burials and the survival of skeletal material.

Several features of the cemetery at Forteviot have social implications. The existence of two cemeteries, and the concentrations of barrows and long graves within them, suggests that burials were organised deliberately. These clusters suggest the burial of individuals belonging to groups with a common identity, perhaps families or communities, within specific areas. This hypothesis could be tested by DNA analysis of any surviving skeletal remains.

The formal arrangement of the long graves, reflected in their orientation and concentration, provides evidence of social organisation and implies organised burial for a specific, probably Christian, community. Bede (*Historia Ecclesiastica*, III.4) records that the Southern Picts were converted to Christianity 'long before' Columba's mission to convert the Northern Picts in 565, although the date concerned is unclear. The apparent absence of long graves within the southern cemetery suggests that there was no deliberate attempt to 'Christianise' what may have been perceived as a pagan site, the prehistoric henge monuments, by reusing it as a Christian cemetery. Although the immediate focus of the long graves appears to have been the northern barrow cemetery, they also suggest the proximity of a place of worship. This may have been the *basilica* at Forteviot (Chap. 4) or an earlier church on Haly Hill, about one third of a mile (300m) east–north-east. The sanctity and status of the *basilica* would have attracted not only pilgrims but also the burial of high-status individuals. This was probably promoted by the church, which would have benefited from its popularity as a burial place through the income generated from controlling the cemetery. The burial of kings and other members of the royal kin group would have been particularly prized because these probably brought with them certain privileges and substantial endowments, as in early medieval Ireland (Ó Floinn 1995: 251).

The largest barrows at Forteviot measure about 33ft (10m) across and, although dwarfed by the prehistoric henges, must still have been very impressive monuments. Those constructed on the surviving earthworks of the large palisaded enclosure must have been even more conspicuous. The ability to mark a burial by covering it with an earthen barrow, whether round or square, demonstrates a confident control of the resources – land, labour and materials – required. These barrows were permanent displays of prestige. The status of their occupants – and their builders, as mortuary rites and monuments reveal more about the living than the dead – would have been reinforced by their exclusive setting, beside a royal centre and within a prehistoric monumental landscape. As such, these monuments were powerful statements not only of local significance but also addressed a wider audience, probably including potentates attending Forteviot on royal business. The location of the southern group of barrows, within and around the large palisaded enclosure is significant here and implies that it was a focus of more than just mortuary rites but also other rituals of royalty (above). These monuments may also reflect a greater security of social status and a more rigid and/or extended social hierarchy. Reflecting their prestige and sanctity, the burial places of high-ranking individuals frequently attracted secondary burials within or around them. This may account for the grouping of barrows, the conjoined square barrows and the proximity of the long graves to the barrows at Forteviot. These features distinguish the barrows as the funerary monuments of members of a socio-political élite, perhaps Pictish kings or members of the royal kin group.

That Forteviot was the burial place of high-status individuals may be supported by the early medieval sculpture found there. In particular, Forteviot no. 1 belongs to a cross-slab, probably a commemorative monument or grave marker (Chap. 5). Pictish kings and members of the royal kin group may have been buried inside the royal church at Forteviot by the ninth century, as its status as a *basilica* suggests (Chap. 4). In particular, Forteviot was probably the burial place of Cináed mac Ailpín, who died there in 858, and possibly of Giric mac Dúngail, who may have been killed there in 889 (Chap. 1). Although some versions of the Scottish regnal lists claim that Cináed and Giric were buried on Iona (Lists D, F, I, K, N; ed. Anderson 1973: 266, 267, 273, 274, 282, 283, 288, 290), the formulaic manner in which they record the burial of most early Scottish kings there, regardless of the place and circumstances of their death, does not inspire confidence and suggests an attempt at aggrandisement by the later community of Iona.

PRODUCTION AND CONSUMPTION

Early medieval royal centres lay at the centre of an extensive landscape that was bound together in a complex network of social, economic and political relationships of dominance and dependency, duty and obligation, right and prerogative. Fiscal administration was an important function of royal centres, which were central places for the control of resources from the surrounding landscape. This primarily involved the production, collection, redistribution and consumption of agricultural produce. The fertility of Strathearn could not only have supported the periodic presence of the Pictish king and his household but also generated an agricultural surplus, which the king controlled through his lords and officials. The ability to produce an agricultural surplus was probably a key factor in the emergence of Strathearn as the heartland of Fortriu, the pre-eminent and most powerful kingdom of the Southern Picts. From their royal centre at Forteviot, the Pictish kings would have been able to survey the agricultural and social basis of their authority, the lands of lower Strathearn worked by their subjects that both symbolised and maintained those relations of authority between them.

As the central place of a surrounding royal estate, Forteviot was the administrative and fiscal centre where the king's tribute was collected and stored. The Latin term used by historians to describe such a place is a *caput*, although there are no historical references to Forteviot by this term. This estate was probably managed by a lesser-ranking noble or royal official who, unlike the king, was probably a permanent resident at Forteviot. The title of this official is unclear. However, three named *exactatores* were killed in the battle of *Monid Carno* in 729 (AU s.a. 728.2), when one competitor for the Pictish kingship may have attempted to impose his overlordship on, and exact tribute from, another (Aitchison 2003: 41). The recording of their deaths and names reveals that these *exactatores* were men of status. Significantly, this title is closely paralleled by that of the *exactores*, administrative officers responsible for managing Carolingian royal estates (Airlie 1990: 197; 1994: 26). The keeping of written accounts may have been used to record such transactions. Although there is no evidence for this at Forteviot, the St Andrews foundation legend (ed. Skene 1867: 188) refers to the presence of a scribe in the *villa*, presumably a royal vill (*villa regia, villa regis*), at Meigle (*Migdele*), Perthshire, during the reign of Uurad son of Bargoit (*Pherath son of Bergeth*) (839-42) (Clancy 1993: 350; Ritchie 1995: 4).

An important function of the royal progress was the consumption by the king and his court of the dues or tribute paid by subjects as food renders. These were collected at royal centres where the king resided as he travelled around his kingdom. This was not simply a matter of subsistence but, because power was ultimately derived from the land and its reproductive capacity, was fundamental to the maintenance of those social relations upon which royal power rested. Food renders supported the royal household, the king's warband and the specialists patronised by the king, including members of the learned classes and craftsmen. In this manner, the king displayed and maintained his royal status and power through lavish feasting and the giving of hospitality.

Although there are no historical records of this at Forteviot, feasting features prominently in early medieval Insular sources, particularly the north British epic poem *The Gododdin*, and must have been one of the principal contexts in which affairs of state were conducted. Although subsequently associated with Scone, Forteviot was the original setting of Scotland's most infamous feast (Hudson 1991: 18-19), the subsequent shift in location probably reflecting their contrasting fortunes as royal centres (Chap. 10). This episode appears in several sources from the eleventh century and relates how the Pictish nobility invited their Scottish counterparts to a feast. The Scots waited until their Pictish hosts were drunk, removed the bolts supporting the seats of their benches within the royal hall so that they fell into the pits below and slayed them. This mythological episode provided a convenient means of explaining how the Scots 'conquered' the Picts by reducing a long and complex process to a single dramatic event. Nevertheless, it is of interest that this myth portrays Forteviot (originally) as a place of feasting suitable for entertaining the élite of a neighbouring nation.

The principal unit of royal demesne in Scotland north of the Forth during the medieval period was the thanage (Skene 1880, vol. 3: 245-83; Grant 1993; Barrow

2003: 7-56). Although the terminology used during the early medieval period is unclear, the thanage almost certainly has Pictish origins, as the distribution of thanages is confined to north-eastern Scotland, the territory of historical Pictland. The official responsible for the management of a thanage, as well as the local organisation of military service and administration of justice, was the thane. Originally appointed by the king, the office of thane probably became hereditary over time.

Most of the evidence for thanes and thanages is late and Forteviot is no exception (Grant 1993: 80). The earliest record is not until 1264x66, when a thane of Forteviot (*thanus de Forteuiot*) had to account for 20 merks (*Exchequer Rolls*, vol. 1: 18). However, the thanage of Forteviot was probably in existence a century earlier, when a Gillechrist of Forteviot (*Gillecrist de Ferteuieth*) witnessed a charter of William I issued at Dunfermline in 1165x69 (RRS, vol. 2: 138, no. 28). This reveals that Gillechrist was a man of status who moved in royal circles. His name attests a close association with Forteviot, suggesting that he was its thane, although he is not recorded explicitly as such. The thane of Forteviot probably did not owe all the agricultural produce from his thanage to the king but paid a fixed or 'firm' amount, known as a *ferme*, annually. In 1358-9, the crown fermes of Forteviot were worth £5 (*Exchequer Rolls*, vol. 1: 558). Forteviot was not unique in being both a royal centre and a thanage, a status it shared with Scone.

An attempt to reconstruct the hypothetical extent of the pre-feudal thanage or shire of Forteviot from modern parish boundaries was made by Professor Stephen Driscoll (1991: 102-3), following Professor Geoffrey Barrow's maps of other shires (Barrow 2003: 7-56; see also Driscoll 1991: 99-100). However, this omitted the northern portion of the parish, thereby missing placename evidence of the division of the thanage into dependent estates, and also overlooked extensive changes to the parish lands over time, principally the addition of the adjoining parish of Muckersie in 1618 (Groome 1903, vol. 1: 610; Meldrum 1926: 182-3). The pre-thirteenth-century parish of Forteviot was not only large but also displays some distinctive features (*17*). Unusually, the parish boundaries are not defined by those natural boundary-markers provided by the River Earn and the Water of May. Instead, the parish of Forteviot straddles both watercourses. This is paralleled at other early medieval royal centres. For example, at Govan, an important ecclesiastical centre associated with the kings of the Strathclyde Britons, the large medieval parish straddled the River Clyde (Driscoll 2003: 77).

The medieval parish of Forteviot comprises a cross-section of lower Strathearn, stretching from the lower slopes of the Ochil Hills to the south, across the Forteviot terrace and the floodplain of the Earn, and onto the Gask Ridge north of the river, where it incorporates Dupplin and Pitcairnie lochs. This territory

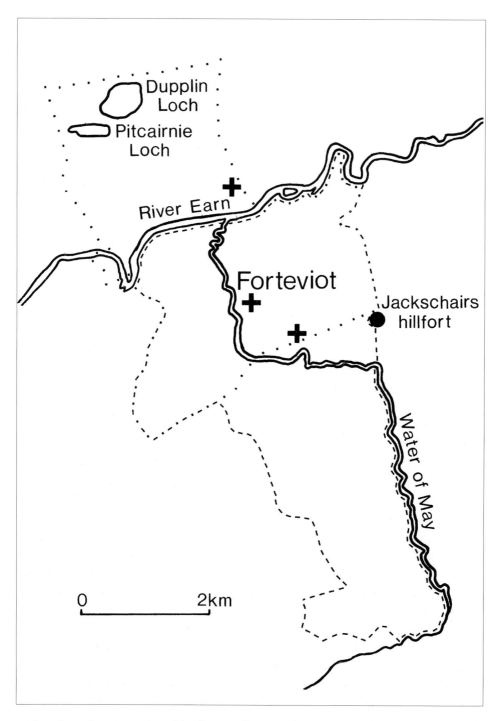

17 A conjectural reconstruction of the thanage of Forteviot by Professor S.T. Driscoll (dashed line) and based on the pre-thirteenth-century parish of Forteviot here (dotted line)

comprised good-quality agricultural land, including meadow and arable land but with ready access to hill grazing on the Ochils, and measured approximately 4.75 x 2.75 miles (7.6 x 4.4km) with an area of around 5059 acres (12,496 ha). The lochs and watercourses within the estate enabled the exploitation of a wider range of ecological zones, optimising self-sufficiency throughout the seasons by providing fishing and wild-fowling. And, befitting the function and status of a *caput*, Forteviot occupies a central location within this territory. These features suggest that the medieval parish of Forteviot originated as, and probably fossilises the territory of, an early medieval royal estate or thanage with an economy based on mixed farming.

The land would have been worked through several outlying dependent estates within the thanage of Forteviot, two of which may be identified. One of the most commonly surviving Pictish placename elements is *pet(t)*, literally a 'piece', 'portion' or 'share' of land, but probably denoting a dependent estate and, implicitly, part of a larger entity (Watson 1926: 407-14; Jackson 1955: 146-8; Whittington and Soulsby 1968; Whittington 1974; Nicolaisen 1976: 151-8; 1996: 6-17; Cox 1997: 47-53; Fraser, D. 1998; Fraser, I. 1999: 201). This survives in *Pit-* placenames, of which there are over 300 in north-east Scotland and one, Pitcairnie, in Forteviot parish. Pitcairnie's name survives in Pitcairnie Loch (NO028197) and the adjacent Cairnie Braes, Cairnie Moor, Cairnie Wood and the farms of Upper Cairnie and Wester Cairnie, all on the Gask Ridge. This location is characteristic of *pit-* placenames: well drained, south facing and away from the heavy soils of the floodplain of the Earn. Pitcairnie provides evidence of the division of the thanage of Forteviot into *pet(t)* places or dependent estates. Supporting this, 'all our lands of *Cardny* and *Dolcorachy* in the thanage of Forteviot with their appurtenances' were granted by Robert I in 1314 (RRS, vol. 5: 327-8, no. 39). *Cardny* is an early name form and reveals that Cairnie is not derived from Gaelic *carn*, a (burial) mound of stones, but Pictish *card(d)en*, 'brake', 'copse', 'thicket' (Watson 1926: 352-3; Nicolaisen 1976: 158-9; 1996: 24-6; Fraser 1987: 69, 70). This estate was presumably located on the edge of a wooded area.

Dolcorachy no longer survives as a placename, but its link with *Cardny* suggests that it may be identified with the adjacent estate, now occupied by the farm of Bankhead (Watson 1926: 418). *Dolcorachy's* name reinforces the agricultural significance of this dependent estate. The first element is Pictish *dol*, 'water meadow', 'haugh', a word borrowed into Gaelic as *dail*, while the original vowel survives in the cognate Welsh *dôl* (Watson 1926: 414; Nicolaisen 1996: 26; Fraser 1987: 68; 1999: 204; Taylor 2003). This was coupled with the genitive of Gaelic *corrachadh*, 'odd-field' or 'taper field' (Watson 1926: 418). This haughland lay in the floodplain of the River Earn. *Dolcorachy* probably took its name from a distinctively-shaped meadowfield in a bend in the Earn, such as that south of Wester Cairnie (at NO034177) (*colour plate 13*). They also support the interpretation of an economy based on mixed agriculture, with cereal production on the lighter soils and livestock farming on the rich grazing provided by the meadows along the floodplain of the Earn.

Although evidence of these dependent estates is limited and late, Forteviot may have conformed to the early medieval economic organisation known as the multiple estate (on which see Jones 1979; 1984; 1985; Kapelle 1979: 50-85; Davies 1982a: 43-7; but see Gregson 1985). The multiple estate comprised a principal settlement, the *caput*, supported by a hierarchy of several outlying and subsidiary settlements or farmsteads, forming a single grouped unit of administration, and owing rents, tributes or services. However, the precise forms of land ownership and estate organisation remain unclear and may have varied in space and time. Despite the interest in *pit-* placenames, Pictish agricultural organisation and royal estates remain little studied (but see Driscoll 1991).

Evidence for the royal control of resources at Forteviot is also sparse and late, although the granting of 4 acres of arable land at Forteviot by William I in 1178x88 (RRS, vol. 2: 259, no. 208) reveals the use to which at least some land was put. The milling of crops harvested within the thanage would have featured prominently in the control, collection, redistribution and consumption of agricultural produce. Reflecting this, a mill was probably closely associated with the royal centre and may have influenced its siting beside the Water of May. A mill is not recorded at Forteviot until 1383 (RMS, vol. 1: 271, no. 730) but may have existed at an earlier date. The location concerned is probably Milton of Forteviot, only one third of a mile (0.5km) north-west of Forteviot.

As a centre of agricultural production and distribution and, presumably, of those crafts patronised by the king and his court, Forteviot may also have been a trade centre. This would have been facilitated by its nodal location within the landscape, with good communication routes along and across lower Strathearn and its proximity to both a ford across, and the tidal limit of, the River Earn.

DEFENCE

Another defining quality of royal palaces is defence, reflecting the turbulent nature of early medieval society and politics, or at least enclosure, defining a royal residence from its hinterland in a symbolic statement of royal status. In addition, the church at Forteviot, with its wealth and relics of St Andrew (Chap. 4), may also have required a defensive site. The defensive quality of a location may be derived from its natural strength and/or the provision of man-made fortifications. Pictish fortifications vary considerably in construction and form but typically involved one or more enclosing ramparts of earth or stone, sometimes of massive proportions and occasionally timber-laced, with or without one or more external ditches (Alcock 1981; Aitchison 2003: 94-9; Ralston 2004).

Documentary sources may imply that the royal centre was fortified, particularly its description as an *urbs* (below) and a reference to 'the strong house' at Forteviot (*Prophecy of Berchán*, §139; ed. and trans. Hudson 1996: 45, 86). This may support the antiquarian tradition that the royal centre was fortified (Chap. 2). However, the former presence of fortifications at Forteviot has been rejected because they are not recorded in late eighteenth- or early nineteenth-century accounts made before the destruction of Haly Hill (Alcock 1982: 229). However, this is of uncertain relevance because Haly Hill had largely disappeared by then and any defences may also have been swept away by the Water of May. Moreover, little can be inferred from the absence of references to defences in these few laconic and imprecise antiquarian accounts. The remains of slight or poorly preserved defences may have attracted little interest in an area rich with hillforts. The systematic field survey of hillforts in Perthshire did not begin until a century after the destruction of Haly Hill and it is not surprising, therefore, that Forteviot is absent from these (Christison 1898; 1900). In addition to that part of the site swept away by the Water of May, another area of the royal centre probably lies beneath the modern hamlet of Forteviot. Present-day Forteviot occupies an area of approximately 10.8 acres (4.4ha), which could easily accommodate a great enclosure comparable to the double-palisaded examples that are characteristic of Anglian royal centres, such as Sprouston (1.7 acres (0.7ha)) and Yeavering (1.85 acres (0.75ha)). This should not be confused with the Neolithic palisaded enclosure, which predates the church at Forteviot by some three millennia (Chap. 2).

Paralleling a debate about Carolingian palaces (Gauert 1965), scholars remain divided about whether Forteviot was fortified or not. This debate has probably been prompted by the openness and accessibility of Forteviot's location, which contrasts with that of most Pictish royal centres. Could Pictish kings have lived in an unfortified or even unenclosed place when most of their royal centres were hilltop or coastal fortresses? Not surprisingly, therefore, Forteviot is claimed to have been fortified (Ritchie and Ritchie 1998: 28) and the site of a fortress (Anderson 1922, vol. 1: 266; Hudson 1996: 118), rath or cashel (Duncan 2002: 10). In contrast, others maintain that the royal centre was unfortified (Foster 1998: 16, 19), unenclosed (Sutherland 1994: 67) and even 'totally unenclosed' (Foster 1992: 225). Although the royal centre may have been enclosed by some form of bank or palisade of which no trace survives, there is no antiquarian or archaeological evidence that Forteviot was fortified (Driscoll 1998a: 47; 2001: 242; 2002: 35).

Forteviot does not occupy a position of great natural strength, revealing that defence was not a primary requirement in the siting of the royal centre. Of greater importance was its ability to meet the requirements of a focus of royal power and ritual, with the royal halls, church, assembly place(s) and cemeteries this required, particularly if these were associated with prehistoric monuments. Nevertheless, the location of the royal centre on a knoll at the edge of a steep escarpment dropping to the Water of May would have provided some measure of natural defence, at least on the west. Its strength would have been greater if, as suspected, the Water of May flowed around the north of the site to form a promontory (Chap. 2). Maximising its defensive potential and minimising the resources required for its construction and defence, a palisade may have cut off an area on the edge of the Forteviot terrace to form a small promontory fort. This need not have enclosed the entire royal centre, but may have defended a relatively small but significant area, presumably including Haly Hill.

In the absence of evidence that Forteviot was fortified, Skene believed that the requirement for defence was met by nearby hillforts. The closest hillfort to the royal centre is at Jackschairs Wood (NO072168). This occupies a foothill of the Ochils on the eastern boundary of the former parish and conjectural thanage of Forteviot, only 1.25 miles (2km) east-south-east of Forteviot. Although now poorly preserved and obscured by trees, this hillfort is roughly circular in plan and enclosed by four concentric ramparts with medial ditches, except where steep slopes provide natural defences on the west, and with an entrance on the east (Skene 1857: 276–7; Christison 1900: 106). Skene (1857: 277) identified this as the 'citadel' of an extensive royal centre at Forteviot and claimed that it lay at the centre of a circle of large hillforts occupying hilltops to the north and south of Forteviot, which, 'from the extensive prospect they command, would effectually guard against the unseen approach of an enemy'.

However, all these hillforts are unexcavated and undated and they may range widely in date and function. In particular, the form and location of those larger hillforts occupying elevated sites in the Ochil Hills are more consistent with late Bronze Age or early Iron Age than early medieval activity and may date from c. 1000–300 BC. However, the Jackschairs Wood hillfort and the royal centre may be linked by more than proximity. The location of this hillfort, on an eminence rising from the valley floor and at a relatively low altitude (311ft (95m)), is more consistent with that of early medieval fortifications. Nevertheless, before afforestation, the hillfort commanded extensive views of Forteviot and lower Strathearn. Moreover, the hillfort and royal centre may have been linked by a 'covered way', presumably a sunken or hollow track, that led from the hillfort 'a considerable distance in the direction of the village' of Forteviot (Skene 1857: 276). Perhaps paralleling the relationship between the royal centre and prehistoric monuments at Forteviot, the remains of a large cairn lie immediately north of the hillfort. The hillfort at Jackschairs merits further investigation, including survey and trial excavation.

PALACIUM AND URBS

The description of Forteviot as a *palacium* and *urbs* is of potential relevance to the fortified status of the royal centre. These specialised terms therefore require examination. An alternative interpretation of *palacium* is that it refers to the pale or palisade (Latin, *palata*), a defensive barrier of stout wooden stakes set closely together, around a royal site (Cowan 1981: 9). Although this etymology is unconvincing (Alcock and Alcock 1992: 222), so little is known about the characteristics of *palacia* that it is worth reconsidering. Remarkably, there is documentary and sculptural evidence for the construction of a palisade at Forteviot during the mid-ninth century, although this was not defensive in function (Chap. 8). Although *palacium* probably means 'palace' in this context, the royal centre at Forteviot, or part of it, may have been enclosed within a palisade.

The more impressive fortifications tend to dominate perceptions of early medieval fortified sites, but not all were enclosed by ramparts of earth or stone. For example, the Anglian royal centres at Milfield, Sprouston and Yeavering included massive double-palisaded enclosures (Hope-Taylor 1977; Gates and O'Brien 1988; Smith 1991: 272-4; Alcock 2003: 234-8), while the inner of either a double palisade or two successive palisades at Kirk Hill, St Abb's Head, Berwickshire, yielded radiocarbon dates centred on the seventh century (Alcock *et al.* 1987: 273). Palisaded defences, though on a smaller scale, are also found in north-east Scotland. The multi-phase defences of the promontory forts at Inchtuthil and The Welton (*18*), both Perthshire, include palisades (Ross 1902: 230-4; RCAHMS 1994: 48, 50, 52). Although undated, both forts may include an early medieval phase. One rampart at Inchtuthil incorporated masonry from the nearby Roman legionary fortress (Ross 1902: 232; RCAHMS 1994: 55), while The Welton is associated with a cemetery that includes square barrows.

Forteviot is one of only two *palacia* recorded in early medieval Scotland, emphasising its status as a place of exceptional importance. Although associated with Forteviot during his reign (Chap. 1 and above), Domnall mac Ailpín died not there but in *palacio Cinnbelathoír* on 13 April 862 (CKA, ed. and trans. Hudson

18 Aerial photograph of the multi-phase defences of the promontory fort at The Welton, Perthshire, including palisades. Outside the defences is a cemetery that includes square barrows. *Crown copyright: Royal Commission on the Ancient and Historical Monuments of Scotland*

1998: 148, 153). This royal centre may be identified with that of *Rathinveramon*, at the confluence of the rivers Almond and Tay (Aitchison in prep.). The implications for the *palacium* of Forteviot are uncertain. Not all *palacia* need have been the same and the term may have concerned their royal associations and/or functions rather than their physical form.

With only two examples recorded, use of the term *palacium* is very restricted in early medieval Scotland. Moreover, these references not only occur in the same source but also concern the same reign, the short kingship of Domnall mac

Ailpín (858-62). This suggests that *palacium* may represent the distinctive idiom of a specific scribe and that both entries were recorded by the same hand. The details of the legislative assembly at Forteviot and the precision of Domnall's death record indicate that these entries were made contemporaneously with, or very soon after, the events they record. This need not have implications either for the meaning of *palacium* or the function and status of Forteviot, but it may explain why only two Pictish royal centres are described as *palacia*. The mid-ninth-century date of both references does not imply that either *palacia* in general, or *Cinnbelathoír* and Forteviot in particular, represent a late development in royal centres associated with either the final decades of the Pictish kingship or, in traditional terms, the political ascendancy of the Scots over the Picts. In contrast, its royal associations reveal that Forteviot was already an established royal centre some decades before it was described as a *palacia*, while its barrow cemeteries imply its status as the ritual centre of a socio-political élite from the early or mid-first millennium.

Forteviot's status as an *urbs* is also relevant to the debate concerning its fortification, as well as being of wider significance. Forteviot is described as an *urbs* in the St Andrews foundation legend (ed. Skene 1867: 185). *Urbs*, 'city', seems implausibly grandiose for a Pictish royal centre. What did the scribe mean when he referred to Forteviot as an *urbs*? In contrast to *palacium*, there are several references to *urbes* in early medieval Insular sources. The St Andrews foundation legend itself refers to two, Constantinople (*Constantinopolitana urbe*) and Kilrimont (St Andrews, *urbs Rymont*) (ed. Skene 1867: 140, 188). These *urbes* convey an impression of the status of Forteviot, linking it with the most important ecclesiastical and political centres in eastern Christendom and Pictland respectively. But the implications for the fortified status of Forteviot are unclear because, although Constantinople was defended by some of the most impressive fortifications in the medieval world, it is unclear if St Andrews possessed man-made defences. Perhaps significantly, the other Pictish *palacium*, *Bellethor* (i.e. *Cinnbelathoír*), is also referred to as an *urbs* (*Life of St Cadroe*, ed. Skene 1867: 108).

Other sources provide clearer insights into the defensive significance of the term. Bede employs *urbs* as a translation of Anglo-Saxon *burh* (Campbell 1979: 36-7) and a lost inscription from Shaftesbury, Dorset, refers to the *burh* founded by King Alfred in 880 as an *urbs* (Keynes and Lapidge 1983: 340; Okasha 1983: 98; RCHME 1972: 57; Lapidge *et al.* (eds) 1999: 418; Higgitt 2004: 9). *Burh*, which occurs in modern placenames as *borough*, *burgh* or *bury*, means a defended or fortified place (Cameron 1961: 112-15; Gelling 1978: 143-6). Bede refers to eight *urbes*, including four in northern Britain: *Alcluith*, the fortified royal centre of the Strathclyde Britons on Dumbarton Rock (Alcock and Alcock 1990); *Giudi*, possibly Castle Rock, Stirling (Graham 1959; Jackson 1963: 36-8; 1969: 72, n. 1; 1981; Alcock 1981: 175-6; but see Rutherford 1976); *Bebbanburh*, Bamburgh, the fortified royal centre of Northumbria (Hope-Taylor 1966b; Alcock 2003: 198); and *Colodaesburg*, the monastery on Kirk Hill, St Abbs, occupying the site of an earlier fortification (Alcock 1981: 162-5; 1988: 4; Alcock *et al.* 1987). To Bede at least, fortification was the distinguishing feature of an *urbs*, although the term probably also had a political and administrative significance, rather than just referring to physical characteristics. In Northumbria at least, *urbs* described a fortified site with economic and/or political functions relating to a dependent territory (Campbell 1979: 42, 50). *Urbs* was also employed in the sense of 'castle' or 'fortress' on the Continent (Niermeyer 1976: 1052).

Forteviot's description as an *urbs* may imply that it was a fortified royal site. But, over two centuries later and in Pictland rather than Northumbria, did the St Andrews foundation legend use *urbs* in the same sense as Bede? This is unclear and the destruction of Haly Hill probably means that Forteviot's fortified status will remain unresolved. Whereas Bede refers to several *urbes*, providing a large enough sample from which to identify their principal characteristics, too few *urbes* appear in the St Andrews foundation legend to draw any meaningful conclusions, other than that they were important ecclesiastical and political centres. It has been suggested that the term *urbs* may foreshadow the later thanages (Barrow 2003: 55), but the multiplicity of thanages contrasts with the rarity of recorded *urbes* in Pictland. There is no evidence to suggest a direct link between Forteviot's status as both an *urbs* and a thanage.

Even on the basis of the limited archaeological and documentary evidence available, Forteviot easily meets the criteria of a palace. Despite suggestions that *palacium* does not refer to a palace at all, any uncertainties of translation and interpretation may be dispelled. However, 'palace' is still a value-laden term with unhelpful medieval and modern associations that detract from the understanding of the character and function of early medieval royal power centres. Forteviot is therefore referred to throughout this book not as a 'palace' but a 'royal centre', denoting not only the royal residential buildings and their associated structures but also their wider administrative and monumental contexts, the landscape within which rituals of royalty were performed, providing the agricultural basis on which royal power was founded.

The description of Forteviot as a *palacium* and *urbs* is significant. Although there is some uncertainty about the precise meaning of both terms, they provide insights into the character, functions and status of the royal centre when used in conjunction with other sources and the archaeological record. Forteviot comprised a royal residence, assembly place and church (Chaps 4, 5 and 9), at which some of the great affairs of state were decided and publicly proclaimed. This is tangible evidence of Forteviot's pivotal role in the emergence of statehood in early medieval Scotland. Forteviot also had a less glamorous, but still important, role as a *caput*, a centre for controlling the resources of the royal estate, and later the thanage, of Forteviot.

The royal centre of Forteviot is poorly recorded in documentary sources and its surviving remains await archaeological investigation. Nevertheless, enough is known or may be inferred about the principal components and functions of the royal centre to reveal the physical context of kingship among the Picts during the ninth century. The emergence of Forteviot as a centre of royal authority has been interpreted as a significant development in the practices and powers of early medieval kingship in Pictland (Driscoll 1998b: 170). According to this argument, royal authority, at least among the Southern Picts, began to shift away from the traditional foci of hillforts, such as Dundurn in upper Strathearn (*colour plate 10*). With defence as their primary function, these older, fortified hilltop royal centres were eclipsed because they were less suitable locations for the changing requirements of early medieval kingship, being less accessible and having insufficient space for public assemblies and the monumental structures associated with rituals of royalty. The emergence of Forteviot as an important royal centre by the ninth century represents a move away from those hilltop sites to lower-lying locations.

However, the evidence for any shift in the siting of royal centres is limited and the situation may have been more complex. Archaeological evidence may attest Forteviot's function as a high-status site at a much earlier date than the limited documentary sources suggest. Although Forteviot's status as a royal centre is only confirmed by the ninth century, the presence of square barrows may indicate its association with a socio-political élite from the early or mid-first millennium. There is also documentary evidence for the late use of hillforts. Giric mac Dúngail (878-89) may have died at Dundurn (Regnal Lists D, F and I; ed. Anderson 1973: 267, 274, 283), indicating that he was in residence at the time, although another source places his death at Forteviot (Chap. 1). Giric's successor, Caustantín mac Dúngail (d. 890?) was also associated with Dundurn (*Prophecy of Berchán*, §141; trans. Hudson 1996: 86). Activity at Dundurn as late as the ninth century may be supported by a calibrated radiocarbon date of AD 640-910, although the excavator believed this came from the citadel besieged in 683 (Alcock *et al.* 1990: 201). Later still, the hillfort on Dunsinane Hill, Perthshire, is linked with Cináed mac Máel Choluim ('Kenneth II') (971-95) (Regnal Lists F and I; ed. Anderson 1973: 275, 284) and, most famously of all, Macbeth (1040-57)

(Aitchison 1999: 166-79). Although limited, this evidence suggests that fortified royal centres continued in use into the eleventh century, although on what basis is unclear. Moreover, the great medieval royal castles of Edinburgh and Stirling may have developed from earlier hillforts, revealing that the requirement for fortified royal centres never disappeared.

If there was a shift to royal centres occupying more open sites by the ninth century, then it was either a gradual process or one that saw periodic reverses, with kings reverting to fortified royal centres during less stable times. But the variety of types and locations of royal centre probably continued to be occupied according to the political circumstances, personal preferences and activities of kings. This is not to underestimate the importance of the emergence of lower-lying and more accessible royal centres. With the investment of royal authority in these central places, churches emerge as integral components of royal power centres for the first time, including at Forteviot (Chaps 4 and 9). Forteviot attests fundamental developments in early medieval kingship, changes that involved kings increasingly seeking authority and legitimacy from the Church and the law and that came to characterise medieval kingship.

4

THE CHURCH AT
FORTEVIOT

The kingships of early medieval Britain and Ireland frequently enjoyed a close and mutually supportive relationship with the Church. Kings sought legitimacy for their rule and royal office in the divine sanction that only the Church could confer and this was manifested most overtly in royal inauguration rituals. At the same time, the Church was dependent on royal patronage for its lands, wealth and protection. In keeping with this, a symbiotic relationship existed between kingship and Church in early medieval Scotland (Hudson 1994b; Clancy 1996) and, although poorly recorded, in Pictland. Indeed, the nature of this relationship appears to have been stronger or more direct among both the Picts and early Scots than among other Insular peoples, with kings founding churches and being closely involved in liturgical matters. This was the case in Pictland from at least *c.*710, when Nechtan son of Derilei arranged for the Pictish Church to adopt the cult of St Peter and the Roman liturgy and built a stone church (Bede, *Historia Ecclesiastica*, V.21).

As a result of the close relationship between Insular kingships and the Church, political and religious authority were closely interlinked, including in Pictland. With the growing importance of more accessible centres of political power, churches emerged as integral elements of royal centres for the first time. This reflects the increasingly prominent role of the Church in conferring political legitimacy, not only through royal inauguration rites but also by promoting concepts of Christian kingship and providing access to the appropriate rituals. The Church also benefited from this arrangement, receiving the king's protection and support, increased ceremonial visibility and possibly an administrative role, giving the Church a powerful influence in law and government. As a result, the Church not only fulfilled a spiritual role within society but also exerted political power.

In keeping with this, Forteviot was not only a centre of secular power but also a focus of religious activity. This chapter examines the ecclesiastical component of the early medieval royal centre, although the evidence, archaeological and textual, is very sparse. Research is further hampered by the problems of interpretation posed by the main documentary source, which relates the foundation of a church at Forteviot by a Pictish king. As this source is central to the study of Forteviot as an ecclesiastical centre, it requires an introduction and assessment.

THE ST ANDREWS FOUNDATION LEGEND

The key source concerning the church at Forteviot is the St Andrews foundation legend (ed. Skene 1867: 138-40, 183-93, 375-77; for commentary see Skene 1862: 303-7; 1876-77, vol. 1: 296-9; vol. 2: 261-7; Anderson 1974a: 7-13; Ash and Broun 1994: 16-20; Macquarrie 1997: 181-2; Broun 2000b; Taylor 2000; Broun and Taylor in prep.). This source has long been of interest to historians studying the origins of the cult and church of St Andrew in Scotland, although its wider implications for Pictish studies in general, and Forteviot in particular, remain unexplored.

The St Andrews foundation legend survives in two versions that possess a similar basic structure but share few details. It concerns events during the reign of *Ungus filius Urguist* or *Hungus filius Forso* (or *Ferlon*), 'a great king of the Picts'. These are hybrid names, derived from the equivalent Gaelic and Pictish forms of the same name, Oengus son of Fergus and Unuist son of Uurguist respectively. This legendary character is referred to here as Hungus in order to distinguish him from his historical counterpart. The legend relates how Hungus led a Pictish army into southern Britain where it wintered at *campus Merc*, probably Mercia rather than the Merse in the Scottish Borders (Anderson 1974a: 8), or to the mouth of a River Tyne, presumably either the Northumbrian or East Lothian Tyne. Surprised and surrounded by the army of Athelstan, king of the Saxons, the Pictish army faced overwhelming odds and near-certain defeat when St Andrew appeared to Hungus in a dream on the eve of battle. The apostle promised Hungus victory and that his relics would arrive in Hungus' kingdom if Hungus gave a tenth of his inheritance to God and St Andrew. The Picts went on to defeat the Saxon army and behead Athelstan. Hungus then returned home to fulfil his vow.

Separately, the legend relates how some of St Andrew's bones were hidden by a monk or bishop called Regulus before Patras was sacked by Constantine the Great in 345 in revenge for the martyrdom of St Andrew there. Regulus then translated the relics of St Andrew from Patras to Constantinople, where he had a vision urging him to set sail with the relics until he reached a place called *Rigmund*, the 'royal mount', a variant form of Kilrimont. Arriving soon after Hungus' victory but failing to find the king there, Regulus and his party travelled on to Forteviot, where they found Hungus' three sons, who were staying there while their father was away campaigning in Argyll. In exchange for guaranteeing Hungus' protection, his sons granted a tenth part of the *urbs* of Forteviot to God and St Andrew for the foundation of a church and erected a cross.

Regulus and his companions then proceeded to *Moneclatu*, 'now called' *Monichi*, where Hungus' queen gave Regulus a royal hall in return for Hungus' safe return. *Monichi* is unlocated but has been variously identified as Monikie or Monifieth, both Angus, or Mondynes, Kincardineshire (Skene 1862: 306; 1876, vol. 1: 298; Anderson 1892: 436; Spearman 1993: 141; Taylor 2000: 115). Regulus next travelled beyond the Mounth to *Doldencha*, 'now called' *Chondrochedalvan*, later Kindrochit, and now Castleton of Braemar, Aberdeenshire (Watson 1926: 468), where he found Hungus. At *Chondrochedalvan*, the king and his nobles prostrated themselves before the relics of St Andrew in veneration and Hungus built a church dedicated to God and St Andrew to house them. Hungus and Regulus then returned together to Kilrimont via *Monichi* and Forteviot, where they built more churches.

The St Andrews foundation legend poses problems of chronology and authenticity. Fundamentally, the existence of two Pictish kings called Unuist son of Uurguist has caused enduring confusion. The later Unuist (820-34) is the king concerned (Chaps 1 and 8). However, the attribution to either king of the foundation of a church at Kilrimont dedicated to St Andrew is weakened by the absence of any evidence for such a church before the tenth century, although this probably reflects the poor survival of documentary sources. The reference to 'Athelstan' is of no assistance here. The most likely Saxon ruler of this name, Athelstan, king of Wessex (924-39), post-dated the later Unuist by a century and invaded Alba, not Pictland, in 934 (Anderson 1974a: 8). A more glaring anachronism is that the legend relates how Regulus left Patras in 345, arriving in Scotland a year and a half later, several centuries too early to have met either Unuist. The mythological nature of the legend is detectable in the eastern Mediterranean origin of the mission to Pictland, which parallels the Scythian origin of the Picts themselves in their origin myth (Bede, *Historia Ecclesiastica* I.1). The legend also incorporates a list of alleged witnesses to Hungus' endowment of the church of Kilrimont, whose names are claimed to have been copied from a corrupted Pictish regnal list (Anderson 1973: 99-100).

These mythological elements and chronological discrepancies inevitably raise doubts about the historical veracity of the St Andrews foundation legend. Indeed, it has been claimed that 'It is difficult to find anything in the legends that can be treated as history, apart perhaps from the name of the founder' (Anderson 1974a: 7). Another assessment maintains that this source is 'dramatically satisfying rather than historically accurate' and that 'so much of the legend's detail is palpably fictional ... that it is difficult to know whether any of it is factual' (Ash and Broun 1994: 18). These views have prevailed (e.g. Alcock 1982: 216; Macquarrie 1997: 181) and scholars, understandably, have been reluctant to place any reliance upon this source, although it still features prominently in studies of the origins of the cult of St Andrew in Scotland. As this source provides unique insights into the study of the royal centre at Forteviot and the interpretation of its arch (Chap. 8), its origins, date and historical reliability require examination.

The St Andrews foundation legend has a complex textual history (Anderson 1973: 236; 1974a: 6-13; Miller 1982; 142; Ash and Broun 1994: 18; Barrow 2003: 222, n.57). All surviving texts of the legend belong to one of two versions. Both versions were produced in Kilrimont and their earliest extant accounts date from the twelfth century. The 'Augustinian' account belongs to an ecclesiastical history of Kilrimont written by an Augustinian canon in the priory of St Andrews sometime between its foundation in 1144 and the death of David I in 1153. The 'Poppleton' account is named after the manuscript in which it is preserved, a fourteenth-century compilation of Scottish historical items, assembled between 1165 and 1184, perhaps at Scone. This version refers to Kilrimont as 'here' and was composed by a member of the *Céli Dé* ('Culdee') community at Kilrimont before *c.*1130, on the basis of the variation in the element 'Kin-' or 'Kil-' in Kilrimont (Anderson 1974a: 1), and may date mostly to the eleventh or even the tenth century.

Like most sources of early Scottish history, both versions survive only in later manuscript copies (Anderson 1974a: 9-11; Broun 2000b: 109-11; Taylor 2000: 119-20), ranging in date from the late twelfth to early eighteenth centuries. The Augustinian version was the better known of the two in medieval Scotland and John of Fordun (*Chronica Gentis Scotorum*, II, 46-48, IV, 13-14; trans. Skene 1872: 69-72, 144-7), Walter Bower (*Scotichronicon*, II, 58-60, IV, 13-14; gen. ed. and trans. Watt 1982: 304-11; 1993: 310-17) and Andrew of Wyntoun (*Orygynale Cronykil*, ed. Amours 1906, vol. 4: 169-73) all used it in their chronicles.

Although both versions are claimed to have been derived from a common source, now lost (Anderson 1974a: 7-8), the relationship between them is obscure.

More fundamentally, the extent of the differences in detail between the versions – for example, in their accounts of Hungus' victorious battle – indicate that these are not simply different recensions of an earlier text (Ash and Broun 1994: 18-19). Instead, their similarities may attest a common purpose rather than a common source. Structural features also indicate that the text is not derived from a single source. The Poppleton version does not read smoothly and even its record of the arrival of St Andrew's relics can be read as two separate accounts (Skene 1877, vol. 2: 264; Ash and Broun 1994: 19). Although Hungus' expedition to Argyll is claimed to sit so incongruously in the narrative that it must be a later interpolation (Anderson 1974a: 7), this isolated reference is more likely to have resulted from the abridgement of a longer and more detailed original. These features suggest that the legend was not created as a single homogenous source in the twelfth century, but is considerably older.

Indeed, both versions claim not only earlier, but Pictish, origins. The Augustinian version states that 'These things ... we have transcribed just as we found in old books of the Picts'. More convincingly, the Poppleton version records that it was written by Thana son of Dudabrach in *Migdele* (Meigle), during the reign of king Pherath son of Bergeth (ed. Skene 1867: 188). This king may be identified in the regnal lists as *Ferath filius Bargoit* or Uurad son of Bargoit (and variant spellings of both) (839-42?) (Lists A, B, D, F, I, K; ed. Anderson 1973: 249, 263, 266, 273, 281, 287), suggesting that this account was made within a decade of the reign of the second Unuist son of Uurguist (820-34). Although surviving only in twelfth-century forms, there is a growing realisation that the origins of the legend are considerably earlier and may lie in the mid-ninth century (Ash and Broun 1994: 19-20).

A range of internal evidence, including personal names, supports a Pictish origin for elements of the St Andrews foundation legend. *Forso*, Hungus' patronymic in the Augustinian version, may originally have read *Forgusso* (Anderson 1974a: 8). This is an early name form and displays two archaic linguistic features. Its genitive -*o* ending is very rare after 863 (ó Máille 1910: 62-8), while *For-*, in preference to the later *Fer-*, is probably even earlier (Anderson 1974a: 7). Although Anderson believed that this was weak evidence for an early date on its own, *For[gus]so* is not the only early name form preserved in the legend. The name of the scribe to whom the legend is attributed, Thana or Chana, is early and rare and cannot be a twelfth-century invention (Ash and Broun 1994: 20). The name recorded is probably Cano, which first appears in the seventh century. Moreover, the prominence accorded to the emperor Constantine in the legend points to a link with the Pictish king Causantín (789-820) or his dynasty. This has been interpreted as evidence that Causantín was named with the Constantine of the legend in mind (Ash and Broun 1994: 18). However, the reverse could be true and Constantine's appearance within the legend could have been inspired by Causantín. This suggests a direct dynastic link between the later Unuist, Causantín's brother, and the legend.

Placename evidence also indicates the antiquity of the legend. Of the 11 places in eastern Scotland named in the Augustinian version, it gives earlier names for five. The use of the formula *qui nunc dicitur* reveals that twelfth-century scribes were inserting the current equivalents for archaic placenames mentioned in the text, in order to make it intelligible to contemporary readers. This high degree of redundancy indicates that scribes were copying a much earlier source. The date of this source is unclear, although at least one of these earlier placenames, *Doldechena*, is Pictish, or incorporates the Pictish element, *dol* (Chap. 3). The legend appears to record the replacement of Pictish placenames by Gaelic ones. Although this does not, in itself, prove the Pictish origin of the legend, it does support it. Reinforcing this, another placename recorded in the legend, *Hyhatnachten Machehirb* (*àth Nechtain meic Irb*), preserves the Gaelicised name of the Pictish king Naiton son of Erp (Taylor 2003).

But the most persuasive evidence for an early date of composition for the St Andrews foundation legend, or rather elements within it, is the detail it contains, particularly about Hungus' family. This includes the names of Hungus' queen and three sons, that his queen gave birth to a daughter, who is also named and her places of birth and burial given, and that his three sons were staying at Forteviot while Hungus was away campaigning in Argyll. These details perform no identifiable function within the legend but are entirely incidental to the narrative. Although uncorroborated by other sources, there is no reason to doubt the veracity of this information, which is unparalleled among Pictish and early Scottish kings and attests the familiarity of the compiler with Unuist son of Uurguist and his family. The only possible discrepancy is that the legend does not mention another son of Unuist, Bran, who was killed in battle in 839 (Chap. 10) with his brother Eóganán (Uuen), who is referred to. But this single omission could be explained in several ways, including Bran's absence from Forteviot, perhaps while he was campaigning with his father.

Although surviving in twelfth-century form, the St Andrews foundation legend is a complex and compound source that was either based on, or at least preserves within it, a much earlier text or texts. Internal evidence, comprising personal names, placenames and incidental detail, indicate that part(s) of the legend was compiled by an associate of Unuist's or at least someone who had access to such information. These features indicate the contemporary, or nearly contemporary, nature of this source with Unuist's reign and its historical reliability. This is corroborated by the iconography and dating of the Forteviot arch. The arch depicts an episode from the St Andrews foundation legend, revealing the existence of the legend, or at least part of it, during the mid-ninth century (Chaps 7 and 8).

The St Andrews foundation legend performs several ideological functions. The original text appears to have been concerned primarily with recording the possessions of lands and churches given by Hungus and his family and dedicated to God and St Andrew at Kilrimont, Forteviot, *Monichi* and *Chondrochedalvan*. This may be paralleled by a small group of terse foundation legends for Pictish churches, notably Abernethy and Deer, which may draw on charters confirming their royal foundation (Jackson 1972: 30, 33; Anderson 1973: 247; Davies 1982b: 272, n.47, 273, n.55). The legend also lists the tithes paid and land given to the Church of Kilrimont by Pictish kings, other members of the royal family and nobles.

The foundation of the church at Forteviot has been accepted as described in the legend (Alcock 1982: 215-16; Spearman 1993: 141). However, its account of the progress of Regulus and his companions may have been intended to explain the rights enjoyed by Kilrimont over the churches at Forteviot, *Monichi* and *Chondrochedalvan* (Anderson 1922, vol. 1: 267, fn; Alcock 1982: 216) or even reflect an attempt to claim these rights in the first place. The legend attempts to establish and/or legitimise a historical claim by St Andrews over the church of Forteviot by documenting its possession which was either contested or not yet established. This suggests that the legend originated at a time when rival churches in Pictland were vying for influence, land and patronage. By recording the royal origin of those gifts of land and churches and by placing the meeting between Regulus and Hungus at the king's royal hall in Kilrimont, the Church of Kilrimont was flaunting its close relationship with the Pictish kingship to bolster its claims over other churches and make those claims less open to challenge from rival foundations.

The St Andrews foundation legend reflects the expansionist ambitions of the Church of Kilrimont at a stage when it was extending its influence throughout Pictland. The legend documents the expansion, real or aspirational, of the *paruchia* of Kilrimont. *Paruchiae* were monastic federations of churches founded by the same saint, or his disciples, and were usually under the abbatial rule of the church where that saint was buried. In Ireland, the more powerful *paruchiae* were attempting to incorporate more churches within their spheres of influence from the mid-seventh century (Hughes 1966: 57-90; 1972: 71-5; Ó Corráin 1981: 334-5; Sharpe 1984a; Etchingham 1999: 105-30). The churches claimed were often early foundations without existing obligations and some distance from the principal church of the *paruchia* concerned.

The St Andrews foundation legend only survived because it was adapted to suit twelfth-century political circumstances. The Poppleton version asserts St Andrews' archiepiscopal status in opposition to York's claim of metropolitan jurisdiction over Scotland and northern England (Broun 2000b). In contrast, the Augustinian version promotes the establishment and endowment of a house of Augustinian canons founded at St Andrews in 1144 by documenting the status, territorial and jurisdictional rights of the Church and bishopric of St Andrews (Taylor 2000). The Augustinian version displays a strong interest in documenting the various rights and possessions of the Church of St Andrews, defining its expanding *paruchia*. Some earlier material was probably preserved in these later versions because their compilers believed that this supported the cases they were trying to advance. As it records the lands and churches dedicated to St Andrew by Hungus and his family, it was almost inevitable that the St Andrews foundation legend should display some interest in them and their activities, even if only to provide background information.

SAINTS, CULTS AND RELICS

The primary function of the St Andrews foundation legend is to explain the adoption of St Andrew as the patron saint of the Picts. It does this by relating Hungus' dream about, and vow to, St Andrew before battle and, separately, how the relics of St Andrew reached Pictland, were taken around the kingdom and then installed in churches built specially to house them. The relics of St Andrew comprised the bones of three fingers of his right hand and an upper arm, a patela and a tooth, according to the legend (ed. Skene 1867: 183).

The cult of relics was widespread in the medieval West. Relics featured prominently in early Christian ritual and were integral to the most common manifestation of popular religion, praying for the remission of sins and the intercession of the saints. By attracting patronage, pilgrims and burials, relics also generated income for the churches keeping them. Moreover, relics were invested with ideological and political power and churches manipulated the possession, display and giving of relics to reinforce and extend their power and status, as the Church of Armagh did with the cult and relics of St Patrick (Doherty 1984a). Displaying close parallels with this, the St Andrews foundation legend records the ideological use of the relics of St Andrew by the Church of Kilrimont.

The possession of the relics of its founding saint was central to a church's efforts to establish its antiquity and status as the head of that saint's *paruchia*. Although both churches had expansionist ambitions, neither Armagh nor

Kilrimont possessed the bodies of their patron saints. Despite this handicap, Armagh claimed to hold the principal Patrician relics, the insignia of St Patrick and a wide range of relics of the martyrs, saints and of Christ himself, which were said to have been brought from Rome (Doherty 1984a: 92-3, 99; Sharpe 1984b). Similarly, the St Andrews foundation legend relates how the relics of St Andrew were brought from Constantinople to Kilrimont. The bearing of relics described mirrors the practice of papal missions, providing a powerful testament to the authority of the Church of Kilrimont and evidence of its direct links with two of the most important centres of Christian authority, Rome and Constantinople.

The primatial aspirations of the Church of Kilrimont and the ideological importance of relics are expressed by the St Andrews foundation legend's claim that the church holding St Andrew's relics is the 'head and mother of all the churches in the kingdom' (Ash and Broun 1994: 18). Indeed, the legend has been interpreted as originating from a new church at Kilrimont in order to claim an antiquity superior to that of Iona, the cult centre of St Columba (Skene 1876, vol. 1: 299). In Pictland, the possession of relics by churches may have been considered essential for founding a church, as in early medieval Ireland (Lucas 1987: 35). It is no coincidence that, on Regulus' circuit around Hungus' kingdom, the relics of St Andrew were displayed and venerated at those places where churches were then founded. The churches at Forteviot, *Monichi* and *Chondrochedalvan* were probably built specifically to house the relics of St Andrew. These relics were probably enshrined in reliquaries that were displayed on, or incorporated in, the altars of these new churches.

Relics also played an important ideological role in establishing or reinforcing relationships of indebtedness between churches. Mirroring papal practices, the giving of relics was one strategy by which a mother church and cult centre, holding the remains of its founding saint, could bring other foundations under its ecclesiastical authority as dependent churches and, in this manner, expand its *paruchia*. The St Andrews foundation legend records how Kilrimont, the cult centre of St Andrew in Pictland, used the relics of its patron saint to solicit grants of land and the building of churches by Hungus and his queen at their royal centres. The manipulation of relics was central to the ideological strategy by which the Church of Kilrimont established and maintained its close relationship with the Pictish kingship, extended its *paruchia* within Pictland and eventually gained the status of a national cult in Scotland.

The St Andrews foundation legend provides the earliest evidence of the cult of St Andrew in Scotland. Yet the origins of his cult in Scotland are obscure (Skene 1862; 1876, vol. 1: 296-9, vol. 2: 261-75; Reeves 1864: 33-5; Henderson 1967: 86-8; Anderson 1974a; 1974b; Ash and Broun 1994; Hall 1994; Turnbull 1997). The current trend is to interpret this evidence cautiously. As a result, the origins of the cult of St Andrew in Scotland cannot be dated any earlier than the twelfth-century date of the earliest surviving text. A historical context has been suggested for the adoption of St Andrew as the patron saint of the Scots. This may have been prompted by a 1072 agreement between the archbishops of Canterbury and York to divide the church in Britain between them, with the intention of impressing Rome and using St Andrew as a match for York's St Peter (Ash and Broun 1994: 20-1).

While the cult of St Andrew in Scotland was clearly of enduring ideological and political significance, the evidence points firmly to its Pictish origins. The use of relics it describes is more consistent with an early medieval context and the ideological significance attached to the relics of St Andrew is readily paralleled by the manipulation of relics by other powerful ecclesiastical centres, notably Armagh. The antiquity of the relics of St Andrew has been inferred from the Gaelic name of their probable reliquary, *Mór Breac*, 'Great Reliquary' (*Liber Cartarum*, ed. Thomson 1841: 329; Ash and Broun 1994: 17). More fundamentally, the identification of a ninth-century text within the legend provides the clearest evidence to date that the cult of St Andrew was adopted by the Picts. Indeed, the references to the apostle, his churches and relics are so integral to the legend that they must be an original feature. Moreover, the legend's account of the progress of these relics and the building and endowment of churches to house them, is very plausible. The background to the legend's concern about the adoption of St Andrew as the 'national' saint of the Picts is provided by the shifting political and ecclesiastical relations that led the Picts to adopt and reject a series of patron saints.

The period between *c.*710 and *c.*850 saw the dominant saintly cults among the Southern Picts shifting from St Columba, firstly to St Peter and then to St Andrew, before reverting to Columba. Around 710, closer political and ecclesiastical links between the Pictish king Nechtan son of Derilei (?706-24, 728-9) and Northumbria led to the Picts rejecting the Celtic liturgy in favour of the Roman liturgy, which differed significantly in several respects, notably the calculation of the date of Easter and the form of tonsure (Bede, *Historia Ecclesiastica*, V.21). Linked to this, and at around the same time, the Picts abandoned the cult of St Columba and Nechtan placed his kingdom under the patronage of St Peter, the apostle traditionally associated with Rome. These changes weakened the influence of Iona in Pictland and resulted in the expulsion from Pictland of the monks of Iona by Nechtan in 717 (AT s.a. 717.3; AU s.a. 716.4; CS s.a. 713; but see Veitch 1997). The cult of St Peter was subsequently rejected by the Picts, possibly because of its strong Northumbrian associations. The political background to this may be provided by the tradition, recorded in the St Andrews foundation legend, of warfare between the Picts and Anglo-Saxons during Hungus' reign.

Although the circumstances of St Andrew's adoption as the 'national' saint of the Picts are unclear, the process involved presumably followed an established pattern. As with the adoption and rejection of other cults, the cult of St Andrew was probably elevated to 'national' status as a result of the influence exerted by Pictish kings over the Pictish Church, but was ultimately inspired by external contacts and influences. As this is what the St Andrews foundation legend describes, it should only be rejected as later propaganda with care. The legend records a tradition explaining how Hungus incurred a personal debt to St Andrew from his victory in battle and discharged this by giving land and building churches dedicated to the apostle at four of his royal centres.

The dominant cult in Pictland appears to have changed again by or during the reign of Cináed mac Ailpín (843-58) with the reintroduction of the cult of St Columba. Cináed transferred the relics of St Columba from Iona, which had suffered from Viking attacks during the first half of the ninth century, and built a church to house them at Dunkeld (CKA; ed. and trans. Hudson 1998: 148, 152; on which see Clancy 1996: 111, 114; 1999: 28-9; Hudson 1998: 152, n.5; Bannerman 1999: 88-94; Broun 1999: 98-9, 104-6, 108-9). Traditionally, this was interpreted as the Scots transferring their institutions of kingship and its associated cults eastwards from Dál Riata into Pictland following the eclipse of Pictish power (Chap. 1). Under royal patronage, the cult of St Columba was invested with special significance in Pictland, and subsequently Alba, in general and Fortriu in particular. For example, the men of Fortriu went into battle parading a relic of St Columba, a crozier known as the *Cathbuaidh* ('battle-triumph'), and twice defeated Viking armies while carrying it (FAI, §429 [?909]; Aitchison 2003: 160-1).

Given the strength of the attachment of the kings of Alba and the men of Fortriu to the cult of Columba, why was the church of Forteviot dedicated to, and why did it house the relics of, St Andrew? In the absence of corroboratory evidence, it has been suggested that the cult of St Andrew was not always celebrated at Forteviot but that it replaced an earlier cult. Cináed mac Ailpín's association with Forteviot (Chap. 1), according to one theory, would also have led him to build a church, or at least re-dedicate an existing church, to house the relics of St Columba at Forteviot (Spearman 1993: 140-1). This theory proposes that the association of the church of Forteviot with the relics of St Andrew, as described in the St Andrews foundation legend, was a later fiction intended to establish St Andrews' historical claim over the church of Forteviot. But there is no evidence to support Forteviot's status as a cult centre of St Columba. It has also been proposed that the saint who was most closely associated with the royal and, in effect, religious centre of the Picts, was regarded as their patron saint (Ash and Broun 1994: 20), and that this was why, according to the legend, the relics of St Andrew were brought to Forteviot.

The prominence of the cult of Columba in Fortriu reflects the ecclesiastical allegiances of a new political order, the dynasty of the sons of Alpín, and need not preclude the presence at Forteviot of a church founded by an earlier king and dedicated to St Andrew. However, other interpretations are possible. Although the church of Forteviot may have retained is dedication to St Andrew throughout the ascendancy of the cult of Columba, it could be a medieval borrowing, inspired by the St Andrews foundation legend.

Although its precise nature is unclear, the St Andrews foundation legend reveals much about the nature of the relationship, real or aspirational, between the church of Forteviot and the cult centre of St Andrew at Kilrimont during the ninth century. Their close association is not surprising, as both churches were associated with, indeed were integral elements of, two of the principal royal centres of Unuist son of Uurguist. In addition, Unuist's patronage of both ecclesiastical centres was presumably a significant factor in establishing and maintaining their close relationship. The legend uses various hagiographical conventions to demonstrate or claim that the church at Forteviot belonged to the *paruchia* of the Church of St Andrew: Regulus and his companions arrived in Pictland at St Andrews, symbolising its primacy, before travelling to Forteviot, where the church founded by Hungus was dedicated to St Andrew, whose relics it housed. This was intended to convey that the church at Forteviot was, or at least should have been, under the abbatial rule of St Andrews. The St Andrews foundation legend attests an attempt by the Church of St Andrews to establish a historically-based claim of ecclesiastical primacy over specific churches, including the church at Forteviot.

BASILICA: THE ROYAL CHURCH

The status of the church of Forteviot as a royal church, housing important relics, is supported by the term used in the St Andrews foundation legend. The legend uses different terms for the three churches founded by Hungus. Although *Monichi* and *Chondrochedalvan* are both described as *ecclesia*, 'church', the foundation at Forteviot is referred to as a *basilica* (ed. Skene 1867: 186). What was a *basilica* and what is the significance of this term for nature and function of the church at Forteviot?

1 The inscription linking past and present above the main entrance to the houses in The Square, Forteviot

2 Houses in the Arts and Crafts style in The Square, Forteviot

5 Forteviot, viewed from the edge of the Forteviot terrace, south of the village. St Andrew's Church lies at the centre, the Water of May on the far left and the Gask Ridge in the background. Haly Hill probably stood in the area of the small conifer plantation to the left of the church

6 St Andrew's Church, Forteviot (left) and the Forteviot terrace from the floodplain of the Water of May. A relict river channel is faintly visible, sweeping across the centre ground. Haly Hill probably stood in the area of the road or the small conifer plantation (not in view) on the other side of it

Opposite above: 7 St Andrew's Church, Forteviot: from the north-west

Opposite below: 8 St Andrew's Church and graveyard, Forteviot: from the south

9 An aerial photograph of fields south-east of Forteviot reveals a rectangular enclosure, sub-circular enclosure, linear ditch round, square barrows and long graves. *Crown copyright: Royal Commission on the Ancient and Historical Monuments of Scotland*

10 Dundurn, the *Dùn Duirn* of the Irish annals, in upper Strathearn. The craggy location of this royal hillfort contrasts with that of Forteviot

11 The Moot Hill at Scone, the low mound on which the Scottish kings were inaugurated

12 Redcastle, Lunan Bay, Angus: a Pictish square barrow before excavation. The enclosing ditches, gapped corners and central grave pit are all visible as patches of darker soil. *CFA Archaeology Ltd*

13 The floodplain of the River Earn, from the north. *Dolcorachy* ('taper field meadow') may have gained its name from a distinctively-shaped meadowfield in a bend in the Earn, such as this one south of Wester Cairnie

14 A surviving *basilica*: St Rule's Church, St Andrews, a reliquary church of probably the early twelfth century

15 The Dupplin cross in its new location, Dunning Church

16 The Invermay 'cross': a nineteenth-century pillar sits in an early medieval cross-base

Above: 17 The Invermay cross: the early medieval cross-base

Left: 18 The Forteviot hand-bell

19 The Forteviot arch. © *Trustees of the National Museum of Scotland*

20 The Forteviot arch displayed above the inner entrance to the Kingdom of the Scots gallery in the National Museum of Scotland

21 A canon table in the Book of Kells: Canon I (Matthew, Mark, Luke and John, fol. 2r). *The Board of Trinity College, Dublin*

Above: 22 The lintel above the entrance to the round tower at Brechin

Right: 23 The Saxon tower of All Saints' Church Earls Barton, Northamptonshire

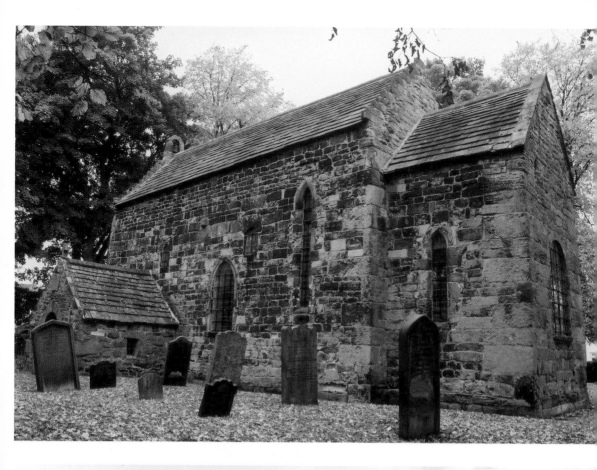

Opposite above: 24 St John's Church, Escomb, Co. Durham, from the south-east. The porch and lancet windows are later additions

Opposite below: 25 St Laurence's Church, Bradford-on-Avon, from the south

26 An elaborately decorated church illustrated in the Book of Kells ('The Temptation of Christ', fol. 202v). *The Board of Trinity College, Dublin*

27 St John's Church, Escomb, Co. Durham: interior looking east towards the chancel

Latin *basilica* is derived from the Greek, βασιλεύς, 'king', 'prince' or 'ruler', and means literally 'royal palace'. This is not a functional description, but refers to a church as the home of Christ the eternal king, according to the dedication service in the tenth-century Romano-German Pontifical (ed. Vogel 1963: 92). *Basilica* also has a more specialised meaning. In the early church in Gaul, Ireland and possibly Britain during the fifth and sixth centuries, a *basilica* was a church holding the tombs of martyrs and was, therefore, a centre of missionary activity (Leclerq 1925; Delehaye 1930; Battisti 1960; Doherty 1984a: 92; 1984b). The use of *basilica* as an ecclesiastical term later declined, being reserved for churches of special status, specifically early foundations housing major relics (Doherty 1984a: 92). Complicating matters further, *basilica* is also an architectural term (Chap. 9). Does the church at Forteviot meet the definition of a *basilica*? For this, it is necessary to examine parallels with other Insular *basilicae*.

Underlining their importance, *basilicae* are recorded at only three ecclesiastical centres in Pictland. The St Andrews foundation legend records the existence of more than one *basilica* at Kilrimont, referring to Hungus' gift of a large area to God and St Andrew for the construction of an unspecified number of *basilicas et oratorias* (ed. Skene 1867: 186). Another reference in the same source to the *basilicae Sancti Apostoli* at Kilrimont (ed. Skene 1867: 186) reveals that at least some of these *basilicae* were dedicated to the apostles, with St Andrew presumably foremost among them. This is supported by an eleventh-century reference to a *basilica* of St Andrew at Kilrimont (*ad basilicam sancti Andree Apostoli; basilice beati Andree*) (*Life of St Cadog* §26; ed. Wade-Evans 1944: 80, 82). This *basilica* was described as a place of pilgrimage comparable only with Rome and Jerusalem, presumably because of the relics it contained. One *basilica* at St Andrews, referred to in the St Andrews foundation legend (ed. Skene 1876: 191), survives as St Rule's Church, a reliquary church of probably the early twelfth century (Fernie 1986: 407; Cameron 1994: 371-2; Heywood 1994) (*colour plate 14*).

The only other record of a *basilica* in Pictland appears in the *Aberdeen Breviary* (pars estiva, fol. clxiiii; Mackinlay 1914: 211), a compilation of saints' lives and information on their shrines collected by travelling researchers and published by Bishop Elphinstone of Aberdeen in 1509-10. According to this, St Fergus founded a *basilica* at Inverugie, now St Fergus, in Buchan. *Basilicae* are even rarer outside Pictland. The only other example in what is now Scotland is from Strathclyde. Paisley (Gaelic, *Paislig*), Renfrewshire, preserves the term *basilica* in its name (Watson 1905; 1926: 194). This was an early and important church and monastery which, according to tradition, was founded in the sixth century by St Mirren from Bangor in Ulster. Unlike Forteviot, both St Andrews and Paisley were early ecclesiastical foundations that flourished during the Middle Ages.

Central to their success was the possession and display of relics, which attracted pilgrims and royal patronage, providing important sources of income.

The close relationship they enjoyed with royal dynasties is a distinguishing feature of *basilicae*, indicating that their status, power and wealth were derived from royal patronage. This is apparent from the dedication stone commemorating the foundation of the church at Jarrow in 685, which records the 'Dedication of the *basilica* of St Paul on the Kalends of May in the fifteenth year of king Ecgfrith and the fourth year of abbot Ceolfrith and founder under God of the same church' (Higgitt 1979; 2004: 21).

The close association of *basilicae* and kingships is also evident in early medieval Ireland. *Basilica Sanctorum*, whose name survives as Baslick, Co. Roscommon, the principal church of the Uí Briúin high-kings of Connachta until the eighth century, was located close to Cruachan, the monumental royal centre of the province of Connachta (Connaught) (Byrne 1973: 247, 250-1; Doherty 1984a: 92; 1984b: 309-10, 314-15). Similarly, the *basilica* of Kildare, near the royal centre of Knockaulin, was the principal church of the Uí Dúnlainge high-kings of the province of Laigin (Leinster) (Doherty 1984a: 94-5; 1984b: 312-14). And Armagh, the pre-eminent church of the province of Ulaid (Ulster), had at least one *basilica*, where relics of Peter, Paul, Stephen, Laurence and other saints were kept, and was also located near a monumental royal centre, Navan Fort (Doherty 1984a: 92-3; 1984b: 310-11; Aitchison 1994: 231, 240, 249, 276, 288).

The specialised status of the *basilica* in early medieval Ireland is revealed by Irish sources, although some of these are late. *O'Davoren's Glossary* (ed. Stokes 1904: 238, §258), compiled in the sixteenth century from earlier laws, defines a *basilica* as an *eclais rígh*, 'king's church'. In Ireland, at least, a *basilica* was a royal church. More specifically, a *basilica* is defined as the burial place of kings in the *Collectio Canonum Hibernensis* (chap. 44, §20; ed. Wasserschleben 1885: 179), compiled in the early eighth century from earlier canons. Indeed, *O'Mulconry's Glossary* (ed. Stokes 1898: 240, §128), compiled in the mid-seventeenth century from earlier laws, claimed that the *basilica* gained its name 'because only kings are buried in them'. Tomb shrines, although of saints rather than kings, feature prominently in a mid-eighth-century description of the *basilica* of Kildare (Cogitosus, *Life of St Brigit*, 32, §1; trans. after Connolly and Picard 1988: 25):

> the glorious bodies of ... Archbishop Conleth and our most flourishing virgin Brigit are laid on the right and left of the ornate altar and rest in tombs adorned with a refined profusion of gold, silver, gems and precious stones with gold and silver coronae hanging from above and different images presenting a variety of carvings and colours.

A *basilica* is also defined as a grave (*Collectio Canonum Hibernensis*, chap. 18, §7; ed. Wasserschleben 1885: 58). This is of particular interest given the close proximity of the *basilicae* at Armagh, Baslick and Kildare to major monumental complexes, including funerary monuments. And at *Baisliocán*, 'little *basilica*', now Baslickane, Co. Kerry, the remains of a small church containing tombs lies just outside a large stone circle (Henry 1957: 141-2; Doherty 1984b: 314-15), possibly attesting the 'Christianisation' of a prehistoric monument that was, or was perceived to have been, a place of pagan worship.

The status and function of the *basilica* in early medieval Ireland provides close and instructive parallels with the church at Forteviot. As in Ireland, the *basilica* at Forteviot was a royal church, its status revealed by its foundation by a Pictish king, Unuist son of Uurguist, at his royal centre and on land given by him or his sons expressly for this purpose. This *basilica* was presumably a reliquary church, a shrine or martyrium containing major relics, including those of the apostle Andrew that Regulus reputedly brought to Pictland. Those relics may have been enshrined within the church, providing both a focus for worship and making the *basilica* an important place of pilgrimage. Another striking parallel between the church at Forteviot and Irish *basilicae* is their association with monuments and burials (Chaps 2 and 3). Forteviot was probably a royal burial place and may have held the tombs of Pictish kings and other members of the royal dynasties which, in turn, attracted other burials (Chap. 3). The income generated from pilgrims and burial rights, combined with its royal patronage, ensured that Forteviot was a wealthy church. This church owed its foundation, status and wealth to the patronage of Pictish kings. Its royal patronage is probably reflected in its associated sculpture (Chap. 5), its stone construction and, more certainly, in the iconography of the Forteviot arch (Chaps 6-8). The form and appearance of the *basilica* at Forteviot may be inferred from the arch and by inference from other early medieval churches (Chap. 9).

Although primarily a reliquary church, other factors may have contributed to Unuist's foundation of a church at Forteviot. Two of the most common motives for founding early medieval churches were so that they could serve as a chantry for the spiritual benefit of the soul of a named individual, often the founder or his wife, or to celebrate victory in battle. The St Andrews foundation legend provides clear evidence for the latter motivation in the founding of the church at Forteviot, although the former may have been implicit. The *basilica* at Forteviot, and the other churches, were founded after Hungus won a battle against the Anglo-Saxons, when he pledged a tenth part of Forteviot to God and St Andrew in return for victory, and returned from a presumably successful campaign in Argyll. The other motive for founding a *basilica* was ideological (Chaps 8 and 9).

ECCLESIASTICAL ORGANISATION

Despite the insights provided by the St Andrews foundation legend, many aspects of the church at Forteviot remain unclear. In particular, it is not known if Unuist's church represents a new building on an earlier ecclesiastical site or a new foundation altogether. Although an important church of elevated status, the nature of the ecclesiastical organisation to which the church of Forteviot belonged, and therefore the character of its ecclesiastical community, is also unclear. There is no record of either an abbot or bishop at Forteviot, making it unclear whether the church was episcopal or monastic in character. It may have been a community of priests serving the residents of the royal centre and its estate by ministrating for the cure of their souls under the jurisdiction of a bishop or, alternatively, a community of monks engaged in private contemplation and study under the authority of an abbot. This community may have been small. As at Govan (Davies 1994: 99-101), comparatively few clerics would have been required to oversee the *basilica* at Forteviot and even a large cemetery associated with it. The sculpture from Forteviot may provide some clues about the status of the church (Chap. 5).

A possible analogy to the church at Forteviot is provided by another Pictish church founded under royal patronage, Nechtan's foundation of *c*.710. Bede's (*Historia Ecclesiastica*, V.21) reference to 'all ministers of the altar and monks' has been interpreted as implying that Nechtan's church was staffed by priests and monks and had an extensive jurisdiction (Macquarrie 1992: 115). Although Bede was probably referring to the Pictish Church as a whole, it is tempting to see the church at Forteviot in similar terms, befitting its status and associations, with its jurisdiction possibly covering Strathearn or even Fortriu as a whole.

However, the status of the church at Forteviot within Strathearn is also unclear. Abernethy is traditionally regarded as the principal early medieval ecclesiastical foundation in Strathearn, although its early history is obscure. Moreover, the episcopal centre of Strathearn moved over time, from Abernethy to Muthill, before eventually settling just outside Strathearn, at Dunblane, in Menteith, *c*.1234 (Macquarrie 1992: 117-18, 128-9). It is unclear why there was no settled see before that date. It may have been as mundane as the bishops of Strathearn, as they were styled in the twelfth and early thirteenth centuries, choosing to reside at an ecclesiastical centre of their choice, a situation paralleled in the diocese of Moray. Alternatively, it may reflect shifting patronage, as the focus of royal and lordly power within Strathearn moved over time. But, during the ninth and tenth centuries, it could have been in response to Viking raids, with episcopal centres that were vulnerable to attacks from the Firth of Tay being abandoned in favour of others further up Strathearn. Regardless of the factors involved, the episcopal centre moved westwards up Strathearn and it may be significant here that Forteviot lies equidistant between Abernethy and Muthill. Under royal patronage, Forteviot may have been the episcopal centre of Strathearn for a time, presumably when the royal centre of Forteviot was at its height, and the church was under royal patronage, during the ninth century.

Forteviot may have had a small *Céli Dé* community sometime between the tenth and twelfth centuries. Although unrecorded, this is supported by analogy with other ecclesiastical sites, particularly those associated with royal centres, in eastern central Scotland during this period. The *Céli Dé*, 'Clients of God' or 'Culdees', was an ascetic revival movement that originated in Ireland during the eighth century (O'Dwyer 1981). There was a *Céli Dé* community at St Andrews by the 940s and several others in Scotland by the twelfth century (Reeves 1864; Macquarrie 1992; Clancy 1996). *Céli Dé* communities varied in character, some sharing larger foundations, often bishops' churches, with corporations of secularised monks and others forming their own communities.

Later evidence can often provide clues about earlier ecclesiastical organisation but there are disappointingly few medieval records of the church at Forteviot. As a result, the relationship between the Church of St Andrews and Forteviot is also obscure and is thought to have been a late one. Forteviot parish is claimed not to have been incorporated within the diocese of St Andrews until the late fifteenth century (Cowan 1967: 69). Two mid-twelfth-century charters recording royal grants of the church (Chap. 1) have attracted interest in this context. Before the reappraisal of the St Andrews foundation legend, these were traditionally believed to be the earliest contemporaneously-recorded references to a church at Forteviot. These grants make no reference to the rights of the Church of St Andrews. This has been interpreted as evidence that St Andrews enjoyed no rights over the church of Forteviot during the mid-twelfth century and, therefore, was not within the diocese of St Andrews before that date (Spearman 1993: 141).

Whatever the reason for the absence of such a record, Spearman's conclusion conflicts with other evidence. The consecration of the parish church of Forteviot by David de Bernham, bishop of St Andrews, in 1241 is strong evidence that Forteviot belonged to the diocese of St Andrews by that date. That Forteviot was a detached parish within the medieval diocese of St Andrews is even more revealing. The fragmented geography of the medieval dioceses of Brechin, Dunkeld, Muthill and St Andrews resulted from the fossilisation of a patchwork of early medieval ecclesiastical landholdings during the episcopal reorganisation of the twelfth century (Donaldson 1974; Ash 1996: 361). Those detached parishes reflect early medieval patronage, with kings and nobles making piecemeal endowments of land and churches to the major monastic churches, including St Andrews.

What is clear is that the church at Forteviot was a major ecclesiastical foundation during the ninth century. Its elevated status is revealed by a wide range of independent evidence, archaeological, documentary and topographical. Its location within or adjacent to the royal centre at Forteviot and its description as a *basilica* attest the status of this foundation as a royal church. This is confirmed by a near-contemporary source, preserved within the St Andrews foundation legend, which attributes the foundation of the church at Forteviot to a Pictish king who may be identified as Unuist son of Uurguist. Forteviot's status as a major ecclesiastical foundation is also corroborated by its association with a remarkable artefactual assemblage. That assemblage now merits detailed study.

5

SCULPTURE AND
METALWORK

With the notable exception of the arch examined in Part 2, no traces of the early medieval church at Forteviot appear to have survived and the site itself has probably been swept away by the Water of May (Chap. 2). As a result, the only physical evidence for the former presence of a Pictish ecclesiastical site at Forteviot is a collection of early medieval sculptural fragments and a single item of metalwork. The study of these artefacts potentially provides important clues about the nature and date of activity at the royal centre in general and its ecclesiastical dimension in particular. They are therefore studied in some detail here, although this chapter makes no claim to be a definitive corpus. In addition, two high-crosses from the vicinity of Forteviot are briefly discussed here because of the unique evidence they provide about the royal associations, status and date of the royal centre and its church.

THE SCULPTURAL ASSEMBLAGE

Several items of early medieval sculpture have been found at Forteviot over the past two centuries (Stuart 1867: xlv, 58-60, pl. CIII; ECMS, vol. 2: 321-7; Alcock and Alcock 1992: 22-3; Sutherland 1997: 46-7). It is unclear if any of these were discovered *in situ* and, as a result, their original provenance is unclear. The three fragments first recorded in the churchyard and adjacent manse garden at Forteviot in the nineteenth century offer the best prospect for having been *in situ*. Even if they were not, this concentration implies that these stones were discovered nearby and almost certainly within Forteviot or its immediate environs. This is consistent with the interpretation that the churchyard, on the edge of the escarpment cut by the Water of May, occupies part of the site of the Pictish church or that it was at least nearby. Alternatively, the church may have been regarded as an appropriate place for depositing stones found over a wider area for safekeeping, as it is today. At least two stones were found in secondary contexts, reused in the walls of farm buildings at Milton of Forteviot, and their original findspots are unrecorded. Nevertheless, these fragments may realistically be assumed to have originated at Forteviot and this is supported by an antiquarian account (below).

With the exception of the Forteviot arch, two which are now lost and Forteviot no. 7, which was moved to the Session House within the graveyard in 2005, these sculptures are displayed inside the porch of the church at Forteviot. All appear to be of local sandstone and are in a fragmentary condition. With better-preserved groups and complete items of early medieval sculpture attracting most attention in Scotland, sculptural fragments are understudied and, therefore, are often poorly understood (Henderson 2005). Nevertheless, surviving fragments can still be significant and informative. As a result of their incomplete state, with only limited decoration surviving, most fragments are conventionally assigned to the catch-all Class III of early medieval sculpture in Scotland; that is, relief sculpture without any Pictish symbols. This is also the case with the fragments from Forteviot. These stones are usually referred to by the numbers assigned to them in J. Romilly Allen and Joseph Anderson's corpus of early medieval sculpture in Scotland, *Early Christian Monuments of Scotland*, published in 1903. This convention is followed here and fragments of sculpture discovered since 1903 are numbered sequentially in the order in which they were found and/or first recorded.

Forteviot no. 1 is the lower part of a free-standing cross-slab and, with the exception of the arch, is the most complete and best-preserved item of early medieval sculpture from Forteviot. This stone formerly stood in the churchyard at Forteviot, where it was first recorded in 1856 (Stuart 1856: 17) (*19*). Although John Stuart (1856: 17; 1867: 59–60) identified this fragment with the Invermay cross (below), it clearly belongs to a cross-slab and not a high-cross. This fragment measures 24 x 19in (61 x 48cm) and is up to 6in (15cm) thick. Both faces and sides are decorated in shallow relief. The quality of the sculpture, in both composition and execution, is high and this fragment has been described as 'accomplished' (Hall *et al.* 1998: 134). The lower 8in (21cm) of the slab is undecorated and tapers slightly, presumably to facilitate its setting in a socket, either in the ground or in another monument.

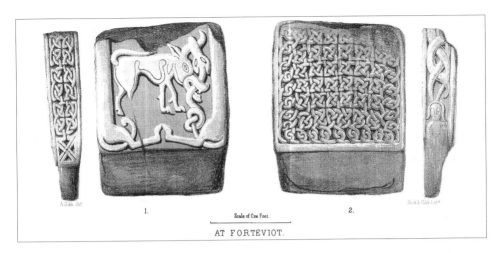

AT FORTEVIOT.

19 The Forteviot no. 1 cross-slab fragment, as illustrated in Stuart's *Sculptured Stones of Scotland* (1856)

The front face of this cross-slab is completely covered with an elaborate carpet of intricate interlace (*20*). Framed by a narrow and plain moulding, this is made up of tightly-spaced knot-work in four different styles of interlaced decoration. A pair of looped cords, with the loops facing each other and linked together (ECMS, vol. 1: 215, no. 553), define a border around the base and lower sides of the cross-slab. Within this, an interlace panel at the base of the slab comprises four vertical rows of crossed oval rings, with cords running horizontally and vertically as well as diagonally (ECMS, vol. 1: 273, no. 692B). Above this is an internal border comprising figure-of-eight-shaped knots, formed by combinations of symmetrical loops in pairs facing to the right and left, with two cords passing through the centres of the loops and crossing at right angles (ECMS, vol. 1: 219, no. 566). This inner border probably defines the outline of the base of a cross. Within this is a small fragment of another panel of interlace. This is a simpler form of circular knot-work which, when intact, would have consisted of circular curves with two diagonals crossing each other at right angles (ECMS, vol. 1: 188, no. 407).

This fragment epitomises what has been described as 'the Pictish preference for the decorated cross', in which a cross is composed entirely of panels of key-patterned or interlaced decoration (Henderson 1993: 213). Although the styles of interlace on Forteviot no. 1 are different, the overall effect is similar to that on St Orland's Stone at Cossans, Angus (ECMS, vol. 2: 216-18, fig. 230A), where the cross comprises different panels of knot-work within an interlaced border. The cross on a cross-slab at Applecross, Ross and Cromarty, is also formed of panels of interlace (Fisher 2001: 88-9, no. 1).

20 The Forteviot no. 1 cross-slab fragment: the front face

On the reverse of the cross-slab, the lower parts of the attenuated bodies of two beasts form a moulding, up to 2in (5cm) wide, along the sides of the stone and their hind legs provide a raised border to the base (21). Two of the beasts' feet, both with exaggeratedly long, single claws, meet in the centre at the base of the cross-slab. The tails of both beasts curl between their hind legs. The tail of the left-hand beast has a bulbous and curled end but the right-hand creature has a much longer tail, tied in an overhand or Stafford knot, that terminates in the head of a carnivore or reptile. This hybrid creature has the body of a snake but a head with ears and a long snout.

21 The Forteviot no. 1 cross-slab fragment: the reverse

Mirroring the opposing claws at the bottom of the cross-slab, the heads of the beasts forming this moulding probably confronted each other at the missing top. This arrangement is readily paralleled in Southern Pictland. Pairs of guardian beasts or sea monsters frame the reverses of the cross-slabs from Dunfallandy (Perthshire), Aberlemno no. 2, Farnell, Monifieth no. 2, and St Orland's Stone (all Angus) and also feature on a cross-slab from Bressay, Shetland (ECMS, vol. 2: 5–10, 209–11, 216–18, 219–21, 229–30, 286–9, figs 4, 227B, 230B, 232B, 242B, 305B). Unusually, the cross-bearing face of the Meigle no. 4 cross-slab is also flanked by a pair of beasts (ECMS, vol. 2: 299–300, fig. 313A; RCAHMS 1994: 102, fig. A; Ritchie 1997: 19). The distinctively elongated 'ball and claw' design of the feet of the beasts on Forteviot no. 1 is paralleled on the cross-slabs from Woodrae, Invergowrie no. 1 (both Angus), Dunfallandy, Gask and Rossie Priory (all Perthshire) (ECMS, vol. 2: 242–5, 255–6, 286–9, 290–1, 306–8, figs 258A, 258C, 266B, 305A, 305, C307, 307A, 322A; Henderson and Henderson 2004: 81).

The panel enclosed by this beastly border is filled by a fantastic horned creature with the body of an ox but the head of a carnivore. The hunched back, belly, haunches and head of this beast are emphasised by an inset line, while its front and rear shoulders are indicated by lobate scrolls forming schematic joints. Although its hind legs are hoofed, its front legs are of the 'ball and claw' variety. Reinforcing its hybrid nature, a single long, curved horn projects from its forehead and it has elongated and toothed jaws. This creature is locked in combat with the serpentine-headed tail of the attenuated beast framing the right-hand side of the cross-slab. It grasps the neck of the snake-like creature in its jaws and the serpent, in turn, grips the horn of the hybrid beast in its jaws. This is an example of the 'beast versus snake' motif found on the Gask and Rossie Priory cross-slabs (Henderson and Henderson 2004: 79–81).

The right-hand side of the stone is decorated with the interlaced tails of three serpentine creatures, their backs decorated with a barbed or serrated pattern (*22*). The tails of two of these snakes emerge from the head or hair of an incomplete human figure, as if forming horns or antennae. This figure has long hair and lentoid, staring eyes. He may represent a naked man, symbolising the fate of the wicked or the pursuit of the damned or lustful evil to hell (Hall *et al.* 1998: 134, 136). This motif is typically positioned on the narrow sides of Pictish cross-slabs, such as the example on the end of the arm of a free-standing cross from Strathmartine (no. 8), Angus (ECMS, vol. 1: 266–7, fig. 277B). The peripheral location and possible symbolism of such figures are in deliberate opposition to the prominent cross, a symbol of salvation, on the front face. However, as the figure on Forteviot no. 1 does not survive below the waist, it does not display the characteristic features of wrist-holding, touching the genitals or the genitals

Right: 22 The
Forteviot no. 1 cross–
slab fragment: right–
hand side

Far right: 23 The
Forteviot no. 1 cross–
slab fragment: the left–
hand side

being attacked by a snake. As a result, the precise parallels and interpretation of
this figure remain uncertain.

The left-hand side of Forteviot no. 1 is decorated with an interlace panel,
with cords running horizontally and vertically as well as diagonally (*23*). These
terminate in a square of knot-work formed by repeating a symmetrical loop-
knot in each of the four triangles formed by dividing the square diagonally into
quarters (ECMS, vol. 1: 272, 286, nos 691 and 724).

Forteviot no. 2 is the arch discussed in Part 2.

Forteviot no. 3 was first recorded in the garden of the manse at Forteviot in
1903 (ECMS, vol. 2: 324). This fragment, measuring 10in (0.25m) across, belongs
to the arm of a free-standing high-cross. Only most of one face and parts of the
end and sides of this arm survive. Nevertheless, this yields enough information to
enable the form of the high-cross, or at least its cross-head, to be reconstructed.

The cross arm is of the wedge-shaped or expanded end form, that is, it widens slightly towards the terminal. The arm–pit or angle where the arm meets the cross-shaft is of the round hollow or circular variety. The presence of part of the quadrant of a connecting ring that joined the arms of the cross reveals that this was a ringed high-cross (24). This fragment belonged to a large, elaborately-carved and impressive monument.

The roughly rectangular front face of the cross arm comprises a single panel, filled with interlace in wide bands comprising repeating triangular Stafford knots in the four corners and with small round pellets filling the spaces between the bands (ECMS, vol. 1: 287, no. 731; Henderson and Henderson 2004: 193) (25). The end of the cross arm is decorated with the surviving part of a rectangular panel, each quarter of which was filled with triangular interlace (26). The pattern repeated is a triangular Stafford knot of cords and with two cords at the bottom crossed over each other (ECMS, vol. 1: 288, no. 733). This interlace is formed with a cord of a type that is variously described as double-beaded, two-ply, median-grooved or median-incised. The surviving stump of the connecting ring has a T-shaped or stepped section (27). The inner face and sides are decorated with a simple two-strand interlace within a moulding and the outer edge of its projecting rib is decorated with a key-pattern of step-shaped bars (ECMS, vol. 1: 331, no. 887).

The form and decoration of Forteviot no. 3 bears several distinctive features and the monument to which it belonged must have been unusual. Its slightly expanded arms contrast with the more common square-armed crosses of Pictland, although crosses of this form are depicted on cross-slabs at Migvie (Aberdeenshire), Mortlach (Banffshire) and Skinnet (Caithness) (ECMS, vol. 2: 30-3, 155-6, 191-2, figs 28, 29, 162, 208). Inserted pellets are rare in Pictish interlace. This is the only recorded example in Southern Pictland and one of only two in Pictland as a whole, the other being on the Rosemarkie no. 2 panel (ECMS, vol. 2: 85-6). The T-shaped section of the connecting ring is unparalleled in Pictland and Dál Riata. The only recorded Irish example, on the Terrace Cross at Tynan Abbey, Co. Armagh (Harbison 1992, vol. 1: 180-1, vol. 2: figs 631, 633), differs subtly in that the projecting part of the ring, the 'foot' of the 'T', is on the inside of the ring while on Forteviot no. 3 it is on the outside.

Forteviot no. 4 was also in the manse garden at Forteviot by 1903 (ECMS, vol. 2: 324). Although poorly preserved and dismissed by the Alcocks as a 'mere fragment' (Alcock and Alcock 1992: 223), this belongs to a once-impressive monument whose eroded appearance belies its significance.

This fragment measures 13.5 x 15.25in (35.5 x 39cm) and is up to 7in (18cm) thick. Carving survives on parts of one face and one side only. The face comprises

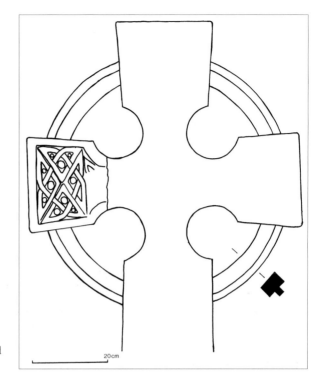

Right: 24 The reconstruction of a free-standing high-cross from the Forteviot no. 3 fragment

Below: 25 The Forteviot no. 3 fragment: the front face, showing the distinctive and unusual pelleted interlace

26 The Forteviot no. 3 fragment: interlaced panel on the end of the cross arm

27 The Forteviot no. 3 fragment: the surviving stump of the connecting ring that joined the arms of the cross has a T-shaped or stepped section. This feature reveals that this fragment belonged to a free-standing ringed high-cross

most of a panel depicting a mounted warrior in low relief (*28*). This horseman is very similar to that on the Dupplin cross (below) and is characteristic of the Benvie-Dupplin school of sculpture (Chap. 6). The top left-hand side of this panel is defined by a narrow moulding decorated with a stepped key-pattern. The horseman faces left and holds a spear in his right hand, its spearhead dipped towards to ground. The reigns are visible and were presumably held in his left hand, although this is obscured by what initially appears to be a blank area at the centre of the image. However, closer inspection reveals a roughly-incised circular area, outlined by a simple groove and with a small indentation at its centre, possibly caused by a compass point. This represents the warrior's shield.

28 The Forteviot no. 4 fragment: a panel, depicting a mounted warrior, from a high-cross

Mounted warriors appear on the reverse of several Pictish cross-slabs, either alone or within more extensive, usually hunting, scenes. This fragment appears to belong to the former and parallels may be identified with two small cross-slabs from Meigle, nos 3 and 5 (ECMS, vol. 2: 298-9, 300-301, figs 312B, 314B; RCAHMS 1994: 102, figs E and I; Ritchie 1997: 18, 20). However, closer study of the surviving side of this fragment leads to a different interpretation. The most obvious feature here is part of an interlace panel, with a moulding around it and a broad beaded moulding above. It is unclear what pattern this interlace belongs to because only a corner survives. Above this, the side of the fragment appears to be irregular and badly damaged but is actually scalloped or double-curved. This scalloped edge appears clearly as a moulding framing the left-hand side of the panel containing the mounted warrior. However, the point at which the outside edges of the curves meet, which may have been decorated with a cusp, as on the Dupplin cross (below), is damaged. In Pictland, this scalloped appearance is found only on the Dupplin cross and the Kirriemuir no. 17 cross-slab fragment (RCAHMS 2003).

The scalloped edge and its close similarity to that of the Dupplin cross enables this fragment to be identified as part of a high-cross. The part concerned depends on how similar these crosses were. The head and shaft of the Dupplin cross display different decorative styles. Only its arms have the scalloped edging and these are filled with interlace or vinescroll. In contrast to Forteviot no. 4, the mounted warrior on the Dupplin cross appears on the top panel on the cross-shaft, which has straight rather than scalloped edges (29, 30). The Forteviot fragment therefore belongs either to the upper or lower arm of a high-cross similar to that from Dupplin or the shaft of a high-cross that also has scalloped edges. The contrasting sculptural styles displayed by this fragment reveal that it belonged to a different high-cross from the Forteviot no. 3 stone.

As a mounted warrior depicted on an impressive monument, the person concerned is evidently of high social status, probably a king. The presence of such an unambiguously secular scene on a high-cross suggests lay patronage of the church at Forteviot, the monuments perhaps commemorating or being commissioned by the individual portrayed on it. This is even clearer in the case of the Dupplin cross (below).

Forteviot no. 5 is a small block, now lost (31). When first recorded in 1903, this fragment was built into the wall of the mill at Milton of Forteviot (ECMS, vol. 2: 324). This sculpture was probably brought with rubble from the site of the royal centre at Forteviot (below), one third of a mile (0.6km) to the south. A single decorated face, measuring 1ft x 6in (30 x 15cm) bears part of a panel of interlaced decoration, with cords crossing each other horizontally and vertically as well as diagonally (ECMS, vol. 1: 272, no. 691). Although this interlace was dismissed by the Alcocks as 'rather confused' (Alcock and Alcock 1992: 223), this impression is simply created by the small area of interlace surviving and the pattern of knotwork is similar to that found on the Forteviot no. 1 cross-slab. Although the mutilated state and small size of this fragment makes analysis difficult, Forteviot no. 5 probably belonged to a cross-slab.

Forteviot no. 6 was lost sometime before 1903 and no description or illustration of it exists. This fragment had also been reused in the wall of an outhouse at Milton of Forteviot, but was lost when the building was demolished and its rubble reused to construct a retaining wall along the east bank of the Water of May (ECMS, vol. 2: 324).

Forteviot no. 7 is a large slab, measuring 25 x 16.5 x 8in (64 x 42 x 20cm), and was first recorded in 1997 (Simpson 1997). Its face was originally decorated, but is now so worn that only the faintest traces are visible (32). One side is better preserved and bears part of an interlace panel, within a moulding (33).

Although very eroded, a typically Pictish scene was tentatively identified on the face of this stone by Nick Simpson (1997) (34). This comprises a human figure, dressed in a knee-length tunic, raising an elongated object, possibly a sword, in his left hand as he strides forward. In front of him stands a hybrid creature comprising the body, legs and tail of an unidentified quadruped, possibly a dog or wolf, with the head of a man. Its head is turned backwards to face the human figure. Immediately in front of this creature is a small, apparently human, figure, which may have been dropped from the jaws of the creature before it looked back. Above the human figure are the front and rear legs of an incomplete quadruped. Simpson's interpretative description of this scene may be modified in the light of subsequent examination. The human figure, his knee brought up as he lunges forward, raises an axe in both hands above his head. His blow is aimed at the rounded back or rump of a quadruped, probably a bear, with its head lowered. This animal appears to be carrying, or colliding with, an elongated object, possibly a post or stake. Above them, the lower jaw, neck and foreleg of a horse are visible and possibly the left leg of its rider.

The combination of men and beasts on this fragment is readily paralleled in Pictish sculpture. Simpson's interpretation implies that it echoes the powerful images of animal aggression and mythological violence found on the sculpture at Meigle (on which see ECMS, vol. 2: 296-305; Ritchie 1997). However, the interpretation presented here suggests that it belongs to a hunting scene, although there are no clear parallels. This fragment clearly belonged to a much larger monument, probably a cross-slab or the shaft of a high-cross.

29 The front and left-hand side of the Dupplin cross, as illustrated in J. Romilly Allen and Joseph Anderson's *Early Christian Monuments of Scotland* (1903)

30 The reverse and right-hand side of the Dupplin cross, as illustrated in J. Romilly Allen and Joseph Anderson's *Early Christian Monuments of Scotland* (1903)

31 The Forteviot no. 5 fragment, now lost, as illustrated in J. Romilly Allen and Joseph Anderson's *Early Christian Monuments of Scotland* (1903)

32 The Forteviot no. 7 fragment. The images on this worn sculpture are only faintly visible

33 The Forteviot no. 7 fragment: part of an interlaced side panel

Above: 34 The Forteviot no. 7 fragment: Nick Simpson's interpretation of the scene (left) and as reinterpreted here (right)

Right: 35 The Forteviot no. 8 fragment: front face

Forteviot no. 8 is a large slab, measuring 22in (56cm) x 18 in (46cm) and 6.5in (16.5cm) thick, and is previously unrecorded (*35*). Carved decoration in false relief survives on one face and one side. A narrow panel, one edge of which is emphasised by an incised line, runs across the face of this slab, which is otherwise undecorated. This panel is filled with thick-corded interlace in a four-cord plait with vertical breaks in the middle vertical row of crossing-points, with two crossing-points between each break (ECMS, vol. 1: 205, no. 513). The side bears part of a rectangular panel, its edges defined by a beaded moulding. This panel contains interlace derived from an eight-cord plait and comprising Stafford knots with extra cords interwoven through the outer parts of the loops, arranged in a double row, with the knots facing right and left towards each other (ECMS, vol. 1: 236, no. 610). This design indicates that the slab, when complete, was almost twice as thick as it is now.

It is unclear what this fragment belonged to, although it appears to have been part of a complete, rather than composite, monument. The presence of decoration on two faces suggests that it belonged to a free-standing monument rather than an architectural fragment and the relationship between the panels may imply that the monument concerned was a cross-slab. This would make the interlace panel on the face of the stone a transverse arm, although it seems too narrow for this and there are no identifiable parallels.

LOST SCULPTURE

The number of sculptured stones from Forteviot is relatively small in comparison to those from other Pictish ecclesiastical sites and, at least initially, appears distinctly unimpressive when contrasted with the rich collections from Meigle or St Vigeans, for example. However, these fragments simply represent accidents of survival and their present condition attests the destructive processes to which the sculpture at Forteviot has been subjected over the centuries. The high quality and poor condition of the surviving sculpture indicates that this is only a small proportion of what once existed at Forteviot (Ritchie 1995: 7). Nevertheless, comparisons with other ecclesiastical centres in Southern Pictland suggests that this assemblage may be a broadly representative sample of the sculpture originally at Forteviot.

The former presence of a more extensive sculptural assemblage at Forteviot is supported by antiquarian sources. The earliest of these may be the *Liber Floridus* of Lambert of St Omer, dating to 1120. This intriguingly refers to the 'palace of the soldier Arthur in Britain, in the country of the Picts, constructed with marvellous art and variety, in which may be seen sculptured all his deeds and wars' (trans. Padel 1994: 6 and nn 18-20). The structure concerned has been identified as Arthur's O'on (Padel 1994: 6; Henderson and Henderson 2004: 220-1), a Roman shrine at Carron, near Falkirk, which was demolished in 1743 (Steer 1958; 1976; RCAHMS 1963: 118, no. 126; Brown 1974; Brown and Vasey 1989). However, Arthur's O'on was undecorated, as eighteenth-century accounts and illustrations reveal, and was neither a palace nor in Pictland. The *Liber Floridus* may refer to Forteviot instead (Ritchie 1995: 9, n. 2), although this is uncorroborated. More fundamentally, the passage may be mythological in nature and not concern an actual site.

Antiquarian sources suggest that extensive losses of early medieval sculpture occurred at Forteviot during the eighteenth century. In 1772, the schoolmaster at Forteviot noted that 'Tradition informs us that some houses in the neighbourhood have been built, or rebuilt, of the stones of the palace at Halyhill; and some of these are easily distinguished by the antiquated figures cut thereon' ('T' 1772). According to a later, although possibly derivative, account, the ruins on Halyhill 'were used as a quarry for the building of minor structures' (Marshall 1880: 103). This is confirmed by the reuse of Forteviot nos 5 and 6 in the walls of the mill and an outbuilding at Milton of Forteviot, although both fragments subsequently disappeared. Although the nature of the sculptures referred to in 1772 is unrecorded, their provenance, reputed association with the 'palace', 'antiquated' appearance and presence of (presumably human) figures strongly suggests that they were early medieval. The present whereabouts of these sculptures are unknown, unless they comprise or include the fragments now in the church at Forteviot.

All traces of sculpture at Forteviot appear to have disappeared by 1832, when the arch was described as 'the only remnant now to be found of the ancient capital of the kings of Scotland' (Skene 1857: 279). In contrast, a source of 1845 claims that the sculptured stones reused in buildings in Forteviot were 'in the possession of Lord Ruthven' (Robertson 1845: 1174). And in 1880 it was claimed that 'some choice specimens of the sculpture which adorned the Palace of Forteviot have been preserved at Freeland House', Forgandenny, the residence of Lord Ruthven (Marshall 1880: 103). However, these accounts presumably refer to the Forteviot arch, which was kept at Freeland House until 1874 (Chap. 6). There are no other records of early medieval sculpture at Freeland House and no sculpture is listed in the sale catalogue prepared when the house and estate were sold in 1919 (Chartres, pers. comm.). However, any sculpture may have been dispersed when Freeland House was sold in 1873 and the arch was moved to Edinburgh (Chap. 6). No examples of early medieval sculpture remain today at Freeland House (Ross, pers. comm.), which is now the Main Building of Strathallan School.

THE DUPPLIN AND INVERMAY CROSSES

Early medieval sculpture from the environs of Forteviot may be of relevance to the study of the royal centre and its church. Two sculptures originally sited a short distance from Forteviot are of particular significance.

The Dupplin cross
The Dupplin cross is a magnificent and exceptional item of Pictish sculpture, 8ft 7in (2.62m) high and the only Pictish high-cross to survive intact (*colour plate 15; 29, 30*) (ECMS, vol. 2: 319–21, figs 334A-D; Alcock and Alcock 1992: 238, 240; 1996; Henderson 1999a; Henderson and Henderson 2004: 189-91; MacSween

2002; Alcock 2003: 231-2, 391-3). It formerly stood in a field known as the Cross Park (NO05051896), on the shoulder of the Gask Ridge (at 295ft (90m) OD), which rises steeply from the north bank of the River Earn, a quarter of a mile (0.4km) east-north-east of Bankhead and just under a mile (1.5km) north of Forteviot. The cross was removed in 1998, when it was taken into the care of Historic Scotland for conservation work and then displayed in the Royal Museum of Scotland in Edinburgh. Following considerable controversy over its most appropriate place and means of display, the cross was returned to Strathearn in 2002 and installed in St Serf's Church, Dunning.

The provenance of the Dupplin cross is the subject of debate. There is uncertainty that the cross stood in its original position (Henderson 1999b: 95, n.72). When exhibited in Edinburgh, the National Museum of Scotland claimed that the cross was 'almost certainly' from Forteviot. And it has been suggested that the cross was originally erected at Forteviot, before being moved by a landowner in the modern period (Driscoll 2001: 242; 2002: 13). However, there is no evidence to substantiate this. Excavations conducted both before and after the removal of the cross proved inconclusive about its original site, although they revealed that it had stood in the same general location since at least the late seventeenth century (Radley and Dunn 2000). However, its roughly-shaped cross-base (*36*) appears to be original and is certainly of early medieval date, as the presence of a fragmentary and unintelligible ogham inscription (Forsyth 1995: 237-9) along one edge reveals. This, combined with the massive size (5ft 5in x 3ft 8in x 1ft 10in high (1.37 x 1.12 x 0.55m)), and weight of the base, indicates that the Dupplin cross stood in its original position until 1998. The significance of this location is that it affords extensive views across lower Strathearn and overlooks Forteviot.

This account focuses only on those aspects of the Dupplin cross that are relevant to the study of the royal centre at Forteviot and its sculpture. Each face of the cross-shaft is divided into two or three panels. The top panel on the east face depicts a warrior on horseback, armed with a spear (*37*). This warrior has a prominent, block-like nose and a long, curved and drooping moustache. In the panel below the horseman are four closely-set and elongated foot soldiers, all clean-shaven and each armed with a small round shield and spear. Another two spearmen, their shields suspended around their necks by *guiges* or shield-straps, occupy the lower panel on the south side of the cross-shaft. These foot soldiers are distinguished from those on the east face by their long, drooping moustaches and by the hems on their tunics, which are decorated with stepped key-work. Lower borders of key-work, in diagonal, stepped and T-shaped designs, are used to emphasise and separate the principal panels on the cross-shaft, including the mounted warrior, four foot-soldiers and inscription.

36 The Dupplin cross: the roughly-shaped cross-base

37 The mounted warrior and foot soldiers on the east side (front) of the shaft of the Dupplin cross. *Crown copyright: Royal Commission on the Ancient and Historical Monuments of Scotland*

A badly weathered inscription in Roman letters was identified in 1990 on the west face of the cross-shaft (Forsyth 1992; 1995: 239-42). This is one of only four Latin inscriptions on Pictish sculpture and, comprising seven lines, the longest surviving Latin inscription on an early medieval sculpture in Scotland. Although mostly illegible, the first two lines can be read as CU [...] NTIN/FILIUSFIRCU/ S. This name is identifiable as that of Causantín son of Uurguist (Constantine mac Fergusa), king of the Picts (789-820) and of Dál Riata (811-20). This identifies the Dupplin cross as a Pictish monument. The rest of the inscription is illegible.

The nature of the relationship between Causantín and the Dupplin cross is unclear because monuments were not necessarily erected during the lifetime of the individuals named on them (Forsyth 1995: 242). However, references to named lay persons in early medieval Insular inscriptions usually record either the patronage or death of the individual named. This inscription probably records that the cross either commemorates Causantín or was erected under his patronage and that it was therefore erected either during his reign or shortly afterwards. Moreover, enough of the inscription survives to enable its form to be inferred. Inscriptions on Anglo-Saxon churches typically begin with the name of the patron, followed by the verb of ordering, then details of his command and sometimes a dedication and the motive for erecting it (Higgitt 1986: 133-4; 2004: 3, 9). The inscription on the Dupplin cross may have been similar in form. Causantín's name appears at the start of the inscription, not only emphasising it but also revealing that the king must be the subject of a sentence which probably continued 'ordered the erection of this cross/monument' (compare Alcock and Alcock 1996: 455; Alcock 2003: 305, 391-2). This inscription records an act of royal patronage, the erection of the cross by Causantín.

According to an alternative theory, the Dupplin cross was erected by Cináed mac Ailpín or one of his sons to commemorate Causantín, who, like Cináed, had held the kingship of both the Picts and the Scots (Spearman, cited in Sutherland 1994: 238; Johnston and Duncan 2005). This is an inventive attempt to reconcile new evidence with the traditional mid- or late ninth-century date for the cross, but there is no evidence to support it.

By linking the Dupplin cross with a named individual, this inscription enables the cross to be dated much more closely than is normal for Pictish sculpture. But unfortunately for dating purposes, Causantín (789-820) enjoyed a long reign by early medieval standards. Although an element of uncertainty remains, this evidence has been used to date the cross much more closely than previously, to at least the first half of the ninth century (Henderson and Henderson 2004: 209). Others have proposed more precise dates, variously assigning the cross to 'round about 800' (Bannerman 1999: 91), 'the beginning of the ninth century' (Forsyth

1995: 243), 'early ninth century' (Henderson 1999a: 164), 'the opening decades of the ninth century' (Forsyth, cited in Wormald 1996: 146), 'the period before 820' and 'not later than 820' (Alcock and Alcock 1996: 455), 'about 820' (NMS display label), 'c 820' (Alcock 2003: 305), 810–830 (Alcock and Alcock 1996: 457; Alcock 1998: 522) and 'c 820+' (Laing 2000: 82). These dating brackets may be refined further. Causantín must have been at the height of his powers during the last decade of his reign, when he held the kingships of both the Picts and the Scots of Dál Riata (but see Broun 1998b). This suggests a narrower dating bracket, the second decade of the ninth century, making the Dupplin cross the most precisely dated example of Pictish sculpture.

That the Dupplin cross was, in part at least, a monument to Causantín's expanded kingdom is supported by the iconography of several scenes on the cross-shaft (Alcock and Alcock 1992: 238, 240). Causantín is portrayed as an equestrian warrior-king, reflecting awareness of Late Antique and early Christian iconography of the mounted ruler as a symbol of authority and divine victory (Carrington 1996: 464). In addition, the scenes portraying the Biblical King David rending the lion's jaws and playing the harp expressed the divine sanction of Causantín's royal power. The cross also displays an overtly military iconography in its two scenes of ranked infantrymen and perhaps performed a function as a record of a great victory. Reinforcing its triumphalist imagery, the Dupplin cross was probably intended to be seen against the sky (Henderson and Henderson 2004: 190-1). The Dupplin cross was a public and monumental expression of royal power and of the spiritual and military basis upon which that power rested, as well as of royal patronage of the Pictish Church and an explicitly Christian kingship. High-crosses not only demonstrate the power of the Church, but also, through some of the inscriptions and images they bear, the combined power and patronage of Church and state.

The inscription probably complements the iconography of the Dupplin cross and names one of the figures depicted. The most likely candidate is the most prominent figure depicted on the cross, the mounted warrior, whose portrait occupies the corresponding panel on the reverse face of the cross-shaft. This inscription makes the Dupplin cross the most closely dated item of Pictish sculpture and the mounted warrior the earliest identifiable portrait not only of a Pictish king, but of any ruler in northern Britain.

The Invermay cross
Just as the Dupplin cross overlooked Forteviot from the north, another high-cross formerly stood on rising ground to the south of the royal centre. Unfortunately, this sculpture has fared less well than the Dupplin cross. Although usually referred

to by scholars as the Invermay cross, after the estate it stood on, it is known locally as the Dronachy cross. This cross formerly stood in North Hallbank Park (NO166059), on a low hill that rises on the north side of the Water of May at Dronachy, 0.75 mile (1.2km) south of Forteviot. The Invermay cross 'was, by some accident ... broken over at the middle', 'not many years' before 1772 ('T' 1772: 332) and was described in 1796 as 'lying broken over at the pedestal, on which are many emblematical figures' (*Statistical Account* 1797 (1976: 200)).

The original cross-base survives. Although considerably damaged and crudely repaired (*colour plate 16, 38*), this cross-base is of much higher quality than that of the Dupplin cross. Formed from a large pyramidal block, measuring 4ft x 4ft 4in and around 2ft high (1.22 x 1.33 x 0.6m), the flat and carefully-dressed sides of the cross-base slope in towards the top. A projecting lip surrounds the socket on the upper surface. The cross-base probably occupies its original location but is, strictly speaking, no longer *in situ* because repeated ploughing has loosened it from the soil and it is now sitting on the ground surface. The study of cross-bases is largely neglected but can reveal much about constructional techniques and the crosses they supported (Fisher 2005). The size and quality of the Invermay cross-base indicates that this belonged to an impressive monument and held a substantial and elaborate high-cross. A plain stone pillar (*colour plate 17; 39*), 9ft (2.74m) high, was erected in the original cross-base *c.*1840 (*Name Book* 1860, vol. 30: 57).

Already felled, the Invermay cross suffered further indignities during the nineteenth century: 'When the cross was broken up the fragments were thrown away as rubbish into the field, and afterwards, being in the way of the plough, were heaped up with other loose stones in the wood hard by' (ECMS, vol. 2: 327). The wood concerned was the Long Plantation, 0.25 mile (0.4km) north of the cross site and 0.75 mile (1.2km) south-east of Forteviot. There, in 1891, Romilly Allen was shown 'three fragments of the destroyed cross ... lying in a fir wood, on a heap of stones which had been collected from the adjoining field'. Two of these fragments lay outside the porch of the church at Forteviot until they were moved into the Session House in 2005, although the third is lost. The mutilated state and small size of these fragments makes analysis difficult and, as a result, the Invermay cross is of uncertain form.

Invermay no. 1 is a small block of sandstone, its roughly squared form and traces of mortar indicating that it has been reused in a building (*40*). This is decorated on only one face, measuring 1ft x 6in (35 x 12cm), with part of a relief panel of tightly interwoven knotwork comprising an eight-cord diagonal plait with a cruciform break in the centre (ECMS, vol. 1: 186-7, no. 403A; vol. 2: 327-8, fig. 340).

Above: 38 The Invermay cross. Although damaged, the original base that held the early medieval cross still survives

Right: 39 The Invermay 'cross': the nineteenth-century pillar in its early medieval base

40 The Invermay
no. 1 fragment

Invermay nos IA and IB are two adjoining fragments, although one is now lost. Again, only one face is decorated, divided into three panels of relief decoration (ECMS, vol. 2: 327-8, fig. 341) (*41*). The top panel comprises a narrow, horizontal band of stepped key-pattern, below which is a larger rectangular panel of double-beaded diagonal key-pattern and with one corner of a panel of diagonal key-pattern below that (ECMS, vol. 1: 331, 346, nos 887, 952).

Close stylistic parallels exist between the Dupplin and Invermay crosses and the sculpture from Forteviot. This is particularly apparent in the appearance of the human figures, with their exaggerated noses and moustaches (Chap. 7), and the patterns of interlace. The same double-beaded diagonal key-pattern occurs on both the Dupplin and Invermay crosses (ECMS, vol. 2: 328; Alcock and Alcock 1992: 240-1), while the key-pattern of step-shaped bars on both crosses also occurs on Forteviot no. 3 and on the tunic hem of one of the figures on the Forteviot arch. These stylistic similarities suggest that the crosses and sculpture from the Forteviot area belong to the same sculptural school and are of similar date.

It is unclear if the Dupplin and Invermay cross stood alone or were originally associated with other sculptures or ecclesiastical buildings. The grandeur of the Dupplin cross and its overtly political imagery indicate that it was a focus of royal and ecclesiastical activities. These high-crosses may have marked places of open-air worship or have stood outside small dependent chapels or oratories of the church at Forteviot, although there is no evidence for these. The parallel

41 The Invermay no. IA fragment

provided by the siting of high-crosses at early medieval Irish ecclesiastical centres suggests a more likely function. As potent symbols of divine power and protection, high-crosses were erected around ecclesiastical boundaries or at the entrance to an ecclesiastical enclosure, where they demarcated the *termonn*, the area of sanctuary and within which the abbot's or bishop's rule prevailed (Buckley 1900; Edwards 1990: 106-7, 164; Hamlin 1982: 69; 1987: 139; Harbison 1992, vol. 1: 352-4; Aitchison 1994: 231-6). This may also have been the case in Pictland and is supported by the erection of 12 stone crosses around Kilrimont, as described in the St Andrews foundation legend (ed. Skene 1867: 186).

That the Dupplin and Invermay crosses were boundary-markers is supported by their original locations. These high-crosses stood on hills or ridges overlooking Forteviot, just under a mile (1.4km) equidistant from, and on opposite sides of, the royal centre. This suggests that they marked the northern and southern limits respectively of either the royal estate of Forteviot or the tenth part of the royal estate that, according to the St Andrews foundation legend, Hungus' sons granted to God and St Andrew. These high-crosses were monumental expressions of ecclesiastical ownership of, and jurisdiction over, the land. Although the extent of the ecclesiastical lands at Forteviot and their relationship with the royal estate are uncertain, the locations of the Dupplin and Invermay crosses imply the existence of an extensive territory around the royal centre. This is paralleled elsewhere in Southern Pictland. The high-cross at Mugdrum (NO225182), of which only the shaft and base now survive (ECMS, vol. 2: 367; Proudfoot 1997: 54-6; Henderson 1999a: 164-5; Henderson and Henderson 2004: 189-90), stands 2.5 miles (4.5km) north-east of the major ecclesiastical and royal centre of Abernethy. The proximity of the former locations of the Dupplin and Invermay crosses to the boundaries of the medieval parish of Forteviot supports the interpretation that the parish lands fossilise the extent of the royal estate (Chap. 3). And, although one must beware of circular arguments, this also supports the argument that both crosses stood in their original locations.

High-crosses probably performed a range of symbolic and liturgical functions. That they were not all boundary-markers is indicated by the presence of fragments of another two high-crosses at Forteviot. This may also be paralleled by early Irish ecclesiastical sites, where high-crosses or cross-slabs sometimes stand inside the enclosure, sited in a formalised manner in the open space in front of and beside the principal church (Herity 1983; 1984). Although the interpretation of their function is influenced by later religious practices, these high-crosses may have formed processional stations where mass was celebrated in the open air. The high-crosses at Forteviot may have performed a similar function and were possibly erected in carefully planned locations defined by the position of the church.

The presence of impressive high-crosses at Dupplin and Invermay, their distinctive styles and the Dupplin inscription, enables these monuments and locations to be linked with Forteviot and its kings. Moreover, it is possible that these are the only surviving examples, complete and fragmentary respectively, of what was originally a larger number of high-crosses sited around the boundary of the ecclesiastical lands at Forteviot, the rest of which have been lost. Like Kilrimont and Irish ecclesiastical centres, Forteviot may have been ringed with high-crosses. The church at Forteviot was only one element, although the most important one, within a wider landscape of Christian belief and ecclesiastical and royal power. The Dupplin and Invermay crosses linked the Pictish church at Forteviot with this hinterland by marking the boundary of the ecclesiastical and/or royal estate.

THE STONE BASIN

Although very different in character from the sculptured fragments described above, another stone within the porch of the church at Forteviot is also of interest. Previously unrecorded, this is a hollowed stone basin. This comprises an irregular stone containing a roughly hemispherical depression measuring 9.5in (24cm) across and 5.5in (14cm) deep (42). Although the stone appears to be otherwise unworked, the smoothness and regularity of the bowl indicates that it is not natural but has been shaped by human agency.

Hollowed stones occur throughout Scotland, with a concentration in highland Perthshire (Robertson 1997: 136, 146, n. 21), but have received little attention. They occur mostly on early ecclesiastical sites and, reflecting this, the larger examples are usually interpreted as 'Celtic' baptismal fonts and the smaller examples as stoups for holy water. Scottish examples are comparable with the stone basins that occur widely on early ecclesiastical sites in Ireland, where they are known as bullauns (Crozier and Rea 1940; Hughes and Hamlin 1977: 99-100; Weir 1980: 55-6; Harbison 1991: 223-8). These are found in both portable rocks, as at Forteviot, and large, earthfast boulders. They can occur singly or in groups and around 30 are recorded at Glendalough, Co. Wicklow (Price 1959).

Bullauns are traditionally associated with folk superstitions and, for example, are sometimes attributed to sleeping or praying saints, whose heads or knees are claimed to have left the marks. In particular, the water that collects in bullauns was popularly believed to have healing properties and was doused on the afflicted part of the body. As a result, bullauns are often referred to by the ailment they are supposed to cure, such as 'wart stones'. They are frequently incorporated into

42 The hollowed stone basin at Forteviot

local pilgrimages or patterns and the tendency for many early ecclesiastical sites to become later places of worship and pilgrimage means that it is difficult to be confident about their date. Nevertheless, they appear to be of considerable antiquity and their occurrence on some prehistoric sites suggests that they range widely in date. The original function of bullauns has been the subject of much speculation and remains obscure. Bullauns are claimed to be mortars for grinding a wide range of foodstuffs, animal fodder, pigments or ores, basins for feeding poultry or collecting cows' milk and stoups for holding holy water or preparing ritual meals. Bullauns probably had various functions.

The date and function of the hollowed stone at Forteviot are also obscure. However, like its Scottish and Irish counterparts, its association with an early ecclesiastical site is probably significant and may suggest a religious function. That Forteviot did not survive as a powerful ecclesiastical centre or place of pilgrimage into the high Middle Ages suggests that the hollowed stone is probably early medieval in date and that its function is associated with the *basilica* of Forteviot.

THE FORTEVIOT HAND-BELL

Although only a single item of early medieval metalwork is recorded from Forteviot, what the royal and ecclesiastical centre lacks in quantity it more than makes up for in terms of quality. The artefact concerned is a hand-bell, which is displayed inside the church at Forteviot. This belongs to a very distinctive type of early medieval ecclesiastical metalwork, a class of hand-bells which are widely regarded as 'Celtic', examples of which are found in Scotland, Ireland and Wales (Anderson 1881: 167-215; Allen 1904: 194-7; Bourke 1980; 1983).

Although its history is unrecorded before the late nineteenth century, this bell has probably always been associated with Forteviot and its successive churches. This is paralleled by better documented cases in both Scotland and Ireland. Of the nineteen surviving Celtic hand-bells in Scotland, seven are from Perthshire and all are linked with later churches on early ecclesiastical sites. Some Celtic hand-bells are associated with specific saints and, as saintly relics, were sometimes encased within later shrines. Although the Forteviot hand-bell is not enshrined, it was probably venerated as a saintly relic and its survival is probably attributable to its custodianship by a dewar (Gaelic, *dèoraidh*), a hereditary keeper of relics, during the Middle Ages (Anderson 1891; Dickinson 1941: 103-9). Relics were invested with wide-ranging great powers and were not only believed to cure diseases but used to enforce civil and criminal justice, collect taxes and invoke divine intervention (Yeoman 1999: 90-2; Barrow 2003: 35).

One of only five Celtic hand-bells in Scotland that are cast in bronze, the Forteviot hand-bell is a superb example of the early medieval bronzefounder's craftsmanship (Anderson 1892; Clouston 1992: 482; Purser n.d.) (*colour plate 18; 43*). The bell is quadrangular in form, with four flat and tapering sides and a nearly square mouth with an everted or flared lip. Tall and narrow, it measures 11in (279mm) in overall height with a mouth of 8.6 x 7.6in (219 x 194mm), making it one of the largest Celtic hand-bells in Scotland. Its sides are of uniform thickness, except where they narrow to a sharp edge around the lip. The casting of its round-sectioned handle, at the crown of the bell, was integral with that of the bell itself. The only imperfections in the casting are some small areas of porosity in the handle and around the lip.

Hand-bells performed several functions in the early medieval Celtic church. They were used to mark the canonical hours and call the faithful to mass. As a *sanctus* bell, they may also have had a liturgical role and were used to punctuate the liturgy. Hand-bells were also symbols of ecclesiastical authority, usually associated with a bishop. The bell would originally have been rung by

43 Woodcut of the Forteviot hand-bell. *Proceedings of the Society of Antiquaries of Scotland*

holding it by the handle and hitting it with a hammer or other object. A clapper appears to have been added to the Forteviot bell at a later date, suspended from a staple fitted through the crown of the bell, although it no longer survives. The hand-bell reportedly emits 'a deep haunting sound when struck' (Lines 1992: 38). A more musicologically-informed assessment is that its surfaces produce different notes, covering a minor third, when struck (Purser n.d.). This implies that different notes, or combinations of notes, were produced to convey different meanings.

On one side of the bell its waist bears a motif comprising a stylised letter 'M' (*44*). This has not been inscribed after the bell was cast but is in relief. This is therefore an original feature and must either have been present in the false wax bell used to produce the mould in which the bell was cast or was scratched in the cope or outer mould. The roughness of the symbol suggests the latter interpretation. This feature is unparalleled and its meaning is uncertain. Although reminiscent of medieval masons' marks, it seems too large and prominent to be a bronzefounder's mark and is more likely to be a dedicatory symbol.

The motif has been interpreted as denoting the dedication of the Forteviot bell to the Virgin Mary or its connection with the missionary for whom it was cast (Clouston 1992: 482). The cult of the Virgin Mary flourished in Anglo-Saxon England and early medieval Ireland (O'Dwyer 1976; 1988; Clayton 1991) and may also have been popular among the Picts. This is suggested by a portrait of the Virgin with Child, accompanied by the inscription 'Saint Mary the

44 The Forteviot hand-bell

Mother of Christ' in Latin minuscules, on a cross-slab at Brechin (ECMS, vol. 2: 249, fig. 261; Henderson and Henderson 2004: 148). Alternatively, the letter may signify a dedication to a Celtic saint. This may be paralleled by inscriptions found on some Irish hand-bells. For example, the bell of Clogher, from Donaghmore, Co. Tyrone, bears the dedication PATRICI and the date 1272, although these were inscribed long after the bell's manufacture (Mitchell 1977). If the symbol on the Forteviot hand-bell represents a dedication to a Celtic saint then there are possible candidates within Perthshire, including St Machan and St Madoe, and several others elsewhere within Scotland.

The Forteviot hand-bell is claimed to belong to the reign of Unuist (Lines 1992: 38), although which king of that name is not specified. However, the dating of Celtic hand-bells is considerably less precise than this. The Forteviot hand-bell has been dated variously to the ninth century (Alcock 1982: 218), later ninth century (Bourke 1983: 466), tenth century (Anderson 1892: 435; Clouston 1992: 482) and tenth to eleventh centuries (Purser n.d.). The use of hand-bells in Scotland has been attributed to the activities of the Columban Church in Pictland (Bourke 1983: 465-6), presumably during the period from the mid-ninth century, after the relics of St Columba were translated from Iona to Dunkeld during the reign of Cináed mac Ailpín (843-58). This might appear to support Forteviot's claimed status as a Columban cult centre (Chap. 4). However, the association of hand-bells with the Columban Church is unconvincing and is not consistent with their wider distribution.

The dating of Scottish hand-bells is derived from stylistic parallels with Irish examples. Two distinctive features of the Forteviot hand-bell, the flared lip and horizontal cross-piece of the handle, are paralleled by a hand-bell from Terryhoogan, Co. Armagh. This hand-bell is conventionally dated from a memorial inscription on it to a named individual whose death is recorded in the Irish annals for 909 (AU s.a. 908.6; Bourke 1980: 57-9; 1983: 464). As a result, cast bronze Celtic hand-bells in Scotland are usually dated to around 900. However, the inscription on the Terryhoogan hand-bell is secondary and provides only a *terminus ante quem* for the casting of the hand-bell, which may be earlier. Indeed, cast bronze hand-bells were manufactured in Ireland from *c*.725, with the finest quality examples dating from *c*.825 (Bourke 1980: 59), and there is no reason why this dating should not also apply to examples found in Scotland. Although traditionally attributed to the Scots and their close connections with Ireland, at least some of these hand-bells are probably of Pictish manufacture (Stevenson 1976: 246). As a result, the Forteviot hand-bell may have belonged to a late Pictish church contemporary with the royal centre of Causantín and Unuist.

Like the sculpture and the church itself, the hand-bell may attest royal patronage of the church at Forteviot. The Forteviot hand-bell is an accomplished and prestigious item of bronzework. It would have belonged to an important and wealthy ecclesiastical foundation and may represent part of the endowment of the church by a Pictish king. The presence of the bell is consistent with the status of the church at Forteviot as a *basilica* and reliquary church.

ANALYSIS AND DISCUSSION

The assemblage of sculpture and metalwork from Forteviot and its environs is not only impressive but unique and reveals much about the royal centre in general and its church in particular.

Despite their mostly poor condition, the forms, functions and approximate date of the monuments to which the surviving fragments belonged may be inferred from other, better preserved, items of Pictish sculpture. The sculptural assemblage from the Forteviot area belongs to four high-crosses, at least one cross-slab, possibly three, and a sculptured arch. The distinctive and much-discussed Pictish symbols are entirely absent from this assemblage. This may not be significant, given the fragmentary condition of most of the items, although Pictish symbols occur less frequently on late Pictish sculpture (Chap. 8). On the basis of stylistic evidence, the sculpture appears to be broadly contemporary, dating to the period between around 750 and 850.

The form and decoration are typical of later Pictish sculpture in Southern Pictland. All but one of the knot-work designs may be paralleled by sculpture from several ecclesiastical sites in Southern Pictland, including Logierait, Meigle and St Vigeans. These parallels exhibit a similar geographical range to those of the Forteviot arch, which belongs to the Benvie-Dupplin school of Pictish sculpture (Chaps 6 and 7). Indeed, the fragments from Forteviot display close similarities with sculpture of the Benvie-Dupplin school; for example, in the appearance of the mounted warrior on Forteviot no. 5, while the closest parallel to the interlace on Forteviot no. 8 occurs on the Benvie cross-slab. The only exception to these Southern Pictish parallels is the repeated triangular knot on the Forteviot no. 3 fragment. This pattern is paralleled on cross-slabs from Ulbster (Caithness) and Burghead no. 8 (Moray), both in Northern Pictland, although its currency beyond Pictland is revealed by its presence on a pillar-cross at Minnigaff, Kirkcudbrightshire (ECMS, vol. 1: 288, no. 733; vol. 2: 33-5, 138, 476-7). The northern affinities of this fragment are also attested in the parallels for crosses with slightly wedge-shaped arms that expand towards the terminals.

The number of high-crosses represented at Forteviot and its environs is of particular interest. Free-standing high-crosses were traditionally thought to be rare in Pictland and only one, the Dupplin cross, survives intact. However, high-crosses, ringed or unringed, once stood at several major ecclesiastical sites, particularly in Southern Pictland. The fragmentary evidence includes cross-heads from Edzell (Angus), Kinnedar (no. 9) (Moray), St Andrews (nos 6 and 52) and St Vigeans (no. 9) and complete or fragmentary cross-shafts from Dunkeld (no. 2), Kinnedar (no. 10), Mugdrum (Fife), Reay (no. 2) (Caithness) and St Andrews (nos 14 and 19) (Henderson and Henderson 2004: 182-93). Moreover, the depiction of free-standing high-crosses on many Pictish cross-slabs reveals a familiarity with these monuments, which were presumably more common than these few fragments suggest (Henderson 1999a: 164; Henderson and Henderson 2004: 185, 188, 191).

The free-standing ringed cross is widely believed to have originated in Ireland, where most surviving examples are found. Free-standing ringed crosses in stone first appear there in the eighth century, imitating earlier wooden crosses encased with metalwork plates. Most surviving free-standing ringed crosses in Scotland occur in Argyll, the territory of Dál Riata. Conventionally, the presence of a free-standing ringed cross at Forteviot was attributed to Irish or Scottish artistic influences on Pictland after the eclipse of Pictish power and was therefore dated to the later ninth century (Alcock and Alcock 1992: 223). However, some Irish high-crosses are now dated to the eighth century rather than the ninth (Edwards 1990: 164). Moreover, the ringed cross may have been developed in Pictland and transmitted to Ireland via Iona, rather than the reverse, as traditionally thought (Stevenson 1956; Mac Lean 1990).

Most unusually, there is an early medieval reference to a cross at Forteviot, implying that the royal centre was notable for its sculpture then. Regulus and the sons of Hungus erected a cross at Forteviot, according to the St Andrews foundation legend. As this source originates in a ninth-century account (Chap. 4), this passage may have a basis in reality and either refers to a real cross at Forteviot or reflects a later tradition intended to explain the presence of a prominent cross there. Although the type of cross concerned is not described, it implies a free-standing high-cross. However, it is impossible to determine whether any of the fragments of high-cross from Forteviot and Invermay or the complete example from Dupplin may be identified with the cross referred to.

The sculpture and metalwork provides some clues about the ecclesiastical organisation to which the church at Forteviot belonged. The absence of monastic scenes, such as the tonsured clerics with book-satchels on the St Vigeans no. 11 cross-slab (ECMS, vol. 2: 271-2, fig. 282B), suggests that the sculpture was not the product of a monastic culture. In contrast, the powerful secular imagery of several stones, with their warriors on foot and horseback, suggests the presence of a church ministrating to a lay community. However, the surviving assemblage is probably too small and poorly preserved a sample to draw firm conclusions.

The only indicator that this sculpture was produced within a monastic milieu is the Latin inscription on the Dupplin cross, which may imply access to a monastic scriptorium (compare Bailey 1980: 81-4; Henderson 1999b: 85-6). If so, then Forteviot is the most likely candidate for the monastery concerned, not only on the basis of its proximity to the Dupplin cross, but also from the close artistic links that exist between the high-cross and the sculpture from Forteviot. This issue has also arisen in Northumbria, where the presence of sculpture at early ecclesiastical sites in County Durham has been cited as evidence that these were what Bede would have called *monasteria* (Cambridge 1984). However, it is unclear whether *monasteria* should be translated as 'monastery' or 'minster', or indeed if there was any meaningful distinction between these terms. On this basis, the sculptural assemblage at Forteviot would qualify it as a *monasterium*, although this may be implicit in its status as a *basilica*.

Sculpture provides tangible evidence of royal patronage of the early medieval Church. The association of impressive assemblages of sculpture, ecclesiastical sites and royal kin groups occurs among the early medieval Britons (Davies 1994), notably at Govan (Macquarrie 1990; 1994; Ritchie (ed.) 1994; Driscoll 2003; Driscoll *et al.* 2005; Govan 2005). The evidence for royal patronage of major ecclesiastical or monastic centres is even stronger in Ireland. At Clonmacnoise, for example, artistic activity was concentrated during several short periods when the monastery came under the control of powerful over-kingships, members of which were buried there (Ó Floinn 1995). Similarly, royal patronage of the Pictish Church may be inferred from the vigorous sculptural tradition of Southern Pictland. Large assemblages of sculpture probably attest an early church which was associated with a royal centre and under the patronage of its kings. For example, the impressive collection of cross-slabs and recumbent gravestones at Meigle (ECMS, vol. 2: 329-40; Ritchie 1997) reveal this as an important church site enjoying a substantial level of secular, probably royal, patronage (Ritchie 1995).

The sculpture from Forteviot and its environs also attests an important Pictish ecclesiastical site possessing close royal associations. This exceptional concentration of high-quality, monumental sculpture reveals a centre of artistic skill, production and patronage. Patronage by the Pictish kings is implied by the ideologically-potent iconography of the Forteviot no. 4 cross-slab and the Dupplin cross, with their vivid images of mounted warriors, and is confirmed by the inscription naming *Custantin filius Fircus* on the latter. This interpretation is supported by the prominence attached to the image of the king on the Forteviot arch (Chap. 7). This rich sculptural assemblage denotes the church as a place of worship of special significance, consistent with Forteviot's status as a royal burial place and a *basilica* (Chaps 3 and 4).

More direct evidence of royal patronage of the church at Forteviot is provided by the arch, to which we now turn.

PART 2

THE FORTEVIOT ARCH

6

INTRODUCING
THE ARCH

The most impressive and unusual item of sculpture to have been discovered at Forteviot is an elaborately carved monolithic arch. Although Scotland is rich in high-quality early medieval sculpture, the Forteviot arch is exceptional for several reasons. The arch bears a striking scene that is bold in conception, elaborate in composition and skilled in execution, but is of unknown meaning and uncertain date. Moreover, the arch is an architectural feature and once belonged to a building, in contrast to the free-standing nature of most Pictish sculpture. In addition, the arch is associated with a historically recorded royal and ecclesiastical centre. This unique combination makes the arch of importance not only to the study of Forteviot but also to the wider understanding of Pictish art, architecture, archaeology and history. The Forteviot arch is multi-disciplinary in its implications and its analysis requires a similar approach. What was pieced together about Forteviot's history, function and royal associations in Part 1 provides the context within which the arch and its sculpture can be studied.

Pictish sculpture is often treated as individual and special items, *objets d'art* viewed in isolation from the society that produced them. Part 2 approaches the Forteviot arch as an artefact, studying how the arch and its imagery were used by its makers and consumers and using the results to unlock new interpretations, not only of the arch and its imagery. The following chapters analyse and interpret the sculptural scene on the Forteviot arch, beginning with a detailed reappraisal of the primary evidence, the art and iconography of the arch itself, but also with reference to documentary sources and stylistic parallels from early medieval Scotland and Ireland. The implications of these findings for the date of the arch, the structure it belonged to, and related aspects of Pictish society, including the nature of the relationship between kingship and the Church in Pictland, are then examined. But before doing so it is worth reviewing the recorded history of the arch, including its discovery, display and previous study.

DISCOVERY AND DISPLAY

The discovery of the Forteviot arch is shrouded in mystery. The only record is that the arch 'was discovered ... lying in the bed of the May, immediately under the Holy Hill' at an unrecorded date 'a few years' before 1832 (Skene 1857: 278). This implies that the arch was probably found during the 1820s. The circumstances of its discovery are also obscure. A suggestion that the arch was found during work to canalise the Water of May (Alcock 1982: 217) is unconfirmed and probably unfounded. The only recorded canalisation and revetment of the May at Forteviot was at an earlier date, in or shortly after 1768, and at a different location, adjacent to the parish church and therefore upstream from Haly Hill (Chap. 2).

The findspot and approximate year of discovery indicate that the arch came to rest in the river bed as a result of the erosion of Haly Hill by the Water of May, a process that was complete by 1832. The arch was then presumably spotted in the river bed as a result of its large size, distinctive and obviously man-made shape and/or its sculpture. The river bed concerned was not that occupied by the May today but skirted the foot of the Forteviot escarpment, before the river changed course in 1852 (Chap. 2).

The freshness of the sculpture (*colour plate 19*) reveals that it cannot have been exposed to the elements for any great length of time. This indicates that, for most of its existence, the arch lay preserved in the ground and/or immersed, face down, on the river bed, its sculpture protected by soil or river silts. However, the damage to the left-hand abutment or end of the arch is characteristic of the delamination of sandstone, caused when water penetrates the stonework and then expands as it freezes, splitting the stone along geological bedding planes (on which see Maxwell 1994; 2005: 165). This repeated process probably caused the step-like appearance of this break in the arch and suggests that this end of the arch has been exposed to the elements. This abutment may have been exposed in the eroding face of Haly Hill before the arch collapsed into the Water of May. It is less likely that this effect could have been produced when the building to which the arch belonged collapsed or was destroyed, which would result in the more irregular break found on the right-hand abutment.

45 The Forteviot arch in the museum of the Society of Antiquaries of Scotland in the Royal
Institution, now the Royal Scottish Academy, on the Mound, Edinburgh, c.1890. Joseph Anderson,
the curator, is pictured in the foreground with George Black, his assistant, beside the arch. © *Trustees
of the National Museum of Scotland*

The arch initially formed part of the private collection of James, seventh
Lord Ruthven, owner of the Forteviot estate, and was kept at Freeland House,
Forgandenny. Walter James Hore-Ruthven, ninth Lord Ruthven and great-
nephew of the seventh lord, sold Freeland House in 1873, prompting him to
seek alternative accommodation for the arch. As a result, the arch was moved to
Edinburgh, where it has remained ever since. It was exhibited by Lord Ruthven
at a meeting of the Society of Antiquaries of Scotland in Edinburgh on Monday
8 June, 1874, and donated to the Society's museum the same year (Donations
1875; Catalogue 1892: 262; cat. no. IB36). Housed firstly in the museum's premises
in the Royal Institution, now the Royal Scottish Academy, on the Mound,
the arch formed a centrepiece of the Society's collections during the late
nineteenth century (45). The collections of the Society of Antiquaries of
Scotland formed the basis of those of the National Museum of Antiquities
of Scotland on the foundation of the latter in 1892. There, the arch was latterly

mounted above a monumental entrance to the Dark Age sculpture room in the Museum's Queen Street premises. This reconstructed doorway, with the arch interpreted as less than a full semi-circle and rising from splayed jambs, was based on those of the probably eleventh-century round towers at Abernethy, Perthshire, and Brechin, Angus (Close-Brooks 1980b: 3). The arch remained there until moved to the new National Museum of Scotland in Chambers Street, Edinburgh, in 1998. Regrettably, given the unique opportunity this presented, the arch is poorly displayed there: dimly lit, inaccessibly high and partially obscured within the entrance to the Kingdom of the Scots gallery (*colour plate 20; 46*).

DESCRIPTION

The Forteviot arch is not a true arch, which is made from several radiating wedge-shaped blocks or voussoirs supporting each other and held in place by a keystone. Instead, it is carved in the shape of a semi-circular arch from a single block of stone, with the curve of the arch-head cut into both its lower and upper faces (*colour plate 19; 47, 48*). The arch is therefore a false or pseudo-arch and is more accurately described as a round-arched monolithic lintel. However, it has traditionally been described as an arch and this is how it is referred to throughout this study.

46 The Forteviot arch displayed within the entrance to the Kingdom of the Scots gallery in the National Museum of Scotland, Edinburgh

47 The Forteviot arch. © *Trustees of the National Museum of Scotland*

48 The well-dressed intrados (lower edge or inside) of the Forteviot arch

The Forteviot arch is carved from a block of Old Red Sandstone. This was presumably quarried from one of the lower Old Red Sandstone deposits in Strathearn. Geological analysis might enable the source of the stone to be identified. This would involve comparing the results of physical and chemical analyses of the arch, including colour, grain size, mineralogy, magnetic susceptibility and chemical composition, with signatures derived from the analysis of groups and formations (stratigraphical units) of Old Red Sandstone in the region. These techniques can distinguish between potential sources, potentially enabling the quarry from which the arch was cut to be identified (compare Hall 2000; Miller and Ruckley 2005). This could open up new lines of enquiry into the socio-economic context of the production of the arch.

Both the extrados and intrados or soffit, the outer and inner faces respectively, of the arch curve in a slightly irregular manner. The span of the arch is approximately 4ft (1.2m) while the extrados, the outer curve of the arch, is about 7ft (2.1m) in diameter. These imperial measurements were probably selected deliberately by the mason. The surfaces of the arch were dressed using a punch and hammer and the tooling marks are still visible. The quality of the dressing of the front surface and intrados is superior to that of the extrados (49), revealing that the former were intended to be seen while the latter was not. The arch is 1ft 2in (0.36m) thick and its rough, undressed back (50) reveals that it has been split from a thicker block. In its present state the arch weighs 17cwt (870kg).

Both abutments of the arch have been damaged, but it is unclear if this occurred in antiquity or more recently, possibly when the arch fell into the Water of May, while it was exposed or during its recovery and subsequent movement. The complete arch probably formed a full semi-circle (Alcock and Alcock 1992: 224). However, the reconstructed doorway in the National Museum of Antiquities of Scotland interpreted the arch as comprising an arc of less than 180 degrees, while the reconstructed abutments in the National Museum of Scotland give a distinctly lopsided appearance. A semi-circular arch would not only have been easier to carve and erect, but would also have been more stable and is paralleled by the semi-circular arches found in some Anglo-Saxon churches (Chap. 9).

As the arch probably formed a complete semi-circle, segments of approximately 20 degrees are therefore missing from each end, although a precise figure is difficult to calculate because neither break is clean, either laterally or transversely. If the now defaced cross originally occupied the crown, the highest point at the centre of the arch, as it appears to have done (Chap. 7), then slightly more of the right-hand abutment of the arch has been lost than the left. The left-hand abutment has suffered delamination of the stone (above), resulting in the surface of the arch becoming detached. Assuming that this was originally a semi-circular

49 The roughly-dressed extrados (top or outer side) of the Forteviot arch. © *Trustees of the National Museum of Scotland*

50 The undressed back of the Forteviot arch. © *Trustees of the National Museum of Scotland*

arch, then approximately 22 per cent of the total surface area of the arch and its sculpture has been lost. This is a significant proportion, but the impact of this loss is probably mitigated by the peripheral contexts of the damaged areas within the overall composition. Although both abutments are missing, not only does most of the sculpture survive but the surviving elements are also the most important ones. Despite the damage it has received, the arch has survived remarkably well, in marked contrast to the fragmentary and weathered state of the other Pictish sculpture from Forteviot (Chap. 5).

The arch is carved on one face only. Most of this surface is well preserved, unworn, with both sculptural detail and tooling marks readily visible. The carving has a crisp appearance, giving it an immediacy that is not normally found in early medieval sculpture. The only damage is localised to the abutments, moulding and most prominent features. The sculpture forms a single panel occupying the entire face of the arch. This scene is framed by a square moulding that is grooved towards its inner edge and is slightly wider on the lower edge than on the upper edge of the arch. The moulding around the upper edge has been damaged badly and some lengths have disappeared entirely, presumably as a result of its prominence and exposed location.

In contrast to true relief sculpture, where the subjects project from a flat background, the arch is carved in false relief. That is, its subjects appear to be in relief only because their background has been lowered by carving it out to form a flat, recessed surface sunk below the level of the surrounding moulding. This false relief is both shallow and fairly uniform. The figures produced using this technique are flat, essentially two-dimensional, and do not stand proud of the surface of the arch but are level with it. This, combined with the linear character of the figures, reveals that the scene began as an engraving on the flat surface of the arch.

This carving appears to have been produced using only a single and simple tool. The marks left on the arch indicate that this was a fine punch. The use of a punch, rather than a chisel, to produce such detailed sculpture may seem surprising but was common practice, as the punch-marks on many Pictish sculptures attest. In the hands of a skilled sculptor, a fine punch is a versatile tool, ideally suited to carving fine detail. The punch was evidently used delicately and the carving of the arch would have been a long and laborious process. These features all confirm the Forteviot arch as the work of a highly skilled and artistic craftsman.

The surface of the arch was also prepared with a fine punch and then appears to have been smoothed by mechanical abrasion. The front face of the arch in particular is so smooth that an abrasive, probably a flat piece of sandstone, may have been used. Despite this, many toolmarks are still visible. These small punch-marks, scattered across the face of the arch, give it a stippled appearance. These probably remain from dressing the stone and cutting out the recessed background. This gives the impression of either carelessness during the preparation of the surface or the poor quality of the abrasion work. However, it is more likely that it simply reflects the fact that the punch-marks would not have been visible when the arch was *in situ*.

The sculpture comprises a mixture of symbols, human figures and animals. What appears to be a damaged cross occupies the crown of the arch, with a quadruped in an upright position, facing the cross to its right. In contrast, the three human figures depicted all face away from the cross. To the left of the cross, and occupying most of this side of the arch is a large figure in a reclining position, grasping an elongated object in both hands and with a horned quadruped beneath his feet. Two smaller figures occupy the right-hand side of the arch, the smallest depicted only from the waist up, the other with his legs bent at the knees and drawn up in front of him. All these figures, animal and human, are depicted in profile and were executed with pecked or punched lines and many of the sculptor's original tooling marks are still visible.

Although aesthetically pleasing, the Forteviot arch does not, at first viewing, appear to display the artistic or technical proficiency that is usually associated with Pictish sculpture. The flatness of the technique contrasts with Pictish relief sculpture and the frozen appearance of the figures on the arch contrasts with the vigorous hunting scenes that adorn several cross-slabs. The scene does not include any Pictish symbols and this has traditionally influenced the dating and identification of the cultural context of the arch (Chap. 8). Indeed, the arch does not immediately invite comparison with Pictish sculpture at all and it is understandable that the arch has often been attributed to the Scots instead. This may be because the sculptor displays a high level of originality in addition to technical competence.

The contrast between the Forteviot arch and other sculpture from Scotland has traditionally been viewed in terms of standards, with the conclusion that the arch is not only of inferior quality but belongs to a declining phase of early medieval art. Indeed, the arch has been described as 'very rudely executed' (Skene 1857: 278) and decorated with 'some rude carvings', including 'exceedingly crude and unlifelike' figures (Meldrum 1926: 17, 18). A more detailed assessment claimed it to be 'a rough, awkward, and rather impressive piece of work, hacked rather than carved out of the stone, the figures clumsily bent to fit inside the curve and their clothes depicted by a series of lines which gives then a strangely ribbon-like appearance' (Curle and Henry 1943: 270-1).

The figures on the Forteviot arch display a close stylistic affinity to those portrayed on several other sculptures from Southern Pictland, notably those belonging to what is widely referred to as the Benvie-Dupplin 'school' of sculpture. The work of this school has also been assessed unfavourably. In particular, its figural sculpture has been criticised as 'stilted and mannered' (Alcock 2003; 393), 'stiff and lifeless' and the overall results described as 'far from happy' (Radford 1942: 17–18). The Benvie cross-slab (51), for example, was described as 'a barbarous production' and the 'very poor' David on the Dupplin cross attributed to 'local' tastes (Stevenson 1955: 126), implying a geographically-limited aberration and decline from high artistic standards.

Such judgements are not comparing like with like. The Benvie-Dupplin school of sculpture, including the Forteviot arch, may lack the flowing lines and confident design that is characteristic of 'classic' Pictish sculpture, as displayed on symbol stones and cross-slabs (or 'Class I' and 'Class II' stones respectively in the scheme devised by Allen and Anderson for ECMS). This, however, does not attest a decline in the quality of Pictish sculpture but belongs to a different artistic style found on several sculptures in Perthshire and Angus. These sculptures are characterised by the absence of Pictish symbols (Henderson 1978; Hicks 1993a: 100, 218) and the distinctive naturalism and liveliness evident in the animals and human figures depicted in 'classic' Pictish sculpture. Contrasting with the slender elegance of the animals that appear so prominently in other Pictish sculpture, the animals depicted by the Benvie-Dupplin school have lost the naturalism exhibited by earlier sculpture and are more stylised in appearance, with short necks, heavy limbs and exaggerated features. They are also smaller in size and tend to be relegated to subsidiary positions and/or restricted spaces within the sculpture. In contrast, these sculptures display an increased emphasis on figural art, in which human figures feature prominently.

However, there is a marked contrast between the naturalistic poses of the incised animals on Pictish Class I stones and the quadrupeds on the arch. While the former are based on close and sympathetic observation and display credible or recognisable characteristics of the beasts portrayed (Gordon 1966; Hicks 1993a: 100, 103; 1993b; Alcock 1993: 230; 1998: 515–28), the latter are stiff, representational images. The sculptor of the arch was clearly more accomplished and confident at depicting people than animals and belongs to a very different tradition from the 'Pictish Animal Master' who produced a high degree of realism in the animal sculpture on Class I stones.

A sculptural tradition or 'school' of sculpture may be defined from the presence of monuments exhibiting many recurring or consistent stylistic characteristics within a geographically discrete area or wider region. Sculpture belonging to a

51 The mounted warriors on the reverse of the Benvie cross-slab, Angus. *Crown copyright: Royal Commission on the Ancient and Historical Monuments of Scotland (Tom and Sybil Gray Collection)*

school often draws upon a common repertoire of themes or motifs, indicating that it was produced according to a similar basic concept. A sculptural tradition has been identified within the region focused on Forteviot and associated with the kings who had their royal centre there (Curle and Henry 1943: 270-1). Although referred to as the Benvie-Dupplin school rather than the 'Forteviot school', the name used to denote this is irrelevant. What is significant is that the sculpture belonging to this tradition is geographically restricted and occurs only in lower Strathearn and Angus (52).

Schools of Pictish sculpture are not only little studied but also largely unidentified (Henderson and Henderson 2004: 212-13). This is unfortunate, as sculptural schools may reflect secular patronage (Driscoll 2000: 242) and could assist the understanding of the social context of artistic production and the manner in which that sculpture was used to advance ideological agendas. The Benvie-Dupplin school, with its narrow geographical focus and potent images of secular power (Chaps 4 and 7), enjoyed secular patronage. This is supported by the association of two of the most impressive sculptures belonging to this school, the Dupplin cross and Forteviot arch, with a major royal centre. Despite this, the Benvie-Dupplin school and its sculpture require more detailed study.

Some of the features exhibited by the Forteviot arch imply the influence of artistic conventions found in other media. In particular, the two-dimensional appearance of the sculpture and the linear character of the figures, produced by the parallel lines delineating the folds of the drapery, indicates a debt to illuminated Hiberno-Saxon manuscripts. The figures on sculpture belonging to the Benvie-Dupplin school have been claimed to imitate manuscript drawings and what was perceived to be their poor artistic quality has been attributed to the difficulties encountered in translating elaborate manuscript exemplars into stone (Radford 1942: 17-18). In addition, the ribbon-like appearance or 'tram lines' created by the folds of the garments has been likened to the manner in which clothes are frequently depicted in illuminated Hiberno-Saxon manuscripts, notably the St Gall Gospel Book (St Gall, Stiftsbibliothek Cod. 51), the Vitellius Psalter (London, British Library Cotton MS Vitellius F.xi) and the Southampton Psalter (Cambridge, St John's College MS C.9(59)) (Curle 1940: 110; Henderson and Henderson 2004: 145; on which see Alexander 1978: nos 73, 74, pls 348-52). Similarly, the stylised animals may be derived from artistic conventions found in manuscripts or metalwork (Hicks 1993a: 218) and this is also apparent from the manner in which the figures are accommodated within the arch (Chap. 8). These analogies suggest that the sculptor was familiar with illuminated gospel books and was either working from such an exemplar or had one in mind.

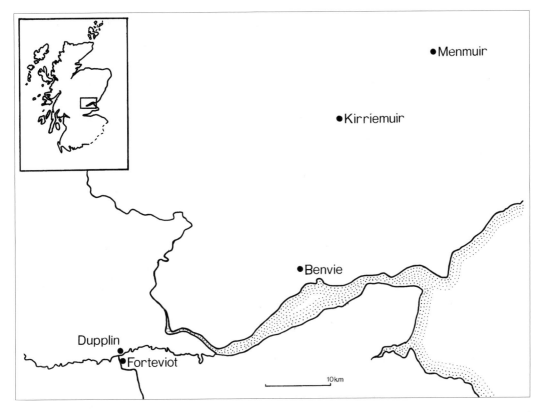

52 Distribution of sculpture belonging to the Benvie-Dupplin school. This tradition is geographically restricted and is represented only in lower Strathearn and Angus

The Benvie-Dupplin school attests a complex process involving the departure from those naturalistic artistic traditions inherited from 'classic' Pictish sculpture in favour of a more figural or representational sculpture that is characterised by its flattened, linear style. This represents an important stage in the later development of Pictish sculpture. It defines a divergent Pictish artistic tradition with a strong local character but displaying external influences. Rather than attesting the descent of pan-Pictish naturalism into local barbarism, sculpture belonging to the Benvie-Dupplin school is the product of a local artistic tradition that is distinctive, subtle and sophisticated. Reflecting a shift in perceptions, more recent assessments of the artistic quality of sculpture belonging to the Benvie-Dupplin school have been more favourable. The Forteviot arch itself has been described as 'superbly carved' (Sutherland 1997: 47), while the Dupplin cross is claimed to demonstrate 'a sophisticated awareness that style in itself can be a bearer of meaning' (Henderson 1999a: 173).

The Forteviot arch certainly displays a technical virtuosity in its execution. This is evident in its originality, boldness, mastery of line and close attention to detail. The latter is apparent from the prominence attached to textures, with elaborate hairstyles, the drape of clothing and the patterning on the cross-shaft all emphasised by surface decoration. This highly-textured treatment is characteristic of the Benvie-Dupplin school and is also found on the Kirriemuir no. 2 and Menmuir no. 1 (both Angus) cross-slabs (ECMS, vol. 2: 227-8, 263-4, figs 240B, 273B).

Any residual doubts surrounding the artistic quality of the Forteviot arch should be dispelled by the vigour and detail of the largest figure. This individual is characterised by his purposeful and energetic stance, bold facial features, ringleted hair and impressive moustache. His flowing clothes, with their decorated hem and the rhythmical repetition of the soft curves of lightly-incised parallel lines delineating the folds of the drapery, give the figure a stylised, linear character. And, in an imaginative stylistic touch, the end of his drooping moustache merges into the gently curving folds of his cloak. Although different in style, the artistic quality of the Forteviot arch is the equal of any other example of Pictish sculpture.

Regardless of its overall artistic standards, the scene on the Forteviot arch displays several distinctive qualities. Above all, the boldness of its images, the stylised figures with their mesmerised stare and the enigmatic meaning of the scene all combine to attract and hold the viewer's gaze. This scene displays great originality, making it unique not only among Pictish sculpture, but also within Insular art in general. The visual impact of the arch is such that it displays an arresting quality and exerts a kind of magic over its audience, as the remarks of several scholars reveal (below).

Although more than compensated for by other characteristics, the quest for originality that is evident in the Forteviot arch was a complex one and was not achieved without some artistic sacrifices. For example, the treatment of the human figures is standardised, with little difference in their, particularly facial, appearance. The depiction of the quadrupeds is so simplistic that the species portrayed are not immediately apparent (Chap. 7) and may be imaginary, symbolic or simply imperfectly executed portraits of actual beasts. In particular, the emphasis on detail and decorative effect is at the expense of the overall composition of the scene. The figures are placed in a curved frame, with their spatial relationships obscured or rendered in an imperfect or schematic manner, and lose much of their compositional value as a result. This impression is strengthened by the apparently randomly mixed combination of human figures, Christian symbols and animals. Most noticeably, there is an inconsistency between the positions of the human figures and quadrupeds, which, unusually for Pictish sculpture, face different directions. The sculptor has made no attempt to unify these elements, which appear disconnected as a result, although some are linked by proximity. The scene initially appears to suffer from a weak overall composition, an impression that is only dispelled by detailed iconographic analysis, including the identification of parallels and taking its physical context into account (Chaps 8 and 9). In mitigation, however, it must be recognised that the sculptor faced considerable constraints imposed by the shape and size of the arch.

PREVIOUS STUDIES

Scholarly interest in the Forteviot arch began a few years after its discovery. The earliest recorded reference to the arch was a paper by the founding father of Celtic studies in Scotland, William Forbes Skene (on whom see Sellar 2001), which he read before the Society of Antiquaries of Scotland in Edinburgh on 23 January 1832. Although not published until 1857, this contains the only, albeit terse, description of the discovery of the arch. The arch subsequently featured in the great studies of 'early Christian' art and architecture in Scotland during the latter half of the nineteenth century, notably John Stuart's *Sculptured Stones of Scotland* (1867, pl. CIII), David MacGibbon and Thomas Ross' *Ecclesiastical Architecture of Scotland* (1897, vol. 3: 623) and J. Romilly Allen and Joseph Anderson's *Early Christian Monuments of Scotland* (1903 (ECMS, vol. 2: 325-6, fig. 336)). The arch is sometimes referred to as 'Forteviot no. 2' after the catalogue number assigned to it by Allen and Anderson. The arch also featured in a wider study, J. Romilly Allen's *Early Christian Symbolism in Great Britain and Ireland* (1887: 239).

The arch was illustrated in all these publications. Skene's paper of 1832 included a woodcut which exaggerates the curve of the arch and, although linear in style, used hatching to create a sense of relief carving (53). This illustration records the arch in more or less the same condition as it is today. It omits some details, such as the moustaches of all figures and the decorated hem of the largest figure but also depicts others that no longer survive, such as the snout of the quadruped beneath the large figure, the hint of an eye and eyebrow on the lower of the two smaller figures and the nose of the figure above him. However, it is unclear if these were still present or if the illustrator was simply reconstructing their former appearance. That this illustration attempts to rationalise the appearance of these figures rather than depict them accurately is supported by the manner in which the noses of all three figures have been rendered in a much less pronounced form than on the arch.

Two lithographic illustrations of the arch by A. Gibb, of Keith and Gibb, Aberdeen, appeared in Stuart's *Sculptured Stones of Scotland* (1856: i; 1867, pl. CIII) (54, 55). These were also somewhat schematic, particularly the illustration adapted to fit the opening page. In addition, these illustrations mistakenly included a third, vestigial, figure at the right-hand end of the arch. The upper part of the head and right eye of this third figure also appeared in the sketch in Romilly Allen's *Early Christian Symbolism* (1887: 239, fig. 82) (56), and still influences the description and interpretation of the arch (Chap. 7). All of these are reasonable representations, although the artistic flourishes in the earlier examples reveal a tension between the requirements of recording and illustration. The woodcut in McGibbon and Ross' *Ecclesiastical Architecture of Scotland* (1897, vol. 3: 624) is not only more accurate but also illustrates the arch from an angle and is therefore more three-dimensional in character, conveying the bulk of the arch (57). Allen and Anderson were the first to illustrate the arch with the aid of photography (58).

Despite its unique form, impressive appearance and prominent display since 1874, the Forteviot arch has received surprisingly little study since 1832. The arch was referred to, although only briefly, in several studies from the mid-twentieth century. But, continuing a theme begun by Joseph Anderson's *Scotland in Early Christian Times* (1881), the arch is surprisingly conspicuous by its absence from many later works on the Picts, their sculpture and wider surveys of the archaeology, art and architecture of early medieval Scotland. The arch was probably ignored because it was unclear how to interpret a sculpture that was undated, of uncertain cultural associations and carried a scene of unknown meaning. Moreover, the arch was not only divorced from the building it once belonged to, but the structure concerned and its site had completely disappeared. Architects, archaeologists and art historians alike had no clear context within which to study the arch. The arch defied straightforward classification and analysis and, as a result, was less well known and studied than its quality and significance deserved.

It was not until 1982, exactly 150 years after Skene's paper, that the study of Forteviot and its arch was placed on a modern, scholarly footing with a multi-disciplinary study by Professor Leslie Alcock, a subject he and the late Mrs Elizabeth Alcock returned to a decade later with the publication of his excavations at Forteviot (Alcock 1982; Alcock and Alcock 1992: 218-41). The Alcocks' pioneering studies brought the arch to the attention of a wider scholarly community, enhancing awareness and understanding of it. But although several subsequent publications mentioned the arch, most of these are no more than token references and the arch has attracted little subsequent study. This may be because the Alcocks' work was considered to be definitive and that there was nothing more to be said on the subject. As a result, there has been little progress

Right: 53 The
Forteviot arch as
illustrated in W.F.
Skene's paper of
1832. *Archaeologia
Scotica*

Below: 54 The
Forteviot arch
as illustrated
by A. Gibb,
of Keith and
Gibb, Aberdeen,
in Stuart's
*Sculptured Stones
of Scotland* (1867)

in understanding the symbolism of the arch and its wider architectural, artistic
and historical implications since the Alcocks' research. This is surprising given
the recent surge of interest in early medieval, and particularly Pictish, art and
archaeology. But it also reflects the continuing legacy of scholarly neglect that
the arch had suffered from archaeologists and art and architectural historians
throughout most of the twentieth century. Although the Alcocks' studies remain
invaluable, the pace of progress in the study of Pictish sculpture and history
is such that a reappraisal of the Forteviot arch is called for, encompassing its
iconography, date, structural role and wider socio-political significance.

FRAGMENT AT FORTEVIOT

PREFACE.

HE Sculptured Stone Monuments of Scotland may be considered the earliest existing expressions of the ideas, and the most genuine records of the skill in art, of the early inhabitants of Scotland; but they have been so long neglected, that now, when attention has been awakened to their interest, we find them diminished in number, and, in many cases, mutilated in their form.

The sculptured or painted tombs of early nations often furnish the only key to their modes of life which we possess; and these memorial stones, if they may not in all cases be classed with sepulchral records, must yet be considered as remains of the same early time when the rock was the only book in which an author could convey his thoughts, and when history was to be handed down by memorials which should always meet the eye, and prompt the question, " What mean ye by these stones ? " *

The erection of pillars, to commemorate events of various kinds, seems to have been common in all parts of the world, and from the earliest times.

Many, curious illustrations of the early use of pillars occur in the Old Testament. Thus we find that when Rachel died, Jacob " set a pillar upon her grave" (Genesis xxxv. 20); and, in the time of Samuel, Rachel's sepulchre is referred to as a well-known place (1st Sam., x. 2.) Again, when Jacob and Laban made a covenant between themselves, the former "took a stone, and set it up for a pillar," and, surrounding it with a cairn of stones, called the place Galeed, or the heap of witness, or Mizpah, which means a beacon or watch-tower (Genesis xxxi. 47, 49), recognising it as a boundary which neither party should overpass. The place seems afterwards to have become the place of rendezvous of the Israelites (Judges x. 17, xx. 1, 1st Samuel, vii. 5, 6.) A stone had been erected over Bohan, the son of Reuben, which afterwards appears to have been recognised as a boundary (Joshua xv. 6, xviii. 17.) Jacob erected a stone at Bethel for a religious purpose (Genesis xxviii. 18.) Joshua also erected a pillar under an oak for a religious purpose, and as a witness against the people (Joshua xxiv. 26–7.)

In Scotland, as in other countries, there are to be found many rude unsculptured

* Joshua iv. 6.

b

55 The opening page of Stuart's *Sculptured Stones of Scotland* (1856), incorporating a stylised illustration of the Forteviot arch, adapted to fit the page, by A. Gibb, of Keith and Gibb, Aberdeen. This misinterpreted the raised upper leg of the right-hand cleric as the upper body of a third figure

Right: 56 The Forteviot arch as illustrated in J. Romilly Allen's *Early Christian Symbolism* (1887). This included a vestigial third figure, or at least the top of his head, eye and upper nose

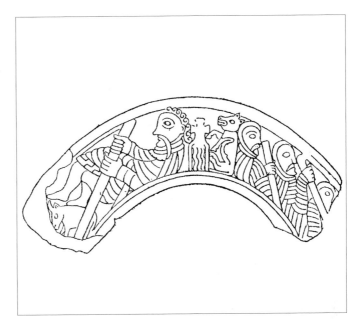

Below: 57 The Forteviot arch as illustrated in McGibbon and Ross' *Ecclesiastical Architecture of Scotland* (1897) is not only more accurate but also illustrates the arch from an angle and is therefore more three-dimensional in character, conveying the bulk of the arch

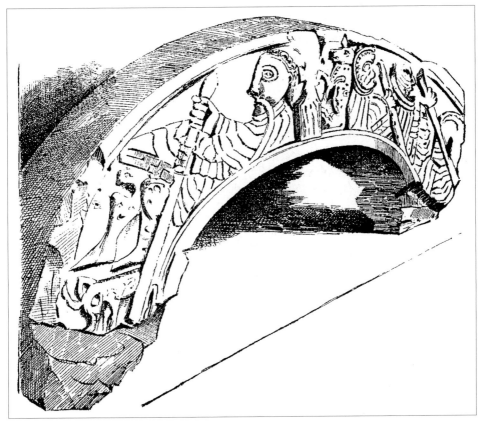

58 The earliest published photograph of the Forteviot arch, in J. Romilly Allen and Joseph Anderson's *Early Christian Monuments of Scotland* (1903)

Despite scholarly neglect and criticism, the Forteviot arch has clearly impressed and intrigued some observers. It has very justifiably been described as 'a very singular stone' (Skene 1857: 278), 'a very curious specimen of early carving' (Allen 1887: 239) and 'a remarkable specimen of early Scottish sculpture' (MacGibbon and Ross 1897, vol. 3: 623). Even some of the art historians who criticised its quality nevertheless found the arch a 'rather impressive piece of work' (Curle and Henry 1943: 270-1). Some modern commentators have also been intrigued by the arch, describing it as 'strange and wonderful ... a remarkable thing ... of no ordinary interest' (Cruden 1986: 24), 'a remarkable carved and curved archstone' (Duncan 2002: 9) and 'a magnificent ... arch' (Macquarrie 2004: 73).

7

IMAGERY AND
INTERPRETATION

Although the iconography of the Forteviot arch has been the subject of previous interpretations (Chap. 8), its symbolism and wider significance have remained elusive. As the most complete item of sculpture from Forteviot and the only surviving evidence of a building belonging to the royal centre, the analysis and interpretation of the sculptural scene on the arch presents a unique opportunity for studying the royal centre.

The analysis conducted in this and the following chapters begins with the assumption that the meaning of any work of art must lie in its form and context, in this case the appearance of the scene on the Forteviot arch, its constituent elements and the physical and socio-political settings in which it was displayed and viewed. These therefore require detailed examination in order to decipher the symbolism of the arch. The sculpture is most readily described and interpreted by examining its constituent elements individually in this chapter before considering the iconography of the scene as a whole in the next chapter. A fundamental requirement of this approach is that it should cover all the components of the sculpture and their possible meaning(s), including any of symbolic significance. The difficulty here is that there may be both practical and symbolic interpretations of the same image, with little to choose between them. This is because the interpretation of images is largely dependent on context, either within the sculptural scene itself or its wider setting. In order to assist the interpretation of these images, this analysis draws on artistic and symbolic parallels from sculpture elsewhere within Pictland where they are available but also, in the absence of these, from early medieval art within the Insular and wider early Christian worlds.

Any description is inevitably influenced by the perceptions of the observer and their interpretation of the meaning(s) of what they are viewing. A completely objective description is impossible and this is particularly true in art history when there is no independent record of the thoughts and intentions of the artist. Accepting that it is impossible to make a meaningful distinction between the processes of description and interpretation, this chapter both describes the images on the Forteviot arch and interprets their meaning, including their symbolic significance. Adopting this principle from the outset, but also for ease of reference, the components of the sculpture are referred to by labels that are both descriptive and interpretative in nature.

A fundamental, but neglected, methodological dilemma confronts the iconographical study of more complex scenes in early medieval sculpture. Should the interpretation of the iconography of a sculpture be influenced by perceptions of the piece overall or should all its constituent elements be identified before seeing what sort of whole they comprise? The disadvantage of the former approach is that modern interpretations of early medieval art are inevitably influenced, even distorted, by our own limitations and preconceptions concerning the sculpture and the wider cultural and historical contexts to which it belonged. In support of the latter approach, the component parts of a scene must be subservient to a narrative sequence or to a theme, or both, if sculpture was invested with any iconographic significance.

THE CROSS

The central element in the sculpture is also the most badly damaged and appears to have been defaced deliberately (Chap. 10). This is a Latin cross, of which only the shaft now survives (59). The cross-head has been removed almost completely and only its outline survives. However, this reveals that the cross had square-headed arms, with the transverse or side arms shorter than the top arm. The damage to the cross-head also extends to the adjacent moulding around the extrados, suggesting that the upper arm overlapped the moulding. The moulding is wider at this point, probably to emphasise the cross. The cross is claimed to have been 'nimbed' (Richardson 1964: 7). Christ's head is typically surrounded by a nimbus or halo in Christian iconography, but there are no detectable traces of such a feature around this cross. Nor are there any indications that this was originally a ring-headed cross which, if poorly executed or observed, might be mistaken for a cross within a nimbus. The tall and broad cross-shaft is as wide as the transom of the cross-head. The cross-shaft is shouldered in form, narrowing from a point about two-thirds of the way up the shaft to form a concave pedestal with a neck that supports the cross-head.

59 The defaced Latin cross, of
which only the shaft survives,
on the Forteviot arch

Although poorly preserved, the cross depicted on the arch is both distinctive and significant in form. Short-armed crosses, both ringed and unringed, occur widely on cross-slabs and less frequently as free-standing crosses in both Pictland and Dál Riata. However, the shouldered form of the cross-shaft is unusual and has no Pictish parallels. The closest parallel is from Applecross, Wester Ross, the site of a major monastic centre founded in 673 by Maelrubha, a monk of Bangor. Although probably dating to a couple of centuries later, a massive cross-slab, 8ft 8in (2.63m) in visible height, is incised with a ringed or 'Celtic' cross on a short shaft rising from a concave-sided pedestal, which is itself supported by a tall rectangular base (Fisher 2001: 90). The top corners of the slab have been cut away, shaping it to the outline of the upper part of the cross head, indicating that this is an unfinished free-standing cross.

The cross-shaft displays the same emphasis on texture that is found elsewhere on the arch. The edge of the cross-shaft is outlined and represents a moulding, a common feature of both free-standing crosses and crosses on cross-slabs. The body of the cross-shaft is decorated with four incised vertical wavy lines, a feature that is not readily paralleled in Insular sculpture. These lines may be an artistic convention, perhaps representing the interlaced decoration found on the shafts of real crosses or the grain of a wooden cross (Alcock 1982: 218). This prompted the interpretation of the cross-shaft as a 'high base' (Close-Brooks 1980b: 3) or a draped altar or pedestal, on which the cross stood (PAS 1997; Henderson 1999a: 177). But, although the cross-head is defaced, it and the shaft were clearly integral elements of the same, unitary, structure, a high-cross. This is revealed most clearly by the line representing the moulding, which, at the shoulder of the cross-shaft, curves inwards and upwards towards the cross-head.

Alternatively, the wavy lines may hold a symbolic significance, possibly symbolising the four rivers of Paradise that flowed from Mount Zion and watered the Garden of Eden. The rivers of Paradise were, in turn, an early symbol of the four Evangelists and their Gospels (Allen 1884: 396; Murray and Murray 1996: 433). This imagery is of particular interest given the proximity of the cross and Agnus Dei within the scene (below). The arch may depict the Agnus Dei on Mount Zion (Revelation 14.1). This is a popular scene in early Christian art and occurs, in the form of the Agnus Dei lying in front of the cross, on a mosaic in the apse of the church of Saints Cosmas and Damian at Rome, built by Pope Felix IV in 526-30 (Parker 1866: 7-8; Krautheimer 1937: 137-43; Oakeshott 1967: 90-2; Osborne and Claridge 1996: 94-5, no. 15) (*60*). The Cross of Calvary, set on a base on a mount and with the rivers of Paradise flowing below it also appears on a large medallion from the base of a fourth-century gilded glass vessel, now in the Vatican Library, Rome (Northcote and Brownlow 1869, vol. 2: 317) (*61*).

60 The Agnus Dei, lying on an altar in front of the cross, on a mosaic in the church of Saints Cosmas and Damian, Rome, 526-30. *Parker,* Pictures in Mosaic Rome and Ravenna *(1866)*

If the Forteviot arch expresses this symbolism, then the rivers of Paradise have been assimilated with the cross, presumably because of the limited area available on the front of the arch.

The lower end of the cross-shaft rests directly on the lower moulding of the arch, without the stepped base often depicted on Pictish cross-slabs. In this case, the moulding itself may have formed the base of the cross, giving the impression of a cross standing on top of a hill or mound. This resembles the arched or domed cross-bases, formed from half an annular ring, found on Pictish cross-slabs at Farr (Sutherland), Edderton (Ross-shire), Abercromby no. 3 (Fife) and St Vigeans no. 12 (ECMS, vol. 2: 53-4, 83-4, 272, 349, figs 51, 51A, 82, 283, 363). Like the stepped cross-base, which is depicted more commonly in Pictish sculpture, the domed cross-base is expressed as an architectural feature and suggests a visual reference. Both forms of cross-base probably express the same symbolism and represent the True Cross upon which Christ was crucified on the hill at Calvary (compare Henderson and Henderson 2004: 191).

The presence of a cross on the arch is of both architectural and symbolic significance. The cross is one of the oldest and most universal of Christian symbols, first adopted as the sign of the Christian faith by the Roman emperor Constantine the Great (d. 337). In addition to being an object and symbol of confession, devotion, meditation and penitence, the cross symbolises the Passion of Christ and, as a result, is one of the few symbols that must be incorporated into a church (Gordon 1963: 32-3). A cross or crucifix is carved on the lintels over the entrances to several early medieval churches and round towers in Ireland and the round tower at Brechin (*62*). This reflects both the symbolism surrounding the act of entering a holy place and the symbolic status of the entrance itself, as reflected in Christ's words, 'I am the door; by me if any man enter in he shall be saved' (John 10: 9).

Left: 61 The Agnus Dei, set on a base on a mount and with the rivers of Paradise flowing below it, as depicted on a medallion from the base of a fourth-century gilded glass vessel. *Northcote and Brownlow,* Roma Sotterranea *(1869)*

Below: 62 The lintel above the entrance to the round tower at Brechin

In contrast to the early Christian sculpture of other Insular peoples, and in what must reflect a deliberate iconographical convention, the figure of Christ crucified is never depicted on Pictish cross-slabs (Simpson 1965: 113-14). But, although now badly damaged, the cross occupies the most prominent location on the arch, the crown or highest point, and forms the centrepiece of the arch, around which the rest of the scene is composed. This cross, and other crosses in Pictish sculpture, not only represents the Holy Cross but is itself both a symbol of Christ and Christ's Passion. Reinforcing the Cross as a symbol of the Passion, the juxtaposition of the cross with the Agnus Dei (below) clearly identifies it as the Cross of Christ. The presence of the cross is fundamental to the interpretation of the arch, both the iconography of the scene depicted on it and the function of the building to which it belonged. The cross attests the Christian context and meaning of the scene.

THE AGNUS DEI

Two animals are depicted on the arch. Both are clearly quadrupeds but are represented in a stylistic fashion that may appear simplistic and below the highest standards of Pictish animal art (Chap. 6). Consequently, there is some uncertainty about the species concerned and, therefore, their symbolic significance.

The most prominent of these animals is depicted in profile immediately to the right of, and facing, the cross (63). This quadruped occupies an awkward, vertical position, a feature paralleled by the calf-symbol in the Book of Kells (Trinity College Dublin MS 58, Canon II, f.3v). It is sitting upright on its haunches, its long tail extending in a straight line along the lower moulding of the arch and its straight back pointing upwards. The beast's rear legs are raised together and this contrasts with the impression created by its forelegs, particularly its raised right leg, as if it is walking or pawing the ground. This contrasts with the naturalistic quality of 'classical' Pictish animal sculpture (Chap. 6).

This is not a naturalistic pose but a stiff, almost heraldic, stance. This may be a result of the limited space available on the arch, the limited abilities of the sculptor, a deliberate artistic style or some obscure symbolic meaning. The double outline of the animal's mouth, chest, foreleg and belly is characteristic of Pictish incised sculpture but occurs only very rarely in relief. Its shoulder is marked by the sweeping curve of the outline and its haunch by a small decorative flourish, indicating the musculature. The manner in which these joints are depicted may represent vestigial body scrolls, related to the lobate scrolls used to mark the shoulder and haunch of quadrupeds in Pictish sculpture (on which see Hicks 1993a: 47, 54, 103; 1993b: 197; Alcock 1998: 516, 518). However, this quadruped lacks the exuberant scrolled body markings found in the best examples, such as the bull sculptures from Burghead, Moray (below).

The rounded muzzle, small, pricked ears and absence of horns indicate that this animal is a lamb or sheep and this is how it is usually, if tentatively, interpreted (ECMS, vol. 2: 325; Curle 1940: 110; Richardson 1964: 7; Alcock 1982: 218; Alcock and Alcock 1992: 225, 226). Alternatively, if the uppermost 'ear' is actually a short, stubby horn, the quadruped portrayed may be a bull. However, this animal does not resemble a bull, lacking the characteristic size and bulky musculature. This leaves the possibility that it may be an ox, a neutered bull that does not develop the physical hallmarks of bulls. Like sheep/lambs, oxen are also unusual members of the Pictish bestiary, although examples occur on stone plaques from Inverness and East Lomond, Fife (ECMS, vol. 2: 102-3, figs 106-7; Corrie 1926; Alcock 1993: 230; Mack 1997: 31). But, taking into account its appearance, context and symbolic meaning, the animal depicted on the Forteviot arch is almost certainly a lamb or sheep.

The only other sheep/lambs in Pictish sculpture are the horned sheep on the St Andrews sarcophagus and the cross-slabs at Aldbar, Angus, and Nigg, Easter Ross, although the representation of these examples is more naturalistic and they have curly fleeces (ECMS, vol. 2: 75-83, 245-7, figs 81, 259B). Their rarity suggests that the presence of the lamb on the arch is significant. Skene (1857: 278) first suggested that the animals on the arch had a symbolic meaning, but did not develop this idea. This is certainly true of depictions of sheep in Pictish sculpture, which appear as an attribute of the biblical King David and symbolise his calling as The Shepherd (Allen 1887: 150-2, 203-8; ECMS, vol. 2: 80-1; Henderson 1998a: 132-3; Hawkes 1997: 156). But the lamb holds a wide range of symbolic meanings in Christian art, including sacrifice, innocence and purity, and as an attribute of several saints and, above all, Christ Himself (Ferguson 1954: 20-1, 93, 103, 114, 121, 125; Murray and Murray 1996: 267).

The symbolic meaning of the lamb on the arch is revealed by its context. The lamb occupies a prominent position within the scene, located centrally and next to the cross at the crown of the arch. In addition, its rear legs and extended right foreleg all touch the cross, while the animal is sitting upright, facing the cross. The close relationship between the lamb and the cross confirms its ecclesiastical symbolism and its context on the arch reveals the lamb as the Agnus Dei, the Lamb of God. The Agnus Dei is a common symbol in early Christian art (Allen 1884: 395-404; 1887: 254-62), although early representations, as on the arch, lack the nimbus or halo familiar in later images. Nevertheless, the Agnus Dei on the arch does display a characteristic feature, its bent right foreleg touching the cross. In medieval and modern representations, this takes the form of the Agnus Dei holding with its bent foreleg a flag or pennant with a cross on it as a symbol of victory (*64*).

Right: 63 The Agnus Dei on the Forteviot arch

Below: 64 The tympanum at Parwich Church, Derbyshire. The Agnus Dei holds with its bent foreleg a flag or pennant with a cross on it as a symbol of victory. *Brushfield,* On Norman Tympana

The Agnus Dei is a physical representation of Christ as the Messiah, after John the Baptist's words when he first saw Jesus: 'Here is the Lamb of God, who takes away the sin of the world' (John 1: 29; see also John 1: 36, Revelation 5: 13, I Corinthians 5: 7) and who alone is 'Worthy to receive power, wealth and wisdom and might and honour and glory and blessings' (Revelation 5: 12). The status of the Agnus Dei as the paschal or sacrificial lamb is revealed by the episode of the lamb upon the altar: 'the lamb that was slain from the beginning of the world', spilling 'the blood of the lamb' (Apocalypse 12: 27; 12: 2). The lamb on the arch may also refer to the blood of the lamb daubed on the door lintels of the houses of the Israelites in Egypt at the Passover (Exodus 12: 21-8). The juxtaposition of the Agnus Dei and the cross confirms their symbolism as paired iconographic metaphors for the Passion and the Resurrection. In conjunction, the cross and Agnus Dei symbolise Christ in Majesty, thus forming a symbolic link between heaven and earth. The association of the Agnus Dei with the *Majestas Domini*, Christ in His Glory, is also found in early medieval sculpture in Ireland, for example on the Cross of Saints Patrick and Columba at Kells (Harbison 1992, vol. 1: 110-11, vol. 2: fig. 355).

The Agnus Dei on the arch reinforces the holiness of the cross with which it is associated, physically and symbolically, and, by extension, emphasises the sanctity of the arch and the building to which it belonged.

THE KING

The largest and most prominent figure portrayed on the arch is to the left of the cross and occupies most of this side of the arch (65). This man is shown in profile in a reclining, almost prostrate, pose, his back and bottom resting on the lower border of the arch, with his legs bent at the knee and drawn up towards his body. This has been interpreted as a seated position (MacGibbon and Ross 1897, vol. 3: 623; Curle 1940: 110; Close-Brooks and Stevenson 1982: 40; Lines 1992: 38), although no seat is visible.

This figure has a striking appearance, with a disproportionately large head and exaggerated features. His distinctive nose, eyes, chin, moustache, hair and clothes all attract attention. He has a very prominent, elongated and block-like or rectangular nose, characterised by a high and sharply-protruding nasal bridge, from which the front of the nose drops almost vertically. His left eye, the only one showing, is large, wide and stares out from the scene. The eye is almond-shaped or lentoid, as if viewed from the front, even though the figure is portrayed in profile, giving this and the other figures a curious perspective. Even this eye,

65 The
king on the
Forteviot arch

with its raised pupil and heavy eyelids and/or eyebrow defined by a double
line, displays exaggerated features. The figure sports an impressive curved and
drooping moustache, with the one pointed end showing so long that it reaches
his shoulders. His strong chin is either pointed or sports a neatly-trimmed goatee
beard. In contrast to these enlarged and obtrusive features, he has an improbably
delicate ear, which is very small and kidney shaped.

This figure has been described as wearing 'a head-dress of a more ornamental
description than the other two [figures]' on the arch and interpreted as 'probably
a rude attempt to represent a crown' or a 'sort of rude coronet' (Skene 1857: 278,
279). However, his head is actually uncovered. What was mistaken for a head-
dress or crown is instead five upstanding curls of hair on the top of the figure's
head, with further curls swept behind his ears and/or at the back of his head.
His hair appears originally to have been collar-length but the arch is damaged at
this point. This either portrays an elaborate and highly formal hairstyle, possibly
in the form of a decorative crest of hair twisted into upright curls, or is a stylised
representation of hair, the sculptor using a few ringlets to convey the impression
of a shock of curly hair.

This character's clothing is equally distinctive. Seven concentric lines around his shoulders and upper body suggest the folds of a cloak or the seams of a quilted mantle worn around the shoulders. This is worn over a knee-length tunic, although its exact form and appearance are obscured by the cape worn over it, the figure's hands and the object in them, as well as his awkward position. However, there is no evidence to support claims (ECMS, vol. 2: 325; Lines 1992: 38; PAS 1997) that the figures on the arch are wearing byrnies or hauberks, tunics of quilted armour, or armour itself. One distinctive detail of his tunic is shown clearly, the decorated hem or border, which comprises a stepped or key-work pattern. There is a suggestion of footwear, possibly calf-length boots, although this may be a result of damage to the arch, which has left a diagonal line across the upper calves of the figure. More convincingly, there are faint traces at the base of the shin of the elongated tongues of ankle-length boots or buskins.

All these features are readily paralleled in Pictish sculpture (66). There is evidence of elaborate hairstyles from throughout Pictland. The leading, and apparently most senior, warrior on the symbol stone from the Brough of Birsay, Orkney, and, although now damaged, the upper horseman on the Benvie cross-slab both sport hairstyles of upstanding ringlets, together with a large tress of curled hair at the nape of the neck (ECMS, vol. 2: 247-9, fig. 260B; Ritchie 1994: 13-14, fig. 9). Curled hair also features prominently on two graffiti portraits, once thought to be Viking but now identified as Pictish, from the Broch of Burness, Orkney, and Jarlshof, Shetland (Marwick 1924: 295-7; Stevenson 1981: 289; O'Meadhra 1993: 426-8, figs 27.1-2; Ritchie 1994: 13-14, figs 8 and 9) (67).

The stark and stylised facial appearance of the large figure on the Forteviot arch is a distinctive characteristic of the Benvie-Dupplin school. The rectangular, block-like nose also occurs on the two figures on the right-hand side of the arch (below), on the horsemen on the Benvie cross-slab and Dupplin cross, on David playing the harp on the north side of the Dupplin cross and on the two men fighting on the St Andrews no. 19 cross-shaft (ECMS, vol. 2: 247-9, 319-21, figs 260B, 334C; Henderson 1999a: 172; Henderson and Henderson 2004: 192). The exaggerated appearance of other facial features exhibited by these figures suggests that the block-like nose probably reflects artistic licence and may even represent an artistic convention. This is supported by the occurrence of such noses within other Insular contexts; for example, those of Saints Paul and Anthony in a panel on the north side of the Moone cross, Co. Kildare, Ireland (McNab 1988, fig. 3; Harbison 1992, vol. 2: fig. 518; Henderson 1999a: 172-3). In a Pictish context, the block-like nose may even represent the signature of a sculptor or school of sculpture.

66 Mounted warrior kings and aristocrats of the Southern Picts: (1) Kirriemuir no. 2, Angus; (2) Dupplin cross, Perthshire; (3) Benvie, Angus; (4) Kirriemuir no. 3, Angus. *After Alcock 1998*

67 Dress and hairstyles of aristocratic warriors of the Northern Picts: (1) the Brough of Birsay, Orkney; (2) Jarlshof, Shetland; (3) the Broch of Burness, Orkney. *After Ritchie 1994*

However, block-shaped noses do occur naturally, possibly as genetically inherited features. The distinctive noses of the figures portrayed on sculpture belonging to the Benvie-Dupplin school may therefore suggest a family likeness and the people represented may have been related. This possible genetic link is of particular interest given that the horseman on the Dupplin cross and the individual on the Forteviot arch were not only members of the same royal dynasty, but brothers.

The other facial features are also paralleled in sculpture belonging to the Benvie-Dupplin school. The staring, frontal eyes are similar to those of the figures on the Dupplin cross but also occur widely in Insular art, including in the Book of Kells. The long, drooping moustache is also found on the horsemen on the Aldbar and Benvie cross-slabs and on the horseman and two foot soldiers on the right-hand side of the Dupplin cross (ECMS, vol. 2: 245-9, 319-21, figs 259B, 260B, 334C, 334D). These distinctive moustaches are claimed to have a cultural significance and 'may represent the unfamiliar features of the Scots who were now settling in former Pictish territory' (Hicks 1993a: 219). But while these droopy moustaches depart from the usual appearance of figures in Pictish sculpture, there is no reason why this should be attributed to incoming Scots rather than to a change of fashion among the indigenous Picts.

The clothing worn by this figure is also widely attested in Pictish sculpture. The long-tongued, half-length boots are similar to those worn by the horseman on the Meigle no. 3 cross-slab and the clerics and desert fathers on the St Vigeans no. 7 cross-slab (ECMS, vol. 2: 268, 299, figs 278, 312B; RCAHMS 2003). The cloak or mantle is paralleled by the horsemen on the Kirriemuir no. 2 and Menmuir no. 1 cross-slabs, both Angus (ECMS, vol. 2: 227-8, 263-4, figs 240B, 273B; RCAHMS 2003). The tunic, particularly its textured appearance, is also similar to that on the Menmuir no. 1 cross-slab. The tunic hems of two moustached foot soldiers on the Dupplin cross and a possible cleric on the Rosemarkie no. 4 cross-slab fragment, Ross-shire, are also decorated with a square key-work pattern (ECMS, vol. 2: 87-8, fig. 85). Hems decorated with different designs, including key-work, occur on the tunics of the senior warrior on the Brough of Birsay stone, the graffito portrait from the Broch of Burness, the clerics and biblical characters on the St Vigeans no. 7 and Meigle no. 29 cross-slabs and an angel on the Kirriemuir no. 4 fragment (ECMS, vol. 2: 87-8, 260-1, 268-9, 340, figs 85, 270, 278, 355).

Key-work patterns, including some similar to that on the hem of the figure on the Forteviot arch, are used as borders on sculpture in Southern Pictland, notably the Kirriemuir no. 3, Invergowrie no. 1, St Vigeans no. 10 and Meigle no. 6 cross-slabs (ECMS, vol. 2: 255-6, 258-60, 270, 301-2, figs 266A, 266B, 269B, 281D, 315B). Key-work patterns also form borders around or beneath the principal panels of other Pictish sculptures. On the Dupplin cross, the panels at the top of the cross-shaft containing the inscription on the front, the mounted warrior on the back, beasts on both side panels and the four spearmen below the horseman are all highlighted in this manner. A border of stepped key-work also occurs above the mounted warrior on the Forteviot no. 4 fragment, belonging to a high-cross (Chap. 5). The Benvie cross-slab (ECMS, vol. 2: 247-9, fig. 260B) (*51*) reveals the significance of this feature. Of the two horsemen portrayed, the one surrounded by a key-work border is clearly the more senior, as his superior position, larger size and more elaborate hairstyle reveal. These examples indicate that key-work patterns are not simply decorative but signify the high social status of the figures they are associated with. This makes it a particularly appropriate design for the hem of the tunic worn by the most prominent figure on the arch.

The appearance and exaggerated features of this figure reveal much about his status. Although he has been interpreted as a cleric (Laing and Laing 1993: 28), the figure's uncovered head and full head of hair expose the absence of a Celtic tonsure, in which the front of the head was shaved. This reveals that he was a lay person. Despite misinterpreting this individual's hairstyle as an ornamental head-dress or crown, Skene (1857: 278) concluded that this feature 'marks him out as a higher dignity' and identified him as a 'royal person'. The identifications proposed for this king are assessed within the context of the date of the arch (Chap. 8).

The figure's royal status is supported by his facial hair. The curled hair and long moustache led to his identification as a 'warrior chief' (Stevenson 1955: 127). Flamboyant moustaches are also an indicator of rank in Insular, including Pictish, sculpture (Hawkes 1996: 30; Henderson 1999a: 172; Aitchison 2003: 75-6; Alcock 2003: 149). This is apparent on the Dupplin cross, where a moustached horseman appears above a panel containing four foot soldiers. The lower status of the infantrymen is unambiguously expressed by their portrayal on foot rather than horseback, their lower – literally subordinate – position on the cross-shaft and clean-shaven appearance. Clothing, like hairstyles and facial hair, is also an indicator of status. Here, the combination of a mantle, a tunic with a decorated hem and, as their ribbon-like appearance suggests, the generous use of fabric in their manufacture, all reveal the wearer as a man of elevated social status.

Size, place and space are used to convey status in Pictish sculpture. The figures on cross-slabs are carefully-arranged, frequently with the largest figure at the top centre (Alcock 1993: 232). Particular precedence is given to the depiction of biblical heroes in Pictish sculpture (Henderson 1986; Alcock 1995; Carrington 1997; Hawkes 1997; Henderson and Henderson 2004: 129-37), as revealed by the towering presence of the King David figure on the St Andrews sarcophagus (Henderson 1998a: 101, 103, 105-8; 1998b: 23-4) (68). The Forteviot arch depicts a similarly heroic figure of literally enlarged proportions. Indeed, his greater size and prominent position ensure that he occupies most of the left-hand side of the arch. The unmistakable emphasis on this figure reveals his pre-eminent status. In addition, his close proximity to the cross at the crown of the arch elevates him above the ground and emphasises the divine source or sanction of his power. This figure expresses the ideals of Pictish physical appearance and emphasises the tastes to which the Benvie-Dupplin school of sculpture aspired. It also encapsulates the grammar of Pictish figural sculpture and the rich symbolic meaning invested in personal appearance.

The lay people portrayed most prominently in Pictish sculpture are of high social status because they usually appear on cross-slabs that presumably commemorate them and marked their graves. The resources required, in terms of quarried stone, sculptural expertise and rights of burial at ecclesiastical sites, suggests that the individuals concerned were people of substance, probably nobles or members of royal kin groups. But, in conjunction, and reinforced by the association of the arch with a royal centre, the features displayed by this figure indicate that he was a person of exceptional social status, a king. This conclusion is supported by the similar appearance, including the clothing, hairstyle and moustache, of the

68 The St Andrews sarcophagus, with the enlarged King David figure on the right

mounted warrior depicted on the Dupplin cross. This horseman is Causantín son of Uurguist, king of the Picts (789-820) (Chap. 5).

Identifying the activity in which the king portrayed on the arch is engaged is more problematic. He is shown gripping an elongated object in both hands. This artefact has been interpreted in various ways, the most common of which is that it is a staff or sword (Allen 1887: 239-40; Anderson 1892: 437; ECMS, vol. 2: 325; Close-Brooks 1980b: 3: Alcock 1982: 220; Alcock and Alcock 1992: 225; Lines 1992: 38; PAS 1997; Sutherland 1997: 47; Henderson 1999a: 177; Duncan 2002: 10). The Alcocks, the strongest proponents of its interpretation as a weapon, described it as 'a large sword in a scabbard which narrows towards the tip' (Alcock and Alcock 1992: 225).

Images of medieval kingship have been used to interpret this figure and support claims that he carries a sword. The figures in the scene have been described as 'seated in the usual royal attitude, with the sword across the knees' (MacGibbon and Ross 1897, vol. 3: 623). The image cited in support of this interpretation is the miniature portrait of Malcolm IV (1141-65) in the illuminated initial of the foundation charter of Kelso abbey, in which the king is seated, with his sword lying across his knees (ECMS, vol. 2: 325; see also Lines 1992: 38) (*69*). Parallels have also been drawn with the kings in the twelfth-century Norse chessmen from Lewis, who sit grasping with both hands a scabbarded sword lying across their knees (Close-Brooks and Stevenson 1982: 40). However, these images belong to a different era and form of

69 The portrait of Malcolm IV (1141-65) in the illuminated initial of the foundation charter of Kelso abbey. *National Library of Scotland courtesy of the Duke of Roxburghe*

kingship, in which the sword of state and the sceptre symbolised the king's powers. The object held by the king on the arch cannot have possessed this role because the two smaller characters on the right-hand side of the arch also hold similar items, but each with one hand rather than both. Although the main figure appears to be a king, he does not hold a sword of state. Nevertheless, the Kelso charter portrait has influenced recent interpretations of the scene on the arch (Chap. 8).

More fundamentally, the artefact held by the king does not resemble a sword. It is implausibly large, in both length and thickness, and has none of the features or fittings that one would expect to find on a sword, including a pommel, hand-grip, cross-guard or blade. Instead, this object is straight-sided for most of its length, although it does taper slightly towards its lower end. This cannot represent a sword rendered by either Pictish artistic convention or clumsiness because swords are depicted clearly in other Pictish sculptures, for example the Inchbrayock, Angus, cross-slab (ECMS, vol. 2: 223-4, fig. 235B).

Claims that the item depicted is a sheathed sword (Anderson 1892: 437; Alcock and Alcock 1992: 225) are equally unconvincing because, with the exception of only the blade, the sword's distinguishing features should still be visible. Indeed, most swords depicted in Pictish sculpture, including that on the Inchbrayock cross-slab, are still in their scabbards. Moreover, there are no traces of a sword chape, the decorative mount at the tip of the scabbard. These distinctive and sometimes elaborate scabbard fittings are depicted on several Pictish cross-slabs and two examples survive in the St Ninian's Isle hoard, Shetland (Wilson 1973: 58-60, no. 11, 118-21). Strengthening the argument against this identification, a sword is unlikely to have been held in the two-handed manner shown on the arch. Illustrating the confusing nature of this scene, the figures on the arch have been described as holding swords but sitting as if 'rowing backwards' (Lines 1992: 38).

Although identified as a 'warrior chief' (Stevenson 1955: 127), this figure is not depicted in this role. This contrasts with the many armed and frequently mounted figures portrayed in Pictish sculpture, including on the reverse of the Forteviot no. 4 cross-slab and on the Dupplin cross (Chap. 5). In the absence of any identifiable swords, spears or shields, the standard arms and armour of the Picts (Aitchison 2003: 47-62), the figures portrayed cannot be either fighting or hunting.

The final argument against the identification of this artefact as a sword is that it would be out of place in what is essentially a religious scene. Although the sword is invested with some Christian symbolism – for example, as an instrument of martyrdom and symbol of St Paul (Gordon 1963: 79) – none of these meanings appears to be relevant to the arch. While senior lay persons probably carried a sword as a symbol of their status, it is unclear why the principal figure on the Forteviot arch should be portrayed wielding a drawn sword. It is even more out of keeping for the clerics on the right side of the arch (below) to be carrying swords. The cumulative evidence that none of the figures on the arch are carrying swords is overwhelming.

The interpretation of these objects as shepherds' crooks is also unlikely. A symbol of pastoral calling and ecclesiastical status within the Celtic church, the *bachall* or cambutta was sometimes a reliquary enshrining the crook of a founding or patron saint (Bourke 1987). Shepherds' crooks appear in Pictish sculpture, where they are held by clerics on the Bressay, Papil, St Vigeans nos 4 and 7 and Meigle no. 29 cross-slabs (ECMS, vol. 2: 5-8, 10-12, 240-1, 268-9, 340, figs 4, 4A, 7, 255B, 278, 355). These crooks are easily identified by their curved or hooked heads or, occasionally, a knobbed terminal, as on the St Vigeans no. 11 cross-slab (ECMS, vol. 2: 271-2, fig. 282B). The absence of these distinctive features from the objects depicted on the arch reveals that these are not ecclesiastical crooks.

Another possible interpretation of these artefacts, as oars, may also be rejected. This is clear from the manner in which the principal figure grips the shaft, with both thumbs pointing up instead of towards each other, as he would if was rowing. Moreover, no ship is depicted on the arch, although Pictish sculptors were perfectly capable of depicting oared ships, as demonstrated by the fine example on St Orland's Stone (ECMS, vol. 2: 216–18, figs 230A, 230B; Aitchison 2003: 124–5, 126, 128). There is no evidence to support the interpretation that the figures on the Forteviot arch hold oars or are in a ship.

An alternative interpretation, that the object represents a staff or stave, seems more plausible, but the manner in which it is gripped and the king's stance are curious. He grasps the staff firmly with both hands, as if applying great force to it, apparently pulling it upwards or downwards. This is also implied by his crouched posture. Stretched out, almost flat on his back, with his legs bent at the knees, he appears to be putting his whole body weight into whatever he is doing. The sculptor has vividly captured the energy of this figure, giving him the appearance of a Pictish pole-vaulter. However, the oddly contorted position of the figure may not depict a realistic posture but might reflect artistic licence. This is a result of the sculptor's struggle to accommodate the image of an upright figure within the restricted field available on the arch. The limitations imposed by this affect the placing of the figure within the scene and its composition (Chap. 8).

THE BULL

The second quadruped depicted on the arch is smaller than the Agnus Dei and occupies a more peripheral location, a restricted space below the king and near the left-hand abutment (70). This animal is partly obscured by the king's staff and is also slightly damaged. Its snout and lower legs are missing, a result of the loss of detail due to delamination of the surface of the stone. Nevertheless, enough survives for the quadruped and its symbolic significance to be identified.

The quadruped is depicted in profile, has a straight back and stands horizontally on all fours. It faces towards the left, as is normal for animals in Pictish sculpture (Hicks 1993a: 44–5, 47, 49). It has a more angular head than the Agnus Dei and a single, wide and triangular pricked ear is visible. Its mouth is indicated with a simple line and its eye by a circle. The animal's most distinctive feature is a single long and curved horn, apparently projecting from its forehead. The position of its front legs, with the right slightly in front of the left, suggests that the beast is either ambling or at rest. This peaceful pose is reinforced by its tail, which hangs vertically.

70 The bull on the Forteviot arch

Like the Agnus Dei, this is a stiff, representational image and, as a result, the species portrayed is not immediately apparent. However, this quadruped has been interpreted as a sheep because of its similarity to the Agnus Dei (Curle 1940: 110; Richardson 1964: 7; Henderson and Henderson 2004: 145). However, this resemblance is only superficial and may be attributable to the stylised quality of the representation rather than the intention of the sculptor. This animal has also been identified as a simpler form of the more elaborate horned beast found on the Forteviot no. 1 cross–slab (Alcock 1982: 227; Chap. 5). But that hybrid beast, a cross between a carnivore and a bovine, is obviously mythical. The Second Vision of Daniel, in which a goat with a single horn attacks a two-horned ram (Daniel 8: 3–8), suggests another possible interpretation of the quadrupeds. However, this is weakened by the fact that the beasts are not associated with each other but with the figure above and the cross beside them.

The size and shape of the horn reveal that this quadruped is neither a sheep nor a goat but a bovine. The animal is either a bull or a castrate, that is, an oxen or steer. However, its sexual characteristics are unclear, in contrast to other bovines in Pictish sculpture (on which see Alcock 1993: 230). A simple curved line at the shoulder implies its musculature, although the relatively slight body and long horn may suggest that this is an ox rather than a bull. But the stylised nature of this image makes it difficult to distinguish its sex and the king's staff passes in front of the animal's groin, obscuring any testicles. On balance, the solidity of the animal, coupled with the prominence of its horn, indicate that the sculptor intended this to be a bull. However, it lacks both the naturalistic quality and sheer animal energy of other bulls depicted in Pictish sculpture, notably those on the stone plaques from Burghead (ECMS, vol. 2: 118-24; Alcock 1993: 230; Cessford 1995; Mack 1997: 30, 98-100; Scott 2005).

The small size, peripheral location and relatively simple execution of this quadruped may suggest that it was intended to fill an otherwise blank space on the arch. This is consistent with the *horror vacui* that characterises Pictish sculpture, and Celtic art generally, in which the sculptor has to fill every surface, leaving no area free of decoration. However, the presence of the bull on the arch is unlikely to be coincidental. The bull was sacred to the pagan Celts and retained its significance as a symbol of aggression, strength and virility (Ross 1967: 302-8; Green 1986: 176-9; 1989: 149-51; 1992: 51-2; see also Rice 1999). This is expressed most vividly in the Old Irish epic tale *Táin Bó Cuailnge*, 'The Cattle Raid of Cooley', in which the provinces of Connachta and Ulaid go to war over a bull. The bull is closely associated with kingship in early Irish mythology. The two bulls at the centre of the *Táin* are owned by the warring kings of Connachta and Ulaid. The *tarbhfeis* or 'bull feast' was a divinatory ritual, involving the slaughter and eating of a bull, for selecting the king of Tara, according to *Togail Bruidne Dá Derga*, 'The Destruction of Dá Derga's Hostel' (trans. Gantz 1981: 65).

Vivid images of taurine aggression and power occur in Pictish sculpture, notably the two bulls confronting each other on the Meigle no. 12 recumbent stone (ECMS, vol. 2: 333-4, fig. 346C; Ritchie 1997: 23-4). Some of the Burghead bulls are also depicted in an aggressive stance, pawing the ground and with heads lowered, ready to charge. Reinforcing their association with royal power and warrior-kingship, these sculptures were found in the largest fortified site in Pictland, a coastal promontory fortress with massive timber-laced ramparts (Small 1969; Edwards and Ralston 1978). Burghead was a power centre of exceptional importance and perhaps the fortress of the king of the Northern Picts.

The carefully composed nature of the scene on the arch and its iconography (Chap. 8) indicate that the bull was included deliberately. The bull may be a protective animal associated with a threshold, in this case between the nave and chancel of a church (Chap. 9), symbolically demarcating the safe route into the sacred space (Kitzinger 1993: 4-6). This may be paralleled in Anglo-Saxon architectural sculpture, notably by the long-beaked dragons on the jambs of the entrance to the Church of St Peter at Monkwearmouth (Cramp 1984, part 1: 125-6, nos 8a and b) and the animal heads associated with the doorways and chancel arch of the Church of St Mary, Deerhurst, Gloucestershire (Bailey 2005:

1–7). However, this does not explain the presence of an animal within a more extensive scheme, as on the Forteviot arch.

Like the Agnus Dei, the location of the bull within the composition reinforces its symbolic significance. These quadrupeds are qualifying symbols, reinforcing the meaning of the objects or figures with which they are associated on the arch. While the Agnus Dei is closely associated with the cross, the bull is symbolically associated with the king portrayed immediately above it. Indeed, so closely are they linked in physical terms that the king's feet almost touch the bull, symbolising the royal power upon which his kingship rests. This animal signifies or confirms the status of the figure above it. As a zoomorphic expression of secular power and aggression, the bull on the Forteviot arch symbolises the kingship of this figure and is an attribute of his warrior-kingship.

THE CLERICS

Two closely-positioned figures are portrayed in profile on the right-hand side of the arch (71). Both are smaller than the king, presumably reflecting their lower status but probably also because the sculptor needed to accommodate two figures in a space no larger than that occupied by the king on the opposite side of the arch. The upper or left-hand figure is truncated and shown only above a line running from the middle of his back to his front waist. Although it has been suggested that the knees and feet of this figure are visible among the folds of his clothes (Alcock 1982: 218), there are no signs of these. The second figure, below and to the right of the first, is portrayed in full but is otherwise very similar in appearance. This figure is shown in an awkward squatting position, his legs bent sharply at the knee and his thighs raised up tightly against his torso. However, this is partly obscured by the folds of the figure's cloak and by damage to the abutment of the arch, as a result of which his legs are missing below the tops of his calves.

It is unclear whether the posture of the lower figure is related to the activity he is engaged in. More probably, it reflects artistic licence and the sculptor's attempt to compress these figures into the limited space and curving field available on the arch. The compressed and truncated nature of these figures are unusual, with no obvious parallels in Pictish sculpture. However, this treatment of figures, depicted in profile and with bendy legs doubled back or drawn up, is closely paralleled in the Book of Kells (Canons I and II, ff. iv and 2) (*colour plate 21*), where flexible-limbed human figures are inserted into the arches and columns of the canon tables (Henderson and Henderson 2004: 209).

71 The
clerics on the
Forteviot arch

The combination of the lower figure's bent legs and the missing end of the sculpture has caused enduring confusion about the form and number of figures on this side of the arch. Stuart's (1856: i) reconstruction of the complete arch misinterpreted the raised upper leg of the right-hand figure as the upper body of a third cleric (55). A third figure, or at least the top of his head, eye and upper nose, was included in another illustration of the arch (Allen 1887: 239) (56). Reliance on these incorrect illustrations led to long-standing claims that a third figure was present on this side of the arch (ECMS, vol. 2: 325; Curle 1940: 110; Alcock 1982: 220; Alcock and Alcock 1992: 226; Lines 1992: 38) or that a total of four figures are depicted on the arch (MacGibbon and Ross 1897, vol. 3: 623; Driscoll 2001). Adding to the confusion, it has also been claimed that there is only one figure on either side of the arch (Laing and Laing 1993: 28). According to another suggestion, if the arch originally comprised a full semi-circle, then its missing abutment may have held not only the lower leg and foot of the second figure but also another animal, decorative motif or figure, presumably provided that he was truncated in the same manner as the left-hand person (Alcock 1982: 218; Alcock and Alcock 1992: 225). However, there is no evidence for the presence of another figure or animal here and the form of the sculpture at this end of the arch remains unclear.

The faces of both figures are damaged. Despite this, they clearly resemble each other and have been portrayed in the same manner as the king, with whom they share similar facial characteristics. The upper figure has lost his nose, its prominence presumably resulting in it being broken off, although the void it has left and the protruding nasal bridge reveal it to have been block-like in form. The face belonging to the lower figure has disappeared above the cheek resulting in the loss of his eye and ear, although his elongated and block-like nose remains *in situ*. Both figures have pointed chins and impressive drooping moustaches, although not as long as the king's. The upper figure also has a staring, lentoid eye and a dainty ear. Unlike the king, the hair of both figures is obscured by their clothing.

Both figures are dressed similarly. Their heads are covered with a cowl or hood belonging to a hooded cloak or robe. Details of these garments are picked out with a ribbon-like arrangement of incised lines, in a similar manner to the king's clothes. Like the king, both figures hold an elongated object which has been interpreted variously as a shepherd's crook, staff, sword or oar. But, unlike the king, they hold this in only one hand. The lower figure grasps his staff in his right hand and the upper figure probably in his left.

The smaller size, shorter moustaches and truncated/compressed appearance of these figures reveal that they are of lower status than the king. In keeping with the interpretation of the staves as swords and clothes as hauberks, these figures have been identified as 'followers or guards' of the king (Skene 1857: 278). Alternatively, their hooded cloaks have led to these figures being interpreted as travellers or 'muffled wayfarers' (Henderson and Henderson 2004: 145, 241, n. 115). However, their identification is revealed by the portrayal of figures wearing hooded cloaks on cross-slabs from Bressay, Papil (Shetland), Aldbar, Kirriemuir no. 1, Invergowrie no. 1 and St Vigeans nos. 7, 11 and 17 (ECMS, vol. 2: 5-15, 227, 240-1, 246-7, 255-6, 268, 271-2, 275, figs 4, 4A, 7, 239A, 255B, 259A, 266B, 278, 282A, 282B, 288A). Most of these figures are shown holding gospel books, shepherds' crooks or flabella (liturgical fans), religious artefacts carried by senior ecclesiastics as the tools of their trade and symbols of their status. The cowled heads of both figures on the Forteviot arch therefore distinguish them as clerics, although their precise status, whether as monks or priests, is unclear.

Although their position and the significance of their presence is not immediately apparent, the inclusion of these clerics, together with the cross, reinforces the ecclesiastical theme and context of the scene on the arch.

8

THE ICONOGRAPHY OF
THE ARCH

Having examined the constituent elements of the sculpture on the Forteviot arch, the analysis of the overall scene, its iconography and wider significance may now be attempted. How might this apparently incongruous group of figures, animals and symbols be interpreted? Or is the meaning of the scene on the arch now lost forever?

METHODOLOGY

This analysis of the iconography of the Forteviot arch is based on two fundamental assumptions. The first is that the scene depicted on the arch is not simply decorative in function. That is, it was not intended merely to be aesthetically attractive but instead expressed some intrinsic meaning, if not to every viewer then at least to those who had been initiated into its symbolism. This concept should be familiar to students of medieval art in general and Pictish sculpture in particular. Pictish sculpture is notable for its striking imagery and use of a wide range of rich symbolism. Beasts and enigmatic abstract symbols appear in recurring combinations on symbol stones, revealing that they held some specific meaning (Samson 1992; Forsyth 1997), while cross-slabs bear figures or scenes illustrating a wide range of biblical, ecclesiastical, mythological and secular subjects. Although the interpretation of individual scenes or symbols is rarely straightforward, Pictish sculpture was not simply decorative but clearly conveyed a deeper, symbolic meaning. Similarly, the strong narrative content of the scene on the arch invites interpretation by the viewer.

The study and interpretation of *ex situ* architectural sculpture is often problematic because it is not a single artefact or monument but a component of a more extensive and complex structure. As a result, the interpretation of architectural sculpture is more challenging if it is divorced from its original context and even more so if the structure to which it originally belonged no longer survives, as is the case with the Forteviot arch. However, the second assumption employed here is that the Forteviot arch tells its own story. The key to the meaning of the scene, therefore, must lie in the sculpture itself. The arch was intended to be seen and, therefore, the meaning of the scene carved on it must have been known to at least some elements within that audience. This approach rejects the pessimistic notion that only the original sculptor can reveal what he depicted and the meaning of his images. The unknown sculptor has left enough evidence to enable the scene to be read. Those clues comprise the images themselves and the context in which they occur. Although the building in which the sculpture was displayed has disappeared without record, the scene is on an arch which belonged to a structure at a royal centre within the kingdom of Fortriu in Pictland.

Of fundamental importance to the analysis and interpretation of this sculpture is that it comprises a single, unitary narrative scene rather than a random assortment of unrelated images or more than one scene. This is revealed by the visual unity of the scene, which is broadly symmetrical in layout and arranged around the high-cross and Agnus Dei at the crown of the arch. Skene (1857: 278) remarked that the figures on either side of the arch are separated by the cross. Instead, the cross, with its central position and dominant symbolism, unites them. The cross is fundamental to the interpretation of the scene and of the architectural and liturgical setting of the arch (Chap. 9). This composition displays a fine sense of symmetry, with the large figure of the king and the associated bull on the left-hand side being balanced by the two smaller figures of the clerics on the right. The unity and symmetry of the composition are reinforced by the consistent style, pose and appearance of the human figures. All three lean back or recline with their legs, where visible, bent at the knee, carry a staff, wear flowing tunics and have similar facial features, notably prominent noses, drooping moustaches and staring eyes. This scene has been composed and executed skilfully.

The unity of the scene is emphasised by being framed within a prominent moulding and this effect would have been reinforced by the architectural context of the arch, particularly the substantial impost blocks on which it rested (Chap. 9). Visually, the sculpture on the arch comprises a self-contained unit and this, therefore, is how it may be interpreted. It represents a unitary composition and, as such, presumably portrays a specific event, whether historical or mythological.

Any sculpture or monument is the product of a specific time and place and was erected for a particular purpose, to record and express a message. All sculpture tells a story, but its meaning is dependent on the context(s) of the sculpture concerned. The contexts in which a sculpture is produced and viewed influence the impact it has on its viewers and this, in turn, shapes the observers' interpretation of its meaning(s). Although poorly recorded, what little is known about the wider contexts of the arch has already been covered in the discussion of the royal centre, its church and kings in Part 1. The specific context of the arch is, or rather was, provided by its location within the church at Forteviot. This concerns both the structural function of the arch within the fabric of the church and any liturgical or symbolic associations that particular location may have held (Chap. 9). However, because that contextual evidence no longer survives, greater reliance must be placed on the use of comparative sources to shed some light on the iconography of the arch. This should not be restricted to architectural and sculptural parallels, but as the scene on the arch displays a narrative quality, should be extended to myth and legend.

PREVIOUS INTERPRETATIONS

Before analysing the iconography of the scene on the arch, it is worth reviewing previous interpretations. The inherently enigmatic nature of the scene has proved problematic since the discovery of the arch. Skene (1857) made no attempt to explain the sculpture and even Romilly Allen (1887: 240), the leading authority on early Christian symbolism and sculpture of his day, was perplexed: 'I am unable to suggest any explanation of this subject, as it is quite unlike anything which occurs in the contemporary MSS or on Celtic stonework elsewhere'. As a result, although many identifications have been proposed for individual elements depicted on the arch, there have been fewer interpretations of the overall scene and its meaning. Nevertheless, these theories provide a useful starting point for studying the iconography of the arch.

The earliest and most enduring interpretation of the scene identified the main figure as the Hungus of the St Andrews foundation legend, supported by his three sons (MacGibbon and Ross 1897, vol. 3: 623; Alcock 1982: 220; Alcock and Alcock 1992: 226; Lines 1992: 38). But a specific interpretation relating the sculpture to an episode in the legend was lacking, leaving the association uncorroborated. More fundamentally, this interpretation was undermined by the presence of only two, not three, figures on the right-hand side of the arch, while their dress reveals that these were not high-status laymen but clerics. Also drawing on the St Andrews foundation legend, the figures have been interpreted as Regulus and his travelling companions, their staves attesting their status as itinerant clerics (Duncan 2002: 9-10). This, however, is inconsistent with the secular dress of the main figure.

Biblical imagery features in several interpretations. The scene was claimed to depict shepherds watching their flock (Richardson 1964: 7; see also Wagner 2002: 22). This carries a powerful biblical symbolism, of God as a shepherd of men and of Israel (Psalms 23; 80.1; 100.3; Isaiah 40.11). The scene was also described as comprising 'two clerics on either side of what may be a lamb' although, not surprisingly, its precise meaning remained obscure (Laing and Laing 1993: 28). Recognising his secular status, the principal figure was identified as a Defender of the Faith, his office symbolised by the cross and 'altar' beside him (Henderson 1999a: 177). According to this interpretation, the Defender of the Faith and his attendants are depicted protecting not only his flock but also a cross standing on a draped pedestal or altar. In a biblical interpretation that expresses the imagery of pilgrimage, the largest figure is thought to represent Christ the Good Shepherd, holding a staff and with a sheep at his feet, while the two 'wayfarers' represent either the commission to the apostles to go forth and preach to all nations (Mark 16.15-18) or the two disciples returning to Jerusalem after their encounter with the risen Christ on the road to Emmaus (Luke 24.33) (Henderson and Henderson 2004: 145, 209). Less convincingly, the scene is simply described as comprising several saints (Fawcett 2002: 93), but without elaboration.

Interpretations of the sculpture as a biblical scene are unconvincing because they do not take into account the secular status of the main figure, as revealed by his dress and hairstyle (Stevenson 1955: 127). But despite the identification of the principal figure as a king, the arch does not portray a purely secular sculpture. Instead, the prominence of the cross, Agnus Dei and clerics attest the explicitly religious nature of this scene. Indeed, the scene is composed around the cross and Agnus Dei, symbols of Christ's death and Resurrection. Clearly, the interpretation of the scene must accommodate the presence of both lay and ecclesiastical figures on the arch.

SCULPTURAL AND TEXTUAL PARALLELS

In the absence of parallels in Pictish sculpture, the interpretation of the scene on the Forteviot arch is dependent on the analysis of its contents, composition and context, as well as any parallels, in sculpture or other media, from outside Pictland. Analysis of the human figures on the arch concluded that the implements they are holding are not crosses, shepherds' crooks, oars or swords, but staves (Chap. 7). The search for parallels therefore concentrates on this.

The validity of widening the search for parallels to the scene on the arch throughout the Insular world is supported by the external influences that may be detected in Pictish art. For example, some Pictish crosses and interlace designs display artistic inspiration of Irish and Northumbrian origin. This was a two-way process and the Book of Kells, which may have been produced on Iona, displays Pictish influences (Henderson 1982). But although the presence of Northumbrian artistic influence and builders in Pictland is recorded (Chap. 9), Anglo-Saxon sculpture offers no identifiable parallels to the scene on the Forteviot arch.

In contrast, several Irish parallels, both sculptural and textual, for the scene on the Forteviot arch may be identified. A panel on the east face of the high-cross known as the Cross of the Scriptures, at Clonmacnoise, Co. Offaly, depicts two figures in profile standing on either side of a stake or staff (Harbison 1992, vol. 1: 49) (72, 73). The person on the left is identifiable as a monk or cleric from his long, ankle-length tunic worn under a cloak with either a high collar or lowered cowl. The figure on the right wears a shorter, knee-length tunic and is identifiable as a high-status lay person by the sword suspended from a belt around his waist. The status of both figures is also conveyed by the opulence of their clothes. The cleric's cloak is decorated with a wide hem, while the hems of the tunics of both figures are adorned with pellets. These two figures grasp a stake firmly in both hands, their interlinked hands symbolising their unity of purpose.

The scene on the Cross of the Scriptures is not unique. A similar scene also occurs in a panel on the east face of the shaft of a high-cross originally from Ballyogan but now known as the North Cross at Graiguenamanagh, Co. Kilkenny (Harbison 1992, vol. 1: 96) (74). The panel on the north side of the base of the twelfth-century St Tola's Cross, Dysert O'Dea, Co. Clare (Harbison 1992, vol. 1: 85), depicts four figures, at least one of whom is identifiable as a senior cleric from his crook (75). Although the two central figures are too badly weathered to identify whether they are clerics or laymen, both hold a tau cross or T-headed stake, their legs bent at the knees as they use their weight to drive it into the ground.

The Cross of the Scriptures bears two inscriptions which are now badly eroded, although nineteenth-century records of them survive: 'A prayer [or blessing] for Colmán who made this cross for king Fland' (*Oróit do Cholmán dorroinde in Chrossa ar ind rìg Fland*) on its east face, immediately below the panel described above, and 'A prayer for Fland, son of Máelsechnaill' (*Oróit do Fland mac Maelsechnaill*) on its west (Henry 1980; Ó Murchadha 1980; but see Harbison 1979; 1992, vol. 1: 356-7, 368, 371). This refers to Flann Sinna mac Máelsechnaill, Clann Cholmáin high-king of Ireland (879-916), and Colmán, abbot of Clonmacnoise (c.904-26).

Their cooperation is also recorded in the Irish annals for 908: 'The stone church of Clonmacnoise was built by Flann mac Máelsechlainn and Colmán Conaillech' (CS s.a. 908; see also AClon s.a. 901). The Cross of the Scriptures stands before the west door of the principal church at Clonmacnoise, known as 'the Cathedral' or Tempul Mór, which probably occupies the site of the church built in 908 and may incorporate its foundations (Henry 1970: 39).

72 The Cross of the Scriptures, Clonmacnoise, Co. Offaly. *Office of Public Works, Dublin*

Above left: 73 The foundation scene depicted in a panel on the east face of the Cross of the Scriptures, Clonmacnoise

Above right: 74 The foundation scene depicted on the east face of the shaft of a high-cross originally from Ballyogan but now known as the North Cross at Graiguenamanagh, Co. Kilkenny

75 The foundation scene depicted in a panel on the north side of the base of the twelfth-century St Tola's Cross, Dysert O'Dea, Co. Clare. *Office of Public Works, Dublin*

The scene on the Cross of the Scriptures has attracted a wide range of interpretations. Several of these are biblical, including the episode in the story of Joseph in which the cup-bearer gives the cup to Pharoah (Genesis 40.9–15) (Harbison 1992, vol. 1: 49, 85, 96, 203–4; 1994: 38). Most of these, however, are vague and unconvincing and do not take into account the presence of a high-ranking lay person and cleric. More analyses attribute the scene to an episode from the history of Clonmacnoise (Harbison 1992, vol. 1: 49 and refs). These interpretations vary considerably, although the most common is that the scene depicts the foundation of the Church of Clonmacnoise by either Diarmait mac Cerbaill, high-king of Ireland, and St Ciaran, who founded the Church of Clonmacnoise in 545, or Flann Sinna and Colmán. The act of foundation portrayed is obscure because of uncertainty about the object held by the two figures but has been interpreted as the erection of a cross, possibly during the sanctifying of the site, or planting of a staff, ceremonial stake, pillar, post or rod. A common interpretation is that the scene depicts the erection of the corner-post of a church, presumably one of the stout wooden posts that flank the gable ends and bear most of the weight of the roof.

If accepted at face value and associated with the annalistic entries, the panel may depict Flann Sinna and Colmán building the church erected at Clonmacnoise in 908. But there are discrepancies. The church built by Flann Sinna and Colmán is described in the annals as a *damliac*, a term revealing that it was of stone (Macdonald 1981: 307; Harbison 1982: 620; Hamlin 1984: 118), while the figures are shown driving a wooden stake into the ground. As a result, this scene may appear more likely to represent the foundation of Clonmacnoise in 545. This is supported by two accounts which, although preserved in late sources, are both derived from earlier versions. *Betha Ciarain*, the *Life of Ciarán* preserved in the late fifteenth-century *Book of Lismore*, records that 'Ciarán planted the first stake in Clonmacnoise and Diarmait mac Cerbaill was along with him' (trans. Stokes 1890: 276). The vernacular version of the same episode, in *Aided Dhiarmada (The Violent Death of Diarmait)*, is more detailed (trans. after O'Grady 1892, vol. 2: 76–7 (spelling updated and names rendered in a consistent form)):

> The cleric was there in the act of founding a church.
> 'What is the work you do?', Diarmait asked.
> 'To build a little church', Ciarán answered.
> 'That might as well be its name: *eglais bheg*, that is, "little church"'.
> 'Thrust in the upright with me', Ciarán said to Diarmait, 'and [as we do it] allow me to place my hand over yours, so that your hand and your royal rule shall have been imposed on the men of Ireland forever'.

But rather than building a church, these sources, sculptural and literary, concern a common motif in early Irish hagiography, in which a saint delineates the boundary of the enclosure or wider territory around the church he is founding. This boundary defined the *termonn*, the area of sacred ground within which the abbot's authority and ecclesiastical law prevailed. As a result, this was a fundamental act in the founding of an ecclesiastical site and integral to the consecration of the holy ground enclosed within it. As a sacred act of foundation, delineating the ecclesiastical boundary preceded the construction of the church itself.

Boundaries are inherently ambiguous in nature, occupying a liminal zone between the area enclosed and the outside world, but belonging to neither. As a result, boundaries are often associated with anxieties and taboos and are the setting of rituals and/or symbols intended to sanctify or purify them. In the case of early medieval churches and monasteries, these rituals may have included processions around the ecclesiastical boundary, which was often marked physically by a *vallum*, usually an earthen bank and ditch. For example, a ritual procession, including the circuit of holy relics, features prominently in Patrician hagiography and the spiralling route of a processional way has been identified, fossilised within the street plan of Armagh City (Aitchison 1994: 238, 265-81). Processional rituals were also a periodic re-enactment of a divine archetype, the primordial act of creation, replicating the ritual delineation of the boundary at the foundation of the church. Such processions comprised a ritual reconstitution of the boundary, reaffirming its sanctity, security and status and that of the enclosure, church and ecclesiastical community it demarcated.

The scene on the Cross of the Scriptures depicts and commemorates the foundation of the Church of Clonmacnoise by St Ciarán and Diarmait mac Cerbaill in 545. This event was invested with a renewed significance in the early tenth century because both builders of the church at Clonmacnoise in 908 had direct links with the original founders, Colmán as a successor of St Ciarán in the abbacy of Clonmacnoise and Flann Sinna as a direct descendant of Diarmait mac Cerbaill. It is this later event that is commemorated in the inscription on the cross-shaft. The construction of the church by Colmán and Flann Sinna was a re-enactment of the foundation of the Church of Clonmacnoise almost four centuries earlier. Drawing on the legitimacy conferred by an ancient past and auspicious ancestors or predecessors, the Cross of the Scriptures was also a monument to Clann Cholmáin's enduring patronage of the Church of Clonmacnoise. In particular, the panel portraying Ciarán and Diarmait mac Cerbaill, united in their joint act of founding the church, is a powerful expression of royal patronage.

Although these Irish sculptures occur on high-crosses rather than arches or lintels, this is not significant because, like the Forteviot arch, they also belong to an ecclesiastical context. Moreover, another Irish example of this type of scene occurs on a lintel, which is no longer *in situ*, at Carndonagh, Co. Donegal (Henry 1933, pl 114; Sexton 1946: 84; Lacy 1983: 249, pl 23; Harbison 1995: 274-5, fig. 4) (76). This lintel bears a central ringed high-cross, flanked on the right by a panel of interlaced decoration and on the left by possibly five human figures, four of whom are in pairs, holding stakes or staffs between them in both hands. Although identified as a Romanesque crucifixion scene (Harbison 1995: 275, fig. 4), it neither portrays a crucifixion nor is Romanesque in style. The Carndonagh lintel is another early medieval depiction of the delineation of an ecclesiastical boundary at the foundation of a church.

INTERPRETING THE ARCH

The basic element of the Irish scenes discussed above, high-status lay and ecclesiastical figures driving a stake into the ground, also occur on the Forteviot arch. Another parallel is provided by the central cross on the Carndonagh lintel. The arch depicts a scene that is practically identical but adapted for a semi-circular arch and rendered in the distinctively figural style of late Pictish sculpture. These parallels are too close to be dismissed as coincidental. Similarities of artistic attitude, outlook and milieu existed among sculptors, metalworkers and (presumably) manuscript illuminators on either side of the Irish Sea during the late eighth and early ninth centuries (Edwards 1998: 238-9) and close iconographic parallels have been identified between Irish high-crosses and Pictish relief sculpture (Laing 2000: 103-5). More specifically, an artistic link between Clonmacnoise and the Benvie-Dupplin school is indicated by the similarity of figures on the high-crosses at Clonmacnoise and the cross-slabs at Aldbar, Benvie and Invergowrie (Hicks 1980: 19).

The scene on the Forteviot arch reflects close artistic contacts between Pictland and Ireland. This not only suggests that the Irish parallels have implications for the interpretation of the arch but that the arch expresses the same iconography as those Irish sculptures. Fundamentally, the scene on the arch conforms to the standard iconography of ecclesiastical foundation in Ireland and demonstrates that this was also current among the Picts.

On the basis of these parallels, this scene on the arch may be interpreted as depicting the delineation of an ecclesiastical boundary by a king and two senior clerics inserting wooden stakes into the ground to form a palisade. This

76 The foundation scene depicted on a lintel, which is no longer *in situ*, at Carndonagh, Co. Donegal

would have comprised the *vallum* that marked the boundary of the ecclesiastical enclosure. The sacred nature of this act, and of the area thus enclosed, is revealed by the presence of a cross and the Agnus Dei. The scene on the arch depicts the foundation of a church. The arch was found on or near the site of an important early ecclesiastical centre at Forteviot (Chap. 4) and its size and weight preclude that it could have come from anywhere else. The arch, therefore, depicts the foundation of the church of Forteviot. Supporting this interpretation and the association of crosses with ecclesiastical boundaries (Chap. 5), the arch depicts both a high-cross and the erection of a palisade. The cross depicted may not only be symbolic but may depict an actual high-cross, perhaps even the Dupplin or Invermay cross, that marked either the boundary of the ecclesiastical lands or the enclosure within which the church at Forteviot was located.

The interpretation of this scene is independently corroborated by the St Andrews foundation legend. According to this source, Hungus and his sons granted to God and St Andrew land at the royal centre of Forteviot for the foundation of a church. The scene on the arch depicts the foundation of that church. Indeed, the king, in contrast to the clerics on the other side of the arch, is portrayed grasping his stave in both hands and with his back arched, capturing the very moment at which he plunged the stake into the ground and founded the church at Forteviot. This reading of the arch indicates that the fundamental element in the foundation of the church at Forteviot was the delineation of the ecclesiastical boundary around the land given by Unuist. Symbolising the unity of purpose and interdependence of the Pictish Church and kingship, the boundary was marked out jointly by Unuist and two clerics. Just as the large figure depicts Unuist, the two smaller figures on the right of the arch probably depict real people, albeit in a characteristically stylised or figural manner. But who are they? As the scene depicted appears to be historical rather than legendary in nature, it is unlikely to be Regulus and is more likely to represent high-ranking clerics, possibly the bishops of St Andrews and of Fortriu. The presence of the clerics within the scene also has a deeper symbolism, emphasising the involvement of the Pictish Church in the foundation of the *basilica* and the demarcation of its boundary. More fundamentally, the arch was also a powerful expression of Pictish social identity, the king representing his people and the clerics representing the Church.

Several commentators have linked the foundation legend and the arch (MacGibbon and Ross 1897, vol. 3: 623; Alcock 1982: 220; Duncan 2002: 9), although none have been able to explain the nature of the relationship or interpret the iconography of the arch. The scene on the arch both reveals and provides a visual record of a lost detail from an existing Pictish narrative that concerns, among other things, the foundation and construction of the church at Forteviot by Hungus. The close link between legend and sculpture suggests that the St Andrews foundation legend, or at least some elements within it, has a basis in historical reality.

The scene on the arch is an isolated iconographic survival in Pictland, geographically removed from those Irish sculptures with which it displays close parallels. Differences, where they do occur, may be attributed to the sculptor's attempt to execute a similar scene within the confined space of an arch. The ambitious nature of the sculpture is revealed by the manner in which the sculptor adapted the composition to fit a semi-circular field. This he achieved by tailoring the different components to the scene, each one being individually proportioned for, and accommodated within, the limited space available. This is why the Agnus Dei stands upright, the king slouches awkwardly and the clerics are either truncated or compressed. At the same time, the sculptor managed to comply with the Pictish sculptural convention of placing a large figure at the top centre of the sculpture. These figures have not simply been squeezed into the scene. Restricted by the curving field of the arch, the sculptor displays great skill in making the most effective use of a small and awkwardly-shaped field for carving the scene.

The form of the arch lends itself to, and accentuates, the 'floating composition' that is characteristic of Pictish sculpture (on which see Curle and Henry 1943: 265; Henderson 1998a: 103). In this, several elements of the scene appear to be suspended in mid-air, rather than set on ground lines, and are interlocked, leaving little undecorated background. However, by carving it on a semi-circular arch, the sculptor was forced to introduce one major change. The scene was broken up, with the ecclesiastical and secular dignitaries separated and each inserting their own post instead of jointly planting a single stake. This fragmented arrangement may also be attributed to the origins of the scene, which may lie in the copying of an earlier work of art (Chap. 7), but without reference to the context for which it was designed.

This interpretation of the scene on the arch has possible implications for the meaning of the term *palacium*. Although conventionally translated as 'palace' (Chap. 3), the suggestion that *palacium* refers instead to the palisade marking the boundary around a royal site (Cowan 1981: 9) is of particular interest in this context. But the main weakness of this interpretation is that not only palaces, but also a wide range of ecclesiastical, fortified and domestic sites were also enclosed by palisades, as aerial reconnaissance reveals. As a result, Cowan's interpretation of *palacium* and the depiction of the erection of a palisade on the Forteviot arch are coincidental.

The narrative revealed by this reinterpretation of the scene on the arch sheds new light on several aspects of Pictish history. It illuminates a key episode in the reign of Unuist, one of the most powerful, but poorly understood, Pictish kings, and in the history of Forteviot, one of the most important royal centres in Pictland, but which is poorly preserved and little studied. More widely, it also provides a unique insight into the relationship between structures of secular and religious authority among the Picts, notably royal patronage of the Pictish Church. As a testament in stone, the Forteviot arch makes a powerful statement to the largesse of the Pictish kings, the giving of one tenth of the royal centre of Forteviot and possibly its dependent estate to God and St Andrew for the foundation of a church.

By depicting a central episode in the St Andrews foundation legend, this scene also has important historiographical implications. As a sculptural expression of a central episode in the St Andrews foundation legend, the arch confirms the authenticity and mid-eighth-century date of at least this passage and, more generally, the Pictish core of this source. This is particularly important given the rarity of Pictish documentary sources and the fact that they only survive as much later copies, or embedded in later texts, frequently making it difficult to identify their original form and sometimes hindering their attribution to the Picts. This supports a mid-ninth-century date for this part of the St Andrews foundation legend and also has implications for the dating of the arch.

DATING THE ARCH

The iconography of the arch inevitably raises further questions. Who commissioned the arch, why and when? The date of the arch is fundamental to the understanding of its historical context and wider socio-political significance, including royal patronage of the Pictish Church in general and the Church of Forteviot in particular. Without even an approximate date, it is difficult to identify the king portrayed on the arch and/or responsible for the construction of the building it belonged to.

Dating early medieval sculpture is notoriously difficult. In the absence of analytical methods enabling the absolute dating of sculpture, the traditional approach has been to rely on a hierarchy of inference, using the primary evidence of inscriptions, archaeological associations, historical contexts and, less reliably, the secondary evidence of typology and style (Cramp 1991: xlvii–xlviii; Laing 2000). The rarity of legible and decipherable inscriptions, sculpture recovered in dateable archaeological contexts and relevant historical sources means that this hierarchy is of only limited use in Pictland. As a result, art historians are usually dependent on a relative series of artistic sequences. However, this approach, which is based on the identification of artistic similarities and parallels, is inexact. This imprecision is increased where the corpus of material is small in size, has a narrow geographical distribution and is restricted to the same artistic medium. This applies to sculpture belonging to the Benvie–Dupplin school. Moreover, the Forteviot arch is the only example of architectural sculpture from the Benvie–Dupplin school, potentially making it more difficult to infer a date from other sculptures belonging to this group.

The limitations of this approach are apparent from the wide range of dates proposed for the arch and chronological range of the kings claimed to be portrayed on it. These dates range from the eighth to the twelfth centuries and claim a broad range of art historical analogies in support. Skene (1857: 278-9) dated the arch to the eleventh or twelfth century, influenced by his mistaken belief that the semi-circular arch was not introduced into England until the eleventh century and from there to Scotland, possibly during the reign of Edgar (1097-1107). Skene also claimed an artistic similarity between the king portrayed on the arch and the portrait of Alexander I (1107-24) on his coins, concluding that the arch belonged to an alteration made to an earlier palace by Alexander. Allen and Anderson (ECMS, vol. 2: 325, n.1) claimed another twelfth-century parallel, likening the pose of the king on the arch to the portrait of Malcolm IV (1141-65) in the foundation charter of Kelso abbey (69). Although implying a mid-twelfth-century date for the arch, Allen and Anderson did not draw any conclusions from this. In contrast, Stuart (1867: 59) claimed that the arch 'must be assigned to a very early period, probably not later than the eleventh century'. He was followed by MacGibbon and Ross (1897, vol. 3: 623), who identified the king as the Hungus of the St Andrews foundation legend, adding that the building from which the arch came was unlikely to date to as early as the eighth century but may have been added in a tenth-century rebuild. The Hungus concerned is claimed to be the eighth-century Unuist son of Uurguist (Lines 1992: 38).

Ninth- and/or tenth-century dates were favoured for the arch throughout the twentieth century, with scholars unanimous in identifying it as the work of Scottish rather than Pictish sculptors. Mrs Cecil L. Curle (1940: 110) assigned the arch to probably the late ninth or early tenth centuries, as did the National Museum of Antiquities of Scotland, with more confidence (NMAS 1949: 18). Richardson (1964: 8) also suggested a ninth or tenth-century date for the arch and tentatively proposed 'some degree of authorship' with the Dupplin cross. More precisely, Curle and Francoise Henry (1943: 270-1) believed that the Forteviot school of sculpture, to which they assigned the arch, was fostered by Cináed mac Ailpín (843-58) and his successors. Introducing more securely dated parallels from outside Scotland for the first time, Radford (Radford 1942: 17) suggested that the attention to detail evident in the hairstyles and clothing of the figures was inspired by mid-tenth century the Winchester school of Anglo-Saxon art

In the most detailed examination of the date of the arch, Alcock (1982: 223-9) identified three possible options on historical grounds, primarily documentary evidence of royal activity at Forteviot. These date ranges were:

c.710 x c.750: encompassing the reign of Nechtan (?706-24 and 728-9), when Northumbrian builders were active in Pictland, and the earlier part of the reign of his successor, the first Unuist son of Uurguist (729-61)

c.842 x c.900: the period following the traditional takeover of the Picts by the Scots under Cináed mac Ailpín (843-58)

c.1058 x 1165: covering the reigns of Malcolm III and his successors

The Alcocks used artistic parallels to select from these chronological options (Alcock 1982: 229; Alcock and Alcock 1992: 227). They identified several stylistic similarities between the Forteviot arch and sculpture belonging to the Benvie-Dupplin school, which was then dated to the late ninth or tenth centuries. However, the Alcocks did detect some Pictish influences, notably in the joints and double outline of the Agnus Dei. This led them to conjecture that the arch belonged to the period immediately after the Scottish takeover of Pictland and that the church to which it belonged was erected by Cináed mac Ailpín (843-58) or his brother Domnall (858-62).

The Alcocks' conclusions had the appeal of associating the arch with one of the most famous but obscure kings of early Scotland and prompted subsequent claims that the arch belonged to the reign of Cináed (e.g. Lines 1992: 37). But other studies were more cautious and assigned the arch more generally to one of Cináed's (unspecified) successors in the Scottish kingship (Close-Brooks and Stevenson 1982: 40). Recent studies avoid attributing the arch to specific reigns and give a wider chronological bracket, variously dating it to possibly the eighth or early ninth century (Glendinning and MacKechnie 2004: 28-9), ninth century (Driscoll 1998b: 174; Duncan 2002: 9), late ninth century (Foster 1996: 48-9; Fawcett 2002: 93), late ninth or early tenth centuries (Small 1999: 52), late ninth or tenth century (Close-Brooks and Stevenson 1982: 40) or tenth century (Close-Brooks 1980b: 3; Walker and Ritchie 1987: 133). Although overlapping, the wide range of dates proposed reveals the extent of the uncertainty concerning its date.

The assumption behind all these dates rests on Pictish symbols. So central are Pictish symbols to perceptions of Pictish art and, indeed, of the Picts themselves that their presence is widely regarded as an indicator of 'Pictishness'. As a result, Pictish symbols have also been invested with chronological significance, their disappearance traditionally attributed to the socio-political changes occasioned by the Scottish 'conquest' of the Picts, conventionally dated to 843 (Curle 1940: 105; Stevenson 1955: 122, 126-7; Henderson 1975: 11; 1978: 56-7; Laing and Laing 1993: 140; but see Radford 1942: 2-3). The accession of the mac Ailpín dynasty was believed to provide a closely-dated art-historical horizon for sculpture north of the River Forth. The absence of Pictish symbols from the arch has been interpreted as evidence that it dates to after the Scottish takeover of Pictland, c.850 (Alcock and Alcock 1992: 227). In contrast, several stylistic features displayed by the arch point to strong Pictish artistic influences at the very least, if not its production within a Pictish cultural context. These include the form of interlace on the king's hem, the moustaches, clothes, hairstyles and overall artistic style, all of which share traits with sculpture in Southern Pictland. On artistic grounds, therefore, the arch is intimately associated with the Picts.

The only feature portrayed on the arch which is potentially dateable with reference to other sculpture is the cross. Its shouldered shaft and short transverse arms are consistent with crosses of the ninth and tenth centuries. But, in the absence of Pictish symbols, these sculptures have also been interpreted as combining Pictish sculptural characteristics with Scottish artistic influences and are traditionally dated, therefore, to the later ninth century. In the absence of any absolute dating evidence for the Forteviot arch, the only approach available was comparative dating, based on artistic similarities with other sculptures. The problem with this approach is that sculpture belonging to the Benvie-Dupplin school is no more securely dated than the Forteviot arch.

The source of inspiration for the scene on the arch is unclear. It could have been a sculpture, either architectural or free-standing, although surviving Irish examples depicting the foundation of a church all appear to be later than the Forteviot arch. Alternatively, it may have been in another medium. Stylistic parallels or influences have been noted between the figures on the arch and those depicted in some manuscript illuminations (Chap. 6 and above). The *St Gall Gospel Book* belongs to the mid-eighth century and the Book of Kells was produced between 750 and 800. In contrast, Anglo-Saxon manuscript parallels are later, sometimes considerably later, in date. The Winchester school of late Saxon art (on which see Wormald 1971; Wilson 1984: 154-7, 180-90; Laing and Laing 1996: 170-6) belongs to the mid-tenth century, the Southampton Psalter is dated palaeographically to the second half of the tenth or early eleventh centuries, while the Vitellius Psalter dates to *c.*1060. These are later than the Pictish artistic influences or context of the arch, suggesting that they cannot have influenced the scene on the arch. The Book of Kells should provide a more relevant indication of the date of the arch because it displays Pictish artistic influences (Henderson 1982) and was probably produced on Iona, closer to Pictland than these other manuscript parallels. Although its date, like its provenance, has been the subject of much debate, the Book of Kells probably belongs to the late eighth or possibly early ninth centuries (Edwards 1990: 155-6).

The Irish parallels to the scene depicted on the Forteviot arch may provide a new source of dating evidence. These scenes occur on sculpture that is claimed to range from the ninth to twelfth centuries, although most are poorly dated. The most precisely dated of these is the Cross of the Scriptures at Clonmacnoise, which may be dated from the two individuals who are named in the inscription on it. The absence of the formula *oróit ar anmin*, 'pray for the soul of ...', reveals that this high-cross was erected during the lifetimes of Flann Sinna (879-916) and Colmán (*c.*904-26). The date range of *c.*904-16 may be further refined by the spatial relationship between the high-cross with a church built in 908 (above). Another interpretation, based on an alternative reading of its inscription and iconography, dates the high-cross to around the period 830-50 (Harbison 1992, vol. 1: 368, 371), although this has not been widely accepted.

Although the Cross of the Scriptures may imply an early tenth-century date for the related scene on the Forteviot arch, the latter need not have been derived from an Irish exemplar. As with the ringed high-cross (Chap. 5), there is no reason why this motif of the delineation of the ecclesiastical boundary must have originated in Ireland and then spread to Pictland. Moreover, the validity of any comparative dating derived from the Cross of the Scriptures is complicated by the fact that royal involvement in the erection of high-crosses in Ireland is not recorded until the mid-ninth century (Harbison 1994: 104; Forsyth 1995: 243), later than in Pictland (below). The Cross of the Scriptures implies a ninth- or tenth-century date for the scene on the arch. However, uncertainty about the date of the Cross of the Scriptures and the nature of the relationship between the foundation motif on the Forteviot arch and those on Irish sculpture, makes it impossible to be any more precise than this.

The existence of two Pictish kings named Unuist son of Uurguist, who ruled in different centuries, has posed a dilemma for the study of the royal centre of Forteviot in general and its church in particular (Chap. 1). New evidence is provided by the reinterpretation of the iconography of the arch as depicting the erection of the palisade marking the ecclesiastical boundary, a fundamental element in the founding of the church at Forteviot, which the St Andrews foundation legend attributes to Hungus and Regulus. The link between the scene on the arch and the St Andrews foundation legend has implications for the dating of both and, therefore, for identifying the Unuist responsible for founding the church at Forteviot. It is accepted that the legend must have been in existence when the arch was carved and that the interpretation of the scene is independent of the historical veracity of the source, but simply relies on the legend being known when the arch was carved (Alcock 1982: 220; Alcock and Alcock 1992: 226; Duncan 2002: 9). The chronological implications of this have remained unrealised because the earliest elements of the legend remained unrecognised. However, the core of the legend is a mid-ninth-century source, composed during or shortly after the reign of the later Unuist son of Uurguist (820–34) (Chap. 4). This is the king portrayed on the arch. In turn, this identification provides a much closer date for the arch and the foundation of the church of Forteviot than would be expected from archaeological or art historical evidence. However, the status of this evidence is unclear, as either the sculpture or the legend could have been inspired by the other at a later date.

The Dupplin cross (Chap. 5) also has major implications for the dating of the arch and there are good art historical grounds for assigning a similar date to both sculptures. The close artistic similarities between the arch and the Dupplin cross (Chaps. 5 and 6) indicate that they are of a similar date. This is supported by the geographically restricted nature and the small number of sculptures belonging to the Benvie-Dupplin school, which includes both the arch and the Dupplin cross. Reinforcing their close relationship, the Dupplin cross formerly stood only a mile (1.6km) north of Forteviot.

The person who commissioned the arch may be identified from this combination of evidence. The close artistic relationship between the Dupplin cross and the arch indicates that the arch dates to *c.*810–20. This enables the identification of the Unuist son of Uurguist to whom the foundation of the church at Forteviot is attributed by the St Andrews foundation legend because it corresponds closely with the reign of the later Unuist son of Uurguist (820–34). The king portrayed on the arch and who founded the church at Forteviot was the later Unuist of the two kings of this name. No other king is so intimately associated with Forteviot and its church. This Unuist was responsible for building the church of Forteviot and his image dominates the arch that occupied such a prominent position within that church.

The reinterpretation of the iconography and date of the Forteviot arch and the historical core of the St Andrews foundation legend provide new insights into Unuist son of Uurguist (Óengus son of Fergus or 'Óengus II'), King of the Picts. The ninth-century Unuist has long been claimed to be so much more obscure than his earlier namesake that almost nothing is known about him (Skene 1876, vol. 1: 298; Anderson 1973: 99; 1974a: 7). In contrast, a critical reappraisal of the sources reveals that this Unuist, far from being one of the most obscure and poorly documented of Pictish kings, is exactly the opposite. Although his reign remains tantalisingly sketchy, due the St Andrews foundation legend more personal information is known about him than any other Pictish or early Scottish king.

The achievements and reign of this Unuist have long been overshadowed by those of his eighth-century namesake, a celebrated warrior-king who seized the Pictish kingship in battle in 729. Indeed, so great is the reputation of the earlier Unuist that references to an unspecified Unuist son of Uurguist are assumed to refer to the earlier king simply because he was the better known (compare Anderson 1974a: 7). In a self-perpetuating process, references to the later Unuist tend to be misattributed to his earlier namesake, resulting in the apparently more fully recorded Unuist becoming a convenient peg on which to hang any references to a king of that name. This is understandable, given the long reign of the first Unuist and the fact that he is already well documented, by Pictish standards, as a result of his wars against neighbouring peoples. But the conflated sources relating to these kings need to be separated and the mistakenly interwoven lives of the two Unuists disentangled. The reappraisal of both the Forteviot arch and the St Andrews foundation legend (Chap. 4) requires a reassessment of both the source material relating to this king and of the king himself. This would enable the later Unuist to emerge from under the shadow of his more famous and supposedly better-documented earlier namesake for the first time.

An example of the source reappraisal required is of particular relevance to the study of Unuist's patronage of the Church. Three Pictish kings are recorded as patrons of an unidentified Northumbrian church or monastery, probably Monkwearmouth/Jarrow or Lindisfarne, in the *Liber Vitae* of the Church of Durham, which was originally compiled in the mid-ninth century (fol. 12; ed. Stevenson 1841: 2; ed. Gerchow 1988: 304, nos 43, 80, 100; Rollason *et al.* 2004; see also Chadwick 1949: 19; Airlie 1994: 41-3). The kings named are *Custantin* (Causantín), *Unust* (Unuist) and *Uoenan* (Uuen/Eóganán). Although the Unuist concerned is consistently identified as the eighth-century king of that name, the listing of the brother and son of the ninth-century Unuist strongly indicates that the later king is intended. This source records a close dynastic link between these kings and the Northumbrian Church, with Unuist maintaining the relationship begun by Causantín, his brother. This sheds new light on these kings as patrons not only of the Pictish church but as rulers with much wider, even international, perspectives and profiles.

This reinterpretation of the iconography and date of the arch provides independent corroboration of the ninth-century date of the core of the St Andrews foundation legend as well as unique insights into the association of Unuist son of Uurguist with Forteviot, particularly his foundation of a church at the royal centre and his status as an ecclesiastical patron. The Forteviot arch is a graphic and potent testament to royal patronage of the Pictish Church.

9

THE ARCH, ARCHITECTURE AND LITURGY

The structural role of the Forteviot arch reveals that it was a fundamental component of a greater structure. Having examined the iconography of the Forteviot arch, its wider significance may now be investigated. Only by studying the arch within its architectural context will its potential for contributing to our knowledge of Pictish society be realised. In particular, the iconography and structure of the arch provide clues that can assist the interpretation of the form and layout of the church at Forteviot and, through this, the nature of the liturgy celebrated there. What does the arch reveal about the architecture of, and activities performed within, the church at Forteviot?

PREVIOUS INTERPRETATIONS AND PARALLELS

Medieval sculpture and architecture are traditionally studied separately and even treated as disconnected subjects. But the Forteviot arch is undeniably an item of architectural sculpture. This inevitably raises questions and provides clues about the type of structure the arch belonged to. There has been little consensus on this and both ecclesiastical and secular buildings have been proposed previously. Skene (1857: 278) claimed that the arch 'has every appearance of having formed a part of the ancient palace, probably the top of the gateway'. This is echoed in its recent interpretation as 'a magnificent ceremonial entrance arch' to the 'great palace' of Forteviot (Macquarrie 2004: 73) and less specific claims that the arch belonged to a palace (Lines 1992: 37; Oram 2004: 37).This illustrates the ambiguity surrounding the term 'palace' because, although the arch was found on the site of a royal centre, there is no evidence that it belonged to a royal residence. These claims have been influenced by parallels with Carolingian royal palaces (Henderson 1994: 52), particularly that of Louis the Pious at Ingelheim, which was adorned with frescoes portraying hunting scenes, according to his court poet, Ermoldus Nigellus, writing around 826 (Nelson 1992: 137–80).

In contrast, the prominent display of a cross and Agnus Dei on the arch attests its ecclesiastical context and significance, indicating that the arch belonged to a religious building.The arch was first claimed to have come 'from [the] ruins of an ancient church at Forteviot' in 1892 (Catalogue 1892: 262; see also MacGibbon and Ross 1897, vol. 3: 623) and this has been accepted by several subsequent commentators. The Alcocks went further, not only suggesting that the arch belonged to a chapel-royal, but also speculating that this was the western of two churches at Forteviot, that it had a specific association with Easter and was where kings celebrated this major festival in the Christian calendar (Alcock 1982: 220, 222; Alcock and Alcock 1992: 236). However, others have been unable to decide whether the arch belonged to an ecclesiastical or secular building (Close-Brooks 1980b: 3; Cruden 1986: 24; Canmore; NMS exhibit label).

Although the iconography of the scene points to the ecclesiastical context of the arch, comparative material is almost completely absent. Not only is the arch unique, but also no pre-twelfth century churches survive in Scotland. Nevertheless, parallels have been sought for the arch. It has been compared with the arched heads of the doorways of the round towers at Abernethy and Brechin (Richardson 1964: 9). But although the broad moulding around the entrance to the Brechin round tower is sometimes mistaken for a semi-circular arch (e.g. Glendinning and MacKechnie 2004: 28), this megalithic lintel is actually flat-topped, with only its underside carved to give a round-headed opening (*colour plate 22*).This is also the case with the lintels over the doors of the round tower at Abernethy, the south door of the porch-tower at Restenneth Priory, Angus (*77, 78*), and many early Irish churches and round towers. Of 55 Irish round towers with surviving doorways, only one, Glendalough, Co. Wicklow, has a semi-circular megalithic arch (Barrow 1979: 197-200). However, round towers probably date to the eleventh or twelfth century, three centuries later than the Forteviot arch, and had a very different function from the church at Forteviot. There is therefore no discernible link, architectural, artistic or chronological, between the doorways of round towers and the Forteviot arch. As a result, alternative structural parallels must be sought.

Above: 77 Restenneth Priory, Angus

Right: 78 The interior of the narrow
south door of the tower porch at
Restenneth Priory, Angus, showing the
megalithic lintel, rebated to hold a door

No parallels are forthcoming from early medieval Irish churches and the only parallel in Irish architectural sculpture is on a straight lintel from a church that no longer survives (Chap. 8). However, Northumbrian and wider Anglo-Saxon influences in Pictish ecclesiastical architecture (below) and sculpture, including the Dupplin cross (Stevenson 1955: 126; 1971: 73; Mac Lean 1998; Henderson 1982: 83-4; 1999a: 163, 167-70; Wilson 1984: 114-19; Henderson and Henderson 2004: 190-1) suggest that parallels should be sought in Anglo-Saxon England in general, and Northumbria in particular. Facilitating the search for parallels, many examples of Anglo-Saxon church fabric survive and these are well studied (e.g. Taylor and Taylor 1965; 1978; Cherry 1976; Fernie 1983; Butler and Morris (eds) 1986; Gem 1993; 2003). Moreover, our understanding of Anglo-Saxon churches is augmented by recent studies of the symbolic and liturgical significance of their architecture and art (Gem 1983; 1993; 2005; Gameson 1995).

However, there are no close parallels to the Forteviot arch in Anglo-Saxon ecclesiastical architecture. The megalithic arches above the door- and window-heads of about 10 Anglo-Saxon churches are, like the Scottish and Irish examples above, also flat-topped lintels with curved undersides (Taylor and Taylor 1978, vol. 3: 808-12, 847-8). The only semi-circular megalithic arches identified in an Anglo-Saxon church are the inner and outer arches above the west door of the tower at Earls Barton, Northamptonshire, dating to 950-1000 (Taylor and Taylor 1965, vol. 1: 222-6, fig. 99) (*colour plate 23* (*73*)). Shaped megalithic lintels are also used above the lower and bell-storey windows of the tower at Earls Barton and above the windows in the nave and the bell-storey windows of the tower of the Church of St John the Baptist at Kirk Hammerton, West Yorkshire, dating to *c.*1050 (Taylor and Taylor 1965, vol. 1: 361-4). These lintels, however, are not semi-circular in form but betray their origins as square or rectangular masonry blocks, resulting in either a squat or elongated appearance. In addition, no examples of arches bearing sculptural scenes are recorded, although there is evidence that arches within the interior of some Anglo-Saxon churches were used to make public statements (below).

THE ARCHITECTURE OF THE CHURCH AT FORTEVIOT

The ecclesiastical architecture of early medieval Scotland is poorly understood, reflecting the scarcity of evidence. No Pictish churches are known to survive, either as upstanding monuments or even as ground plans. Not surprisingly, Pictish ecclesiastical architecture remains almost completely obscure as a result. However, our poor understanding is also the product of assumptions concerning

79 The tower of the church at Earls Barton, Northamptonshire, showing the curved megalithic lintels

the 'primitive' character of Scottish and Pictish churches. The ecclesiastical architecture of early medieval Scotland has traditionally been perceived as backward in comparison to that of Ireland and Anglo-Saxon England. Indeed, early ecclesiastical centres in Scotland have been claimed to be 'chiefly notable for their simplicity ... scatterings of rude huts around an equally unambitious oratory', with the result that 'there are few signs of any striving after architectural effects in Scotland before the eleventh century, even though the adjacent areas had already seen the emergence of a more monumental approach to [church] design before then' (Fawcett 1985: 28).

This simplistic view is not consistent with the evidence, limited though it is. The Southern Picts had a tradition of stone churches, built under royal patronage, from at least the early eighth century. Bede (*Historia Ecclesiastica*, V.21; eds and trans Colgrave and Mynors 1969: 532, 533) relates how, *c*.710, Nechtan, king of the Picts, successfully appealed to Ceolfrith, abbot of Monkwearmouth/Jarrow, for builders (*architectos*) to construct a church of stone in the Roman manner (*morem Romanorum ecclesiam de lapide*). This contrasted with the traditional technique of church building that Bede (*Historia Ecclesiastica*, III.25; eds and trans Colgrave and Mynors 1969: 294, 295) describes as 'in the manner of the Irish' (*in more Scottorum*), but which prevailed throughout the Insular peoples: 'not of stone but of hewn oak ... with a roof thatched with reeds' (*non de lapide, sed de robore secto*). This stone church remains unlocated, although it may have been near Restenneth (Barrow 1983: 8). Nevertheless, Nechtan's patronage suggests that it was at a royal centre in Southern Pictland.

Marking the inception of the Pictish tradition of ecclesiastical architecture in stone, Nechtan's church was probably a small and simple structure, unicameral (single-cell) or with a small chancel. But this injection of Northumbrian architectural expertise and influence may have stimulated a tradition of church building in stone in Pictland. As a result, Pictish ecclesiastical architecture may have become more confident and ambitious, with later churches growing in size and/or displaying greater architectural and artistic elaboration. A degree of architectural grandeur and opulent ornamentation may be inferred from the status of the church at Forteviot as a *basilica*.

The *basilica* originated in the public building found in the forum of Roman towns and cities, where it formed the municipal administrative centre. This comprised a central nave, essentially a rectangular hall, divided from flanking side aisles by arches or columns supporting the roof. On the adoption of Christianity as the official religion of the Roman Empire, the *basilica* was adopted by the early Church as the model for its places of worship and some *basilicae* were converted into churches. However, in an early medieval Insular context, *basilica* refers to function rather than form, a church of special status rather than meeting the classical architectural definition of a *basilica* as an aisled building.

Nevertheless, Northumbrian *basilicae* comprised aisled churches of stone from the seventh century (Taylor and Taylor 1965, vol. 1: 297-312; vol. 2: 516-18; Fernie 1983: 59-63). Wilfrid's *basilica* at Ripon, North Yorkshire, was 'a church of dressed stone (*basilicam polito lapide*), supported by various columns and complete with side aisles' (Eddius Stephanus, VSW §17; ed. Colgrave 1927: 36; trans. after Colgrave 1927: 37; Webb 1983: 123). And the scale and magnificence of Wilfrid's church at Hexham, Northumberland, left Eddius Stephanus (VSW §22; trans. Webb 1983: 128) awe-struck:

> My poor mind is at quite a loss for the words to describe it – the great depth
> of the foundations, the crypts of beautifully dressed stone, the vast structure
> supported by columns of various styles and with numerous side-aisles, the walls
> of remarkable height and length, the many winding passages and spiral staircases
> leading up and down. Without doubt it was the spirit of God who taught our
> bishop to plan the construction of such a place, for we have never heard of its
> like this side of the Alps.

As the aisled stone church appears to have been the favoured form for *basilicae* in Northumbria, it may also have been introduced to Pictland with Northumbrian influences on ecclesiastical architecture. But there is no evidence that the Forteviot arch belonged to an aisled church, for example, as one of several arches belonging to an arcade dividing the nave from an aisle. Instead, this church, like smaller Northumbrian examples, probably had an aisleless nave. However, one cannot be confident arguing from negative evidence when so little is known about the church at Forteviot and early medieval churches in Scotland generally.

The status, function and royal associations of a *basilica* were discussed in Chapter 4. Their possession of holy relics and association with kings ensured that *basilicae* were richly endowed through royal patronage and with the gifts of pilgrims. As a result, *basilicae* were no ordinary churches but were instead impressive structures, their grand scale and richness of ornamentation expressing their power, wealth, status and connections. As a *basilica*, the church at Forteviot would have been designed to accommodate not only holy relics but also the rituals and pilgrims associated with them. The importance attached to the keeping and veneration of relics probably exerted a strong influence on the planning and form of this church. At its most elaborate, this may have included multiple altars, perhaps in side chapels or aisles, and a crypt to accommodate the storage of relics and the procession of pilgrims who came to venerate them.

Such churches must have been impressive sights, regardless of their material of construction. But what did the *basilica* at Forteviot look like? In the absence of any other evidence, the appearance of the church at Forteviot can only be inferred from descriptions of other *basilicae*, surviving early medieval churches outside Pictland and the arch itself. Of these categories, only the arch comprises direct evidence.

It has been claimed that no significant conclusions can be drawn from the arch (Cruden 1986: 24) and that we can 'only regret the loss ... of a very interesting building' (Alcock 2003: 285). But the arch is the only fragment of church fabric to have been recovered at Forteviot to date and also comprises the best physical evidence, not only for this but for any Pictish church. To dismiss the architectural implications of the arch is to reject the best, and possibly only, opportunity for understanding the form and appearance not only of the church at Forteviot but of Pictish ecclesiastical architecture in general. Although a single fragment can, inevitably, only enable limited conclusions to be drawn, the arch provides significant clues about the church it belonged to, as well as unique insights into its socio-political and liturgical contexts and significance. Inference based on detailed observation and appropriate parallels not only has a legitimate role here but is the only way in which knowledge of the arch may be advanced. Any information that can be deduced from the arch is of value given our profound lack of knowledge about Pictish ecclesiastical architecture and practices.

Even in its present, decontextualised, state the arch reveals much about the church at Forteviot. Fundamentally, the monolithic nature and high-quality carving and decoration of the arch indicate that it belonged to a prestigious church that was both grand in scale and rich in ornamentation. The arch must have come from a church that was not only built of stone but was a substantial structure. Stone walls would have been required not only to support such a heavy architectural feature as the arch but also to maintain the architectural and visual integrity of the building. The arch therefore attests the presence of a masonry church, providing the best physical evidence of ecclesiastical architecture in stone in Pictland. If the quality and scale of the arch were replicated throughout the church then this indicates that the walls were of good-quality dressed stonework in large blocks. The requirement for a level mounting for the arch implies that this masonry was laid in regular courses. The use of a monolithic arched lintel has structural implications for the church. Arches are stronger than straight lintels, enabling them to support heavier loads. The use of an arch implies a requirement for a greater load-bearing strength, capable of withstanding a considerable downwards thrust, such as that produced by a high wall. Although forming the head of a comparatively small entrance, the monumental proportions of the Forteviot arch indicate that it belonged to a substantial structure.

The width of the church walls is indicated by the undressed back of the arch. Its rough appearance reveals that this was not visible, but was concealed within the thickness of the wall. Although the arch did not continue through the full thickness of the wall, the masonry above it would also have required support on the other side of the wall. As a result, the arch probably backed onto another monolithic arch, only the dressed or sculptured front face of which would have been exposed on the other side of the wall. The head of the archway was therefore formed by not one but two carved stone arches placed alongside each other. Assuming the same width for the paired arch gives an overall wall thickness of at least 2ft 4in (0.71m). This, in turn, reveals that at least one of the walls of the church was faced with masonry on both sides and the others walls were presumably similar. The walls of St John's Church at Escomb, Co. Durham (colour plate 24), dating to c.680, are also double-skinned, and also have a uniform thickness of about 2ft 4in (Taylor and Taylor 1965, vol. 1: 209-11; Fernie 1983: 54-6).

The church at Forteviot probably had a very distinctive and impressive appearance, not only distinguishing it from secular structures but also marking it out as a church of elevated status, specialised function and enjoying royal patronage.

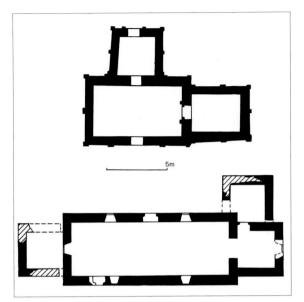 

Above left: 80 Ground plans of St Laurence's Church, Bradford-on-Avon, and St John's Church, Escomb, Co. Durham.

Above right: 81 The interior of the nave of St John's Church, Escomb

This would have been conveyed in various ways, including its prestigious construction, in terms of its fabric, size and proportions. Probably reflecting Irish influences, Northumbrian churches tend to be tall and long relative to their width. For example, the nave at Escomb has an internal width-to-length ratio of 1:3 and the presence of the chancel accentuates this impression of length and narrowness (*80, 81*). This lofty church has an internal width-to-height (at the wall-head) ratio of just over 1:1.5. These proportions contrast with the 'Augustinian' style displayed by churches elsewhere in Anglo-Saxon England, such as the Church of St Laurence at Bradford-on-Avon, Wiltshire (Taylor and Taylor 1965, vol. 1: 86-9; Fernie 1983: 145-50) (*colour plate 25; 82*). These churches are generally twice as long as they are broad, that is, with an internal width-to-length ration of only 1:2.

The interpretation of the arch as a chancel arch (below) reveals that the church was at least bicameral, that is, its interior was divided into two compartments, a nave and chancel. The double-celled church represents either an adaptation of traditional vernacular architecture for ecclesiastical purposes or a simplified distillation of classical architectural forms (Cherry 1976: 160). Constructed of either stone or wood, the bicameral church was a simple structural form and was widespread throughout early medieval northern Europe. Although dependent on the analysis

82 St Laurence's Church, Bradford-on-Avon, from the south-east

of the function and context of the arch (below), the church at Forteviot probably comprised a long and narrow rectangular nave connected to a small square chancel by a tall and narrow chancel arch. This would have distinguished the church by its great height and length relative to its width. The distinction between nave and chancel was clearly marked and would have been readily apparent, both externally and internally. This would have produced an exquisite building with a most distinctive and impressive appearance, the long, narrow and lofty proportions of its nave readily apparent from the exterior. Once inside, its interior space would have been characterised by its compressed plan and soaring height, combining to create an impression of sanctity and dignity. Within this, the chancel was entered through an arch of sublime beauty and grace.

If the form of the Forteviot arch was echoed throughout the church, then its doors and windows, like the surviving arch, were probably also small and narrow for aesthetic, structural and social reasons. Mirroring the arch, doors and windows may also have had semi-circular heads in the form of monolithic false arches. The location of the entrance to the church is unclear, but was presumably either in the west wall, as in Irish churches (on which see Leask 1955; Harbison 1982), or the west end of the south wall, as in Anglo-Saxon churches. Windows were probably set high in the walls and splayed widely on the interior because of the thickness of the walls, maximising the amount of light admitted while keeping out most of the wind and rain. The roof was probably steeply pitched for both aesthetic and structural reasons, complementing the loftiness of the church but also reducing lateral thrust against the wall-heads and assisting the run-off of rainwater. The roof covering was probably thatch or wooden shingles but, for such a prestigious building, may have been of stone. The locally available Old Red Sandstone splits readily along bedding planes into flat slabs to provide ideal roofing material that would have been in keeping with the fabric of the church.

The appearance of the interior of the church is even less certain. Surviving Anglo-Saxon churches often have an air of austerity. However, this impression is probably misleading and attributable to the poor survival of fixtures, fittings and decorations. In contrast, early medieval sources reveal that some churches were structures of considerable grandeur and opulence (Radford 1977; Harbison 1982). For example, the seventh-century timber-built *basilica maxima* at Kildare was described (Cogitosus, 32, §3, 8; trans. Connolly and Picard 1988: 26) as:

> a church with its spacious site and its awesome height towering upwards. It is adorned with painted pictures and inside there are three chapels which are spacious and divided by board walls .... The first of these walls ... is painted with pictures and covered with wall hangings .... This church contains many windows and one finely-wrought entrance ... who can express in words the exceeding beauty of this church?

This is presumably the type of elaborately-decorated church illustrated in the Book of Kells ('The Temptation of Christ', fol. 202v) (*colour plate 26*). Wilfrid's church at Hexham was also richly adorned (Eddius Stephanus, VSW §22; trans. Webb 1983: 128):

> Bishop Acca ... decked out this superb edifice with splendid gold and silver ornaments, precious stones and silks and purples for the altars. What description could do justice to the fabric he installed?

These commentators were almost certainly biased as a result of their close association with the churches whose praises they were singing. But, although they had a vested interest in exaggerating the ornate appearance of their own churches, the general tenor of these accounts is probably accurate. Although limited, archaeological and architectural evidence provides tantalising glimpses of the opulent decoration, rich colours and ornate furnishing of some early medieval Insular churches. The interiors of some Anglo-Saxon churches were decorated with painted wooden panels and coloured plasterwork (Cather *et al.* 1990), while decorated wooden architectural fragments survive from Ireland and Northumbria (Karkov 1991). The ornate appearance and high quality of fixtures and fittings are indicated by a magnificent early eighth-century bronze zoomorphic-headed door handle from an ecclesiastical site at Moynalty, Donore, Co. Meath, Ireland (Ryan 1987; Youngs 1989: 68-9, no. 64). These features would have added character and humanity to churches which were otherwise distinguished by their simplicity of form. Their role, however, was not simply decorative. By contributing to the sanctity and splendour of the interior, they celebrated the glory of God and, in many cases, also conveyed symbolic meaning or liturgical messages.

But the most durable artistic medium in which the status of the church at Forteviot and its associated iconography were conveyed was sculpture. The arch demonstrates that the rich sculptural tradition found in Pictish cross-slabs and high-crosses, including the assemblage from Forteviot and its environs, was also employed by the Picts in architectural contexts. It also reveals that sculptors worked closely with architects during the construction of the church in order to integrate art and architecture. Adding to the richness of its appearance, Pictish sculpture, including architectural sculpture, may not have been intended to be seen in its present state but was possibly decorated with gesso and paint, as Anglo-Saxon sculpture was (Cather *et al.* (eds) 1990; Bailey 1996: 5-7).

The Alcocks suggested that at least one of the recently discovered fragments at Forteviot appeared to be architectural in nature (Alcock and Alcock 1992: 223), but did not identify the sculpture(s) concerned or offer any supporting argument. In contrast, other than the arch, none of the fragments from Forteviot appear to belong to architectural sculpture (Chap. 5). Despite this, the arch attests a strong, confident and skilled tradition of architectural sculpture at Forteviot. This indicates that sculpture played an important role in whatever decorative and iconographic schemes existed within the interior of the church. As a result, the church may have been richly decorated with architectural sculpture. If so, this sculpture may have continued or complemented the iconography of the arch, possibly continuing around the church to form a more extensive iconographic scene. The most likely context for any additional sculpture may have been in the false arches over doors and windows and/or in a string-course, a continuous horizontal moulding set in, or projecting from, a wall surface.

Fragments of *ex situ* architectural sculpture, carved on one face only, are recorded from many early ecclesiastical sites in Pictland, suggesting that they once adorned churches (Hall *et al.* 1998: 136; Henderson and Henderson 2004: 208-9). However, these have received little study, making this an unexploited resource in terms of its implications for Pictish ecclesiastical architecture. These fragments often belong to elongated panels, decorated with sculptural scenes on one side only. Meigle no. 22, for example, is decorated with a two-tailed merman flanked by two beasts (ECMS, vol. 2: 337; Ritchie 1997: 25). Although interpreted as a lintel (Henderson and Henderson 2004: 208-9), this is too slight and probably belonged to a string-course or a wall frieze. Conventions borrowed from architectural sculpture may be reflected on a Pictish cross-slab. The adjoining panels of different styles of interlace – comprising a ten-cord plait of two-ply cord, a diagonal key-pattern of T- and Z-shaped bars and zoomorphic interlace – on the edge of the Dunblane no. 2 cross-slab (ECMS, vol. 2: 317) parallels the juxtaposition of different decorative styles on fragments of friezes from Breedon-on-the-Hill, Leicestershire (Jewell 1986: 111; Henderson and Henderson 2004: 209). Made up of separate panels, this form of decoration could be extended or repeated as required and, as such, would have been ideally suited as a string-course.

String-courses, in plain, chamfered or moulded forms, feature in several Anglo-Saxon churches (Taylor and Taylor 1978, vol. 3: 902-14). Only one early sculptured string-course survives *in situ* in an Anglo-Saxon church, on the west porch at Monkwearmouth, but is too weathered to interpret. Fragments of *ex situ* Anglo-Saxon string-courses or wall friezes survive. Sections of at least two elaborately sculptured and extensive friezes, possibly carved under the patronage of the kings of Mercia in the early ninth century, have been reused in different parts of the church at Breedon-on-the-Hill (Clapham 1927: 219-38; Cramp 1977: 194-210; Wilson 1984: 80-4; Jewell 1986). The mounted warriors, spiral ornaments, key and fret patterns and foliate strands inhabited by birds, men and horsemen display stylistic parallels with Pictish sculpture (Henderson and Henderson 2004: 28, 52, 57, 208-9). Sections of zoomorphic friezes, including a fish, cow, boar and carnivore, survive from Hexham and Monkwearmouth (Taylor and Taylor 1965, vol. 1: 303; Cramp 1984, pt 2: 621-5, 1007-15, 1027, pls 117, 184-5). Friezes are readily paralleled in eastern Christianity, notably in Armenia and Georgia, where relief sculpture decorates the facades, altars and surrounds of early medieval churches (Mepisashvili and Tsintsadze 1979: 221-5; Beridze *et al.* 1984: 31-44, 162-85).

Its status as a *basilica* and the quality of the surviving arch suggest that the church at Forteviot was richly decorated with a wide range of fixtures and fittings, possibly including ornate woodwork, fine metalwork fittings and hanging fabrics. In combination, these may have formed a coherent iconographical programme that encompassed the entire church. An obvious theme would be the life of Christ, with scenes illustrating or symbolising important events from His life being displayed around the church (below). However, if the arch is the sole surviving fragment of such an iconographical programme, it suggests a greater concern with Pictish ecclesiastical and secular subjects, reflecting the interests of the patron and his clients (below). As a result, the iconographic theme within the church may have been provided by the St Andrews foundation legend, with sculptures around the church depicting episodes from it.

Symbolism and location would have been integral to any iconographical programme. Like the arch, these works of art were integral elements of the building, with individual items probably designed to be displayed in specific spaces. These items were probably intended to be viewed in an appropriate context, presumably one that displayed them to their best advantage and maximum iconographic impact. As the focus of the church, much of this decoration was probably concentrated on and around the altar, which was presumably richly furnished. Pictish sculpture provides evidence of this in the form of decorated altar-slabs, panels, shrines and recumbent gravestones, examples or fragments of which have been found at several Pictish ecclesiastical sites (Henderson and Henderson 2004: 197-210).

The adornment of Pictish churches with sculpture is in itself significant. Architectural sculpture performs two main functions. It conveys ideological meaning, enabling a building – or rather its builders and patrons – with ambitions of aggrandisement to signal its status through artistic embellishment. The sculpture in the church at Forteviot was an explicit reflection of its royal patronage, enabling the church to project its royal associations in a conspicuous manner. Sculpture is also a manifestation of power, reflecting the availability and command of the resources required for its production. This includes the stone from which the arch was quarried, the labour required to quarry and transport the stone and the specialised artistic, sculptural and architectural expertise required to design, produce and erect the arch. The scale and quality of the arch attest an ambitious and sophisticated project and the ability to command the resources required has significant social implications. Only a patron of considerable wealth could afford the great costs of building a church that was not only of stone but also decorated with sculpture.

The church at Forteviot received its lands from, and was built by, Unuist, king of the Picts. It is therefore appropriate that the architecture and sculpture of this church reflected the ambition and investment that royal patronage brought. Although the church at Forteviot may still have been fairly small by Northumbrian and later standards, this was nevertheless an ambitious and prestigious church, reflecting its status as a *basilica* and its royal patronage. Its stone construction and lofty proportions would have ensured that it was an impressive structure, dominating the royal centre and the surrounding landscape and visible throughout lower Strathearn. In combination, these various architectural features would have left no doubt about the function, status, and power of the church at Forteviot. Unuist's church at Forteviot was a foundation of both status and architectural accomplishment. The surviving arch from Forteviot is consistent with an impressive, stone-built and highly decorated royal church, fit for a royal centre and a prestigious place of worship of the king of the Picts.

THE ARCHITECTURAL CONTEXT OF THE ARCH

Any further inferences about the form or layout of the *basilica* at Forteviot are dependent on the architectural function and context of the arch. The arch clearly sat above an opening within a wall, but what sort of feature and where? Alcock (1982: 222; 2003: 285) pessimistically claimed that the former location of the arch within the church is impossible to identify and that speculation about its architectural setting is pointless. But despite the loss of both the building to which the arch belonged and its site, the size, form and appearance of the arch all provide clues.

The narrowness of the opening spanned by the Forteviot arch, about 4ft (1.22m), initially suggests that it was a window head. However, this would be unusually wide for an early medieval window, which were rarely glazed and therefore tended to be narrow in order to keep out the elements. One suggested explanation for the small size of the arch is that it belonged to a doorway with splayed-sides, in which the jambs sloped towards each other as they rose, making the doorway wider at the bottom than at the top. Based on the doorways of the Abernethy, Brechin (*colour plate 22*) and Irish round towers (Close-Brooks 1980b: 3), this was the form of the reconstructed doorway formerly used to display the arch in the National Museum of Antiquities of Scotland. But the jambs of splayed doorways slope very subtlely, making little practical difference to the width of the entrance. Moreover, the doorways of round towers provide a poor parallel for the Forteviot arch (above). It is unlikely, therefore, that the Forteviot arch belonged to a splayed doorway.

Despite its small size, the dimensions of the arch are consistent with a doorway or entrance. Indeed, approximately 4ft was a common width for the doorways of Anglo-Saxon churches, regardless of whether they gave access through a porch or tower or directly to the nave (Taylor and Taylor 1978, vol. 3: 818, fig. 664). Moreover, the dimensions of the doorways at Earls Barton are even smaller than those implied by the Forteviot arch: the west doorway is 3ft 3in (0.99m) wide and 8ft 7in (2.62m) high to the crown, while the south doorway on the first floor is only 2ft 6in (0.76m) wide and 7ft 5in (2.27m) high. The south doorway of the porch at Restenneth (72) is also 2ft 6in wide. Although narrow, the size of the Forteviot arch is consistent with that of a door head. However, the arch is not rebated, cut with a groove or recess around the intrados to receive the top of the door when shut, although this may have been in the arch it was paired with. There is no evidence that the arch sat above a doorway. Indeed, the monumental scale and iconography of the arch indicate that it belonged to an even more prominent location within the church.

The surfaces of the arch are in good physical condition and display little evidence of prolonged exposure to the elements while the arch was *in situ*. The extrados is unweathered and retains the mason's original tooling marks, presumably because it was protected by the wall it supported. Despite suffering localised damage, the front surface of the arch and its sculpture are also unweathered. This reveals either that the arch occupied a sheltered position or that the building it belonged to was not standing for long before it was destroyed and the arch buried. The unweathered condition of the arch indicates that it was located within the interior of the church.

Different locations within the church at Forteviot have been proposed for the arch. The arch has been interpreted as forming the top of a doorway and it has been suggested that the doorway concerned belonged to a church porch (Close-Brooks and Stevenson 1982: 40) or the west door of the church and inside a tower porch (Alcock and Alcock 1992: 226-7; Ritchie 1995: 5-6). These interpretations were presumably influenced by the narrow south doorway and megalithic lintel of the tower porch at Restenneth (*78*). But although the lower courses of the tower porch at Restenneth were traditionally claimed to be the remains of the stone church built for Nechtan by Northumbrian builders *c.*710 (Simpson 1963; Donaldson 1974: 1-2; Cruden 1986: 5-6), this fabric is now dated to the eleventh or twelfth centuries (Brown 1925: 67; Fawcett 1985: 28; 2002: 93; Fernie 1986: 397; Cameron 1994: 375). Restenneth is therefore of doubtful relevance because the lintel there is different in form (above) and the porch is three or four centuries later than the church at Forteviot. Reinforcing the case against the siting of the Forteviot arch within a porch, this location would have restricted access to its sculpture, making it visible only momentarily before worshippers entered the church. This would have weakened the impact of the iconography on its intended audience. Its decoration and iconography indicates that the arch occupied a more prominent and readily visible location within the church.

The interpretation that the arch graced the main entrance to the church may also have been influenced by the tympana above the south doorways of Norman churches in the Romanesque style. Tympana, the semi-circular area between the lintel of a doorway and the arch above it, are sometimes elaborately decorated, usually with biblical scenes and/or symbols (Allen 1887: 253-87; Brushfield 1900;

Keyser 1927; Givans 2001). Moreover, the cross and Agnus Dei are the most commonly-occurring symbols on tympana in Norman churches in England (Allen 1887: 253-4). Some tympana, such as that at Beckford, Worcestershire, include a central cross and/or Agnus Dei. This recalls the symbolic components, if not composition and style, of the scene on the Forteviot arch. However, these churches date mostly to the twelfth century and belong to very different architectural, cultural and historical contexts to the Forteviot arch, making this analogy of doubtful relevance.

A location above the exterior of the entrance to the church may be paralleled by some Anglo-Saxon dedicatory inscriptions. Originally, the inscription at Kirkdale, West Yorkshire, was probably set over the south door, but on the exterior, making it visible to anyone approaching the church from that side (Higgitt 2004: 7). The inscription from Odda's Chapel at Deerhurst (Taylor and Taylor 1965, vol. 1: 234-8), which dates the construction of the chapel to 1056, was originally mounted on the wall above the door, according to a medieval chronicle, although the door and wall-face – interior or exterior – concerned are not recorded (Higgitt 2004: 3). Alternatively, the Hendersons' interpretation of the scene as representing the commission to the apostles to go forth to preach to all nations led them to conclude that the arch sat above the interior of the entrance to the church (Henderson and Henderson 2004: 209). As the sculpture would have met viewers' gaze as they left the church, they claimed this as an example of the architectural symbolism identified in some Anglo-Saxon churches.

Other interior locations for the arch have been proposed. It may have sat over the doorway to an eastern annexe (C.A.R. Radford, cited in Alcock 1982: 222), such as those in the pre-conquest St Alkmund's Church, Derby, and Ine's church at Glastonbury, Somerset, which dates to the early eighth century (Taylor and Taylor 1965, vol. 1: 250-7; Radford 1976; 1981). Such a chamber may have comprised a side chapel, possibly containing the shrine and relics of a saint or a royal tomb.

But the most enduring interpretation of the arch is as a chancel arch (MacGibbon and Ross 1897, vol. 3: 623; Driscoll 2002: 35; Alcock 2003: 231, 285). A chancel arch provided access between a rectangular nave, which held the laity, and a smaller chamber, the chancel, sometimes also known as the choir or quire, which was traditionally reserved for the use of the priest. The chancel forms the eastern end and most sacred part of a church and may have housed the altar, the area immediately around which is known as the sanctuary. The focal point of any church is its altar, at which Holy Communion is celebrated. In the case of a reliquary church, as at Forteviot, the chancel probably also held holy relics, in tombs and/or elaborate metalwork reliquary caskets, probably kept on or near the altar. This would have been the focus of a range of devotional acts by worshippers, including pilgrims drawn by the presence of the relics of St Andrew. This area within the church would have provided an appropriately prominent location for such an elaborately carved and monumental arch. In particular, the symbolic references on the arch to Christ's Passion and Resurrection (Chap. 7) reveals that the probable location of the arch, therefore, was over the entrance between the nave of the church and the chancel.

A possible objection to the chancel arch interpretation is the narrow span of the arch. At only about 4ft (1.22m) wide, this is unusually but not impossibly narrow in comparison to Anglo-Saxon chancel arches (Alcock and Alcock 1992: 224). For example, the chancel arches at Escomb (*colour plate 27; 83*), Kirk Hammerton and Odda's Chapel are 5ft 3in (1.6m), 5ft 10in (1.63m) and 7ft (2.13m) wide respectively (Taylor and Taylor 1978, vol. 3: 797, fig. 654). However, the width of Anglo-Saxon chancel arches is determined by both structural requirements and aesthetic qualities, linked to the form and scale of the churches concerned. Odda's Chapel could accommodate a relatively wide chancel arch because of the small size of the overall structure and its relatively squat proportions. In contrast, the loftier church at Escomb necessitated a chancel arch that was considerably narrower in order to support the weight of its higher walls. Moreover, the chancel arch at Bradford-on-Avon is only 3ft 6in (1.07m) wide (Taylor and Taylor 1965, vol. 1: 89) (*84*), even narrower than the Forteviot arch. Although only a single surviving example, this must be regarded as significant in view of the great number of Anglo-Saxon churches that have been lost over time. Bradford-on-Avon demonstrates beyond doubt that the dimensions of the Forteviot arch are consistent with those of an early medieval chancel arch.

The narrowness of the Forteviot arch may be explained in several ways. It may reflect a Pictish architectural style or tradition. Alternatively, it may attest Pictish liturgical practices or ecclesiastical organisation, with the narrow arch obscuring, and therefore mystifying, the rites performed within the chancel and/or the celebrants of those rituals. This might, for example, reflect the strong control that Pictish kings exerted over the Pictish Church. Or there may be a more mundane, structural explanation. Although it seems unlikely on the basis of the arch, the Picts may have lacked architectural expertise or confidence, limiting their ability to design and build more complex features. The use of a false arch, instead of a voussoired arch, supports this interpretation. As any opening in a wall creates a point of weakness, a narrower arch would ensure greater stability than a wide one. In addition, it is also easier to construct narrow arch-heads, whether those involve true or false arches. Finally, the symbols on the arch, its iconography and its liturgical significance all support its interpretation as a chancel arch (below).

Above left: 83 The chancel arch of St John's Church, Escomb

Above right: 84 The chancel arch of St Laurence's Church, Bradford-on-Avon

The height of the chancel arch at Forteviot is uncertain. Northumbrian churches tend to be tall and narrow and this is mirrored in their chancel arches, with those at Escomb and Kirk Hammerton being 15ft (4.57m) and 13ft (3.96m) high respectively (Taylor and Taylor 1965, vol. 1: 237, 364). These tall, narrow chancel arches are the most impressive feature of Anglo-Saxon churches. Anglo-Saxon influence on ecclesiastical architecture in Pictland suggests that the Forteviot arch may have been of comparable height. This may explain the character of the sculpture on the arch. In Anglo-Saxon churches, the amount of applied carved ornament a sculpture carries may reflect how high up it was placed, the more elevated sculptures requiring less additional decoration (Gem 1993: 53, 55). In the case of the Forteviot arch, this may explain why punch-marks were left visible on the surface of the arch, particularly in the recessed background. These marks may not have been visible from ground level, possibly because they were obscured by shadows in the poor light.

The arch was probably sprung from imposts, blocks of stone that distributed the weight of the arch evenly on the supporting wall (85). These may have projected beyond the arch and the jambs, a characteristic feature of Anglo-Saxon ecclesiastical architecture (Taylor and Taylor 1965, vol. 1: 11-12). The monumental nature of the arch reveals that the imposts must have been substantial. It is unclear if they were decorated, although Anglo-Saxon impost blocks are usually either plain and square, chamfered or ornamented with a simple motif. If the church at Forteviot displayed strong Anglo-Saxon influences, the jambs of the archway between nave and chancel may have been constructed using the characteristic 'long-and-short-work', comprising monolithic quoin stones laid alternately flat and upright. This arrangement is sometimes referred to as 'Escomb fashion', after one of the best examples of its type, where it is used in the chancel arch and corners of the church (86). Quoins not only strengthened the chancel arch, an important consideration when supporting a monolithic arch, but also added a decorative effect by emphasising the arch and its edges. If present, the combined effect of these architectural features would have been to frame the arch with monumental masonry, adding to its visual impact, architectural impressiveness and prestige.

The scene on the arch was positioned for ease of reference, an accessible icon. Its elevated location ensured that the sculpture on the arch was the dominant image seen on entering the church and remained visible throughout mass, regardless of how many celebrants there were. The chancel arch and its sculpture performed a range of symbolic functions. Fundamentally, they attracted the attention of the observer to the most important and sacred part of the interior of the church. They also marked the entrance to the chancel and, therefore, the route to the altar and the relics kept there. This entrance, surmounted by the arch, emphasised the sanctity of the altar by forming an architectural frame through which it was viewed. This would have drawn the viewer in as a participant in the rituals celebrated in front of the altar. Equally importantly, the siting of the arch maximised the impact of its iconography on viewers. The simple shape of the narrow entrance into the chancel would have attracted the eyes of observers towards the sculptural scene on the arch. Located above and in front of the altar, the arch reinforced those impressions of space and dignity created by the church and drew the eyes of celebrants upwards to its imagery and towards heaven. The lofty location of the arch and its sculpture must have impressed viewers, who would have encountered nothing even remotely comparable in vernacular architecture. The iconography of the arch transfixed the viewer in front of a frozen moment from a historical narrative depicting the foundation of the church at Forteviot. In conjunction, the location, height and imagery of the arch reinforced its symbolism of royal power and its iconography of royal patronage.

Above: 85 The chancel arch of St John's
Church, Escomb, showing quoins resting
on projecting impost blocks

Right: 86 The jambs of the archway
between nave and chancel at Escomb,
showing long-and-short-work

READING THE ARCH

The interpretation of the arch as a prominently and publicly displayed sculpture depicting the foundation of the church at Forteviot inevitably raises questions about the audience and status of the sculpture it bears. The scene on the arch presumably had a practical function and was intended to be read. But who was communicating through the sculpture, what message or messages did it convey and who were the recipients of those messages? How was the arch read and who was its audience? The architectural context of the arch assists this analysis.

This decorated chancel arch probably fulfilled several functions. Although the context of the arch and some of its components are undeniably ecclesiastical in nature, the scene emphasises the founder rather than the foundation, the king who commissioned the work rather than his commission, the church he built. As a result, the sculpture reflects the perspective of the secular founder, Unuist, and not the beneficiary of his patronage or a third party. The scene speaks on behalf of the king, giving him an active role as the patron of the church. This has major implications for the interpretation of the function of the sculpture.

The Forteviot arch refers to real people, emphasising its iconographic significance and maximising its ideological impact. The most prominent figure portrayed on the arch is Unuist son of Uurguist, the founder of the church at Forteviot, the prominence accorded to him in the scene attesting not only his royal status but also his role as patron. By displaying the image and benefaction of a royal building patron, the scene emphasises that the church was founded and built on Unuist's initiative. The act of delineating the ecclesiastical boundary at Forteviot comprised an explicit, and presumably public, acknowledgement of royal patronage of the church at Forteviot and, by extension, the Pictish Church generally. But this ceremony was a transitory act, occupying only a brief moment in time. Only by recording it in stone was it possible to create a lasting record. Sculpture is a particularly effective medium of communication for the rich and powerful to display acts of patronage in a public and permanent way. As a graphic statement of the foundation of the church, and of the identity and role of its royal patron and protector, the primary function of the scene on the arch was to record Unuist's initiative and achievement. The arch records Unuist's patronage, the foundation and endowment of the church through his gift of part of the royal centre or its estate. The enclosure of that royal land by Unuist is depicted on the arch.

Unuist is depicted on the arch as the *dominus fundi*, literally the 'lord of the estate' or 'landlord', the endowing patron. The scene expresses the theme of *praesentatio*, the presentation of the patron or patron saint to Christ, who is symbolised on the arch by the cross and Agnus Dei. As well as proclaiming the king's largesse, the deliberate inflation of his image would have conveyed to both Unuist and his subjects that the king had received a good return on his investment. A Pictish audience would have understood the significance of this figure's size, appearance and the symbolism of a flamboyant moustache and decorative hem.

The benefits for Unuist of his patronage of the church at Forteviot and portrayal on the arch were both spiritual and secular. An analogy may be drawn between the iconography of the arch and some foundation inscriptions recording acts of patronage in Anglo-Saxon churches. Those from Odda's Chapel and Kirkdale both begin with a cross and the name of the patron (Higgitt 2004). Similarly, the Forteviot arch begins with a cross and the image of Unuist, if read from the crown to the left and according to its most visually arresting elements. The scene invokes the cross as a symbol of salvation, its proximity to Unuist's image revealing the status of the royal patron as a spiritual beneficiary. Unuist probably founded his church in the expectation of receiving certain spiritual benefits in return and had his image displayed prominently inside the church with this in mind. Benefactions to the medieval church were often linked with the welfare of the soul of the founder or patron. Unuist may have believed that a clearly displayed record of his patronage would attract prayers for his soul after his death and his prominent image on the chancel arch was perhaps intended to serve as an implicit call for such prayers.

Kings had other, secular, motives for recording their benefactions in this way. The arch was not only structural in function but also provided ideological support to the king. Early medieval kings were expected to display their wealth and power through conspicuous consumption, including gift-giving and patronage. In an ecclesiastical context, few acts could rival the giving of royal land, the building of a new church and its adornment with monumental sculpture when it came to the display of royal power and patronage. The impression created would have been even greater when associated with a masonry church, which were presumably rare in Pictland. The chancel arch proclaimed Unuist's status and achievements as a Pictish building patron *par excellence*. Moreover, by bearing symbols of Christ's Passion and from its location within the church, the arch invoked God as a holy witness to Unuist's patronage and symbolised the divine sanction for his kingship. As a focus for the display and maintenance of political power, the church at Forteviot celebrated both God and Unuist's own power. Other sculpture and furnishings within the church, and indeed the church itself, probably reinforced this. Paralleling the function of the prehistoric henge monuments and the importance of ancestors at Forteviot, the church was a theatre for the performance of rituals of royalty and laden with ideological meaning. The arch was both an architectural expression of royal power and a source of ideological support to Unuist and his dynasty.

Despite this, the recipients of Unuist's patronage, the church and its clerics, may have had some influence over the sculpture, perhaps in its religious symbolism and/or the inclusion of the clerics in the scene. The church at Forteviot would also have had an interest in displaying this prominent statement of royal patronage. As a public and permanent record of the close royal associations of the church at Forteviot, the scene on the arch may have been intended to reinforce respect for the immunity of the church and the ownership of its lands. In addition, the sculpture was probably displayed with the intention of maintaining the close relationship that existed between the church at Forteviot and Unuist and, therefore, the benefits that this brought in the form of royal protection and patronage. However, the arch did not simply record a transaction in which the Church was the principal beneficiary, but is a product of a symbiotic relationship within which both parties were mutually interdependent.

The Forteviot arch displays a concern with the ownership and patronage of churches and with the context of secular power. The sculpture graphically proclaims the royal patronage and, by implication, ownership of the church at Forteviot. But who was the king trying to impress and why? What audience was addressed by the scene on the arch? As monumental sculpture, prominently and permanently displayed, the arch was presumably intended to be seen and read by as many people as possible, although it may have been directed at an influential rather than a wide audience. Speaking through the sculpture, the patron used the arch to articulate his power and status.

That Unuist's act of patronage is recorded graphically, in a sculptural scene, may suggest a non-literate or partially literate social context (on Pictish literacy see Forsyth 1998), implying that the intended recipients of the message(s) conveyed by the scene comprised a lay audience. But this patronage may also have been recorded in an inscription elsewhere in the church or on an associated monument. The Dupplin cross attests the combined use of both imagery and an inscription to convey royal patronage and power to both literate and non-literate viewers. The Forteviot arch and Dupplin cross comprise records of royal patronage and their close association in space and time may attest a newly active class of church patron and represent a new phase of church building by the sons of Uurguist.

The size of the audience of the iconography of the arch is unknown, but may be equated with the celebrants, whether as participants or observers, of those rituals performed within the church. This may appear to be small by modern standards of size and comfort, but even small early medieval churches could hold substantial numbers. For example, it is estimated that the nave at Escomb could have accommodated a standing congregation of about 84 adults (Alcock 2003: 276) while the Irish annals record the burning of as many as 300 people in churches (Lucas 1967: 191-2).

The interpretation this audience attached to the arch is also unclear. Early medieval audiences may have been experienced at interpreting different levels of meaning in public sculpture. But, just as early medieval iconography requires analysis and interpretation today, contemporary audiences may also have required an explanation of the arch in order to achieve a coherent and consistent message. Bede (*Historia Ecclesiastica*,V.7) refers to an inscription that was addressed to both those who read it and those who heard it, implying that inscription texts were read aloud (Higgitt 1997: 72-3). This may also have been the case with sculptural scenes, particularly those of more complex symbolic and/or ideological significance, which may have required explanation to an audience. Indeed, one function of early medieval sculpture depicting biblical passages was to assist preaching and the teaching of the gospels (Alcock 2003: 75-8). The narration of important sculptural scenes might explain why the foundation legends of Forteviot and Clonmacnoise survive in both sculptural and textual forms.

ARCHITECTURE AND LITURGY

The most likely way in which the meaning of a sculpture within a church may have been explained to an audience was by its incorporation in the liturgy. The liturgy is the order for the celebration and administration of the Eucharist, the sacrament commemorating the last supper, in which bread and wine are consecrated and consumed. This is particularly relevant in this case, because mass would have been led by a cleric standing in front of the altar and below the chancel arch. Moreover, the liturgy would have been celebrated in the presence of the king and senior clerics portrayed on the arch, or their successors.

The Forteviot arch is a chancel arch carrying a graphic record of royal patronage, Unuist's foundation of the church at Forteviot. Studying the relationship between symbolism and setting, the iconography and location of the arch, offers the potential for increasing our understanding of its liturgical and ideological significance. Here it is assumed that the church at Forteviot, together with its furnishings and sculpture, were planned and arranged in the best manner possible to carry out the functions for which they were intended. As the principal function of churches is the performance of divine worship, they may be expected to reflect the liturgical uses for which they are built (Parsons

1989: 1). What does the architectural context of the arch reveal about Pictish liturgy and the manner in which its iconography was used and read?

Symbols are incorporated into churches to enrich them with meaning, to emphasise the tenets of the Christian faith and to hold the interest of worshippers at focal points within the church. Symbols and symbolism reinforce the message of the Church, making the experience of worship more intense and the place of worship more meaningful, attractive and distinctive (Gordon 1963: 83). The nature and function of ecclesiastical symbolism in general, and the iconography of the Forteviot arch in particular, suggest that the arch was displayed prominently within the interior of the church in order to maximise its impact on observers. This is consistent with its function as a chancel arch.

The use of arches to convey liturgical messages is attested in Anglo-Saxon England. The arch over the south portico at St Mary's Church, Breamore, Hampshire (87), bears a runic inscription expressing the covenant between God and man (Genesis 9, 8–17) (Gameson and Gameson 1993), while Bede (*Lives of the Abbots*, 6; trans. Webb 1983: 190–1) describes the attachment of icons around a chancel arch:

> He [Benedict Biscop] brought back [from Rome, in 680] many holy pictures of the saints to adorn the church of St Peter he had built [at Monkwearmouth]: a painting of the Mother of God, the Blessed Mary Ever-Virgin, and one of each of the twelve apostles which he fixed round the central arch on a wooden entablature reaching from wall to wall; pictures of incidents in the gospels with which he decorated the south wall, and scenes from St John's vision of the apocalypse for the north wall. Thus all who entered the church, even those who could not read, were able, whichever way they looked, to contemplate the dear face of Christ and His saints, even if only in a picture, to put themselves more firmly in mind of the Lord's incarnation and, as they saw the decisive moment of the Last Judgement before their very eyes be brought to examine their conscience with all due severity.

Although these examples differ in nature and function from the scene on the Forteviot arch, they convey the visual impact of prominently and deliberately sited works of art within a church interior and their liturgical and ideological importance. The Forteviot arch, whether alone or combined with other sculptures or images, in other media, may have had a similar impact on viewers.

In all this, the church itself constructs both the scene and the viewpoint. The location and iconography of the arch suggests that these informed the viewer about the meaning of the building. Architectural sculpture works in conjunction

87 The inscribed arch over the south portico at St Mary's Church, Breamore, Hampshire

with architecture itself, articulating the building and conveying a specific reading of the structure. The use of sculpture as an integral element of buildings is significant because it elucidates the meaning of architecture itself. If sculptures are signposts then they should be visible and intelligible. In the case of Forteviot, this approach is hindered by the destruction of the church and the absence of information about the nature of the audience, how it looked at the building and how capable it was at reading sculpture. There were, however, several categories of people who knew that buildings contained signs and how to read them: those who commissioned, designed and produced them and those who funded their construction. These parties, each with their own vested interests, probably used the iconography of sculpture to enhance their status and/or that of the church with which they were so closely associated.

The prominence of the cross and Agnus Dei on the arch add to the intensity of the message of the Church and reinforce the building's sanctity and function. But the iconography of the arch is not only ecclesiastical in nature. It also bears symbols of royal power and images of both secular and ecclesiastical figures. The combined royal and ecclesiastical character of the scene makes explicitly political statements about royal power and royal patronage of the Church (Chap. 8). This iconography was reinforced by the location of the arch, which stood beyond the body of the nave and within the eastern 'clerical' area, rather than the western 'communal' part of the church. Moreover, the arch sat above the threshold to the most sacred precinct within the church, the area that housed the altar and, presumably, holy relics and reliquaries. The viewer was being informed about the meaning of the building, the status of those clerics and kings associated with it, and their relationship with God.

The symbolic importance of religious art is demonstrated by the arch and the interpretation of it above. The nature of this symbolism and its relationship to the liturgy now needs to be explored. Very little is known about Pictish liturgy, hindering the interpretation of the liturgical context and significance of the arch. With no surviving Pictish churches or liturgical texts, the only source of evidence is Bede (*Historia Ecclesiastica*, V.21). Although an elaborate church such as that at Forteviot may have had a liturgy to match, the arch inevitably provides only very partial insights. Nevertheless, it throws light on liturgical practices for which there is no evidence from other sources, in particular the relationship between church structure and liturgy.

A direct link between the arch and the Mass supports this interpretation. The Picts adopted the Roman liturgy *c.*710, together with the Roman practice for calculating the date of Easter and the Roman tonsure. A link between liturgy and architecture among the Picts is revealed by Nechtan's request for guidance on liturgical matters at the same time as Northumbrian builders, indicating that they were both sought and provided as a package. The simultaneous adoption of the Roman rite and the construction of a church *in more Romanorum* suggest that the church concerned was designed and built with the requirements for celebrating the Roman rite in mind. Furthermore, this may have initiated a tradition of ecclesiastical architecture in stone which, with its associated sculpture, was influenced by these liturgical requirements.

A more explicit link between architecture and liturgy may also be identified. The Agnus Dei is depicted prominently at the crown of the arch. *Agnus Dei* is also the name given to the formula recited three times by a priest at mass in the Roman liturgy, except on Good Friday and Holy Saturday. It occurs at the Fraction, towards the end of the canon and after the prayer '*Haec commixtio*', which accompanies the *commixtio* or commixture, when a small portion of the consecration bread is placed in the chalice and mixed with the consecrated wine, symbolising the reunion of Christ's body and soul at the Resurrection. In the Roman rite, after completing this prayer, the priest covers the chalice with the pall, genuflects, rises, inclines his head towards the altar and, with his hands joined in front of his chest, says in a loud voice, '*Agnus Dei, qui tollis peccata mundi, miserere nobis*' ('Lamb of God, Who takest away the sins of the world, have mercy upon us'). The priest then repeats the formula unchanged, but on the third recitation substitutes '*dona nobis pacem*' ('Grant us peace') for '*miserere nobis*'. The Celtic rite is very similar and contains the line '*Ecce agnus dei*' ('Behold the lamb of God'). This is preserved in the Stowe Missal (fol. 34b; ed. Warren 1881: 242), which was compiled between 792 and 812 (Kenney 1929: 699).

This three-fold petition to the Lamb of God was adopted by the Roman rite during the papacy of Sergius I (687-701) (Duchesne 1886, vol. 1: 376). The *Agnus Dei* was therefore an element of the Roman rite when it was adopted by the Picts and the fact that it had only recently been adopted suggests that it may have been given a special emphasis. The scene depicted on the pediment above the cross on the cross-slab from Nigg, Easter Ross (ECMS, vol. 2: 75-83; Henderson 2001; Alcock 2003: 77; Henderson and Henderson 2004: 139-41) is of particular interest in this context (*88*). This illustrates an episode from St Jerome's Latin *Life of St Paul the Hermit*, in which the fourth-century desert fathers Saints Anthony and Paul share a meal of bread brought miraculously from heaven in the beak of a raven, symbolising the Holy Spirit. The loaf concerned is the Eucharist, the consecrated host symbolising the body of Christ, as revealed by a missing segment in its lower left-hand quarter, and the descending raven is depicted placing the broken host in a chalice. This chalice stands on the top arm of the cross, which forms a decorated altar front. This scene refers to the *commixtio* (Ó Carragáin 1988: 7-14) and its prominent iconographic representation here attests the significance of this rite among the Picts.

References to royal patronage, possibly including Unuist's foundation of the church at Forteviot, may have been incorporated in the liturgy in Pictland. Although there is no direct evidence for this, one of the spellings of Unuist's name used in the St Andrews foundation legend suggests that Unuist son of Uurguist may have been referred to in the Pictish liturgy. Ungus may represent the sound of his name as it continued to be known, perhaps liturgically (Anderson 1973: 98). Its possible incorporation within the liturgy may also explain the preservation of the St Andrews foundation legend. The scene portrayed on the arch and the liturgy complemented each other. A similar liturgical practice is recorded in Northumbria. At the consecration of his church at Ripon, sometime between 671 and 678, Wilfrid stood in front of the altar and recited a list of those lands given to the church by the Northumbrian kings, who were present (Eddius Stephanus, VSW §17; trans. Webb 1983: 123-4):

> Like Solomon's temple it was consecrated on completion to the Lord and dedicated to St Peter, prince of the Apostles, to gain the help of his prayers for all who might enter. The altar was dedicated and covered in purple woven with

gold. The people participated in the ceremony and everything was carried out according to the canons. Those most devout and Christian kings, Ecgfrith [king of Northumbria] and Aelfwine [Ecgfrith's brother and possibly sub-king of Deira], the kings beneath them, the abbots and sheriffs, and all kinds of dignitaries besides were present. Wilfrid stood in front of the altar, facing the people, and in the kings' presence read out in a clear voice a list of lands which previous monarchs and now themselves had given him for their souls' salvation with the consent and signature of the bishops and all the ealdormen .... God would indeed be pleased with the good kings for the gift of so much land to our bishop. They gave Wilfrid land round Ribble, Yeadon, Dent and Catlow, and in other places too. When the sermon was over the kings started a feast of three days and nights in which all the people took part.

Like Wilfrid's church at Ripon, the church at Forteviot was also founded by royal patronage, the granting of lands belonging to the royal centre or estate of Forteviot by Unuist, king of the Picts. That event is depicted on the Forteviot arch and the message of royal patronage that it conveyed may have been reinforced by the liturgy. The architectural context of the arch, between nave and chancel, provided a meaningful backdrop for the celebration of the Mass incorporating a reference to royal patronage. This, in turn, reinforced the close relationship that existed between kingship and the Church in Pictland and emphasised the power of the Pictish kings and the divine sanction through which they held the kingship. By according the king such prominence, the arch and its context created a visual link between the earthly Mass, celebrated by the king, and the Heavenly Mass, presided over by Christ. Royal patronage of the church at Forteviot reinforces the importance of the physical setting of Pictish kingship, its associated rituals and the concept of divine kingship. The arch was a fundamental component of the architectural context for the performance of rituals of royalty within the royal centre of Forteviot.

The Forteviot arch, in addition to the political iconography of the Dupplin cross, is evidence that the Picts used sculpture to make ideological statements. This scene was intended to be viewed in a specific context, providing an appropriate setting in which the sculpture could be displayed to its best effect and maximum iconographic impact. The chancel arch formed the frame through which the celebration of the liturgy, the altar and holy relics were witnessed by worshippers, further emphasising the prominence and significance of the scene on the arch and its iconographic significance. The physical context of this scene is significant and its appearance on an arch above the entrance to a chancel must have given it added resonance for contemporary observers.

88 The scene depicted on the pediment above the cross on the cross-slab from Nigg, Easter Ross.
Crown copyright: Royal Commission on the Ancient and Historical Monuments of Scotland

The arch itself would have supported and enhanced the meaning of the scene.
Specific architectural forms were invested with symbolic meaning during the
early Middle Ages (Krautheimer 1942; Gem 1983). The form of the arch both
alluded to and reproduced the hill on which Christ was crucified. The arch may
have been perceived as a symbol of Calvary and, therefore, of Christ's Passion,
as the cross and Agnus Dei at the crown of the arch confirm. This suggests that
the arch performed the function of a Station of the Passion, perhaps belonging
to a series of stations in the form of sculptural scenes illustrating or symbolising
important events in the life of Christ, that were displayed around the church, and
for which a parallel may be identified in the pre-Reformation church of Saint-
Riquier in Picardy in the form of tableaux mounted over arches within the
church, with the Passion over the chancel arch (Parsons 1989: 8). Alternatively,
this architectural iconography may refer to the vision of the Lamb of God on
Mount Zion (Revelation 14.1-5), symbolising God's temple and expressing the
longing of the pilgrim and worshipper for their spiritual home.

The location of the altar may have given the scene on the Forteviot arch added
significance. Structural and documentary evidence reveals that the principal altar
in several pre-ninth-century Anglo-Saxon churches stood near the east end of
the nave or in the chancel (Taylor 1973; Parsons 1986; 1989: 13, 18-21). These

altars were therefore located some distance from the east wall of the chancel, where they were commonly sited from the high Middle Ages. If this early medieval arrangement was paralleled at Forteviot, the altar would not have been located against the east wall but free-standing and either within the chancel or just inside the nave of the church. The altar would have stood either behind or directly in front of the chancel arch and been framed by it in either case. The liturgical significance of this is that ceremonies could be performed around the altar, notably at the consecration of the church, and that the celebrant/officiant would have celebrated mass facing west and from a position directly under the chancel arch.

This is a very dramatic, even theatrical, arrangement and has implications for the liturgical practices celebrated in the church at Forteviot and for the symbolism of the arch. It implies the dramatic potential of the Pictish liturgy and that the church at Forteviot and its sculpture were arranged with the symbolic actions of the liturgy firmly in mind. That a priest may have recited the liturgy referring to the Agnus Dei, and possibly including the phrase 'Behold the lamb of God', beneath the arch, with its central image of the Agnus Dei, reinforces this point. This is consistent with the dynamic and interdependent relationship that existed between sculpture and architecture evident in early medieval contexts, in which the setting of a sculpture within a building reinforced the message it was intended to convey (Gameson and Gameson 1993; Bandmann 2005). Although the Hendersons misinterpret the iconography and location of the Forteviot arch, they correctly acknowledge its sculptor's skilled use of the effect that could be achieved by combining sculptural imagery and architectural form within a church and the understanding of contemporary architectural conventions and their symbolism that this displays (Henderson and Henderson 2004: 209).

The sculptor of the arch and patron of the church must have appreciated the symbolic significance of displaying the scene portraying the foundation of the church in this way. Architecture and sculpture combined to portray the foundation of the church at Forteviot as an act of divine intercession, blessed not only by the Pictish Church, in the form of the clerics depicted on the arch, but by Christ himself. Moreover, through his prominence and proximity to the sacred symbols on the arch, the king was projecting himself as ruling by divine right. The arch made an ideological statement about the king's office, projecting it as rightful and divinely ordained in a deliberate strategy to demonstrate the legitimacy of the kingship of Unuist son of Uurguist and to deter potential challengers. The arch attested a covenant between kingship, Church and God.

PART 3

EPILOGUE

10

THE FATE OF THE ROYAL CENTRE AND ITS CHURCH

The most remarkable thing about the Forteviot arch is that it has survived at all. As one of the most significant components – architectural, artistic and iconographic – of the Pictish church at Forteviot, it is only as a result of the greatest act of good fortune that the arch has been preserved. Its survival is all the more remarkable when one considers that it alone remains while all other physical traces of the church, not only its fabric but also its former site, have disappeared completely. But, although in surprisingly good condition, the arch has not survived unscathed. The condition of the arch, and one feature in particular, may provide evidence of an eventful episode in the history of the royal centre and its church. What does the damage sustained by the arch tell us about its fate and that of the church it belonged to? Once again, the arch potentially provides unique insights, not only into the Pictish church and royal centre at Forteviot, but also into a couple of the most obscure episodes of Pictish and early Scottish history. This concluding chapter also examines the decline and abandonment of the royal centre.

The Forteviot arch tells a story, as the analysis of its iconography and context above reveals, shedding new light on the church and royal centre of Forteviot. However, the story told by the arch is not restricted to that intended by its sculptor and commissioning patron. Sculpture can also acquire other meanings as a result of its later interpretation, reuse or treatment. This is the case with the Forteviot arch.

DAMAGE SUSTAINED BY THE ARCH

The arch was discovered in the bed of the Water of May, where it probably came to rest after the erosion of Haly Hill by the Water of May. Despite this, apart from its truncated ends, the arch has sustained very little damage over the past 1100 years, especially when compared to the fragmentary nature of other Pictish sculpture from Forteviot (Chap. 5).

Most early medieval sculpture in Pictland has undergone some form of reuse, with evidence of stones having been cut down for reuse in building work or as grave markers. That the arch bears no signs of reuse suggests that the church at Forteviot underwent a catastrophic event that prevented its retrieval and subsequent reuse. This makes the condition of the central cross on the arch, which has been almost completely obliterated apart from its shaft, of particular interest. This could be accidental damage, sustained when the church collapsed, and a result of the central and uppermost position of the cross at the crown of the arch. Apparently supporting this interpretation, the moulding around the extrados is damaged extensively at this point. However, although the projecting nature and exposed position of this moulding left it vulnerable to accidental damage, the defaced cross cannot be interpreted in the same manner because the adjacent features are completely unscathed. This includes items of fine detail such as the curly hair of the king to the right and the extended foreleg of the Agnus Dei to the left, both of which are so close to the cross-head as to be practically touching it. This implies that the damage to the cross was deliberate rather than accidental, and directed specifically at the cross, while leaving adjacent features unharmed. The cross appears to have been singled out for treatment and removed deliberately. This has implications for the fate of the church to which the arch belonged. This suggests another new narrative, an event of great importance in the history of the arch and the church it belonged to. But what was it and how may this feature be interpreted?

The damage received by the cross implies that the iconography of the arch was deliberately edited relatively early in its life. This has the potential to reveal something significant about the cultural and therefore chronological contexts of the arch and the church to which it belonged. For example, the deliberate defacement of a cross may suggest a period of apostasy, although none are recorded in Pictland. Hindering its interpretation, however, the treatment suffered by this cross appears to be without parallel among the many other crosses in Pictish sculpture. Only one other cross, on the cross-slab from Woodrae, Angus, appears to have been removed deliberately (ECMS, vol. 2: 242–5, fig. 258A). However, this slab was reused in the floor of a medieval castle, presumably necessitating the removal of the relief-carved cross in order to produce an even surface, while its reverse face is also badly damaged. In this case, the defacement of the cross appears to have been for practical rather than religious or symbolic reasons. This cannot have been the case with the Forteviot arch, where the removal of such a small feature could have had no practical consequences for the reuse of the arch, of which there is no evidence anyway.

The damage inflicted on the cross appears to be evidence of an act of iconoclasm. Why was this cross considered offensive when others on Pictish sculpture were not? This indicates that the cross on the arch was not a victim of an official campaign of iconoclasm. What is striking about the Forteviot arch is that the cross, the most obvious Christian symbol, appears to have been defaced deliberately, in contrast to the Agnus Dei next to it, which survives intact. If the damage inflicted on the cross represents a deliberate act of iconoclasm, then this was presumably done by someone with either a limited knowledge of Christian symbolism or someone with a very specific and prejudiced interpretation of one symbol but not another. No obvious context or interpretation is apparent for the latter. That the cross was singled out for removal suggests that it was regarded as offensive and unacceptable, presumably because of its symbolic significance, but that the rest of the scene does not appear to have provoked a similar response. This might suggest the appropriation of the church by a group hostile to Christianity but ignorant of other Christian symbols.

FORTEVIOT IN THE VIKING WARS

A possible context for the destruction of the church at Forteviot is suggested by events in Southern Pictland during the ninth century. Fortriu was subjected to a succession of Viking attacks from the mid-ninth century (Smyth 1977: 143-9; 1984: 141-74; Crawford 1987: 39-53; Hudson 1991: 16; 1994a: 33-4, 66-71). These incursions reveal that Viking aggression was not confined to coastal raids, but was on a larger and more ambitious scale, using estuaries and rivers to penetrate the Pictish heartland in search of new sources of plunder. The Vikings were fielding armies in Pictland as early as 839, when the men of Fortriu (*fir Fortrenn*) were defeated in battle by an army of Dublin Vikings (AU s.a. 838.9). An enduring confusion of the placenames (Chap. 3) has resulted in claims that Forteviot was the site of this battle. Although possible, there is no evidence for this and no location is recorded. However, the identity of the vanquished side indicates that this battle was fought within Fortriu and the Pictish heartland was the focus of subsequent Viking campaigns. The scale of the Pictish defeat in 839 is revealed by the identities and numbers of the casualties. The dead included Uuen son of Unuist (Eóganán mac Óengusa) (?837-9), king of both Pictland and Dál Riata, his brother Bran and Áed mac Boanta (?835-9), (presumably sub-) king of Dál Riata, while 'others almost innumerable were slain' (AU s.a. 838.9).

This heavy defeat has traditionally been interpreted as fatally weakening Pictish power, paving the way for the Scots, under Cináed mac Ailpín, to seize power in Pictland in 843 (e.g. Anderson 1922, vol. 1: 268, n.3; Anderson 1973: 195). However, this link was not made until the late thirteenth century, when the *Chronicle of Huntingdon* (trans. Anderson 1922, vol. 1: 271) recorded that: 'when Danish pirates (*pirat[a]e Danorum*) ... with the greatest slaughter had destroyed the Picts who defended their land, Kenneth passed into the remaining territories of the Picts'. In reality, the Pictish and Scottish kingships were so closely linked through intermarriage that two earlier kings, Causantín (Constantine) (789-820) and Unuist (Óengus II) (820-34), had held both kingships concurrently (Anderson 1973: 193-5; but see Broun 1998b). Moreover, the death of both Pictish and Scottish kings in the battle of 839 indicates that both kingdoms were allied against the Vikings. If the Vikings did influence the political developments of the mid-ninth century, it seems more likely to have been as a result of their activities in Dál Riata rather than Pictland. Viking raids and settlement on the western coast and isles may have pressured the abandonment of royal centres in Dál Riata and the consolidation of the royal power base east of *Druim Alban*, within the Pictish heartland of Fortriu. This, in turn, may explain why Fortriu came under Viking attack from 839.

Viking raids continued unabated after the accession of Cináed mac Ailpín (843-58), during whose reign 'the Danes ravaged Pictland as far as Clunie and Dunkeld' (CKA; trans. after Hudson 1998: 153), implying that these royal and ecclesiastical centres (on which see Alcock 1981: 161; RCAHMS 1994: 88-91; Broun 1999) were among those plundered on this occasion. Dunkeld's importance during Cináed's reign is attested by his translation of the relics of St Columba from Iona to a church that he had specially built, probably at Dunkeld (CKA; trans. Hudson 1998: 152 and n.5; Chap. 4). The area ravaged indicates the extent of the Viking campaign and suggests that they attacked from the Firth of Tay with a sizeable force and advanced up Strathmore and Strath Tay, cutting a broad swathe through Southern Pictland. Another Viking assault is said to have occurred in the twelfth year of Cináed's kingship, 855 or 856 if calculated from the start of his kingship over both the Picts and Scots (*Chronicle of Huntingdon*). Nevertheless, Forteviot clearly retained its importance after these Viking attacks, as the promulgation of laws there during the reign of Domnall (858-62) attests. But worse was to come.

The Viking onslaught on Pictland was at its most intense during the reign of Causantín mac Cináeda (862-76). A raid led by a joint king of the Dublin Vikings in 866 was unparalleled in its ferocity, duration and aftermath: 'Olaf with his heathens ravaged Pictland and occupied it from the kalends of January to the feast of St Patrick', that is, from 1 January to 17 March (CKA; trans. after Hudson 1998: 153-4). Irish annals record that 'the Vikings laid waste and plundered Fortriu, and they took many hostages with them' (FAI, §328 [for 866]; see also AClon s.a. 864; AU s.a. 865.1; Anderson 1922, vol. 1: 292). This was not just an isolated and opportunistic attack, but one that had longer term, strategic objectives, as the Vikings' overwintering and their taking of hostages reveals. It is unclear if Viking raids on Pictland were focused on Fortriu or if this reflects biases in the sources and that attacks inflicted on the Southern Pictish heartland were more likely to be recorded.

But Fortriu was not the only target and, in 870-1, Olaf (Amlaíb) and Ivar (Ímhar), joint kings of the Dublin Vikings, led what was then the largest Viking attack on northern Britain. Although accounts of this are dominated by the siege and capture of the royal fortress of the Strathclyde Britons at Dumbarton Rock, this assault was much more extensive. The Dublin Vikings also ravaged Pictland until the following year, when they took back to Ireland 200 ships full of captive Angles, Britons and Picts or 'Albans' (AU s.a. 869.6, 870.2; FAI, §393 [871]). The identity of the hostages reveals that the Vikings had plundered not only Dumbarton and the Strathclyde Britons but throughout central Scotland, south-east into Anglian-held Lothian and north-east into Fortriu. The Vikings were still reaping the benefits of their hostages up to five years later. But this was not without its risks and, in 872x5, 'Olaf, while taking tribute, was killed by Causantín' (CKA, trans. Hudson 1998: 154; on the dating see Anderson 1922, vol. 1: 352-3, n.6; Hudson 1994a: 51; Miller 1999).

Olaf's death may have deterred further aggression from the Dublin Vikings but no sooner had they been defeated than a new enemy began their attacks. In 875, the 'dark' or 'black foreigners', as Irish and Scottish sources refer to the Danes, attacked, defeating the Picts in battle and inflicting a 'great slaughter' on them (AU s.a. 874.3; see also ASC s.a. 875). The *Chronicle of the Kings of Alba* (trans. Hudson 1998: 154; also trans. Anderson 1922, vol. 1: 353) provides a location: 'a battle was fought by him [Causantín] at Dollar [*Dolaír*] between Danes and Scots and the Scots were slaughtered as far as *Achcochlam* [i.e. *Athfothlam*, Atholl]. The Northmen spent an entire year in Pictland'. This campaign was on an even greater scale than that of 848/9, with the Danes apparently seizing the area between Dollar to Atholl, a distance of some 40 miles (64km), and overwintering in Fortriu. Fortriu, the heartland of Southern Pictland, was overrun by the Danes.

Dollar is a location of strategic significance at the southern foot of the Ochil Hills, 13 miles (21km) south-south-west of Forteviot. It lies only 3 miles (5km) south-west of the meeting point of two routes through the Ochil Hills at Yetts o'Muckhart, both of which lead to Forteviot. One leads north-west through Glendevon and Gleneagles, following the route of the modern A823 to Auchterarder, 7 miles (11km) west-south-west of Forteviot, while the other heads north along the Glendey Burn and the Dunning Burn, following the route of the modern B934, to Dunning, 3 miles (4.5km) south-west of Forteviot. The proximity of Forteviot to the route followed by this Viking army suggests that the royal centre was probably attacked and plundered. As a conspicuous symbol of Pictish royal power and authority, and a source of considerable portable wealth, Forteviot would have been an attractive target.

Although Causantín survived the Viking attack of 875 to fight another day, that day was not long in coming. Causantín 'and many along with him' were slain in battle by the Vikings in 877 (CGG, trans. Anderson 1922, vol. 1: 351-2, n.7), probably at Inverdovet, Fife (Watson 1926: 445; but see Anderson 1922, vol. 1: 353, n.3, 354, n.3). Possibly conflating these two battles, the scale of these defeats is indicated in the bleak comment of an Irish source: 'That was the occasion when the earth gave way under the men of Alba' (CGG, trans. Anderson 1922, vol. 1: 351-2, n.7). There is no record of warfare between these adversaries for a generation but, when it came, their fortunes were reversed. In 904, the men of Fortriu defeated the Vikings in battle and killed Ivar, a leader of the Dublin Vikings, 'and there was a great slaughter around him' (AU s.a. 903.4). The *Chronicle of the Kings of Alba* (ed. and trans. Hudson 1998: 150, 155) places this battle in Strathearn, although it does not record a specific location. Nevertheless, it has been claimed that Forteviot 'was destroyed by Norwegian pirates in 904' (Stuart 1856: 17) and, once again, the royal centre would have been an attractive target to a Viking army.

The Vikings sought slaves and rich metalwork, the richest sources of which were monastic communities and royal centres. While the Irish annals record some Viking successes at slaving, their appropriation of Pictish metalwork, possibly as plunder, is also apparent. A crescentic bronze plaque, decorated with key-work on one side and double disk and Z-rod and beast's-head symbols on the other, was found at the Laws of Monifieth in 1796 but since lost (Roger 1880; ECMS, vol. 2: 280-1; Henderson and Henderson 2004: 88, 90, 95, 225) (*89*). Although most Pictish metalwork seized by the Vikings was probably recycled, this plaque was inscribed with a runic, probably ownership, inscription comprising a personal name, presumably of the Viking who acquired it in Pictland. Relics played a prominent role in Pictish and Scottish warfare, notably as battle talismans and standards (Aitchison 2003: 77, 161). If so, then the status of the Church of

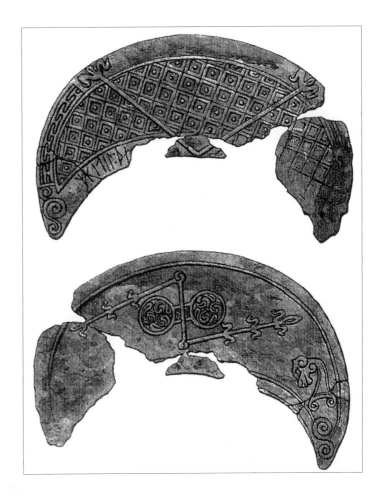

89 The bronze plaque found at the Laws of Monifieth, Angus, in 1796. *Proceedings of the Society of Antiquaries of Scotland*

Forteviot as a repository of relics may have given it added importance in these wars as both a target and muster point.

These events occurred within 50 years of the construction of the church at Forteviot. Uuen, the Pictish king who died in battle in Fortriu against a Viking army in 839 provides a direct link between these events and the construction of the church at Forteviot. Uuen was Unuist's son and direct successor in the Pictish kingship. Moreover, his presence at Forteviot during his father's reign is recorded in the St Andrews foundation legend, revealing a personal link with the royal centre.

The overwintering of Viking armies in Fortriu is recorded on three occasions: in 866, 870-1 and 875. These armies would have needed a base, with quarters. What could have been more appropriate accommodation for them, complete with a ready supply of portable wealth, than the royal centre of the kingdom they had overrun? The church at Forteviot may have been occupied by the Vikings on any or all of these occasions. There may be parallels here with Viking activities in Ireland during the mid-ninth century. When the Vikings seized Clonmacnoise in 845, the wife of the Viking leader desecrated its altar in an act of deliberate profanation: 'And the place where Ota, the wife of Turgéis, used to give her audience was upon the altar of Clonmacnoise' (CGG, trans. Todd 1867: 13). This refers to Ota's celebration of pagan rituals, specifically her oracular recitals (Chadwick 1975: 22-3).

Something similar may have occurred at Forteviot and the abuses to which the church was subjected possibly included the removal of the cross from the arch. Great symbolism can be invested in small acts of iconography or iconoclasm, the significance of which is related to that of the building or item concerned. The neatness with which it was removed and the survival of the Agnus Dei and figures may be explained in several ways, although this inevitably involves some speculation. For example, a Pictish mason may have been forced to remove the cross himself while the Vikings might not have recognised the Christian symbolism of the Agnus Dei and possibly left the figures intact as reminders of their military successes in defeating the Picts and occupying a Pictish royal centre.

FORTEVIOT AND THE SCOTTISH REFORM OF THE PICTISH CHURCH

Another possible context for the damage inflicted on the Forteviot arch is suggested by events in the Pictish Church from the mid-ninth century. The dominant cult in Pictland appears to have changed by or during the reign of Cináed mac Ailpín (843-58) (Chap. 4). Not surprisingly, given the close relationship that existed between kingship and Church, this was accompanied by changes in ecclesiastical organisation and probably the liturgy.

The *Chronicle of the Kings of Alba* attributes the destruction of the Picts by the Scots under Cináed mac Ailpín to divine intervention, claiming that 'God condescended, as reward for their [the Picts'] wickedness, to make them alien from, and dead to, their heritage – they who ... spurned the Lord's mass and precept' (trans. Hudson 1998: 152). This portrays the Picts as heretics and their downfall as divine retribution for their abuses of the Church. The passage is problematical because it reflects later mythological perceptions, dating to no earlier than the 970s, of the conquest of the Picts by the Scots. Nevertheless, the entry may provide important evidence, perhaps of a strategy for replacing Northumbrian ecclesiastical influences in Pictland with Scottish practices (Hudson 1991: 14-5; 1994b: 155-6; 1998: 152, n.2).

Scottish kings were certainly active in reforming the Pictish Church. Giric mac Dúngail (*c.*878–*c.*889) is described as 'the first [king] to give liberty to the Scottish Church, which was in servitude up to that time, after the custom and fashion of the Picts' (Regnal Lists D, F, I, N; ed. Anderson 1973: 267, 274, 283, 290; trans. Anderson 1922, vol. 1: 365). Although paralleled by the freedoms granted by Irish kings to Irish churches, this may be identified as a new dispensation to the Church and one that is intimately associated with the imposition of a new authority (Cowan 1981: 11; Wormald 1996: 142). This suggests a more significant cultural change than that traditionally claimed for the accession of Cináed mac Ailpín in 843, suggesting that Giric, not Cináed, should be regarded as the first of the Scottish kings to rule over Pictland.

But it seems unlikely that the allegedly heretical associations of the Pictish Church provide a plausible context for the defacement of the arch, particularly as Forteviot continued in use as a royal and ecclesiastical centre under the Scottish kings. Moreover, if this was the case, then why have the crosses on other Pictish sculptures not suffered the same treatment? Similarly, it is difficult to detect any association between the damage to the cross and Giric's ecclesiastical reforms, which were presumably administrative and organisational, rather than iconographic, in nature. Although an iconographic difference between Pictland and Dál Riata is suggested by the absence of portraits of Christ on Pictish crosses, crosses without Christ are also recorded in Dál Riata and the cross continued as a religious symbol throughout the Middle Ages. The shouldered cross on the Forteviot arch also occurs on a cross–slab from Applecross (Chap. 7), indicating that its form is unlikely to have offended Scots. A more plausible context for the removal of the cross may have been on the deconsecration of the church. However, the integral role of the church within the royal centre suggests that it is unlikely to have been abandoned or fallen into disuse unless it was replaced. There is no evidence for a second church at Forteviot, although the possibility cannot be excluded. The Scottish reform of the Pictish Church does not provide a plausible context for the defacement of the arch.

FORTEVIOT AND THE SCOTTISH REFORMATION

Damage to the upper part of the cross has also been attributed to an act of iconoclasm during the Scottish Reformation (Alcock 1982: 222; Spearman, cited in Alcock and Alcock 1992: 225). According to this interpretation, the arch was then deliberately demolished and cast into the Water of May, implying that the church to which the arch belonged was still standing until the late sixteenth century.

This claim seems unlikely on two grounds. Firstly, one of the principal grievances of the Reformers was idolatry, the worship of images, and it was against these images and the ecclesiastical institutions associated with them that they vented their anger, wreaking wanton damage and destruction in Scotland on a huge scale (on which see McRoberts 1959). In these circumstances, it seems unlikely that the Reformers would have singled out and carefully removed a cross while leaving untouched the animals and figures on either side of it. More probably, the entire scene would have been defaced and possibly the entire building destroyed, although churches were frequently spared provided that all offending images and objects were removed (Cowan 1982: 190). Secondly, if the church at Forteviot had survived until the mid-sixteenth century, it is surprising that there are no references to it, particularly if it was richly decorated with sculpture.

Nevertheless, the historical and geographical context may lend weight to the interpretation. Perth was a hotbed of Reformation activism and another ancient royal centre also suffered from the reformatory zeal of the townsfolk. Incited by John Knox's preaching in Perth in 1559, Reformers destroyed four monasteries and the altars in the Kirk. A mob from the town then descended on Scone, where they sacked and fired the abbey, church and bishop's palace. But although these events are described in Knox's *Historie of the Reformation* (1587), he makes no reference to Forteviot. Perhaps any action at Forteviot occurred on another occasion, and Knox was unaware of it, or was on such a small scale that Knox and others did not consider it worth recording. But, in the absence of any evidence, it seems unlikely that the church at Forteviot was targeted during the Reformation.

The reason for this is that the Pictish church had not been in use, and may not even have been standing, for some centuries before the Reformation. This conclusion is supported by the good condition of the arch. In pre-Reformation churches, the chancel was usually separated from the nave by a chancel screen, choir screen, rood screen or pulpitum. These were inserted into early churches, their superimposition on the chancel arch often leaving traces. However, there are no signs that such a screen was ever present on the Forteviot arch. Although this is not, by itself, conclusive, it adds weight to the likelihood that the Pictish church at Forteviot did not survive until the Reformation. More fundamentally, the consecration of a parish church at Forteviot in 1241 reveals that the Pictish church had been replaced by that date at the very latest.

THE DECLINE AND ECLIPSE OF THE ROYAL CENTRE

It has been claimed that the Scots abandoned Forteviot after its destruction by the Danes in favour of Scone (Skene 1856: 275-6). In reality, the royal centre survived for another three centuries before its abandonment by the Scottish kings, although the Viking campaigns from the mid-ninth century may have brought about the end of Forteviot's heyday as a royal centre. That Forteviot went into decline after this period is suggested by its absence from the sources until the mid-twelfth century. Forteviot never appears to have recovered from the Viking attacks on Fortriu.

Although Viking raids may have initiated Forteviot's decline as a royal centre, its fate was sealed in the longer term by the rising importance of nearby, and apparently rival, royal centres. In its place merges another royal centre, Scone. Significantly, there are no historical references to Scone before the tenth century and no known early medieval sculpture from the site. Although its origins are obscure, Scone first achieves prominence in 906 (CKA, trans. after Hudson 1998: 155-6), when:

> in the sixth year of his reign, king Causantín [Constantine II] and bishop Cellach, on the Hill of Belief (collis credulitatis) near the royal city/monastery (regali cívítati) of Scone, covenanted to guard the laws and disciplines of the faith and also the rights of the churches and gospels in like manner with [those of] the Scots.

From this point on, Forteviot declined in importance as Scone rose. Scone remained an important royal centre, the inauguration place of the Scottish kings, throughout the medieval period. The contrasting fortunes of these royal centres, located only 7 miles (11km), apart indicates that Scone eclipsed Forteviot as the preferred royal centre of this region around the year 900. This suggests that Scone's construction, or at least its rise to prominence, as a royal centre is a product of the Viking Age. Perhaps paralleling the relationship between the royal centres of the North British kingdom of Strathclyde at Dumbarton and Govan (Driscoll 2003: 82), the new or ascendant royal centre at Scone celebrated the authority of the Scottish royal dynasty which had regrouped and reinvented itself in the aftermath of the Viking onslaught.

The twelfth century also saw the advent and growth of a new form of royal power centre, royal burghs, the first of which were established during the reign of David I (1124-53). One of the most important of these was Perth, which lay even closer to Forteviot than Scone. Perth occupied a location of great strategic importance, beside a ford across the River Tay and with natural defences provided by the small streams running into the river (Duncan 1978: 465, 467-9). Limited archaeological evidence, supported by radiocarbon dates, indicates that Perth's origins as an urban centre began as early as the ninth or tenth centuries (Hall, D. 2004; Hall, M. n.d.). Established as a royal burgh in 1124x27, Perth was an important centre of royal administration and government. This is amply attested by the royal charters issued there and the frequency with which the Scottish parliament met there throughout the Middle Ages. Burghal trade was fundamental to Perth's development, with the Tay providing ready access to a wide range of markets and the customs dues levied from shipping providing an important source of revenue. Forteviot's fate was sealed by its proximity to the royal burgh of Perth and the royal centre and inauguration site at Scone, which retained its importance throughout the Middle Ages. Unable to compete with these contrasting but successful royal centres, Forteviot went into terminal decline and was eventually abandoned by the Scottish kings.

The decline of Forteviot as a royal centre by the twelfth century and its eclipse by Perth and Scone are apparent from the evidence of royal charters. As these attest the frequency with which kings resided at royal centres, the relative importance of Forteviot, Scone and Perth is readily reflected in the numbers of surviving charters issued at these royal centres during the twelfth and thirteenth centuries (eds McNeill and MacQueen 1996: 159-64):

Reign	Place of Issue and Number of Charters Issued		
	Forteviot	Scone	Perth
David I (1124-53)	0	13	5
Malcolm IV (1153-65)	I	0	13
William I (1165-1214)	I	I	46
Alexander II (1214-49)	0	18	8
Alexander III (1249-86)	0	24	3
Guardians of the Realm (1286-92)	0	I	2

The charter evidence attests how the popularity of the royal centres on the River Tay swung between Perth and Scone during different reigns, with Forteviot remaining a distant third. Reinforcing this, the charter granted by William I at Forteviot actually confirms rights on Scone Abbey (Chap. 3). Although few early Scottish royal charters survive, there is no reason to believe that those issued at Forteviot have suffered disproportionately in comparison to those granted at other royal centres. The grants of the Church of Forteviot made by Malcolm IV and William I (Chap. 3) give the impression of the disposal of assets which, although still valuable, were not valued highly by these kings. The impression created by the very small number of royal charters issued at Forteviot, therefore, is that this royal centre had already been eclipsed by Perth and Scone by the early twelfth century.

Although Forteviot's importance as a royal centre had already waned, it still featured in the Scottish Wars of Independence, albeit in a minor capacity. Significantly, the absence of any writs issued at Forteviot reveals that the royal centre was not included in the itinerary of Edward I as he made his triumphalist progress around Scotland during 1303-04 or on his campaign of 1307. Although eclipsed by Perth and Scone, Forteviot's close proximity to them ensured that it featured in the English campaign of 1306. After the defeat of Robert I and his army at Methven on 19 June 1306, the Prince of Wales, the future Edward II, established his headquarters at Forteviot, where he wrote a letter to the Earl of Pembroke on 1 August (CDS, vol. 2: 485, no. 1809). Edward's presence at Forteviot implies the existence of habitable buildings there, while his occupation of a Scottish royal centre may have been of symbolic significance, presumably emphasising the completeness of the Scottish defeat.

The latest recorded royal association with Forteviot, albeit a transient one, was during the Second Scottish Wars of Independence. In 1332, Edward Balliol, son of the deposed King John (1292-96), led a small army to wrest the kingship of Scotland from the newly enthroned infant king, David II (1329-71) (Nicholson 1974: 125-6; Rogers 2000: 27-47; Brown 2002: 23-36). Supported by Edward III of England, Balliol's army was composed of English archers and those Scots nobles who had been dispossessed by David's father, Robert I. After landing at Kinghorn, Fife, on 6 August, Balliol took Dunfermline. His objective was Perth and the nearby royal inauguration place of Scone, but his advance was blocked by a numerically superior Scottish force, led by David's regent, Donald, Earl of Mar, occupying the Gask Ridge on the north side of the River Earn. Edward and his army were forced to halt on the southern bank of the Earn and camped at the Miller's Acre near Forteviot, on the night before their decisive victory over the Scots at the Battle of Dupplin Moor, 2 miles (3km) north of Forteviot, on 11 August. Balliol then occupied Perth and was crowned at Scone on 24 September.

Balliol's choice of camp may have been borne of military necessity and reflect Forteviot's strategic location near a crossing point on the River Earn. But Balliol's presence at Forteviot – like that of Edward, Prince of Wales, in 1306 – may attest his desire to associate himself with Scottish royal centres, as his occupation of Dunfermline and Perth and coronation at Scone demonstrate. Although there is no evidence that Forteviot was still a functioning royal centre in 1332, or had been for around 150 years, its link with the Battle of Dupplin Moor indicates that an awareness of the site's royal associations still existed then. Balliol may have been seeking to boost the legitimacy of his claim to the Scottish kingship and the morale of his army by occupying the ancient royal centre of the Scottish kings on the eve of battle.

When Forteviot ceased to be a royal centre is unclear, and the gap between the latest royal charter issued there, in 1165x71, and its role in the Wars of Independence, in 1306 and 1332, is considerable. Forteviot's status and function as a royal centre certainly appears to have been eclipsed by the reign of David II, when the baronies of Forteviot and Forgandenny (*Fergundeny*) were granted to John de Lyon.

The end of Forteviot's status as a royal centre, and even the dimming memory of its existence, is further revealed by Andrew of Wyntoun's *Orygynale Cronykil* of *c*.1410. Although perhaps a device to explain Forteviot's importance during the reign of Malcolm Canmore, Wyntoun's tale about Duncan and the miller's daughter does not even mention the presence of a royal centre there. With the sole exception of this episode, Forteviot was not the focus of mythological associations. Forteviot slipped quietly into historical obscurity and popular indifference until it became the subject of antiquarian interest in the late eighteenth century.

Forteviot was not unique as a 'failed' royal centre but may be paralleled by *Cinnbelathoír/Rathinveramon*, located on the other bank of the River Tay from Scone (Aitchison in prep.). Both royal centres occupied sites that were threatened by flooding or riverine erosion and were eventually abandoned in favour of the more suitable nearby royal centres of Perth and Scone. Another factor here was the concentration of royal centres in Fortriu. As the kingdom of the Scots expanded from the tenth century, so the kings of Scots needed to conduct their royal progress around a more extensive circuit, inevitably leading to the redundancy of some of the ancient royal centres in the heart of the kingdom of Alba.

But, unlike Forteviot, the ecclesiastical foundation at Scone thrived throughout the Middle Ages. Its success is attributable to its ability to transform itself into an important ecclesiastical centre and its continued royal patronage, due to its status as the ancient inauguration place of the Scottish kings. The church at Scone and its existing *Céli Dé* community was transformed into an Augustinian priory in 1114, when Alexander I founded a stone-built church there and this was elevated to an abbacy around 1163 (Cowan and Easson 1976: 97–8; Aitchison 2000: 83–4). Scone was another of 'the four heid pilgrimages of Scotland' (Chap. 4). The church at Forteviot enjoyed no comparable developments. This probably reflects a decline in royal patronage during the twelfth century, presumably because the royal centre itself was already in decline by this period.

APPENDIX

VISITING FORTEVIOT
AND ITS ARCH

All information given here is correct at the time of going to press, but readers are advised to check with the relevant organisations before making any plans.

Forteviot and its arch are both readily accessible today.

FORTEVIOT

Forteviot is located 5.5 miles (9km) south-west of Perth. Perth is served with good rail and road links. The nearest First ScotRail station is Perth. For rail enquiries and information, telephone 08457 484950 (24 hours) or for website enquiries consult www. firstscotrail.com or www.nationalrail.co.uk. By road, Forteviot may be reached from Edinburgh and the south by leaving the M90 at Junction 9, Bridge of Earn, and then travelling 5 miles (8km) west along the B935. If travelling from Stirling and Glasgow to the south-west, leave the A9 at Upper Cairnie, 5.5 miles (9km) west-south-west of Perth, and join the B934, then cross the bridge over the River Earn and turn right onto the B935 on the other side of the railway line. The B935 crosses the Water of May and Forteviot is located a short distance on the other side.

The Church of St Andrew in Forteviot (National Grid Reference NO052175) belongs to the Parish of the Stewartry of Streathearn, in lower Strathearn, Perthshire. The church houses the Celtic hand-bell and all the early medieval sculpture from Forteviot with the exception of the arch. The church is kept locked when not in use but is open by arrangement.

FOR INFORMATION AND ENQUIRIES:
Revd Colin Williamson
The Manse, Aberdalgie, Perth PH2 0QD
Tel.:   Manse: 01738 625854 Office: 01738 621674 (9.00am – 12 noon, weekdays)
Fax: 01738 643321
Email: stewartry@beeb.net

THE FORTEVIOT ARCH

The Forteviot arch is on permanent display in the National Museum of Scotland, Chambers Street, Edinburgh EH1 1JF The arch may be found above the inner entrance to the Kingdom of the Scots gallery on Level 1.

OPENING HOURS:
Mon – Sat: 10.00am – 5.00pm, except Tuesday: 10.00am – 8.00pm
Sunday: 12 noon – 5.00pm

ADMISSION CHARGE:
Free

FOR INFORMATION AND ENQUIRIES:
Email: info@nms.ac.uk   Web site: www.nms.ac.uk
Tel.:   0131 247 4422   Fax: 0131 220 4819

THE DUPPLIN CROSS

The Dupplin cross is in the care of Historic Scotland and displayed in St Serf's Church in the centre of the village of Dunning (NO019144), 8 miles (13 km) south-west of Perth and 3 miles (4.5km) south-west of Forteviot. From the A9, Dunning may be reached by turning south onto the B9141. The church is open during summer months only, except by prior arrangement.

OPENING HOURS:
Open summer only
1 April – 30 September: Mon – Sun, 9.30am – 6.30pm

ADMISSION CHARGE:
Free

FOR INFORMATION AND ENQUIRIES:
Web site:
www.historic-scotland.gov.uk/properties_sites_detail.htm?propertyID=PL_270

Tel.: 01764 684497
Historic Scotland visitor information service: 0131 668 8800

BIBLIOGRAPHY

The following abbreviation is used:

RCAHMS – Royal Commission on the Ancient and Historical Monuments of Scotland

PRIMARY SOURCES

Aberdeen Breviary: ed. W. Blew 1854. *Breviarum Aberdonense*, 2 pts, Londini, Bannatyne Club; also Aberdeen, Maitland Club; London, Spalding Club; first pub. Edinburgh, 1509-10

ACamb: ed. J.W. Ab Ithel 1860. *Annales Cambriae*, Rolls Series 20, London, Longman, Green, Longman and Roberts; ed. and trans. E. Phillimore 1888. 'Annales Cambriae', *Y Cymmrodor* **9**: 141-83

AClon: ed. D. Murphy 1896. *The Annals of Clonmacnoise, being Annals of Ireland from the Earliest Period to AD 1408*, Dublin, University Press for the Royal Society of Antiquaries of Ireland; repr. 1993, Felinfach, Dyfed, Llanerch

Adomnán, VSC: *Vita Sancti Columbae*: eds and trans A.O. Anderson and M.O. Anderson 1991. *Adomnán's Life of Columba*, rev. edn, Oxford Medieval Texts Series, Oxford, Clarendon Press; first pub. 1961, Edinburgh, Oliver & Boyd

AI: ed. and trans. S. Mac Airt 1951. *The Annals of Inisfallen (MS Rawlinson B.503)*, Dublin, Dublin Institute for Advanced Studies

Aided Dhiarmada: trans. S.H. O'Grady 1892. *Silva Gadelic (I-XXXI): a Collection of Tales in Irish with Extracts Illustrating Persons and Places*, vol. 2: 76-88, 2 vols, London, Williams and Norgate

ASC: trans. M. Swanton 1996. *The Anglo-Saxon Chronicle*, London, J.M. Dent

AT: ed. and trans. W. Stokes 1895-7. 'The Annals of Tigernach', *Revue Celtique* **16** (1895): 374-419; **17** (1896): 6-33, 119-263, 337-420; **18** (1897): 9-59, 150-97, 267-303; repr. 1993 as *The Annals of Tigernach*, 2 vols, Felinfach, Dyfed, Llanerch

AU: eds and trans S. Mac Airt and G. Mac Niocaill 1983. *The Annals of Ulster (to AD 1131)*, Dublin, Dublin Institute for Advanced Studies

Bede, *Historia Ecclesiastica*: eds and trans B. Colgrave and R.A.B. Mynors 1969. *Bede's Ecclesiastical History of the English People*, Oxford, Clarendon Press; trans. L. Sherley-Price, rev. R.E. Latham 1990. Bede: *Ecclesiastical History of the English People*, revised edition, Harmondsworth, Penguin; trans. B. Colgrave, in J. McClure and R. Collins (eds) 1994. Bede: *The Ecclesiastical History of the English People, The Greater Chronicle, Bede's Letter to Egbert*, 1-295, Oxford, Oxford University Press

Bede, *Lives of the Abbots of Wearmouth and Jarrow*, trans. J.F. Webb 1983. The Age of Bede, 185-208, Harmondsworth, Penguin

Betha Chiaráin: ed. and trans. W. Stokes 1890. *Lives of the Saints from the Book of Lismore*, Oxford, Clarendon Press , 117-34, 262-80 ; ed. and trans. R.A.S. Macalister 1921. *The Latin & Irish Lives of Ciaran*, London, Society for Promoting Christian Knowledge

Book of Leinster: eds R.I. Best and M.A. O'Brien 1965. *The Book of Leinster, formerly Lebar na Núachongbála*, vol. 4, Dublin, Dublin Institute for Advanced Studies

Bower, Walter, *Scotichronicon*: gen. ed. D.E.R. Watt 1989-98. *Scotichronicon, by Walter Bower in Latin and English*, 9 vols, Aberdeen and Edinburgh, Aberdeen University Press

CB: trans. B. Colgrave, 'Continuations [of Bede]', in J. McClure and R. Collins (eds) 1994. Bede: *The Ecclesiastical History of the English People, The Greater Chronicle, Bede's Letter to Egbert*, 296-8, Oxford, Oxford University Press

CDS: ed. J. Bain, *Calendar of Documents Relating to Scotland Preserved in Her Majesty's Public Record Office*, London, vol. 1 (1108-1272), vol. 2 (1272-1307), Edinburgh, General Register House

CGG: *Cogadh Gaedhel re Gaillaibh*: trans. J.H. Todd 1867. *The War of the Gaedhil with the Gaill, or the Invasions of Ireland by the Danes and other Norsemen*, Rolls Series, London, Longmans, Green, Reader and Dyer

Chronicle of Huntingdon: ed. and trans. T. Forester 1853. *Chronicle of Henry of Huntingdon*, London, H.G. Bohn

Chronicle of the Kings of Alba: ed. and trans. B.T. Hudson 1998. '"The Scottish Chronicle"', *Scottish Hist Rev* **77**: 129-61

CKA: see *Chronicle of the Kings of Alba*

Cogitosus, *Vitae Sanctae Brigidae* (*Life of St Brigit*): ed. J.-P. Migne 1849. *Patrologiae Cursus Completus*, Series Latina 72: cols 775-90, Parisiis, Garnier; trans. S. Connolly and J.-M. Picard 1987. 'Cogitosus: Life of Saint Brigit', *J Royal Soc Antiq Ireland* **117**: 11-27

Collectio Canonum Hibernensis: ed. H. Wasserschleben 1885. *Die irische Kanonensammlung*, 2nd ed., Leipzic, Vertag von Bernhard Tauchnitz; first pub. 1874, Giessen, J. Ricker'sche; repr. 1966, Aalen

Críth Gablach: ed. D.A. Binchy 1943. *Críth Gablach*, Mediaeval and Modern Irish Series, Dublin, Dublin Institute for Advanced Studies

CS: ed. and trans. W.M. Hennessy 1866. *Chronicum Scotorum: a Chronicle of Irish Affairs, from the earliest Times to AD 1135*, Rolls Series 46, London, Longmans, Green, Reader and Dyer

Eddius Stephanus, VSW: *Vita Sancti Wilfrithi*: ed. and trans. B. Colgrave 1927. *The Life of Bishop Wilfred by Eddius Stephanus*, Cambridge University Press; repr. 1985; trans J.F. Webb, 'Eddius Stephanus: Life of Bishop Wilfrid', in D.H. Farmer (ed.) 1983. *The Age of Bede*, 103-82, Harmondsworth, Penguin

Exchequer Rolls: eds J. Stuart, G. Burnett *et al.* 1878-1909. *Rotuli Scaccarii Regum Scotorum: The Exchequer Rolls of Scotland*, 23 vols, Edinburgh, HM General Register House

FAI: ed. and trans. J.N. Radner 1978. *Fragmentary Annals of Ireland*, Dublin, Dublin Institute for Advanced Studies

Fordun, John of, *Chronica Gentis Scotorum*; ed. W.F. Skene 1871. *Johannis de Fordun* Chronica Gentis Scotorum, Edinburgh; trans. F.J.H. Skene 1872. *John of Fordun's Chronicle of the Scottish Nation*, Edinburgh, Historians of Scotland; trans. repr. 1993, 2 vols, Felinfach, Dyfed, Llanerch

Liber Cartarum: ed. T. Thomson 1841. *Liber Cartarum Prioratus Sancti Andree in Scotia*, Edinburgh, Bannatyne Club

Liber Vitae of the Church of Durham: ed. J. Stevenson 1841. *Liber Vitae Ecclesiae Dunelmensis*, Publications of the Surtees Society, London, J.B. Nichols and Son; ed. J. Gerchow 1988. *Die Gedenküberlieferung der Angelsachsen: Mit einem Katalog der libri vitae und Necrologien*, Arbeiten zur Frühmittelalterforschung 20, Berlin, Walter de Gruyter

Life of St Cadog (*Vita Sancti Cadoci*): ed. and trans. A.W. Wade-Evans 1944. *Vitae Sanctorum Britanniae et Genealogiae*, 24-141, Board of Celtic Studies History and Law Series no. 9, Cardiff, University of Wales Press Board

O'Davoren's Glossary: ed. W. Stokes 1904. *Archiv für celtische Lexikographie* **2**: 197-504

O'Mulconry's Glossary: ed. W. Stokes, in W. Stokes and K. Meyer (eds) 1898. *Archiv für celtische Lexikographie* **1**: 232-324, 473-81, 629

Prophecy of Berchán: ed. and trans. B.T. Hudson 1996. *Prophecy of Berchán: Irish and Scottish High-Kings of the Early Middle Ages*, Westport, Conn., Greenwood Press

RMS: eds J.M. Thomson *et al.* 1882-1912. *Registrum Magni Sigilli Regum Scotorum: the Register of the Great Seal of Scotland*, 11 vols, Edinburgh, H.M. General Register House

Romano-German Pontifical: ed. C. Vogel, 1963. *Le pontifical romano-germanique du dixieme siècle*, I, Studi e testi 226, Città del Vatticano

RRS: *Regesta Regum Scottorum*: ed. G.W.S. Barrow 1960. *The Acts of Malcolm IV, King of Scots, 1153-1165*, RRS vol. 1; eds G.W.S. Barrow with W.W. Scott 1971. *The Acts of William I, King of Scots, 1165-1214*, RRS vol. 2; ed. A.A.M. Duncan 1988. *The Acts of Robert I, King of Scots, 1306-1329*, RRS vol. 5; ed. B. Webster 1982. *The Acts of David II, King of Scots, 1329-1371*, RRS 6, Edinburgh University Press

Scottish Chronicle: see Chronicle of the Kings of Alba

Togail Bruidne Dá Derga (*The Destruction of Da Derga's Hostel*): trans. J. Gantz 1981. *Early Irish Myths and Legends*, 60-106, Harmondsworth, Penguin

Wyntoun, Andrew of: *Orygynale Cronykil of Scotland*: ed. F.J. Amours 1903-14. *The Original Chronicle of Andrew of Wyntoun*, 6 vols, Edinburgh, Scottish Text Society

SECONDARY SOURCES

Adamson, H. 1638. *The Muses Threnodie, or, Mirthfull Mournings on the Death of Master Gall*, Edinburgh, George Anderson; rev. edn., ed. J. Cant, 1774. 2 vols, Perth, George Johnston

Airlie, S. 1990. 'Bonds of power and bonds of association in the court circle of Louis the Pious', in P. Godman and R. Collins (eds), *Charlemagne's Heir: New Perspectives on the Reign of Louis the Pious (814-840)*, 191-204, Oxford, Clarendon Press

Airlie, S. 1994. 'The view from Maastricht', in B.E. Crawford (ed.), *Scotland in Dark Age Europe*, 33-46, St John's House Papers 5, St Andrews, Committee for Dark Age Studies, University of St Andrews

Aitchison, N.B. 1994. *Armagh and the Royal Centres in Early Medieval Ireland: Monuments, Cosmology and the Past*, Woodbridge, Cruithne Press/Boydell & Brewer

Aitchison, N.B. 1999. *Macbeth: Man and Myth*, Stroud, Sutton

Aitchison, N. 2000. *Scotland's Stone of Destiny: Myth, History and Nationhood*, Stroud, Tempus

Aitchison, N. 2003. *The Picts and the Scots at War*, Stroud, Sutton

Aitchison, N. in prep. 'Bellethor/Cinnbelathoír: a lost *palacium* and *urbs* of King Domnall mac Ailpín'

Alcock, E. 1992. 'Burials and cemeteries in Scotland', in N. Edwards and A. Lane (eds), *The Early Church in Wales and the West: Recent Work in Early Christian Archaeology, History and Place-Names*, 125-9, Oxbow Monograph 16, Oxford, Oxbow Books

Alcock, L. 1981. 'Early historic fortifications in Scotland', in G. Guilbert (ed.), *Hillfort Studies: Essays for A.H.A. Hogg*, 150-80, Leicester, Leicester University Press

Alcock, L. 1982. 'Forteviot: a Pictish and Scottish royal church and palace', in S.M. Pearce (ed.), *The Early Church in Western Britain and Ireland: Studies Presented to C.A. Ralegh Radford*, 211-39, BAR British Series 102, Oxford, BAR

Alcock, L. 1988. *Bede, Eddius, and the Forts of the North Britons*, Jarrow Lecture 1988, np

Alcock, L. 1993. 'Image and icon in Pictish sculpture', in Spearman and Higgitt (eds) 1993: 230-6

Alcock, L. 1995. 'What is David doing to a lion?', *Pictish Arts Soc J* **7**: 1-2

Alcock, L. 1998. 'From realism to caricature: reflections on Insular depictions of animals and people', *Proc Soc Antiq Scotland* **128**: 515-36

Alcock, L. 2003. *Kings and Warriors, Craftsmen and Priests in Northern Britain, AD 550-850*, Monograph Series no. 24, Edinburgh, Society of Antiquaries of Scotland

Alcock, L. and Alcock, E.A. 1990. 'Reconnaissance excavations on early historic fortifications and other royal sites in Scotland, 1974-1984. 4, Excavations at Alt Clut, Clyde Rock, Strathclyde, 1974-5', *Proc Soc Antiq Scotland* **120**: 95-149

Alcock, L. and Alcock, E.A. 1992. 'Reconnaissance excavations on early historic fortifications and other royal sites in Scotland, 1974-84; 5: A, excavations & other fieldwork at Forteviot, Perthshire, 1981; B, excavations at Urquhart Castle, Inverness-shire, 1983; C, excavations at Dunnottar, Kincardineshire, 1984', *Proc Soc Antiq Scotland* **122**: 215-87

Alcock, L. and Alcock, E.A. 1996. 'The context of the Dupplin cross: a reconsideration', *Proc Soc Antiq Scotland* **126**: 455-7

Alcock, L., Alcock, E.A. and Driscoll, S.T. 1990. 'Reconnaissance excavations on early historic fortifications and other royal sites in Scotland, 1974-84: 3, excavations at Dundurn, Strathearn, Perthshire, 1976-77', Proc Soc Antiq Scotland 119 (1989): 189-226

Alcock, L., Alcock, E.A. and Foster, S.M. 1987. 'Reconnaissance excavations on early historic fortifications and other royal sites in Scotland, 1974-84: 1, excavations near St Abb's Head, Berwickshire, 1980', *Proc Soc Antiq Scotland* **116** (1986): 255-79

Alexander, D. 2000. 'Red Castle, Lunan Bay, Angus', *Discovery and Excavation in Scotland, 1999*, 111

Alexander, D. and Dunwell, A. 2003. 'Red Castle', *Discovery and Excavation in Scotland* (new series) **3** (2002): 144

Alexander, J.J.G. 1978. *Insular Manuscripts, 6th to the 9th Century*, A Survey of Manuscripts Illuminated in the British Isles 1, London, Harvey Miller

Allen, J.R. 1884. 'Notes on early Christian symbolism', *Proc Soc Antiq Scotland* **18** (1883-4): 380-464

Allen, J.R. 1887. *Early Christian Symbolism in Great Britain and Ireland before the Thirteenth Century*, The Rhind Lectures in Archaeology for 1885, London, Whiting & Co

Allen, J.R. 1904. *Celtic Art in Pagan and Christian Times*, London, Methuen & Co

Anderson, A.O. (ed. and trans.) 1908. *Scottish Annals from English Chroniclers, AD 500 to 1286*, London, David Nutt; repr 1991, Stamford, Paul Watkins

Anderson, A.O. (ed. and trans.) 1922. *Early Sources of Scottish History, AD 500 to 1286*, 2 vols, Edinburgh, Oliver and Boyd; repr. 1990, Stamford, Paul Watkins

Anderson, J. 1881. *Scotland in Early Christian Times*, Rhind Lectures in Archaeology for 1879, Edinburgh, David Douglas

Anderson, J. 1891. 'The dewars or hereditary keepers of relics of the Celtic church in Scotland', *Highland Monthly* **2** (1890-1): 84-96

Anderson, J. 1892. 'Notice of a bronze bell of Celtic type at Forteviot, Perthshire', *Proc Soc Antiq Scotland* **26** (1891-2): 434-9

Anderson, M.O. 1973. *Kings and Kingship in Early Scotland*, Edinburgh, Scottish Academic Press; 2nd edn, 1980

Anderson, M.O. 1974a. 'St Andrews before Alexander I', in G.W.S. Barrow (ed.), *The Scottish Tradition: Essays in Honour of Ronald Gordon Cant*, 1-13, Edinburgh, Scottish Academic Press

Anderson, M.O. 1974b. 'The Celtic Church in Kinrimund', *Innes Rev* **25**: 67-76; reprinted in D. McRoberts (ed.) 1976. *The Medieval Church of St Andrews*, 1-10, Glasgow, J. Burns

Anderson, M.O. 1982. 'Dalriada and the creation of the kingdom of the Scots', in Whitelock *et al.* (eds) 1982: 106-32

Anderson, M.O. 2004a. 'Oengus mac Forgusso', in Matthew and Harrison (eds) 2004, vol. 41: 540

Anderson, M.O. 2004b. 'Picts, kings of', in Matthew and Harrison (eds) 2004, vol. 44: 243-6

Ash, M. 1996. 'Lands and churches of the See of St Andrews' in McNeill and MacQueen (eds) 1996: 361-2

Ash, M. and Broun, D. 1994. 'The adoption of St Andrew as patron saint of Scotland', in Higgitt (ed.) 1994: 16-24

Ashmore, P.J. 1980. 'Low cairns, long cists and symbol stones', *Proc Soc Antiq Scotland* **110** (1978-80): 346-55

Ashmore, P. and Maxwell, G.S. 1996. 'Pictish and earlier archaeological sites', in McNeill and MacQueen (eds) 1996: 48-9

Bailey, R.N. 1980. *Viking Age Sculpture in Northern England*, London, Collins

Bailey, R.N. 1996. *England's Earliest Sculptors*, Publications of the Dictionary of Old English 5, Toronto, Pontifical Institute of Mediaeval Studies

Bailey, R.N. 2005. *Anglo-Saxon Sculptures at Deerhurst*, Deerhurst Lecture 2002, np, The Friends of Deerhurst Church

Bandmann, G. 2005. Early Medieval Architecture as Bearer of Meaning, trans. K. Wallis, New York, Columbia University Press

Bannerman, J. 1973. *Studies in the History of Dalriada*, Edinburgh, Scottish Academic Press

Bannerman, J. 1999. 'The Scottish takeover of Pictland and the relics of Columba', in Broun and Clancy (eds) 1999: 71-94; first pub. *Innes Rev* **8** (1997): 27-44

Barclay, G.J. 1983. 'Sites of the third millennium b.c. to the first millennium a.d. at North Mains, Strathallan, Perthshire', *Proc Soc Antiq Scotland* **113**: 122-281

Barrow, G.L. 1979. *The Round Towers of Ireland: a Study and Gazetteer*, Dublin, Academy Press

Barrow, G.W.S. 1983. 'The childhood of early Scottish Christianity: a note on some placename evidence', *Scottish Stud* **27**: 1-15

Barrow, G.W.S. 2003. *The Kingdom of the Scots: Government, Church and Society from the Eleventh to the Fourteenth Century*, second edn, Edinburgh, Edinburgh University Press; first pub. 1973, London, Edward Arnold

Battisti, C. 1960. 'Il problema linguistico di basilica', *Le chiese nei regni dell'Europa occidentale e i loro rapporti con Roma sino all'800*, Settimane di studio del centro Italiano di studi sull'alto medioevo 7, vol. 2: 805-47

Beridze, V., Alibegasvili, G., Volskaja, A. and Xuskivadze, L. 1984. *The Treasures of Georgia*, London, Century

Bigelow, G.F. 1984. 'Two kerbed cairns from Sandwick, Unst, Shetland', in Friell and Watson (eds) 1984: 115-29

Blair, W.J. 1996. 'Palaces or minsters? Northampton and Cheddar reconsidered', *Anglo-Saxon England* **25**: 97-121

Bourke, C. 1980. 'Early Irish hand-bells', *J Royal Soc Antiq Ireland* **110**: 52-66

Bourke, C. 1983. 'The hand-bells of the early Scottish Church', *Proc Soc Antiq Scotland* **113**: 464-8

Bourke, C. 1987. 'Irish croziers of the eighth and ninth centuries', in Ryan (ed.) 1987: 166-73

Bourke, C. (ed.) 1995. *From the Isles of the North: Early Medieval Art in Ireland and Britain*, Proceedings of the Third International Conference on Insular Art, Belfast, HMSO

Bradley, R. 1987. 'Time regained: the creation of continuity', *J British Archaeol Soc* **140**: 1-17

Bradley, R. 1993. *Altering the Earth: the Origins of Monuments in Britain and Continental Europe*, Monograph Series 8, Edinburgh, Society of Antiquaries of Scotland

Bradley, R. 2002. *The Past in Prehistoric Societies*, London, Routledge

Breeze, A. 2000. 'Some Celtic place-names of Scotland, including *Arran, Carmunnock, Gogar*, and *Water of May*', *Scottish Language* **19**: 117-34

Broun, D. 1998a. '*Fortriu/Fortrenn*: an editorial confession', *Innes Rev* **49**: 93-4

Broun, D. 1998b. 'Pictish kings, 761-839: integration with Dál Riata or separate development?', in Foster (ed.) 1998: 71-83

Broun, D. 1999. 'Dunkeld and the origin of Scottish identity', in Broun and Clancy (eds) 1999: 95-111; first pub. *Innes Rev* **48** (1997): 112-24

Broun, D. 2000a. 'The seven kingdoms in *De situ Albanie*: a record of Pictish political geography or imaginary map of ancient *Alba*?', in Cowan and McDonald (eds) 2000: 24-42

Broun, D. 2000b. 'The church of St Andrews and its foundation legend in the early twelfth century: recovering the full text of version A of the foundation legend', in Taylor (ed.) 2000: 108-14

Broun, D. and Clancy, T.O. (eds) 1999. *Spes Scotorum: Hope of Scots. Saint Columba, Iona and Scotland*, Edinburgh, T&T Clark

Broun, D. and Taylor, S. in prep. *The Church of St Andrew and its Foundation Legends*,

Brown, C. 2002. *The Second Scottish Wars of Independence, 1332-1363*, Stroud, Tempus

Brown, G.B. 1925. *The Arts in Early England, vol. 2: Anglo-Saxon Architecture*, 2nd edn, London, John Murray

Brown, I.G. 1974. 'Gothicism, ignorance and a bad taste: the destruction of Arthur's O'on', *Antiquity* **48**: 283-8

Brown, I.G. and Vasey, P.G. 1989. 'Arthur's O'on again: newly discovered drawings by John Adair, and their context', *Proc Soc Antiq Scotland* **119**: 353-60

Brown, M. 1992. 'Cropmarks east of Forteviot village: interpretative description', in Alcock and Alcock 1992: 231-4

Brown, W. and Jamieson, J. 1830. *Select Views of the Royal Palaces of Scotland from Drawings by William Brown, Glasgow; with Illustrative Descriptions of their Local Situations, Present Appearance, and Antiquities*, Edinburgh, Cadell & Co.

Browne, M.A.E. 1980. 'Late Devensian marine limits and the pattern of deglaciation of the Strathearn area, Tayside', *Scottish J Geol* **16**: 221-30

Brushfield, T. 1900. 'On Norman tympana', *J British Archaeol Assoc* **6** (NS): 241-70; repr. as *On Norman Tympana: with Especial Reference to those of Derbyshire*, London, Bedford Press

Buckley, M.J.C. 1900. 'Notes on boundary crosses', *J Royal Soc of Antiq Ireland* **30**: 247-52

Burl, H.A.W. 1991. *Prehistoric Henges*, Princes Risborough, Shire

Burt, J.R.F. 1997. 'Long cist cemeteries in Fife', in Henry (ed.) 1997: 64-6

Burt, J.R.F., Bowman, E.O. and Robertson, N.M.R. (eds) 1994. *Stones, Symbols and Stories: Aspects of Pictish Studies*, Proceedings from the Conferences of the Pictish Arts Society, 1992, Edinburgh, Pictish Arts Society

Burton, J.H. 1867-70. *The History of Scotland: from Agricola's Invasion to the Extinction of the Last Jacobite Insurrection*, 7 vols., Edinburgh, William Blackwood and Sons

Butler, L.A.S. and Morris, R.K. (eds) 1986. *The Anglo-Saxon Church: Papers on History, Architecture and Archaeology in Honour of Dr H.M. Taylor*, CBA Research Report 60, London, Council for British Archaeology

Byrne, F.J. 1973. *Irish Kings and High-Kings*, London, B.T. Batsford

Cambridge, E. 1984. 'The early church in Co. Durham: a reassessment', *J British Archaeol Assoc* **137**: 65-85

Cameron, K. 1961. *English Place-Names*, London, B.T. Batsford

Cameron, N. 1994. 'St Rule's Church, St Andrews, and early stone-built churches in Scotland', *Proc Soc Antiq Scotland* **124**: 367-78

Campbell, D. 1888. *The Book of Garth and Fortingall: Historical Sketches Relating to the Districts of Garth, Fortingall, Athole, and Breadalbane*, Inverness, Northern Counties Newspaper and Printing and Publishing Co.

Campbell, E. 2003. 'Royal inaugurations in Dál Riata and the Stone of Destiny', in Welander et al. (eds) 2003: 43-59

Campbell, J. 1979. 'Bede's words for places', in P.H. Sawyer (ed.), *Names, Words and Graves: Early Medieval Settlement*, 34-54, Leeds, School of History, University of Leeds

Cant, J. (ed.) 1774. *The Muses Threnodie: or, Mirthful Mournings on the Death of Master Gall*, by Henry Adamson, 2 vols, rev. edn., Perth, George Johnston

Carrington, A.J. 1996. 'The horseman and the falcon: mounted falconers in Pictish sculpture', *Proc Soc Antiq Scotland* **126**: 459-68

Carrington, A.J. 1997. 'David imagery and the chase motif in Pictish sculpture', *Studia Celtica* **30** (1996): 147-58

Carver, M. 1999. *Surviving in Symbols: a Visit to the Pictish Nation*, Edinburgh, Canongate with Historic Scotland

Caseldine, C. 1983. 'Palynological evidence for early cereal cultivation in Strathearn', *Proc Soc Antiq Scotland* **112** (1982): 39-47

Catalogue 1892. *Catalogue of the National Museum of Antiquities of Scotland*, new edn, Edinburgh, Society of Antiquaries of Scotland

Cather, S., Park, D. and Williamson, P. (eds) 1990. *Early Medieval Wall Paintings and Painted Sculpture in England*, BAR British Series 216, Oxford, BAR

Cessford, C. 1995. 'A bull cult at Burghead', *Pictish Arts Soc J* **8** (autumn 1995): 14-23

Chadwick, H.M. 1949. *Early Scotland: the Picts, the Scots and the Welsh of Southern Scotland*, Cambridge, Cambridge University Press

Chadwick, N.K. 1975. 'The Vikings and the western world', in B. Ó Cuív (ed.), *The Impact of the Scandinavian Invasions on the Celtic-Speaking Peoples, c.800-1100 AD*, 13-42, Dublin, Dublin Institute for Advanced Studies; first pub. *Proceedings of the International Congress of Celtic Studies held in Dublin, 6-10 July 1959*, 1962, Dublin, Dublin Institute for Advanced Studies

Chalmers, G. 1848. *Caledonia: or, a Historical and Topographical Account of North Britain from the Most Ancient to the Present Times*, 3 vols, second edn, London, T. Cadell; first pub. 1807-24

Cherry, B. 1976. 'Ecclesiastical architecture', in D.M. Wilson (ed.), *The Archaeology of Anglo-Saxon England*, 151-200, Cambridge, Cambridge University Press

Christison, D. 1898. *Early Fortifications in Scotland, Motes, Camps and Forts*, Rhind Lectures in Archaeology for 1894, Edinburgh, W. Blackwood & Sons

Christison, D. 1900. 'The forts, "camps", and other field-works of Perth, Forfar and Kincardine', *Proc Soc Antiq Scotland* **34** (1899–1900): 43–120

Churches 2002. *Churches to Visit in Scotland*, Edinburgh, NMS Publishing for Scotland's Churches Scheme

Clancy, T. 1993. 'The Drosten Stone: a new reading', *Proc Soc Antiq Scotland* **123**: 345–53

Clancy, T. 1996. 'Iona, Scotland and the Céli Dé', in Crawford (ed.) 1996: 111–30

Clancy, T.O. 1999. 'Columba, Adomnán and the cult of saints in Scotland', in Broun and Clancy (eds) 1999: 3–33

Clapham, A.W. 1927. 'The carved stones at Breedon-on-the-Hill, Leicestershire', *Archaeologia* **77**: 219–40

Clare, T. 1986. 'Towards a reappraisal of henge monuments', *Proc Prehist Soc* **52**: 281–316

Clayton, M. 1991. *The Cult of the Virgin Mary in Anglo-Saxon England*, Cambridge, Cambridge University Press

Close-Brooks, J. 1980a. 'Excavations in the Dairy Park, Dunrobin, Sutherland, 1977', *Proc Soc Antiq Scotland* **110** (1978–80): 328–45

Close-Brooks, J. 1980b. *Dark Age Sculpture*, Edinburgh, National Museum of Antiquities of Scotland

Close-Brooks, J. 1984. 'Pictish and other burials', in Friell and Watson (eds) 1984: 87–114

Close-Brooks, J. and Stevenson, R.B.K. 1982. *Dark Age Sculpture: a Selection from the Collections of the National Museum of Antiquities of Scotland*, Edinburgh, National Museum of Antiquities of Scotland/HMSO

Clouston, R.W.M. 1992. 'The bells of Perthshire', *Proc Soc Antiq Scotland* **122**: 453–508

Corrie, J.M. 1926. 'Notice of … (2) a symbol stone from East Lomond Hill, recently presented to the National Museum', *Proc Soc Antiq Scotland* **60** (1925–6): 32–4

Cowan, E.J. 1981. 'The Scottish Chronicle in the Poppleton Manuscript', *Innes Rev* **32**: 3–21

Cowan, E.J. and McDonald, R.A. (eds) 2000. *Alba: Celtic Scotland in the Medieval Era*, East Linton, Tuckwell Press

Cowan, I.B. 1967. *The Parishes of Medieval Scotland*, Scottish Record Society 93, Edinburgh, Scottish Record Society

Cowan, I.B. 1982. *The Scottish Reformation: Church and Society in Sixteenth Century Scotland*, London, Weidenfeld and Nicolson

Cox, R.A.V. 1997. 'Modern Scottish Gaelic reflexes of two Pictish words: *pett and *lannerc*', *Nomina* **20**: 49–58

Cramp, R. 1977. 'Schools of Mercian sculpture', in A. Dornier (ed.), *Mercian Studies*, 191–233, Leicester, Leicester University Press

Cramp, R. 1984. *Corpus of Anglo-Saxon Stone Sculpture*, vol. 1: *County Durham and Northumberland*, 2 parts, Oxford, Oxford University Press for The British Academy

Cramp, R. 1986. 'The furnishing and sculptural decoration of Anglo-Saxon churches', in Butler and Morris (eds) 1986: 101–4

Cramp, R. 1991. *Grammar of Anglo-Saxon Ornament: a General Introduction to the Corpus of Anglo-Saxon Stone Sculpture*, Oxford, Oxford University Press for The British Academy; first pub. 1984 as *Corpus of Anglo-Saxon Stone Sculpture: General Introduction*, London, British Academy

Craw, J.H. 1930. 'Excavations at Dunadd and at other sites on the Poltalloch Estates, Argyll', *Proc Soc Antiq Scotland* **64** (1929–30): 111–46

Crawford, B.E. 1987. *Scandinavian Scotland*, Studies in the Early History of Britain, Scotland in the Early Middle Ages 2, Leicester, Leicester University Press

Crawford, B.E. (ed.) 1996. *Scotland in Dark Age Britain*, St John's House Papers 6, Aberdeen, Scottish Cultural Press

Crozier, I.R. and Rea, L.C. 1940. 'Bullauns and other basin-stones', *Ulster J Archaeol* **3**: 104-14

Cruden, S. 1964. *The Early Christian & Pictish Monuments of Scotland: an Illustrated Introduction*, 2nd edn, Edinburgh, HMSO/Ministry of Public Buildings and Works; first pub. 1957

Cruden, S. 1986. *Scottish Medieval Churches*, Edinburgh, John Donald

Cullingford, R.A., Caseldine, C.J. and Gotts, P.E. 1980. 'Early Flandrian land and sea level changes in lower Strathearn', *Nature* **284**: 159-61

Curle, C.L. 1940. 'The chronology of the early Christian monuments of Scotland', *Proc Soc Antiq Scotland* **74** (1939-40): 60-116

Curle, C.L. and Henry, F. 1943. 'Early Christian art in Scotland', *Gazette des Beaux-Arts* (6th series) **24**: 257-72

Darvill, T. 1996. *Prehistoric Britain from the Air: a Study of Space, Time and Society*, Cambridge Air Surveys, Cambridge University Press

Davies, W. 1982a. *Wales in the Early Middle Ages*, Leicester, Leicester University Press

Davies, W. 1982b. 'The Latin charter-tradition in western Britain, Brittany and Ireland in the early medieval period', in Whitelock *et al.* (eds) 1982: 258-80

Davies, W. 1994. 'Ecclesiastical centres and secular society in the Brittonic world in the tenth and eleventh centuries', in A. Ritchie (ed.) 1994: 92-102

Delehaye, H. 1930. 'Loca sanctorum', *Annalecta Bollandiana* **48**: 5-64

Dickinson, W.C. 1941. 'The *toschederach*', *Juridical Rev* **53**: 85-111

Doherty, C. 1984a. 'The use of relics in early Ireland', in Ní Chatháin and Richter (eds) 1984: 89-101

Doherty, C. 1984b. 'The basilica in early Ireland', *Peritia* **3**: 303-15

Donaldson, G. 1953. 'Scottish bishops' sees before the reign of David I', *Proc Soc Antiq Scotland* **87** (1952-3): 106-17; repr. in Donaldson 1985: 11-24

Donaldson, G. 1974. 'Scotland's earliest church buildings', *Records Scottish Church Hist Assoc* **18**: 1-9; repr. in Donaldson 1985: 1-10

Donaldson, G. 1985. *Scottish Church History*, Edinburgh, Scottish Academic Press

Donations 1875. 'Donations to the Museum and Library', *Proc Soc Antiq Scotland* **10** (1872-4): 720-1

Driscoll, S.T. 1988a. 'The relationship between history and archaeology: artefacts, documents and power', in Driscoll and Nieke (eds) 1988: 162-87

Driscoll, S.T. 1988b. 'Power and authority in early historic Scotland: Pictish stones and other documents', in J. Gledhill, B. Bender and M. Larsen (eds), *State and Society: the Emergence and Development of Social Hierarchy and Political Centralisation*, 215-36, London, Unwin Hyman

Driscoll, S.T. 1991. 'The archaeology of state formation in Scotland', in W.S. Hanson and E.A. Slater (eds), *Scottish Archaeology: New Perceptions*, 81-111, Aberdeen, Aberdeen University Press

Driscoll, S.T. 1998a. 'Formalising the mechanisms of state power: early lordship, ninth to thirteenth centuries', in Foster *et al.* (eds) 1998: 32-58

Driscoll, S.T. 1998b. 'Political discourse and the growth of Christian ceremonialism in Pictland: the place of the St Andrews Sarcophagus', in Foster (ed.) 1998: 168-78

Driscoll, S.T. 1998c. 'Picts and prehistory: cultural resource management in early medieval Scotland', *World Archaeol* **30**: 142-58

Driscoll, S.T. 2000. 'Christian monumental sculpture and ethnic expression in early Scotland', in W. O. Frazer and A. Tyrrell (eds), *Social Identity in Early Medieval Britain*, 233-52, Leicester University Press

Driscoll, S.T. 2001. 'Forteviot', in Lynch (ed.) 2001: 242-3

Driscoll, S.T. 2002. *Alba: the Gaelic Kingdom of Scotland, AD 800-1124*, The Making of Scotland, Edinburgh, Birlinn/Historic Scotland

Driscoll, S.T. 2003. 'Govan: an early medieval royal centre on the Clyde', in Welander *et al.* 2003: 76-83

Driscoll, S.T. 2004. 'The archaeological context of assembly in early medieval Scotland – Scone and its comparanda', in Pantos and Semple (eds) 2004: 73-94

Driscoll, S.T., O'Grady, O. and Forsyth, K. 2005. 'The Govan School revisited: searching for meaning in the early medieval sculpture of Strathclyde', in Foster and Cross (eds) 2005: 135-58

Duchesne, L. 1886-92. *Liber Pontificalis: texte, introduction et commentaire*, 2 vols, Paris, Bibliothèque des Écoles Françaises d'Athènes et de Rome

Dumville, D. 2000. 'The Chronicle of the Kings of Alba', in Taylor (ed.) 2000: 73-86

Duncan, A.A.M. 1978. *Scotland: The Making of the Kingdom*, The Edinburgh History of Scotland 1, rev. edn, Edinburgh, Oliver & Boyd; first pub. 1975

Duncan, A.A.M. 1996. 'The Church: early Christianity', in McNeill and MacQueen (eds) 1996: 330-2

Duncan, A.A.M. 2002. The *Kingship of the Scots, 842-1292: Succession and Independence*, Edinburgh, Edinburgh University Press

ECMS: Allen, J.R. and Anderson, J. 1993. *The Early Christian Monuments of Scotland*, 2 vols, repr., Balgavies, Angus, Pinkfoot Press; first pub. 1903, Edinburgh, Society of Antiquaries of Scotland

Edwards, K.J. and Ralston, I. 1978. 'New dating and environmental evidence from Burghead fort, Moray', *Proc Soc Antiq Scotland* **109** (1977-78): 202-10

Edwards, N. 1990. *The Archaeology of Early Medieval Ireland*, London, B.T. Batsford

Edwards, N. 1998. 'The Irish connection', in Foster (ed.) 1998: 227-39

Etchingham, C. 1999. *Church Organisation in Ireland, AD 650 to 1000*, Maynooth, Laigin Publications

Fairweather, A.D. and Ralston, I.B.M. 1993. 'The Neolithic timber hall at Balbridie, Grampian Region, Scotland: the building, the date, the plant macrofossils', *Antiquity* **67**: 313-23

Fawcett, R. 1985. *Scottish Medieval Churches: an Introduction to the Ecclesiastical Architecture of the 12th to 16th Centuries in the Care of the Secretary of State for Scotland*, Edinburgh, HMSO/ Historic Buildings and Monuments Directorate

Fawcett, R. 1990. *The Abbey and Palace of Dunfermline*, Edinburgh, Historic Scotland

Fawcett, R. 1994. *Scottish Abbeys and Priories*, London, B.T. Batsford/Historic Scotland

Fawcett, R. 2002. *Scottish Medieval Churches: Architecture & Furnishings*, Stroud, Tempus

Fawcett, R. (ed.) 2005. *Royal Dunfermline*, Edinburgh, Society of Antiquaries of Scotland

Ferguson, G. 1954. *Signs and Symbols in Christian Art*, Oxford, Oxford University Press

Fernie, E. 1983. *The Architecture of the Anglo-Saxons*, London, B.T. Batsford

Fernie, E. 1986. 'Early church architecture in Scotland', *Proc Soc Antiq Scotland* **116**: 393-411

Fisher, I. 2001. *Early Medieval Sculpture in the West Highlands and Islands*, Monograph Series 1, Edinburgh, RCAHMS/Society of Antiquaries of Scotland

Fisher, I. 2005. 'Christ's Cross down into the earth: some cross-bases and their problems', in Foster and Cross (eds) 2005: 85-94

FitzPatrick, E. 2004a. *Royal Inauguration in Gaelic Ireland, c.1100-1600: a Cultural Landscape History*, Studies in Celtic History 22, Woodbridge, Boydell Press

FitzPatrick, E. 2004b. 'Royal inauguration mounds in medieval Ireland: antique landscape and tradition', in Pantos and Semple (eds) 2004: 44-72

Forsyth, K. 1992. 'A Latin inscription on the Dupplin Cross', *Proc Soc Antiq Scotland* **122**: 283

Forsyth, K. 1995. 'The inscriptions on the Dupplin Cross', in Bourke (ed.) 1995: 237-44

Forsyth, K. 1997. 'Some thoughts on Pictish symbols as a formal writing system', in Henry (ed.) 1997: 85-98

Forsyth, K. 1998. 'Literacy in Pictland', in H. Pryce (ed.), *Literacy in Medieval Celtic Societies*, 39-61, Cambridge Studies in Medieval Literature 33, Cambridge University Press

Forsyth, K. and Trench-Jellicoe, R. 2000. 'The inscribed panel', in Hall *et al.* 2000: 166-8

Forteviot n.d. *Forteviot Church: where Scotland Began*, guide leaflet [no author stated]

Fortey, N.J., Phillips, E.R., McMillan, A.A. and Browne, M.A.E. 1998. 'A geological perspective on the Stone of Destiny', *Scottish J Geol* **34.2**: 145-52

Foster, J. 1999. 'Strathearn', in Omand (ed.) 1999: 115-23

Foster, S.M. 1992. 'The state of Pictland in the age of Sutton Hoo', in M. Carver (ed.), *The Age of Sutton Hoo: The Seventh Century in North-Western Europe*, 217-34, Woodbridge, Boydell Press

Foster, S. 1996. *Picts, Gaels and Scots: Early Historic Scotland*, London, B.T. Batsford/ Historic Scotland

Foster, S. 1998. 'Before *Alba*: Pictish and Dál Riata power centres from the fifth to late ninth centuries AD', in Foster *et al.* (eds) 1998: 1-31

Foster, S. (ed.) 1998. *The St Andrews Sarcophagus: a Pictish Masterpiece and its International Connections*, Dublin, Four Courts Press

Foster, S. and Cross, M. (eds) 2005. *Able Minds and Practised Hands: Scotland's Early Medieval Sculpture in the 21st Century*, Society for Medieval Archaeology Monograph 23, Leeds, Maney

Foster, S., Macinnes, A. and MacInnes, R. (eds) 1998. *Scottish Power Centres: from the Early Middle Ages to the Twentieth Century*, Glasgow, Cruithne Press

Fraser, D. 1998. 'An Investigation into Distributions of Ach-, Bal- and Pit- Place-Names in North-East Scotland', unpub. MLitt thesis, University of Aberdeen

Fraser, I.A. 1987. 'Pictish place-names: some topographic evidence', in Small (ed.) 1987: 68-72

Fraser, I.[A.] 1999. 'Place-names', in Omand (ed.) 1999: 199-210

Friell, J.G.P. and Watson, W.G. (eds) 1984. *Pictish Studies: Settlement, Burial and Art in Dark Age Northern Britain*, BAR British Series 125, Oxford, BAR

Gameson, R. 1995. *The Role of Art in the Late Anglo-Saxon Church*, Oxford, Clarendon Press

Gameson, R. and Gameson, F. 1993. 'The Anglo-Saxon inscription at St Mary's Church, Breamore, Hampshire', *Anglo-Saxon Stud Archaeol Hist* **6**: 1-10

Gates, T. and O'Brien, C. 1988. 'Cropmarks at Milfield and New Bewick and the recognition of Grubenhaüser in Northumberland', *Archaeol Aeliana* (5th ser.) **16**: 1-9

Gauert, A. 1965. 'Zur Struktur und Topographie der Königspfalzen', *Deutsche Königspfalzen: Beiträge zu ihrer historischen und archäologischen Erforschung* **2**: 1-60

Gelling, M. 1978. *Signposts to the Past: Place-Names and the History of England*, London, J.M. Dent & Sons

Gem, R. 1983. 'Towards an iconography of Anglo-Saxon architecture', *J Warburg and Courtauld Institutes* **46**: 1-18

Gem, R. 1993. 'Architecture of the Anglo-Saxon church, 735 to 870', *J British Archaeol Assoc* **146**: 29-66

Gem, R. 2003. *Studies in English Pre-Romanesque and Romesque Architecture*, 2 vols, London, Pindar

Gem, R. 2005. 'How much can Anglo-Saxon buildings tell us about liturgy?', in H. Gittos and M.B. Bedingfield (eds), 2005. *The Liturgy of the Late Anglo-Saxon Church*, 271-89, London, Boydell Press, Henry Bradshaw Society

Gibson, A. 1998. 'Hindwell and the Neolithic palisaded sites of Britain and Ireland', in A. Gibson and D. Simpson (eds), *Prehistoric Ritual and Religion: Essays in Honour of Aubrey Burl*, 68-79, Stroud, Sutton

Gibson, A. 2002. 'The later Neolithic palisaded sites of Britain', in A. Gibson (ed.), *Behind Wooden Walls: Neolithic Palisaded Enclosures in Europe*, 5-23, BAR International Series 1013, Oxford, Archaeopress

Givans, D.B.C. 2001. *English Romanesque Tympana: a Study of Architectural Sculpture in Church Portals, c.1050-c.1200*, 3 vols, unpub PhD thesis, University of Warwick, Coventry

Glendinning, M. and MacKechnie, 2004. *Scottish Architecture*, World of Art series, London, Thames and Hudson

Gordon, C.A. 1966. 'The Pictish animals observed', *Proc Soc Antiq Scotland* **98** (1964-6): 215-24

Gordon, E. 1963. *A Handbook on the Principles of Church Building: Furnishing, Equipment, Decoration*, Edinburgh, The Church of Scotland Advisory Committee on Artistic Questions

Gourlay, R. 1984. 'A symbol stone and cairn at Watenan, Caithness', in Friell and Watson (eds) 1984: 131-3

Govan 2005. 'Govan Old', *Current Archaeol* **198** (July/August 2005): 276-82 (no author cited)

Graham, A. 1959. 'Giudi', *Antiquity* **33**: 63-5

Grant, A. 1993. 'Thanes and thanages, from the eleventh to the fourteenth centuries', in A. Grant and K.J. Stringer (eds), *Medieval Scotland: Crown, Lordship and Community*, 39-81, Edinburgh, Edinburgh University Press

Green, M. 1986. *The Gods of the Celts*, Stroud, Alan Sutton

Green, M. 1989. *Symbol and Image in Celtic Religious Art*, London, Routledge

Green, M.J. 1992. *Dictionary of Celtic Myth and Legend*, London, Thames and Hudson

Gregson, N. 1985. 'The multiple estate model: some critical questions', *J Hist Geog* **11**: 339-51

Groome, F.H. (ed.) 1903. *Ordnance Gazetteer of Scotland: a Graphic and Accurate Description of Every Place in Scotland*, new edn, 3 vols, London, Caxton Publishing Co.; first pub. 1882-85, 6 vols, Edinburgh, Thomas C. Jack

Hall, D. 2004. '75 High Street, Perth', *Discovery and Excavation in Scotland* (ns) **4** (2003): 164

Hall, M. 2000. 'Landscape context: geology', in Hall *et al.* 2000: 168-9

Hall, M. n.d. 'Towards an understanding of Perth's origin: the Pictish & Gaelic background', conference paper abstract, available at www.tafac.freeuk.com/prthcon/originsnotes.htm

Hall, M.A., Henderson, I. and Taylor, S. 1998. 'A sculptured fragment from Pittensorn Farm, Gellyburn, Perthshire', *Tayside and Fife Archaeol J* **4**: 129-44

Hall, M., Forsyth, K., Henderson, I.B., Scott, I.G., Trench-Jellicoe, R. and Watson, A. 2000. 'On markings and meanings: towards a cultural biography of the Crieff Burgh Cross, Strathearn, Perthshire', *Tayside and Fife Archaeol J* **6**: 154-88

Hall, U. 1994. *St Andrew and Scotland*, St Andrews, St Andrews University Library

Hamlin, A. 1982. '*Dignatio diei dominici*: an element in the iconography of Irish crosses?', in Whitelock *et al.* (eds) 1982: 69-75

Hamlin, A. 1984. 'The study of early Irish churches', in Ní Chatháin and Richter (eds) 1984: 117-26

Hamlin, A. 1987. 'Crosses in early Ireland: the evidence from written sources', in Ryan (ed.) 1987: 138-40

Hanks, P., Hodges, F., Mills, A.D. and Room, A. 2002. *The Oxford Names Companion*, Oxford, Oxford University Press

Harbison, P. 1979. 'The inscriptions on the Cross of the Scriptures at Clonmacnoise, Co. Offaly', *Proc Royal Irish Acad* **79** (sec. C): 177-88

Harbison, P. 1982. 'Early Irish churches', in H. Löwe (ed.), *Die Iren und Europa im früheren Mittelalter*, vol. 2: 618-29, Veröffentlichungen des Europa Zentrums Tübingen, Kulturwissenschaftliche Reihe, Stuttgart, Klett-Cotta

Harbison, P. 1991. *Pilgrimage in Ireland: the Monuments and the People*, London, Barrie & Jenkins

Harbison, P. 1992. The High Crosses of Ireland: an Iconographical and Photographic Survey, 3 vols, RGZM Forschungsinstitut für Vor- und Frühgeschichte, Monographien 17, Bonn, Römisch-Germanisches Zentralmuseum

Harbison, P. 1994. *Irish High Crosses with the Figure Sculptures Explained*, Drogheda, The Boyne Valley Honey Company

Harbison, P. 1995. 'The Biblical iconography of Irish Romanesque architectural sculpture', in Bourke (ed.) 1995: 271-80

Harding, A.F. and Lee, G.E. 1987. *Henge Monuments and Related Sites of Great Britain: Air Photographic Evidence and Catalogue*, BAR British Series 175, Oxford, BAR

Harding, J. 2003. *Henge Monuments of the British Isles*, Stroud, Tempus

Hawkes, J. 1996. 'The Rothbury Cross: an iconographic bricolage', *Gesta* **35**: 77-94

Hawkes, J. 1997. 'Old Testament heroes: iconographies of Insular sculpture', in Henry (ed.) 1997: 149-58

Henderson, G. and Henderson, I. 2004. *The Art of the Picts: Sculpture and Metalwork in Early Medieval Scotland*, London, Thames and Hudson

Henderson, I. 1967. *The Picts*, London, Thames and Hudson

Henderson, I. 1975. 'The monuments of the Picts', in P. McNeill and R. Nicholson (eds), *An Historical Atlas of Scotland, c.400-c.1600*, 9-11, St Andrews, Atlas Committee of the Conference of Scottish Medievalists

Henderson, I. 1978. 'Sculpture north of the Forth after the take-over by the Scots', in J. Lang (ed.), *Anglo-Saxon and Viking Age Sculpture and its Context*, 47-73, BAR British Series 49, Oxford, BAR

Henderson, I. 1982. 'Pictish art and the Book of Kells', in Whitelock *et al.* (eds) 1982: 79-105

Henderson, I. 1986. 'The "David cycle" in Pictish art', in Higgitt (ed.) 1986: 87-123

Henderson, I. 1993. 'The shape and decoration of the cross on Pictish cross-slabs carved in relief', in Spearman and Higgitt (eds) 1993: 209-18

Henderson, I. 1994. 'The Picts: written records and pictorial images', in Burt *et al.* (eds) 1994: 44-66

Henderson, I.B. 1996. 'Pictish territorial divisions', in McNeill and MacQueen (eds) 1996: 52

Henderson, I. 1998a. '*Primus inter pares*: the St Andrews sarcophagus and Pictish sculpture', in Foster (ed.) 1998: 97-167

Henderson, I. 1998b. 'Descriptive catalogue of the surviving parts of the monument', in Foster (ed.) 1998: 19-35

Henderson, I. 1999a. 'The Dupplin cross: a preliminary consideration of its art-historical context', in Hawkes and Mills (eds) 1999: 161-77

Henderson, I. 1999b. 'Monasteries and sculpture in the Insular pre-Viking age: the Pictish evidence', in B. Thompson (ed.), *Monasteries and Society in Medieval Britain: Proceedings of the 1994 Harlaxton Symposium*, 75-96, Harlaxton Medieval Studies 6, Stamford, Paul Watkins

Henderson, I. 2001. 'The cross-slab at Nigg, Easter Ross', in P. Binski and W. Noel (eds), *New Offerings, Ancient Treasures: Studies in Medieval Art for George Henderson*, 129-34, Stroud, Sutton

Henderson, I. 2005. 'Fragments of significance: the whole picture', in Foster and Cross (eds) 2005: 69-84

Henry, D. (ed.) 1997. *The Worm, the Germ, and the Thorn: Pictish and Related Studies Presented to Isabel Henderson*, Balgavies, Angus, Pinkfoot Press

Henry, F. 1933. *La sculpture Irlandaise pendant les douze premiers siècles de l'ère Chrétienne*, 2 vols, Paris, Libraire Ernest Leroux

Henry, F. 1957. 'Early monasteries, beehive huts, and dry-stone houses in the neighbourhood of Caherciveen and Waterville (Co. Kerry)', *Proc Royal Irish Acad* (Sec. C) **58**: 67-172

Henry, F. 1970. *Irish Art in the Romanesque Period, 1020-1170 AD*, London, Methuen & Co

Henry, F. 1980. 'Around an inscription: the Cross of the Scriptures at Clonmacnoise', *J Royal Soc of Antiq Ireland* **110**: 36-46

Herity, M. 1983. 'The buildings and layout of early Irish monasteries before the year 1000', *Celtic Monasticism: Monastic Studies* **14**: 247-84

Herity, M. 1984. 'The layout of Irish early Christian monasteries', in Ní Chatháin and M. Richter (eds) 1984: 105-16

Herity, M. 1995. 'Motes and mounds at royal sites in Ireland', *J Royal Soc Antiq Ireland* **123** (1993): 127-51

Heywood, S. 1994. 'The Church of St Rule, St Andrews', in Higgitt (ed.) 1994: 38-46

Hicks, C. 1980. 'A Clonmacnoise workshop in stone', *J Royal Soc of Antiq Ireland* **110**: 5-35

Hicks, C. 1993a. *Animals in Early Medieval Art*, Edinburgh University Press

Hicks, C. 1993b. 'The Pictish Class I animals', in Spearman and Higitt (eds) 1993: 196-202

Higgitt, J. 1979. 'The dedication inscription of Jarrow and its context', *Antiq J* **59**: 343-74

Higgitt, J. 1986. 'Words and crosses: the inscribed stone cross in early medieval Britain and Ireland', in Higgitt (ed.) 1986: 125-52

Higgitt, J. 1997. '"Legentes quoque uel audientes": early medieval inscriptions in Britain and Ireland and their audiences', in Henry (ed.) 1997: 67-78

Higgitt, J. 2004. *Odda, Orm and Others: Patrons and Inscriptions in Later Anglo-Saxon England*, Deerhurst Lecture 1999, np, Friends of Deerhurst Church

Higgitt, J. (ed.) 1986. *Early Medieval Sculpture in Britain and Ireland*, BAR British Series 152, Oxford, BAR

Higgitt, J. (ed.) 1994. *Medieval Art and Architecture in the Diocese of St Andrews*, Conference Transactions 14, [Tring], British Archaeological Association

Hope-Taylor, B. 1966a. 'Doon Hill, Dunbar, East Lothian', *Med Archaeol* **10**: 175-6

Hope-Taylor, B. 1966b. 'Bamburgh', *Univ Durham Gazette* **8**: 11-12

Hope-Taylor, B.K. 1977. *Yeavering: an Anglo-British Centre of Early Northumbria*, Department of the Environment Archaeological Report 7, London, HMSO

Hope-Taylor, B. 1980. 'Balbridie ... and Doon Hill', *Current Archaeol* **72**: 18-19

Hudson, B.T. 1991. 'The conquest of the Picts in early Scottish literature', *Scotia: Interdisciplinary J Scottish Stud* **15**: 13-25

Hudson, B.T. 1994a. *Kings of Celtic Scotland*, Westport, Conn., Greenwood

Hudson, B.T. 1994b. 'Kings and Church in early Scotland', *Scottish Hist Rev* **73**: 145-70

Hudson, B.T. (ed. and trans.) 1996. *Prophecy of Berchán: Irish and Scottish High-Kings of the Early Middle Ages*, Westport, Conn., Greenwood Press

Hudson, B.T. 1998. '"The Scottish Chronicle"', *Scottish Hist Rev* **77**: 129-61

Hughes, K. 1966. *The Church in Early Irish Society*, London, Methuen

Hughes, K. 1972. *Early Christian Ireland: an Introduction to the Sources*, London, Methuen

Hughes, K. and Hamlin, A. 1977. *The Modern Traveller to the Early Irish Church*, London, SPCK; repr. 1997, Dublin, Four Courts Press

Innes, T. 1729. *A Critical Essay on the Ancient Inhabitants of the Northern Parts of Britain, or Scotland; Containing an Account of the Romans, ... Britains, ... Picts, and Particularly of the Scots*, 2 vols, London, William Innys; repr. ed. W.F. Skene, Historians Of Scotland, 1885, Edinburgh, Paterson

Jackson, K.H. 1955. 'The Pictish Language', in Wainwright (ed.) 1955: 129-66

Jackson, K.H. 1963. 'On the northern Britain section in Nennius', in N.K. Chadwick (ed.), *Celt and Saxon: Studies in the Early British Border*, 20-62, Cambridge University Press

Jackson, K.H. 1969. *The Gododdin: the Oldest Scottish Poem*, Edinburgh, Edinburgh University Press

Jackson, K.[H.] 1972. *The Gaelic Notes in the Book of Deer*, Cambridge University Press

Jackson, K.H. 1981. 'Bede's *Urbs Giudi*: Stirling or Cramond?', *Cambridge Medieval Celtic Studies* **2**: 1-8

James, S., Marshall, A. and Millett, M. 1984. 'An early medieval building tradition', *Archaeol J* **141**: 182-215

Jewell, R.H.I. 1986. 'The Anglo-Saxon friezes at Breedon-on-the-Hill, Leicestershire', *Archaeologia* **108**: 95-115

Johnston, I. 2004. 'First king of the Scots? Actually he was a Pict', *The Scotsman*, 2 October 2004

Johnston, I. and Duncan, A. 2005. 'Plan for monument to "Scotland's birthplace" blocked by landowner', *The Scotsman*, 3 January 2005

Johnston, J.B. 1892. *Place-Names of Scotland*, Edinburgh, D. Douglas

Jones, G.R.J. 1979. 'Multiple estates and early settlement', in P.H. Sawyer (ed.), *Medieval Settlement: Continuity and Change*, 15-40, London, Edward Arnold

Jones, G.R.J. 1984. 'The multiple estate: a model for tracing the interrelationships of society, economy and habitat', in K. Biddick (ed.), *Archaeological Approaches to Medieval Europe*, Studies in Medieval Europe 18, Kalamazoo, Mich., Medieval Institute Publications

Jones, G.R.J. 1985. 'Multiple estates perceived', *J Hist Geog* **11**: 352-63

Kapelle, W.E. 1979. *The Norman Conquest of the North: the Region and its Transformation, 1000-1135*, London, Croom Helm

Karkov, C. 1991. 'The decoration of early wooden architecture in Ireland and Northumbria', in C.E. Karkov and R. Farrell (eds), *Studies in Insular Art and Archaeology*, 27-48, American Early Medieval Studies 1, Oxford, Ohio, Miami University School of Fine Arts

Keevill, G.D. 2000. *Medieval Palaces: an Archaeology*, Stroud, Tempus

Kelly, F. 1988. *A Guide to Early Irish Law*, Early Irish Law Series 3, Dublin, Dublin Institute for Advanced Studies

Kenney, J.F. 1929. *The Sources for the Early History of Ireland*, Vol. 1: *Ecclesiastical: an Introduction and Guide*, New York, Columbia University Press; repr. 1993, Dublin,

Keynes, S. and Lapidge, M. (eds) 1983. *Alfred the Great: Asser's Life of King Alfred and other Contemporary Sources*, Harmondsworth, Penguin

Keyser, C. 1927. *A List of Norman Tympana and Lintels with Figure or Symbolic Sculpture still or till Recently Existing in Churches of Great Britain*, second edn, London; first edn. 1904; rev. edn in prep.

Kitzinger, E. 1993. 'Interlace and icons: form and function in early Insular art', in Spearman and Higgitt (eds) 1993: 3-15

Krautheimer, R. 1942. 'Introduction to an iconography of medieval architecture', *J Warburg and Courtauld Institutes* **5**: 1-33

Krautheimer, R. 1937. *Corpus Basilicarum Christianarum: The Early Christian Basilicas of Rome (IV-IX Century)*, vol. 1, Città del Vaticano, Pontificio Istituto di Archeologia Cristiana

Lacy, B. (ed.) 1983. *Archaeological Survey of County Donegal: a Description of the Field Antiquities of the County from the Mesolithic to the 17th Century AD*, Lifford, Donegal County Council

Laing, L. 2000. 'The chronology and context of Pictish relief sculpture', *Med Archaeol* **44**: 81-114

Laing, L. and Laing, J. 1993. *The Picts and the Scots*, Stroud, Alan Sutton

Laing, L. and Laing, J. 1996. *Early English Art and Architecture: Archaeology and Society*, Stroud, Sutton

Lane, A. and Campbell, E. 2000. *Dunadd: an Early Dalriadic Capital*, Cardiff Studies in Archaeology, Oxford, Oxbow Books

Lapidge, M., with Blair, J., Keynes, S. and Scragg, D. (eds) 1999. *The Blackwell Encyclopedia of Anglo-Saxon England*, Oxford, Blackwell

Leask, H.G. 1955. *Irish Churches and Monastic Buildings*, vol. 1: *The First Phases and the Romanesque*, Dundalk, Dundalgan Press

Leclerq, H. 1925. 'Basilique', in F. Cabrol and H. Leclerq (eds), *Dictionnaire d'archéologie chrétienne et de liturgie*, vol. 2: 525–602, Paris, R.P. dom F. Cabrol

Lines, M. 1992. *Sacred Stones Sacred Places*, Edinburgh, Saint Andrew Press

Lucas, A.T. 1967. 'The plundering and burning of churches in Ireland, 7th to 16th century', in E. Rynne (ed.), *North Munster Studies: Esssays in Commemoration of Monsignor Michael Moloney*, 172–229, Limerick, Limerick Field Club

Lucas, A.T. 1987. 'The social role of relics and reliquaries in ancient Ireland', *J Royal Soc Antiq Ireland* **161** (1986): 5–37

Lynch, M. (ed.) 2001. *The Oxford Companion to Scottish History*, Oxford, Oxford University Press

Mac an Tàiller, I. 2003. 'Ainmean–àite le buidheachas/placenames', available at www.scottish. parliament.uk/vli/language/gaelic/vl-trans.htm#places

Macdonald, A.D.S. 1981. 'Notes on monastic archaeology and the Annals of Ulster, 650–1050', in Ó Corráin (ed.) 1981: 304–19

MacGibbon, D. and Ross, T. 1896–7. *The Ecclesiastical Architecture of Scotland from the Earliest Christian Times to the Seventeeth Century*, 3 vols, Edinburgh, David Douglas

Mackay, G. 2000. *Scottish Place Names*, New Lanark, Geddes & Grosset for Lomond Books

Mackenzie, W.C. 1931. *Scottish Place-Names*, London, Kegan Paul, Trench, Trubner & Co.

Mackinlay, J.M. 1914. *Ancient Church Dedications in Scotland: Non-Scriptural Dedications*, Edinburgh, David Douglas

Mac Lean, D. 1990. 'The origins and early development of the Celtic cross', *Markers (J. Assoc. Gravestone Stud.)* **7**: 233–75

Mac Lean, D. 1998. 'The Northumbrian perspective', in Foster (ed.) 1998: 179–201

McNab, S. 1988. 'Styles used in twelfth century Irish figure sculpture', *Peritia* **6–7** (1987–88): 265–97

McNeill, P.G.B. and MacQueen, H.L. (eds) 1996. *Atlas of Scottish History to 1707*, Edinburgh, The Scottish Medievalists/Department of Geography, University of Edinburgh

MacPherson, D. 1796. *Geographical Illustrations of Scottish History, Containing the Names of Places Mentioned in the Chronicles, Histories, Records, etc*, 4 vols, London, G. Nicol

Macquarrie, A. 1990. 'Early Christian Govan: the historical context', *Records Scottish Church Hist Soc* **24**: 1–17

Macquarrie, A. 1992. 'Early Christian religious houses in Scotland: foundation and function', in J. Blair and R. Sharpe (eds), *Pastoral Care Before the Parish*, 110–33, Studies in the Early History of Britain, Leicester, Leicester University Press

Macquarrie, A. 1994. 'The historical context of the Govan stones', in Ritchie (ed.) 1994: 27–32

Macquarrie, A. 1997. *The Saints of Scotland: Essays in Scottish Church History, AD 450–1093*, Edinburgh, John Donald

Macquarrie, A. 2004. *Medieval Scotland: Kingship and Nation*, Stroud, Sutton

McRoberts, D. 1959. 'Material destruction caused by the Scottish Reformation', *Innes Rev* **10**: 126–72

MacSween, A. 2002. *St Serf's, Dunning and the Dupplin Cross*, Official Guide, [Edinburgh], Historic Scotland

Mack, A. 1997. *Field Guide to the Pictish Symbol Stones*, Balgavies, Angus, Pinkfoot Press

Marshall, W. 1880. *Historic Scenes in Perthshire*, Edinburgh, William Oliphant & Co.

Marwick, H. 1924. 'Two sculptured stones recently found in Orkney', *Proc Soc Antiq Scotland* **58** (1923–24): 295–9

Matthew, H.C.G. and Harrison, B. (eds) 2004. *Oxford Dictionary of National Biography, from the Earliest Times to the Year 2000*, 60 vols, Oxford, Oxford University Press

Maxwell, G.S. 1983. 'Recent aerial survey in Scotland', in G.S. Maxwell (ed.), *The Impact of Aerial Reconnaissance on Archaeology*, 27-40, CBA Research Report 49, London, Council for British Archaeology

Maxwell, G.S. 1987. 'Settlement in Southern Pictland: a new overview', in Small (ed.) 1987: 31-44

Maxwell, I. 1994. 'The preservation of Dark Age sculpture', in Burt *et al.* (eds) 1994: 5-19

Maxwell, I. 2005. 'Scotland's early medieval sculpture in the 21st Century: a strategic overview of conservation problems, maintenance and replication methods', in Foster and Cross (eds) 2005: 159-74

Meldrum, N. 1926. *Forteviot: the History of a Strathearn Parish*, Paisley, Alexander Gardner

Mepisashvili, R. and Tsintsadze, V. 1979. *The Arts of Ancient Georgia*, London, Thames and Hudson

Miller, M. 1982. 'Matriliny by treaty: the Pictish foundation-legend', in Whitelock *et al.* (eds) 1982: 133-61

Miller, M. 1999. 'Amhlaíbh trahens centum', *Scottish Gaelic Stud* **19**: 241-5

Miller, S. and Ruckley, N.A. 2005. 'The role of geological analysis of monuments: a case study from St Vigeans and related sites', in Foster and Cross (eds) 2005: 277-91

Millett, M. and James, S. 1983. 'Excavations at Cowdery's Down, Basingstoke, Hampshire, 1978-79', *Archaeol J* **140**: 151-279

Mitchell, G.F. 1977. 'Bronze bell of Clogher', in P. Cone (ed.), *Treasures of Early Irish Art, 1500 BC to 1500 AD*, 143, no. 44, New York, Metropolitan Museum of Art

Morris, C.D. 1996. 'From Birsay to Tintagel: a personal view', in Crawford (ed.) 1996: 37-78

Murray, D. and Ralston, I. 1997. 'The excavation of a square-ditched barrow and other cropmarks at Boysack Mills, Inverkeilor, Angus', *Proc Soc Antiq Scotland* **127**: 359-86

Murray, P. and Murray, L. 1996. *The Oxford Companion to Christian Art and Architecture*, Oxford, Oxford University Press

Name Book 1860. Ordnance Survey Name Book, unpublished

Nelson, J. 1992. *Charles the Bald*, London, Longman

Ní Chatháin, P. and Richter, M. (eds) 1984. *Irland und Europa: die Kirche im Frühmittelalter/Ireland and Europe: the Early Church*, Veröffentlichungen des Europa-Zentrums Tübingen, Kulturwissenschaftliche Reihe, Stuttgart, Klett-Cotta

Nicholson, R. 1974. *Scotland: the Later Middle Ages*, The Edinburgh History of Scotland 2, Edinburgh, Oliver & Boyd

Nicolaisen, W.F.H. 1976. *Scottish Place-Names: their Study and Significance*, London, B.T. Batsford; 2nd edn, 2001, Edinburgh, John Donald

Nicolaisen, W.F.H. 1996. *The Picts and their Place Names*, Groam House Lecture Series, Rosemarkie, Groam House Museum Trust

Nicolaisen, W.F.H. 1997. 'On Pictish rivers and their confluences', in Henry (ed.) 1997: 113-18

Niermeyer, J.F. 1976. *Mediae Latinatis Lexicon Minus: Lexique Latin médiéval- français/anglais. A Medieval Latin-French/English Dictionary*, Leiden, E.J. Brill

Noddle, B. 2000. 'Animal bone', in Lane and Campbell 2000: 226-8

NMAS 1949, National Museum of Antiquities of Scotland. *A Short guide to Scottish Antiquities*, Edinburgh, HMSO

Northcote, J.S. and Brownlow, W.R.B. 1869. *Roma Sotterranea: or some Account of the Roman Catacombs, Especially of the Cemetery of San Callisto*, London, Longmans, Green, Reader and Dyer

Ó Carragáin, É. 1988. 'The meeting of Saint Paul and Saint Anthony: visual and literary uses of a eucharistic motif', in G. Mac Niocaill and P.F. Wallace (eds), *Keimelia: Studies in Medieval Archaeology and History in Memory of Tom Delaney*, 1–58, Galway, Galway University Press

Ó Corráin, D. 1981. 'The early Irish churches: some aspects of organisation', in D. Ó Corráin (ed.), *Irish Antiquity: Essays and Studies Presented to Professor M.J. O'Kelly*, 327–41, Cork, Tower Books; repr. 1994, Blackrock, Four Courts Press

O'Dwyer, P. 1976. *Devotion to Mary in Ireland, 700–1000*, Dublin

O'Dwyer, P. 1981. *Célí Dé: Spiritual Reform in Ireland, 750–900*, Dublin, Editions Tailliura

O'Dwyer, P. 1988. *Mary: a History of Devotion in Ireland*, Dublin, Four Courts Press

Ó Floinn, R. 1995. 'Clonmacnoise: art and patronage in the early medieval period', in Bourke (ed.) 1995: 251–60

Ó Máille, T. 1910. *The Language of the Annals of Ulster*, Celtic Studies 2, Manchester, Victoria University Publications

O'Meadhra, U. 1993. 'Viking-Age sketches and motif pieces from the northern earldoms', in C.E. Batey, J. Jesch and C.D. Morris (eds), *The Viking Age in Caithness, Orkney and the North Atlantic*, 423–40, Edinburgh, Edinburgh University Press

Ó Murchadha, D. 1980. 'Rubbings taken of the inscriptions on the Cross of the Scriptures at Clonmacnois', *J Royal Soc Antiq Ireland* **110**: 47–51

O'Rahilly, T.F. 1946. *Early Irish History and Mythology*, Dublin, Dublin Institute of Advanced Studies

Oakeshott, W. 1967. *The Mosaics of Rome from the Third to the Fourteenth Centuries*, London, Thames and Hudson

Okasha, E. 1983. 'A supplement to *Hand-List of Anglo-Saxon Non-Runic Inscriptions*', *Anglo-Saxon England* **11**: 83–118

Omand, D. (ed.) 1999. *The Perthshire Book*, Edinburgh, Birlinn

Oram, R. (ed.) 2004. *The Kings & Queens of Scotland*, new edn, Stroud, Tempus; first edn 2001

Osborne, J. and Claridge, A. 1996. *Early Christian and Medieval Antiquities*, vol. 1: *Mosaics and Wallpaintings in Roman Churches*, Series A, pt II, London, The Paper Museum of Cassiano dal Pozzo

Padel, O.J. 1994. 'The nature of Arthur', *Cambrian Med Celtic Stud* **27**: 1–31

Pantos, A. and Semple, S. (eds) 2004. *Assembly Places and Practices in Medieval Europe*, Dublin, Four Courts Press

Parker, J.H. 1866. *Pictures in Mosaic Rome and Ravenna*, Oxford, James Parker & Co

Parsons, D. 1986. '*Sacrarium*: ablution drains in early medieval churches', in Butler and Morris (eds) 1986: 105–60

Parsons, D. 1989. *Liturgy and Architecture in the Middle Ages*, Third Deerhurst Lecture, 1986, Leicester, Friends of Deerhurst Church/University of Leicester Department of Adult Education

Peacock, D. 1849. *Perth: its Annals and its Archives*, Perth, Thomas Richardson

Pennant, T. 1776 [1998]. *A Tour in Scotland and Voyage to the Hebrides, 1772*, Chester, John Monk; ed. A. Simmons, 1998, Edinburgh, Birlinn

Phillips, E., McMillan, A., Browne, M., and Forty, N. 2003. 'The geology of the Stone of Destiny', in Welander *et al.* (eds) 2003: 33–40

PAS 1997. *Pictish Arts Society Field Trip 1997: Abernethy and North Fife*, Pictish Arts Society Field Guide 4, Edinburgh, Pictish Arts Society

Pinkerton, J. 1789. *An Enquiry into the History of Scotland preceding the Reign of Malcolm III, or the Year 1056*, 2 vols, London; 2nd edn 1814

Pococke, R. 1887. *Tours in Scotland, 1747, 1750, 1760, by Richard Pococke, Bishop of Meath*, ed. D.W. Kemp, Edinburgh, Scottish History Society

Pratt, L. 2000. 'Anglo-Saxon attitudes? Alfred the Great and the Romantic national epic', in D. Scragg and C. Weinberg (eds), *Literary Appropriations of the Anglo-Saxons from the Thirteenth to the Twentieth Century*, 138–56, Cambridge Studies in Anglo-Saxon England 29, Cambridge University Press

Price, L. 1959. 'Rock-basins, or "bullauns", at Glendalough and elsewhere', *J Royal Soc Antiq Ireland* **89**: 161–88

Proudfoot, E. 1996. 'Excavations at the long cist cemetery on the Hallow Hill, St Andrews, Fife, 1975–7', *Proc Soc Antiq Scotland* **126**: 387–454

Proudfoot, E. 1997. 'Abernethy and Mugdrum: towards reassessments', in Henry (ed.) 1997: 47–63

Purser, J. n.d. The Forteviot Bell, unattributed and undated display board in St Andrew's Church, Forteviot

Radford, C.A.R. 1942. 'The early Christian monuments of Scotland', *Antiquity* **16**: 1–18

Radford, C.A.R. 1976. 'The church at Saint Alkmund, Derby', *Derbyshire Archaeol J* **96**: 26–61

Radford, C.A.R. 1977. 'The earliest Irish churches', *Ulster J Archaeol* **40**: 1–11

Radford, C.A.R. 1981. 'Excavations at Glastonbury Abbey, 1908–64', in N. Coldstream and P. Draper (eds), *Medieval Art and Architecture at Wells and Glastonbury: British Archaeological Association Conference Transactions for the Year 1978*, 110–34, Leeds, British Archaeological Association

Radley, A. and Dunn, A. 2000. 'Dupplin Cross (Forteviot parish): excavations', *Discovery and Excavation in Scotland 1999*, 70

Rahtz, P. 1979. *The Saxon and Medieval Palaces at Cheddar*, BAR British Series 65, Oxford, BAR

Ralston, I. 1982. 'A timber hall at Balbridie farm: the Neolithic settlement of north-east Scotland', *Aberdeen University Rev* **168** (1981–82): 238–49

Ralston, I. 2004. *Fortifications of the Picts*, Groam House Lecture Series, Rosemarkie, Groam House Museum

Ralston, I. and Reynolds, N. 1981. *Excavations at Balbridie Farm, Kincardine and Deeside District (NO733959)*, Edinburgh, np

RCAHMS 1963. *Stirlingshire: an Inventory of the Ancient Monuments*, 2 vols, Edinburgh, HMSO

RCAHMS 1994. *South-East Perth: an Archaeological Landscape*, Edinburgh, RCAHMS

RCAHMS 2003. *Early Medieval Sculpture in Angus Council Museums*, RCAHMS Broadsheet 11, Edinburgh, RCAHMS

RCHM(E) 1972. Royal Commission on Historical Monuments (England), *Dorset*, vol. 4, *North Dorset*, London, RCHM(E)

Reeves, W. 1864. *The Culdees of the British Islands, as they Appear in History: with an Appendix of Evidences*, Dublin, M.H. Gill; repr. 1994, Felinfach, Llanerch

Reynolds, N. 1980a. 'Dark Age timber halls and the background to excavations at Balbridie', in L.M. Thoms (ed.), *Scottish Archaeol Forum* **10**: *Settlements in Scotland 1000 BC – AD 1000*: 41–60

Reynolds, N. 1980b. 'Balbridie', *Current Archaeol* **70**: 326–8

Rice, M. 1998. *The Power of the Bull*, London, Routledge

Richardson, J.S. 1964. *The Mediaeval Stone Carver in Scotland*, Edinburgh, Edinburgh University Press

Ritchie, A. 1994. *Perceptions of the Picts: from Eumenius to John Buchan*, Groam House Lecture Series, Rosemarkie, Groam House Museum Trust

Ritchie, A. 1995. 'Meigle and lay patronage in Tayside in the 9th and 10th centuries AD', *Tayside and Fife Archaeol J* **1**: 1–10

Ritchie, A. 1997. *Meigle Museum: Pictish Carved Stones*, Edinburgh, Historic Scotland

Ritchie, A. (ed.) 1994. *Govan and its Early Medieval Sculpture*, Stroud, Alan Sutton

Ritchie, A. and Ritchie, G. 1998. *Scotland: an Oxford Archaeological Guide*, Oxford, Oxford University Press

Rivet, A.L.F. and Smith, C. 1979. *Place-Names of Roman Britain*, London, B.T. Batsford

Robertson, N.M. 1997. 'The early medieval carved stones of Fortingall', in Henry (ed.) 1997: 133-48

Robertson, R.J. 1845. 'Parish of Forteviot', *New Statistical Account of Scotland*, vol. 10: 1172-5, Edinburgh, William Blackwood and Sons

Roger, J.C. 1880. 'Notice of a drawing of a bronze crescent-shaped plate, which was dug up at Laws, Parish of Monifieth, in 1796', *Proc Soc Antiq Scotland* **14** (1879-80): 268-74

Rogers, C.J. 2000. *War Cruel and Sharp: English Strategy under Edward III, 1327-1360*, Woodbridge, Boydell

Rollason, D., Piper, A.J., Harvey, M. and Rollason, L. (eds) 2004. *The Durham Liber Vitae and its Context*, Regions and Regionalism in History, Woodbridge, Boydell

Ross, A. 1967. *Pagan Celtic Britain: Studies in Iconography and Tradition*, London, Routledge and Kegan Paul

Ross, D. 2001. *Scottish Place-names*, Edinburgh, Birlinn

Ross, T. 1902. 'Account of the excavation of the Roman station at Inchtuthil, Perthshire, undertaken by the Society of Antiquaries in 1901: (II) Description of the plans', *Proc Soc Antiq Scotland* **36** (1901-2): 203-36

Rutherford, A. 1976. ' "Giudi" revisited', *Bull Board Celtic Stud* **26**: 440-4

Ryan, M. 1987. 'The Donore hoard: early medieval metalwork from Moynalty, near Kells, Ireland', *Antiquity* **61**: 57-63

Ryan, M. (ed.) 1987. *Ireland and Insular Art, AD 500-1200*, 129-37, Dublin, Royal Irish Academy

St Joseph, J.K.S. 1976. 'Air reconnaissance: recent results, 40', *Antiquity* **50**: 55-7

St Joseph, J.K.S. 1978. 'Air reconnaissance: recent results, 44', *Antiquity* **52**: 47-50

Samson, R. 1992. 'The reinterpretation of the Pictish symbols', *J British Archaeol Assoc* **145**: 29-65

Schaller, D. 1974. 'Der heilige Tag als Termin mittelalterlicher Staatsakte', *Deutsches Archiv für Erforschung des Mittelalters* **30**: 1-24

Scott, I.G. 2005. 'The bulls of Burghead and Allen's technique of illustration', in Cross and Foster (eds) 2005: 215-19

Selkirk, A. (citing D. Alexander) 1999. 'Redcastle barrow cemetery', *Current Archaeol* **166**: 395-7

Sellar, W.D.H. 2001. 'William Forbes Skene (1809-92): historian of Celtic Scotland', *Proc Soc Antiq Scotland* **131**: 3-21

Sexton, E. 1946. *A Descriptive and Bibliographical List of Irish Figure Sculptures of the Early Christian Period*, Portland, Maine, Southworth-Anthoensen Press

Sharpe, R. 1984a. 'Some problems concerning the nature of the organization of the Church in early medieval Ireland', *Peritia* **3**: 230-70

Sharpe, R. 1984b. 'Armagh and Rome in the seventh century', in Ní Chatháin and M. Richter (eds) 1984: 58-72

Simpson, N. 1997. 'Rumble in the jungle: Pitcur botany expedition proves a thorn in the side...', *Pictish Arts Soc Newsletter* (summer/autumn 1997) (unpaginated)

Simpson, W.D. 1963. 'The early Romanesque tower at Restenneth Priory, Angus', *Antiq J* **43**: 269-83

Simpson, W.D. 1965. *The Ancient Stones of Scotland*, London, Robert Hale

Skene, W.F. 1857. 'Observations on Forteviot, the site of the ancient capital of Scotland', *Archaeologia Scotica* **4**: 271-9 (paper read 23 January, 1832)

Skene, W.F. 1862. 'Notice of the early ecclesiastical settlements at St Andrews', *Proc Soc Antiq Scotland* **4** (1860-62): 300-21

Skene, W.F. (ed.) 1867. *Chronicles of the Picts, Chronicles of the Scots, and other Early Memorials of Scottish History*, Edinburgh, HM General Register House

Skene, W.F. 1876-80. *Celtic Scotland: a History of Ancient Alban*, 3 vols, Edinburgh, David Douglas

Skene, W.F. 1886-90. *Celtic Scotland: a History of Ancient Alban*, second edn, 3 vols, Edinburgh, David Douglas

Small, A. 1969. 'Burghead', *Scottish Archaeol Forum* **1**: 61-8

Small, A. 1999. 'The Dark Ages', in Omand (ed.) 1999: 47-58

Small, A. (ed.) 1987. *The Picts: a New Look at Old Problems*, Dundee, np

Smith, I.M. 1991. 'Sprouston, Roxburghshire: an early Anglian centre of the eastern Tweed basin', *Proc Soc Antiq Scotland* **121**: 261-94

Smyth, A.P. 1972. 'The earliest Irish annals: their first contemporary entries, and the earliest centres of recording', *Proc Royal Irish Acad* **72** (Sec. C): 1-48

Smyth, A.P. 1977. *Scandinavian Kings in the British Isles, AD 850-880*, Oxford, Oxford University Press

Smyth, A.P. 1984. *Warlords and Holymen: Scotland AD 80-1000*, The New History of Scotland 1, London, E.A. Arnold; repr. 1989, Edinburgh, Edinburgh University Press

Spearman, R.M. 1993. 'The mounts from Crieff, Perthshire, and their wider context', in Spearman and Higgitt (eds) 1993: 135-42

Spearman, R.M. and Higgitt, J. (eds) 1993. *The Age of Migrating Ideas: Early Medieval Art in Northern Britain and Ireland*, Edinburgh and Stroud, National Museums of Scotland/Alan Sutton

Statistical Account 1797. 'Parish of Forteviot', in *The Statistical Account of Scotland*, vol. 20 (1796-7): 117-25 (no author given); reprinted in D.J. Worthington and I.R. Grant (gen. eds), 1976, *The Statistical Account of Scotland*, vol. 11: *South and East Perthshire, Kinross-shire*, 192-200, Wakefield, EP Publishing

Steane, J.M. 1999. *The Archaeology of the Medieval English Monarchy*, 2nd edn, London, Routledge; first edn 1993, London, B.T. Batsford

Steane, J.M. 2001. *The Archaeology of Power: England and Northern Europe, AD 800-1600*, Stroud, Tempus

Steer, K.A. 1958. 'Arthur's O'on: a lost shrine of Roman Britain', *Archaeol J* **115**: 99-110

Steer, K.A. 1976. 'More light on Arthur's O'on', *Glasgow Archaeol J* **4**: 90-2

Stevenson, J.B. 1984. 'Garbeg and Whitebridge: two square barrow cemeteries in Inverness-shire', in Friell and Watson (eds) 1984: 145-50

Stevenson, R.B.K. 1955. 'Pictish Art', in Wainwright (ed.) 1955: 97-128

Stevenson, R.B.K. 1956. 'The chronology and relationships of some Irish and Scottish crosses', *J Royal Soc Antiq Ireland* **86**: 84-96

Stevenson, R.B.K. 1971. 'Sculpture in Scotland in the 6th – 9th centuries AD', in W. Schrickel, V.H. Elbern and V. Milojčić (eds), *Kolloquium über spätantike und frühmittelalterliche Skulptur*, 65-74, Mainz am Rhein, Philipp von Zabern

Stevenson, R.B.K. 1976. 'The earlier metalwork of Pictland', in J.V.S. Megaw (ed.), *To Illustrate the Monuments: Essays on Archaeology Presented to Stuart Piggott*, 246-51, London, Thames and Hudson

Stevenson, R.B.K. 1981. 'Christian sculpture in Norse Shetland', *Frodskaparrit* **28-9**: 283-92

Stuart, J. 1856. *Sculptured Stones of Scotland*, vol. 1, Aberdeen, Spalding Club

Stuart, J. 1867. *Sculptured Stones of Scotland*, vol. 2, Edinburgh, Spalding Club

Sutherland, E. 1994. *In Search of the Picts: a Dark Age Nation*, London, Constable

Sutherland, E. 1997. *A Guide to the Pictish Stones*, Edinburgh, Birlinn

Swift, C. 1996. 'Pagan monuments and Christian legal centres in early Meath', *Ríocht na Midhe* **9.2**: 1-26

'T' 1772. Untitled letter about Forteviot, *The Weekly Magazine, or Edinburgh Amusement* **16** (2 June 1772): 331-2

Taylor, H.M. 1973. 'The position of the altar in early Anglo-Saxon churches', *Antiq J* **53**: 52-8

Taylor, J. and Taylor, H.M. 1965-78. *Anglo-Saxon Architecture*, 3 vols, Cambridge, Cambridge University Press

Taylor, S. 2000. 'The coming of the Augustinians to St Andrews and version B of the St Andrews foundation legend', in Taylor (ed.) 2000: 115-23

Taylor, S. 2003. 'From Tay to Motray – place-names of north-west Fife, unpub. lecture given to the Scottish Place-Name Society day conference, Dundee, 8 November 2003, summarised at www.st-andrews.ac.uk/institutes/sassi/spns/SPNS1103.htm

Taylor, S. (ed.) 2000. *Kings, Clerics and Chronicles in Scotland, 500-1297: Essays in Honour of Marjorie Ogilvie Anderson on the Occasion of her Ninetieth Birthday*, Dublin, Four Courts Press

Topping, P. 1992. 'The Penrith henges: a survey by the Royal Commission on Historical Monuments of England', *Proc Prehist Soc* **58**: 249-64

Turnbull, M. 1997. *Saint Andrew: Scotland's Myth and Identity*, Edinburgh, St Andrew Press

Veitch, K. 1997. 'The Columban Church in northern Britain', *Proc Soc Antiq Scotland* **127**: 627-47

Wagner, P. 2002, *Pictish Warrior, AD 297-841*, Warrior 50, Oxford, Osprey

Wainwright, F.T. 1955. 'The Picts and the problem', in Wainwright (ed.) 1955: 1-53

Wainwright, F.T. (ed.) 1955. *The Problem of the Picts*, Edinburgh, Thomas Nelson; repr. 1980, Perth, Melven Press

Wainwright, G.J. 1989. *The Henge Monuments*, London, Thames and Hudson

Walker, A.D., 1982. Eastern Scotland: *Soil and Land Capability for Agriculture*, Handbooks of the Soil Survey of Scotland 5, Aberdeen, Macaulay Institute for Soil Research

Walker, B. and Ritchie, J.N.G. 1987. *Exploring Scotland's Heritage: Fife and Tayside*, Edinburgh, RCAHMS/HMSO; second edn 1996. *Exploring Scotland's Heritage: Fife, Perthshire and Angus*, Edinburgh, HMSO

Walker, D. 1963. *The Geology and Scenery of Strathearn*, Dundee, Dundee Museum and Art Gallery

Warner, R. 2004. 'Notes on the inception and early development of the royal mound in Ireland', in Pantos and Semple (eds) 2004: 27-43

Warren, F.E. 1881. *The Liturgy and Ritual of the Celtic Church*, Oxford, Clarendon Press; second edn, ed. J. Stevenson, 1987. Studies in Celtic History 9, Woodbridge, Boydell Press

Watson, W.J. 1905. 'Paisley', *Celtic Rev* (1904-05); reprinted in W.J. Watson, Scottish Place-Name Papers, 54, London, Steve Savage

Watson, W.J. 1926. *The History of the Celtic Place-Names of Scotland*, Edinburgh, William Blackwood & Sons; repr. 1993, Edinburgh, Birlinn

Wedderburn, L.M.M. and Grime, D.M. 1984. 'The cairn cemetery at Garbeg, Drumnadrochit', in Friell and Watson (eds) 1984: 151-67

Weir, A. 1980. *Early Ireland: a Field Guide*, Belfast, Blackstaff Press

Welander, R., Breeze, D.J. and Clancy, T.O. (eds) 2003. *The Stone of Destiny: Artefact and Icon*, Monograph Series 22, Edinburgh, Society of Antiquaries of Scotland

Welch, M. 1992. *English Heritage Book of Anglo-Saxon England*, London, B.T. Batsford/English Heritage

Whitelock, D., McKitterick, R. and Dumville, D. (eds) 1982. *Ireland in Early Mediaeval Europe: Studies in Memory of Kathleen Hughes*, Cambridge, Cambridge University Press

Whittington, G. 1974. 'Placenames and the settlement pattern of Dark-Age Scotland', *Proc*

Soc Antiq Scotland **106** (1974-5): 99-110

Whittington, G. and Soulsby, J.A. 1968. 'A preliminary report on an investigation into Pit place-names', *Scottish Geog Mag* **84**: 117-25

Williams, J.H., Shaw, M. and Denham, V. 1985. *Middle Saxon Palaces at Northampton*, Archaeological Monograph 4, Northampton, Northampton Development Corporation

Williams, H. 1998. 'Reuse of prehistoric and Roman monuments', *Med Archaeol* **41**: 1-32

Wilson, A.J. 1993. *St Margaret, Queen of Scotland*, rev. edn, 2001, Edinburgh, John Donald

Wilson, D.M. 1973. 'The treasure', in A. Small, A.C. Thomas and D.M. Wilson (eds), *St Ninian's Isle and its Treasure*, 45-148, 2 vols, London, Oxford University Press for the University of Aberdeen

Wilson, D.M. 1984. *Anglo-Saxon Art: from the Seventh Century to the Norman Conquest*, London, Thames and Hudson

Woolf, A. 2001a. 'Ungus (Onuist), son of Uurgust', in Lynch (ed.) 2001: 604

Woolf, A. 2001b. 'Birth of a nation', in G. Menzies (ed.), *In Search of Scotland*, 24-45, Edinburgh, Polygon

Woolf, A. in prep. *From Pictland to Alba: Scotland 789 to 1070*

Wormald, F. 1971. 'The Winchester School before St Aethelwold', in P. Clemoes and K. Hughes (eds), *England before the Conquest*, 305-14, Cambridge, Cambridge University Press

Wormald, P. 1996. 'The emergence of the *Regnum Scottorum*: a Carolingian hegemony?', in Crawford (ed.) 1996: 131-60

Yeoman, P. 1999. *Pilgrimage in Medieval Scotland*, Edinburgh, B.T. Batsford/Historic Scotland

Youngs, S. 1989. 'Fine metalwork to *c*. AD 650', in S. Youngs (ed.), *'The Work of Angels': Masterpieces of Celtic Metalwork, 6th-9th Centuries AD*, 20-71, London, British Museum Publications

INDEX

Aachen 59
abbeys 25, 38, 60, 179, 180, 202, 252, 254, 256
abbots 20, 25, 96, 98, 100, 130, 193, 197, 213, 238
aber- 65
Abercromby cross-slab 167
Aberdeen 97, 158
Aberdeen Breviary 97
Aberdeenshire 40, 55, 87, 100
Aberlemno cross-slab 108
Abernethy 33, 35, 91, 100-1, 130
round tower 146, 210, 223
Acca, bishop 219
Ada, Countess 52
Adamson, Henry 28, 37-8
administration 52, 61, 71, 73, 76, 82, 86, 214, 233, 251, 254
Áed mac Boanta 246
Áed son of Eochaid 24, 61, 64, 65
Áed Find mac Echdach, king 61
Aelfwine 238
aerial reconnaissance 31, 44-5, 48, 50, 55, 201
Agnus Dei (see also arch, Forteviot) 167, 168, 237, 239-40
Agnus Dei 236-7
agriculture 29, 32, 35, 51, 59, 71, 73, 75-6, 82
Aided Dhiarmada 196
aisles 214-15
Alba 9, 17, 23-5, 87, 95, 248, 256
'Albans' 247
Alcluith 81
Alcock, Mrs Elizabeth 47, 158
Alcock, Professor Leslie 10, 15, 47, 158, 203, 223
Alcocks, Professor and Mrs 110, 115, 159, 203, 210, 220
Aldbar cross-slab 170, 176, 187, 198
Alexander I, king 202, 256
Alexander II, king 254
Alexander III, king 254
Alfred the Great, king 29, 81
Alfred, an Epic Poem 29
Allen, J. Romilly 104, 126, 152, 157-8, 191, 202
Alpín, descendants/sons of 62, 96
altars 93, 98, 100, 166, 172, 192, 215, 219, 221-2, 225, 228, 233, 236-9, 250, 252
Amlaib, see Olaf
Ammianus Marcellinus 16
ancestors 64, 231
Anderson, Joseph 104, *145,* 152, 157-8, 202
Angles 20, 56, 247
Anglo-Saxon England 68, 135, 212-13,
217, 234
Anglo-Saxon(s) 64, 81, 86, 95, 99
Angus 17, 40, 66, 69, 87, 105, 108, 138, 146, 152, 154, 156, 170, 177, 180, 210, 244
animal art (see also arch, Forteviot) 107-8, 115, 152, 156, 169, 182-3, 189, 221, 248
annals 17, 19, 20, 22-3, 25, 53, 136, 194, 196, 233, 247-8
antiquarian accounts/interest 11, 29, 31, 37-41, 47, 77-8, 104, 120, 256
apostles 94-5, 97, 99, 192, 225, 234, 237
apocalypse 234
Applecross 105, 166, 251
arch, Forteviot 9-12, 16, 48, 99, 103-4, 109, 121, 129, 137, 140, 143-240, *145, 146, 147, 149,* 257, **19, 20**
abutments 144, 148, 150, 182, 185, 187
Agnus Dei 166, 169-72, *171,* 182-3, 185, 190, 192, 199-200, 203, 210, 225, 231, 235-6, 239-40, 244-5, 250
animals 154, 156-7, 169-70, 185, 187, 189
architectural context 190, 202-3, 209, 215-16, 218, 223-35, 238, 243-4, 252
architectural implications 11, 159, 167, 243
audience 230-3
bull 170, 182-5, *183,* 190
as chancel arch 217-18, 225-7, 230-1, 234
clerics 185-8, *186,* 190, 192, 200, 240
composition 143, 154, 156-7, 169, 182, 185, 190, 192, 200
condition 144, 150, 166, 224, 243, 252
cross 148, 151, 156, 164-70, *165, 172,* 178, 183, 185, 188, 190, 192, 199, 204, 210, 225, 231, 239, 244-5, 250-2
crown 148, 151, 169-70, 178, 190, 231, 236, 239, 244
damage/defacement 148, 150, 173-4, 182, 224, 235, 243-5, 250-1
date/dating 91, 143-4, 151, 159, 178, 201-8, 244
description 11, 146-51, 158, 164
discovery 11, 43, 144, 157, 191, 244
display 144-6, 158, 234
extrados 148, 164, 224
figures 152, 154, 156-8, *172,* 174, 180-1, 187, 189, 190, 192, 235, 250, 252
historical context/setting 11, 202
iconography 11, 16, 91, 99, 143, 157, 159, 163-4, 169, 172, 184, 189-201, 206-10, 220, 224, 226, 228, 230-5, 243-4
and ideology 230-3, 240
illustrations of 157-8, *159, 160, 161, 162*
interpretation 9, 10, 12, 88, 143, 156, 158, 163-88, 190-2, 198-201, 206, 230, 233, 236, 251
intrados 148, 224
king 140, 156, 172-83, *173,* 185, 187, 190, 192, 200, 202, 206-7, 231, 244
lamb, see Agnus Dei
liturgical context/significance 11, 190-1, 215, 226, 233-40
moulding 150, 164, 166-7, 169, 190, 244
production of 148
quadrupeds, see animals
quality 151-2, 156, 162, 169, 183
sculptor(s) of 11, 157, 173-4, 185, 190, 200, 240, 243
sculptural scene 10-11, 143-4, 150-1, 156, 163, 169, 189-93, 198-200, 203, 205-6, 210, 224, 227-8, 230, 232, 234, 238-40, 252
socio-political context/significance 11, 148, 159, 163, 202, 215, 222, 232
structural role 144, 159, 191, 209
study of 10-11, 144, 157-62
symbols, symbolism 10-11, 159, 163-4, 167, 169-70, 185, 189, 191, 200, 228, 231, 233, 235, 239-40
tooling marks 148, 150-1, 224, 227
archaeological deposits, evidence 11, 39, 47-8, 50, 82, 83, 86, 102, 254
archbishoprics 92
archbishops 94, 98
arches 198, 212, 214-15, 218, 226, *227, 229, 234, 235,* 239
architects 220
architecture 10, 15, 143, 157-8, 209, 212-23, 227-8, 232, 236, 239-40
Argain Rátha Tóbachta, see 'Sacking of the Rath of Tobacht, The'
Argyll 16, 19, 21, 39, 53, 87, 89-90, 99, 138
Armagh, Church of 92-3, 98-9
Armagh City 197
Armenia 221
armies 11, 25, 86, 95, 243, 248-9, 255-6
art 157-9, 163, 170, 212
Anglo-Saxon 203, 205
Pictish 143, 193, 204
Arthur, king 120
Arthur's O'on 120
Arts and Crafts 15, **2**
assemblies 24, 53, 61-4, 81, 83
assembly places 51, 61-2, 65, 78, 83
Athelstan, king 17, 64, 87
Athelstan 86
Atholl 25, 247
Auchterarder 248
authority, see power

bachall 181
Baisliocán, 'little *basilica*' 99
Balbridie 55
Balliol, Edward 39, 255-6
    Ballyogan 193
Bamburgh 82
Banffshire 110
Bangor 97, 166
Bankhead 75, 122
baronies 256
Barrow, Professor Geoffrey 73
barrows 64, 66-70, 67, 79, 80, 81, 83, **9, 12**
basilica 10, 11, 64, 70-1, 96-9, 100, 102, 132, 137, 139-40, 200, 214-15, 219, 221-3, **14**
Basilica Sanctorum 98
basin, stone 131-2, *132*
Baslick 98-9
Baslickane 99
battles 17, 21, 25, 39, 72, 86, 89-90, 92, 95, 99, 207, 245-9, 255-6
Bebbanburh, see Bamburgh
Beckford 225
Bede 16, 53, 70, 81-2, 100, 139, 213, 233-4, 236
bell, see hand-bell
Bellethor, see *Cinnbelathoír*
Benedict Biscop 234
Benvie cross-slab 137, 152, *153*, 174, *175*, 176-7, 198
Benvie-Dupplin school 113, 137, 152, 154-6, *155*, 174, 176, 178, 198, 202-4, 206
Betha Ciarain 196
Biblical imagery, symbolism 192
bishops 40, 61, 87, 97, 100-1, 130, 133, 200, 219, 238, 252
bishoprics 92
bodyguard 52
Book of Lismore 196
book-satchels 138
boots 174, 177
Borders, The 36, 86
boundaries 73, 130-1, 197-201, 205-6, 230
boundary markers 130
Bower, Walter 88
Boysack Mills 66
Bradford-on-Avon, Church of St Laurence 217, *217*, *218*, 226, *227*, **25**
Braemar 87
Bran 90, 246
Breamore, St Mary's Church 234, *235*
Brechin 23, 101
    cross-slab 136
    round tower 146, 167, *168*, 210, 223, **22**
Bred son of Ferat, see Brude son of Wrad
Breedon-on-the-Hill 221
Bressay cross-slab 108, 181, 187
Bridei son of Bile, king 19
Bridei (Brude) son of Maelchon, king 54
Britons 20, 73, 82, 139, 247
Brittonic 17, 37
Broch of Burness graffito 174, *176*, 177
Brough of Birsay symbol stone 174, *176*, 177
Bronze Age 48, 50, 63, 78
bronzefounding 133, 135
Brown, William 43
Brude mac Bili, see Bridei son of Bile

Brude son of Wrad, king 27
Buchan 97
Buchanty 41
builders 203, 213, 224, 236
buildings 53, 54, 69, 222, 250
bullauns 131, *132*
'bull feast' 184
bulls, bull plaques (see also arch, Forteviot) 170, 184
burgh see *burh*
Burghead 137, 170, 184
burghs 253-4
burh 81
burial rights 99, 178
burials 64, 66-71, 75, 92, 98-9, 140
bury see *burh*

Cairnie 70
cairns 50, 68, 79
Caithness 110, 137-8
Caledonii 17
calf symbol 169
Callendar 26
Calvary 166-7, 239
Cambridge University Committee for Aerial Photography 48
Cambuskenneth Abbey 26, 59-60
cambutta 181
campus Merc 86
Cano 89
canons 60, 88, 92, 98, 238
Canterbury 94
capitals 29, 30, 52, 121
caput 71, 75-6, 83
card(d)en 75
Cardny 60, 75
carn 75
Carndonagh lintel 198, *199*
Carolingians 59, 72
Carron 120
cashels 77
castles 37-40, 82, 84, 244
Castletown of Braemar, see Braemar
Cathbuaidh, 'battle triumph' 95
Catlow 238
'Cattle Raid of Cooley' 184
Causantín mac Áeda, king 61, 253
Causantín mac Cináeda (Constantine II), king 247, 248
Causantín mac Dúngail, king 83
Causantín son of Uurguist, king 19, 20, 89-90, 124-5, 136, 139, 179, 208, 246
Céli Dé 41, 88, 101, 256
Cellach, bishop 61, 253
cemeteries 9, 39, 41, 48, 51, 64, 66, 67, 68-70, 78-9, 81, 100
Ceolfrith, abbot 98, 213
Ceolwulf, king 20
ceremonies, see rituals
chalices 236-7
Chana son of Dubabrach 89
chancel arches (see also arch, Forteviot) 226-8, *227*, *229*, 233-4, 238-40, 252
chancels 184, 214, 217-18, 225-6, 228, 238, 240, 252
chancellors 61
Charles I, king 37
charters 25-6, 35, 52, 59, 61, 73, 91, 101, 179-80, *180*, 202, 254-6
Cheddar 56
Chondrochedalvan 52, 60, 87, 90-1, 93, 96

Christ 93, 97, 136, 164, 167, 169, 170, 172, 192, 221, 226, 230, 234, 236-40, 251
    In Majesty 172
Christianity 65, 70, 214, 221, 234, 245
Christison, David 40
Chronicle of Huntingdon 246
Chronicle of the Kings of Alba 17, 23-5, 35, 51, 62, 247, 248, 250
chronicles 88, 225
chroniclers 30
Church, the 64, 84, 85-6, 94, 207, 214, 232, 234-5, 238, 240, 250
Church, Celtic 181
Church, Pictish 10, 11, 85, 95, 100, 125, 139, 144, 199-202, 208, 226, 230, 238, 240, 243, 250-1
churches 29, 61, 78, 84, 87, 91-102, 130, 133, 139, 167, 194, 196-7, 199, 205, 208, 210, 212-15, 219-20, 226, 231-35, 237, 252-3, 256
    Anglo-Saxon 124, 148, 218-19, 221, 223, 225, 227-8, 231, 240
    bicameral 217
    Irish 218, 251
    fixtures, fittings and furnishings 219, 221, 231, 233
    Northumbrian 227
    Pictish 9, 40, 91, 136, 212-13, 222, 236, 243
    Romanesque 224, 225
    stone 9, 85, 99, 194, 213-16, 223, 231, 236, 256
    timber 213-14
Cináed mac Ailpín, king 15, 22-4, 30, 65, 71, 95, 124, 136, 203, 204, 246, 250-1
Cináed mac Máel Choluim, king 83
Cinnbelathoír 79, 81, 256
Cinrighmonai, see Kilrimont
cists 69
Clan MacAlpine Society 30
Clann Cholmáin 193, 197
clergy, clerics (see also arch, Forteviot) 59, 61, 100, 138, 177, 181, 188, 191, 192, 193, 196, 198, 199, 200, 232, 233, 236
Clogher, bell of 136
Clonmacnoise 139, 193, 194, 196, 197, 198, 205, 233, 250
clothing 122, 151, 154, 156, 172, 174, 177, 178, 185, 187, 190, 191, 192, 193, 203, 204
Clunie 246
Coble Haugh 45
coimperta 28
coins 202
Collectio Canonum Hibernensis 98
collis credulitatis, see Scone
Colman, abbot 193-4, 196, 197, 205
Colodaesburg 82
Columban Church 136
commixtio, commixture 236, 237
communities 69, 70, 100, 101, 197
confluences 33, 40, 45, 64, 65
Conleth, archbishop 98
Connachta (Connaught) 98, 184
consecration 101
constables 61
Constantine the Great, emperor 87, 89-90, 167

Constantine mac Fergusa, see
    Causantín son of Uurguist
Constantine son of Aed ('Constantine
    II'), see Causantín mac Áeda
Constantine son of Fergus, see
    Causantín son of Uurguist
Constantinople 81, 87, 93
Continent, the 9, 36
corrachadh 75
Cossans 105
councils 54, 64
courts, royal 52, 54, 60, 64, 72, 76
courts, court sites 61, 63
Cowdery Down 56
craftsmen 72, 150
croft and toft 60
crooks, shepherds' 181, 187-8, 192-3
cropmarks 45, 48, 49, 53, 55, 66, 68-9, 9
cross-bases 122, 123, 126, 127, 167, 195,
    15, 16, 17
Cross of Calvary 166-7
Cross Park 122
Cross of Saints Patrick and Columba,
    Kells 172
Cross of the Scriptures, Clonmacnoise
    193-4, 194, 195, 196-7, 205-6
cross-slabs 71, 104-9, 105, 106, 107, 109,
    110, 114-15, 120, 130, 136-9, 151-2,
    153, 156, 166-7, 169-70, 174, 176-8,
    180-1, 183, 187, 189, 198, 220-1,
    237, 239, 244
crosses (see also arch, Forteviot) 87,
    105, 130, 137, 166, 169, 174, 193,
    196, 198-9, 204, 231, 244, 251
croziers 95
Cruachan 98
crucifixion scenes 198
crypts 214-15
Cuilén (Culen), king 25
Culdees, see *Céli Dé*
Curle, Mrs Cecil L. 203
Custantin filius Fircus, see Causantín son
    of Uurguist

dail 75
Dalcorachy 75
Dál Riata 9, 19-20, 22-3, 39, 61, 65, 95,
    110, 124, 125, 138, 166, 246, 251
damliac 196
Danes 29, 246-7, 253
Daniel, Second Vision of 183
David, Earl of Strathearn 38
David I, king 88, 253-4
David II, king 255-6
death records 16, 17, 20, 21, 23, 25, 72,
    79, 81, 124, 245-6, 247, 248
de Bernham, David, Bishop 40, 101
Deer 91
Deerhurst, Church of St Mary 184, 225
defence, defences 28, 33, 35, 76-9,
    81-4, 253
Defender of the Faith 192
Deira 238
deities, river 65
demesne, royal 72
Dent 238
dèonaidh, see dewar
Derby, St Alkmund's Church 225
desert fathers 177, 237
De Situ Albanie 17
'Destruction of Dá Derga's Hostel,
    The' 184

dewar 133
Dewar, John Alexander, see Forteviot,
    Baron
Diarmait mac Cerbaill, high-king 196-7
Dicalydones 17
diocese 100-1
DNA analysis 69
documentary evidence/sources 77, 82-
    3, 86-7, 102, 143, 201, 203, 239
dol- 75, 90
Dolcorachy 60, 75
Doldencha 87
Dollar 247-8
dominus fundi 230
domus 54
Domnall mac Ailpín, king 24, 61-2, 64,
    79-81, 203, 246
Donaghmore 136
Donald, Earl of Mar 255
Donald mac Alpin ('Donald I'), see
    Domnall mac Ailpín
Donnchad, see Dúnchad
Donore 220
Doon Hill 56
doors, doorways 146, 148, 167, 184, 194,
    210, 212, 218, 220, 223-5
Dorsum Crup, see Duncrub
dress, see clothing
Drest son of Ferat, see Drust son of
    Wrad
Driscoll, Professor Stephen 73
Dronachy 126
Druim Alban 246
Drust son of Wrad, king 21-2, 27
Dubh (Duff), king 25
Dublin 245, 247-8
Dub Tholarg, king 16
dues, see patronage
Dumbarton Rock 82, 247, 253
dùn, see fortress
Dunadd 39, 65
Dunbar 56
Dunblane 44, 100
    cross-slab 221
Duncan, king 27-8, 53, 60, 256
Dúnchad, abbott 23
Duncrub, battle of 25
Dunduff 25
Dundurn 24, 33, 53, 83, **10**
Dunfallandy cross-slab 108
Dunfermline 29, 73, 255
Dun Fother, see Dunottar
Dunkeld 23, 95, 101, 136, 246
    cross-shaft 138
Dunning 248
    St Serf's Church 122
Dunning Burn 248
Dunnottar 17, 35
Dunrobin 68
Dunsinane Hill 83
Dupplin 15
    cross 19, 113-14, 116, 117, 121-6, 123,
        129-31, 138-9, 152, 154, 174, 175,
        176-9, 181, 199, 203, 206-7, 212,
        232, 238, 258, **15**
Dupplin Loch 73
Dupplin Moor, battle of 39, 255-6
Durham, Church of 208
dynasties, royal 62, 89, 96, 98-9, 139,
    176, 178, 204, 232
Dysert O'Dea 193

ealdormen 238
Eamont Bridge 64
Earls Barton, All Saints Church 212,
    213, 223, **23**
*Early Christian Monuments of Scotland,
    The* 104, 157, 162
Early Christian Symbolism 157-8, 161
earthworks, see defences
Easter 94, 210, 236
East Lomond stone plaque 170
East Lothian 56, 86
ecclesia 96
Ecclesiastical Architecture of Scotland, The
    157-8, 161
ecclesiastical centres/sites (see also
    churches) 15, 33, 40-1, 65, 73, 81-2,
    86, 94, 96-7, 100-1, 120, 130-3, 137-
    9, 143, 178, 197, 199, 201, 213, 220,
    222, 246, 251, 256
ecclesiastical organisation 100-2, 138,
    226, 250
ecclesiastics, see clergy, clerics
Ecgfrith, king 53, 98, 238
eclais rígh, 'king's church' 98
economy 75-6
Edderton cross-slab 167
Eddius Stephanus 53, 214
Edgar, king 202
Edinburgh 84, 121-2, 145, 157
Edward I, king 65, 255
Edward II, king 255
Edward III, king 255
Edwin, king 53
Edzell cross-head 138
Egypt 172
élites, socio-political 63, 70, 81, 83
Elphinstone, Bishop 97
*Emigrant's Farewell to the Banks of the
    May, The* 40, 42
Emmaus 192
enclosure(s) 48, 49, 50, 55, 57, 63, 64, 66,
    68, 70, 76-7, 79, 130, 197, 199, 230, 9
endowments, see patronage
Engelram, Chancellor 61
Eóganán mac Óengusa, see Uuen son
    of Unuist
Ermoldus Nigellus 210
Escomb, St John's Church 216-17, 217,
    226-7, 227, 229, 233, **24, 27**
'Escomb fashion' 226
estates 30, 51, 59, 71-3, 75-6, 100, 130-1,
    145, 230, 238
Eucharist 233, 237
Evangelists 166
exactatores 72
excavation(s) 47-8, 55, 66, 69, 79, 122, 158
exchequer rolls 59
execution places 61

Falkirk 120
false relief 150
fans, liturgical, see flabella
Farnell cross-slab 108
Farr cross-slab 167
feasts, feasting 53-4, 72
Felix IV, Pope 166
Ferath filius Bargoit, see Uurad son of
    Bargoit
ferme 73
festivals, Christian 52, 64, 210
Fife 29, 55, 69, 167, 170, 248, 255
Findchaem (*Finchem*), queen 54

INDEX

fir Fortrenn, see Fortriu, men of
Firth of Tay 31, 100-1, 246
fishing 75
flabella 188
Flandrian period 32
Flann Sinna mac Máelsechnaill 193-4, 196-7, 205
'floating composition' 200
fonts, baptismal 131
food renders 59, 72
foot soldiers 122, 125, 176-8
fords 33, 76, 253
Fordun, John of 88
Forgandenny 121, 145, 256
Forso, Forgusso 89
Forteviot 9, 11, 15, 31, 33, *34*, 36, 38, 40-1, *42*, *44*, 45, *46*, 47, 48, *49*, 50, 53, 62, 64, 73, 77, 79, 104, 144, **1, 2, 5, 6**
  Church of St Andrew 38, 40, 43, 96, 126, 131, 133, 144, 252, 257, **6, 7, 8**
  churchyard 43, 103, 104
  Church of 9, 11, 21, 26, 31, 40, 47, 51, 54, 59, 68, 70-1, 76, 83-4, 86-7, 91, 93, 95-6, 99-104, 129-31, 137-8, 140, 191, 199-200, 202, 206-8, 254
  church at 209, 210, 212-24, 228, 230-3, 236-40, 243-4, 248-50, 252
  manse 103, 109, 110
Forteviot, Baron 15
Forteviot Haugh 45
Forteviot, Lord 30
Forth–Clyde isthmus 16, 22, 23
fortifications, see defences
'fort of the birches' 35
Fortrenn, see Fortriu
fortification, fortresses 24, 29-30, 40, 42, 53-4, 77, 79, 82, 247
Fortriu 11, 16-17, 19, 21-2, 24, 35, 71, 95-6, 100, 190, 200, 245-9, 253, 256
fothair 36
Fothuírtabaicht, Fochíurthabaichth 35-7
foundation 91, 93, 196-201, 205-8, 228, 230-1, 233, 237, 240
foundation legends 91, 233
Fraction, The 236
friezes 221
funerals 64
funerary monuments, see monuments
Frebern, Ralph 25
Freeland House 121, 145

Gaelic 37, 86, 90, 94, 97
Gaels 24, 61-2
Gallows Knowe 60-1
gallows placenames 61
Garbeg 68
Garden of Eden 166
Gask cross-slab 108
Gask Ridge 73, 75, 122, 255
gates, gateways 54
Gaul 97
geology 66, 144, 148
geophysical survey 48
Georgia 221
Gibb, A. 158
Gillechrist of Forteviot 73
Giric mac Dúngail, king 24, 71, 83, 251
Giudi 82
Glastonbury 225
Glendalough 131, 210
Glendevon 248
Glendey Burn 248

Gleneagles 248
God 54, 86-7, 91, 97-8, 130, 192, 199, 201, 214, 220, 231, 234, 236, 238-40, 250
Gododdin, The 72
Goídel, see Gaels
Goídel Glas 62
Good Friday 236
gospel books 154, 166, 188, 233-4, 253
Govan 73, 100, 139, 253
governance, royal 60-2
government 52, 86, 254
Gowrie 17
graffiti 174
Graiguenamanagh 193
Grampian mountains 16
grave markers 71, 244
  recumbent gravestones 139, 184, 222
graves 48, 66-7, 69-70, 99, 178, **9**
'Gregor, King of Caledonia', king 29
Guardians of the Realms 254

Haec commixtio 236
hagiography 96, 197
hair, hairstyles 156, 172-4, 177-8, 187, 192, 203-4, 244
Hallow Hill, see St Andrews
'Hallow' placenames 41
halls 54-6, *55*, *56*, *57*, *58*, 72, 78, 87, 91, 214
halo, see nimbus
Haly Hill 38-41, 43, 47-8, 65, 70, 77-8, 82, 121, 144, 244
Haly Mill 41
hand-bells 40, 133-7, *134*, *135*, 257, **18**
heaven 172, 228
Henderson, Prof. George and Dr Isobel 225, 240
henge monuments 45, 48, *49*, 50, 63-4, 66, 68, 70, 231
Henry, Francoise 203
heroic literature 54
Hexham 214, 219, 221
Hiberno-Saxon manuscripts 154
high-crosses 103-4, 109-10, *111*, *112*, *113*, 114-15, *116*, *117*, 121-31, 137-9, 177, 193, *194*, 198-9, 205, 220, **15**
high-kings 98, 193, 196
Highlands, The 32
hillforts 39-40, 77-8, 83-4, **10**
Hill of Belief, see Scone, *collis credulitatis*
Historic Scotland 122
Holy Communion 225
Holy Cross 169
holy days 62
Holy Hill, see Haly Hill
Holy Saturday 236
Holy Spirit 237
holy water 131
Hore-Ruthven, Walter James 145
horror vacui 184
horsemen 113, 122, 174, 176-9, 221
hospitality 59, 72
hostages 247
houses 54
household 52
'Howonam' 21
Hungus son of Forso/Ferlon, king (see also Unuist son of Uurguist) 20, 26, 52, 54, 59-60, 86-7, 89-93, 95-7, 99, 130, 138, 191, 199-200, 202-3, 206, 237

hunting 27-8, 52, 114, 151, 181, 210
Hyhatnachten Machehirb 90

iconoclasm 245, 250
iconography 125, 139, 164, 169, 198, 205, 220-2, 233, 235, 237-9, 250-1
icons 234
ideology 27, 50, 62, 91-4, 99, 139, 154, 222, 231, 233-4, 238
idolatry 252
Ímhar, see Ivar
imposts, impost blocks 190, 228, *229*
inauguration rituals 63-5, 85
inauguration places, sites 22, 30, 65-6, 253-6
Inchaffray abbey 60
Inchtuthill 79
Inchbrayock cross-slab 180-1
Indo-European 36-7
Ine's Church 225
infantrymen, see foot soldiers
Ingelheim 59, 210
inhumations 69
Innes, Thomas 38
inscriptions 15, 19, 81, 122, 124-5, 131, 135-6, 139, 177, 193, 197, 202, 205, 225, 231-4, 248, **1**
interlace 105, *105*, *106*, 108-10, *109*, *111*, *112*, 114-15, *116*, *117*, *118*, 119, *119*, 126, 129, 137, 166, 193, 198, 204, 221
Inverdovet 248
Invergowrie cross-slab 108, 177, 187, 198
Invermay 33
  cross 104, 125-9, *127*, *128*, *129*, 130-1, 138, 199, **16, 17**
Inverness stone plaque 170
Inverugie 97
Iona 20, 71, 93-5, 136, 138, 193, 205, 246
Ireland 9, 48, 61, 63, 65, 70, 85, 91, 93, 97-9, 101, 130-1, 135-6, 138-9, 144, 167, 172, 174, 193, 196, 198, 205, 213, 220, 247, 250
Irish Sea 198
Iron Age 16-17, 66, 78
Israel 192
Israelites 172
íus, see laws
Ivar 247-8

Jackschairs Wood 78
Jamieson, Sir John 38
jambs 146, 223, 228, *229*
Jarlshof graffito 174, *176*
Jarrow 98
Jerusalem 97, 192
John the Baptist 172
John, king 255
Joseph 196
judicial functions/powers 61-3
justice 60-1, 73, 133

Keith and Gibb 158
Kells 172
Kells, Book of 169, 176, 185, 193, 205, 219, **21, 26**
Kelso abbey 179-80, 202
Kenneth MacAlpin ('Kenneth I'), see Cináed mac Ailpín
Kenneth II, see Cináed mac Máel Choluim

key-work/key patterns (see also interlace) 105, 113, 122, 129, 174, 177, 221, 248
Kildare 98-9, 219
Kildrummy, St Bride's Church 40
Kilrimont 20-1, 81, 86-8, 91, 93, 96-7, 130-1
Kincardineshire 16, 17, 35, 87
Kindrochit 87
King David 125, 152, 170, 174, 178, 179
kingdoms 9, 11, 16-17, 19-20, 23, 30, 52-3, 56, 60, 71-2, 86, 92-3, 125, 190, 246, 249, 256
Kinghorn 255
king lists, see regnal lists
kin-groups, see dynasties
kings (see also arch, Forteviot) 9-11, 15, 17, 19-28, 30, 38, 47, 51-4, 56, 59-65, 70-3, 76-7, 84-7, 90-1, 95, 97-9, 102, 114, 121, 124-5, 131, 137, 139, 154, 175, 178-9, 184, 191, 198, 200-1, 203, 206-7, 210, 213, 215, 221-3, 226, 230-1, 233, 236-8, 240, 246, 249, 251, 253-4, 256
kingship(s) 10, 16, 19-20, 22-3, 25, 29-30, 52, 60, 62-4, 72, 80-1, 83-5, 91, 93, 95, 124-5, 144, 179-80, 184-5, 199, 204, 207, 231, 238, 240, 246, 249, 255-6
kinship 62
Kinnedar cross-head/shaft 138
Kirkdale 225, 231
Kirk Hammerton, Church of St John the Baptist 212, 226-7
Kirriemuir cross-slabs 114, 156, 175, 177, 187
knights 25
Knockaulin 98
knot-work, see interlace
Knox, John 252

Laigin 98
Lamb of God, see Agnus Dei
Lambert of St Omer 120
lambs 170, 183, 192
Lammas 43
land, lands 16, 30, 59-60, 71-2, 75-6, 85, 91-3, 95, 99, 102, 130-1, 199, 222, 230-2, 237-8
landscape 11, 33, 47-8, 50, 62-5, 68, 70-1, 76, 82, 131, 222
Last Judgement 234
Lathrisk 55, 56
law, laws 24, 60-2, 36, 61, 64-5, 81, 86, 92, 98, 246, 253
Laws of Monifieth plaque 248, 249
laity, laymen 61, 177, 181, 191, 193, 196, 198
learned classes 72
Leinster, see Laigin
Lewis chessmen 179
Liber Floridus 120
Liber Vitae 208
Life of Bishop Wilfrid 53
Life of Ciarán 196
Life of St Paul the Hermit 237
Lindisfarne 208
lintels 146, 167, 168, 172, 198, 199, 210, 211, 212, 213, 216, 221, 224, 22
literacy 232
literature 11, 26
liturgy 41, 85, 94, 130, 133, 209, 212,

215, 220, 226, 233-40, 250
Loch Earn 31
Loch Leven 28
lochs 75
Logierait 137
'long-and-short-work' 228, 229
Long Plantation 126
lords 59, 60, 71
lordship 65
Lothian 69, 247
Louis the Pious 210
Lyon, John de 256

Maastricht 59
Macbeth, king 27, 83
MacGibbon, David and Ross, Thomas 40, 157-8, 202
Máel Coluim mac Donnchada ('Ceann Mór'), see Malcolm Canmore
Maelrubha, monk 166
'Main Perth Shoreline' 32
Majestas Domini 172
Malcolm III, see Malcolm Canmore
Malcolm IV ('the Maiden'), king 25-6, 59, 179, 180, 202, 254
Malcolm Canmore, king 25, 28-9, 37-40, 52, 203, 256
manuscripts 154, 205
Mar, Earl of 255
Margaret, queen/saint 29
martyrium 99
martyrdom, martyrs 93, 97, 181
masonry 79, 228
masons 148
mass 130, 133, 228, 233, 236, 238, 240, 250
Masterton in Newbattle, see Nebattle
meadows 75-6
Mediterranean 87
meeting places, see assembly sites
Meigle 72, 89
    cross-slabs 108, 114, 177, 181
    recumbent stone 184
    sculpture 115, 120, 137, 221
memory 63-4
Menmuir cross-slab 156, 177
Menteith 17, 100
Mercia 86, 221
Merse, The 86
metalwork 103, 133, 134, 135, 137-8, 154, 198, 221, 225, 248, 249
Methven, Battle of 255
Migdele, see Meigle
Migvie cross-slab 110
Mijas 50
Milfield 56, 57, 79
Military service 73
miller of Forteviot 27-8, 256
Miller, James 15
Miller's Acre 255
mills, milling 60, 76
Milton of Forteviot 28, 76, 104, 114-15, 121
Minnigaff pillar-cross 137
missionaries 97, 135
monasteries 20, 82, 97, 102, 139, 166, 197, 208, 248, 252-3
Mondynes 87
Moneclatu, see Monichi
Monichi 53-4, 87, 91, 93, 96

Monid Carno, battle of 72
Monifieth 87, 248
    cross-slab 108
Monikie 97
monks 28, 87, 94, 100-1, 166, 188, 193
Monkwearmouth/Jarrow 208, 213
    Church of St Peter, Monkwearmouth
Monoth, see Mounth
monuments 9, 48, 50, 62-3, 65-6, 68-71, 78-9, 82-3, 98-9
Moone cross 174
Moot Hill, see Scone
Moray 100, 138, 170
Moray Firth 22-3
Mór Breac 94
mormaer 25
Mortlach cross-slab 110
mortuary ritual(s), see rituals
mottes 40
Mound, The 145
mounds 40, 41, 43, 65
Mounth, The 16-17, 19, 87
Mount Zion 166, 239
moustaches 122, 129, 156-7, 172-3, 176-8, 187, 190, 204, 231
Moynalty 220
Muckersie parish 73
Mugdrum high-cross 130, 138
multiple estate 76
Muses' Threnodie, The 28, 37-9
Muthill 100-1
myths, mythology 11, 22, 26-30, 62-3, 72, 87-8, 115, 120, 184, 189-91, 250, 256

Naiton son of Erp 90
national consciousness/identity 29-30, 63
National Museum of Antiquities of Scotland 145, 148, 203, 223
National Museum of Scotland 146, 148, 20
Navan Fort 98
naves 184, 214-15, 217-18, 217, 223, 225, 228, 233, 236, 238, 240, 252
Nebattle 25
Nechtan son of Derilei, king 85, 94, 100, 203, 213, 224, 236
Neolithic period 48, 50, 55-6, 63, 68, 77
Newmillhaugh 45
Nigg cross-slab 170, 237, 239
nimbus 164, 170
nobles, nobility 22, 52, 59-60, 71-2, 87, 91, 102, 178
Northampton 56
North Britons 253
Northern Picts, see Picts
North Cross, Graiguenamanagh 193, 195
North Hallbank Park 126
North Sea 16
Northumbria 20, 53, 64, 69, 82, 86, 94, 139, 193, 203, 208, 212, 214-15, 217, 220, 222, 224, 236-8, 250
nose, block-shaped 122, 129, 157, 173-4, 176, 187, 190

O'Davoren's Glossary 98
O'Mulconry's Glossary 98
oars 182, 187, 192
Ochil Hills 31, 33, 37, 41, 61, 73, 75, 78, 248

Odda's Chapel 225-6, 231
Óengus son of Fergus, see Unuist son of Uurguist
officials 52, 59-61, 71
ogham 122
Olaf 246
Old Red Sandstone 148, 219
Old Scottish Chronicle, see *Chronicle of the Kings of Alba*
Ordnance Survey 41, 47
Orygynale Cronykil of Scotland 27, 28, 256
Ota 250
Ottonians 59
ownership 59-60
oxen 170, 183

P-Celtic 17, 37
pagans, paganism 65, 68, 99, 184
Paisley, *Paislig* 97
palaces 12, 23, 28, 33, 38-9, 51-6, 59, 76-7, 82, 97, 120-1, 201-2, 209-10, 252
palacium 51-2, 54, 79-82, 201
palisades, palisaded enclosures 48, 50, 68, 70, 77-9, 80, 198-9, 201, 206
Papil cross-slab 181, 187
Paradise, rivers of 166-7
parishes 25, 43, 73, 75, 78, 101, 130
parliament 254
Parwich Church *171*
Passion, the 167, 169, 172, 226, 231, 239
Passover 172
Patras 87
patronage 72, 76, 85, 91-2, 94-6, 98-102, 114, 124-5, 137, 139-40, 154, 197, 201-2, 205, 207-8, 213-16, 221-2, 228, 230-3, 235, 237-8, 240, 243, 256
paruchia 91-3, 96
Pembroke, Earl of 255
Pennant, Thomas 39
Penrith 64
personal names 12, 22, 89-90, 237, 248
Perth 15, 35, 37, 40, 44, 252-7
Perthshire 9, 22, 31, 41, 60, 68, 72, 77, 79, 83, 108, 131, 133, 136, 146, 152, 167
★*pet(t)*, see pit-
Pherath son of Bergeth, see Uurad son of Bargoit
Picardy 239
Picti, see Picts
'Pictish animal master' 152
Pictland 16-17, 19-20, 22-3, 26, 51, 55-6, 61-2, 66, 69, 73, 81-3, 85, 87, 91-8, 108, 110, 114, 120, 130, 136-9, 144, 152, 163, 166, 174, 177, 192-3, 198, 200-6, 214-16, 220, 227, 231, 237-8, 244-8, 250-1
    Northern Picts 16, 54, 70, *176*, 184
pilgrims, pilgrimage 70, 92, 97-9, 132, 192, 215, 226, 239
pit- 75-6
Pitcairnie Loch 73, 75
placenames 11, 21, 31, 33, 35-7, 41, 61, 65, 73, 75-6, 90, 245
planning 15, 53
Pococke, Bishop Richard 38

political/power centres 9, 15, 19, 25, 29, 31, 62
power(s) 16, 22, 24, 33, 60, 62-3, 71-2, 78, 82-6, 92-3, 95, 98, 100, 125, 131, 133, 154, 178, 180, 184-5, 201, 215, 222-3, 228, 231-2, 235, 238, 246, 248
praesentatio 230
priests 100, 188, 225, 236-7, 240
priors, priories 28-9, 88, 256
processions 197, 215
progress, royal 52-3, 60, 72, 91, 255-6
promontory forts 78-9, *80*, 184
Prophecy of Berchán 17, 23, 24
provinces 53, 90, 100, 184
punch 148, 150-1
Pye, Henry James 29

quarries, quarrying 148, 222
queens 87, 90, 93

Radford, Dr C.A.R. Ralegh 203
radiocarbon dates/dating 67-8, 79, 83, 254
Ráith Tobachta 36
rank, see status
Rathinveramon 80, 256
raths 40, 77
raven 237
Reay cross-shaft 138
rechtgae fénechais 61
Redcastle 66, **12**
Reformation 11, 251-2
regali cívitati 253
regia aula 54
Register of St Andrews 28
regnal lists 20-2, 24, 27, 35, 71, 88
Regulus 87, 91, 93, 96, 99, 138, 192, 200, 206
relics 64, 76, 86-7, 89, 92-9, 133, 136, 197, 215, 225-6, 228, 236, 238, 246, 248-9
reliquaries 93-4, 181, 225, 236
reliquary churches 97-9, 137, 225, **14**
rents 76
residence 21, 30, 38-9, 47, 51-9, 61, 64, 76, 83, 210, 254
resources 70-1, 76, 83, 222
Resurrection, The 172, 192, 226, 236
Restenneth Priory 210, *211*, 214, 223-4
retinues 59
rex Fortrenn 17
Richard de Moreuill', Constable 61
Richard of Stirling 26
Richardson, Dr James 203
Ribble 238
rights, see laws
Rigmund, see Kilrimont
Ripon 214, 237-8
ritual(s) 9, 10, 16, 40, 48, 50-1, 62-6, 68-70, 78, 81-3, 85, 92, 132, 184, 197, 215, 226, 228, 231-2, 236-8, 250
River Almond 41, 80
River Clyde 73
River Earn 17, 24, 31-32, 36, 43, 64, 65, 73, 75-6, 122, 255, **13**
River Forth 36, 72, 204
river names 36-7
River Ness 54
River *Tabaicht, Tabaichth* 37
River Tay 36, 80, 253-4, 256
River Teviot 36

River Tyne 86
rivers 65, 245
Robert I ('The Bruce'), king 60, 75, 255
Robert, Master 25
Roman campaigns 16
Roman Empire 214
Romanesque 198
Romano-German Pontifical 97
Rome 93-4, 97, 234
    Church of Saints Cosmas and Damian 166, *167*
Rosemarkie
    cross-slab 177
    panel 110
Rossie Priory cross-slab 108
Rosyth 25
round barrows, see barrows
round towers 146, 167, *168*, 210, 223, **22**
Royal Institution 145, *145*
Royal Museum of Scotland 122
Royal Scottish Academy 145
ruins 38-9, 43
Ruthven, Lord 121, 145

St Abb's Head 79, 82
St Andrew 54, 76, 86-9, 91-7, 99, 130, 199, 201, 226
St Andrews, see also Kilrimont 20-1, 28, 40-1, 54, 81, 88, 91-2, 96-7, 101, 138, 200
    St Rule's Church 97, **14**
    cross-shaft 174
    sarcophagus 170, 178, *179*
St Andrews foundation legend 20-1, 26-7, 51-2, 54, 59-60, 72, 81-2, 86-93, 95-7, 99-102, 130, 138, 191-2, 199-202, 206-8, 222, 237, 249
St Anthony 174, 237
St Brigit 98
St Ciaran 196-7
St Columba 54, 70, 93-96, 136, 246
St Fergus 97
St Gall Gospel Book 154, 205
St Jerome 237
St John's vision 234
St Joseph, Professor J.K.S. 48
St Laurence 98
St Machan 136
St Madoe 136
St Mirren 97
St Ninian's Isle hoard 181
St Orland's Stone 105, 108, 182
St Patrick 92-3, 197, 247
St Paul 98, 174, 181, 237
St Peter 85, 94, 98, 237
Saint-Riquier, Church of 239
St Serf's Island 28
St Stephen 98
St Tola's Cross, Dysert O'Dea 193, *195*
St Vigeans 40, *41*
    cross fragment 138
    cross-slabs 138, 167, 177, 181, 187
    sculpture 120, 137
St Wilfrid 214, 219, 237, 238
'Sacking of the Rath of Tobacht, The' 36
saints 64, 91-3, 95-8, 131, 133, 136, 170, 181, 192, 197, 225, 235
'Sanct Mavane's Mill' 41
sanctuary 225
Sandwick 68

satrap 25
Saxons, see Anglo-Saxons
Scone 22, 25, 28, 30, 61, 65-6, 72-3, 88, 252-6
'Betrayal of' 22
collis credulitatis ('Hill of Belief') 61, 65, 253
Moot Hill 65, **11**
Scotland 10, 16-17, 22-3, 27-9, 39-40, 52, 72-3, 75, 79, 85-90, 92-94, 97, 101, 104, 131, 133, 136, 138, 143-4, 151, 157-8, 202-3, 210, 212-13, 215, 247, 252, 255
Scotland in Early Christian Times 158
Scots 9, 10, 16, 19-22, 27, 30, 33, 37, 39, 61-2, 65, 72, 81, 85, 94-5, 136, 151, 176, 203, 246-7, 250, 253, 256
Scottish Chronicle, see *Chronicle of the Kings of Alba*
scribes 72, 81, 90
scriptorium 139
sculptors (see also arch, Forteviot) 151, 182-3, 198, 220
sculpture 9, 11, 40, 71, 99-100, 103-4, 115, 129, 137-40, 150-2, 155-9, 163-4, 166-7, 169-70, 174, 176-8, 180-5, 189, 191-3, 198, 200, 203-6, 209, 212, 220-2, 225, 227, 230-6, 238, 240, 243-5, 251-3, 257
architectural 190, 202, 204, 209, 212, 220-2, 234-5
classes of 104, 152
dating 124-5, 202
figural 152, 155, 198
Forteviot no. 1 71, 104-9, *105*, *106*, *107*, *109*, 115, 183
Forteviot no. 2, see arch, Forteviot
Forteviot no. 3 109-10, *111*, *112*, 114, 129, 137
Forteviot no. 4 110-14, *113*, 139, 177, 181
Forteviot no. 5 114-15, *118*, 121, 137
Forteviot no. 6 115, 121
Forteviot no. 7 104, 115, *118*, *119*
Forteviot no. 8 119-20, *119*, 137
fragments 114
lost 104, 114-15, 120-1, 126, 129, 131
provenance 103-4
schools of 152, 154, 174, 203
Sculptured Stones of Scotland, The 157-8, *159*, *160*
Sergius I, Pope 237
servants 52
settlements 32, 76
Shaftesbury 81
sheep, see lambs
Shepherd, The 170, 192
shepherds 187-8
Shetland 68, 108, 174, 181, 187
ships 182
shire 73
Simpson, Nick 115
skeletal remains 69
Skene, William Forbes 78, 157, 191, 202
Skinnet cross-slab 110
shrines 97-9, 120, 133, 222, 225
slaves 248
Smith, David 40, 42
social hierarchy 64, 70
social identity 200
society 10, 64, 76, 143-4, 209

Society of Antiquaries of Scotland 145, 157
socio-political organisation 69
Southampton Psalter 154, 205
Southern Pictland, see Pictland
Southern Picts, see Picts
Spearman, Dr Michael 101
Sprouston 56, *57*, 69, 77, 79
square barrows, see barrows
Sraith hErín, see Strathearn
staff, staves 179, 182-3, 187, 190, 192-3, 196, 198-9
Stafford knots 107, 110, 119
stakes 193, 196, 198, 200
statehood 83
Statistical Account of Scotland, The 39
status 177-8, 181, 185, 187, 191-3, 198, 200, 214-16, 220, 222-3, 230-2, 235
Stirling 26, 35, 59, 82, 84
stone circles 99
Stone of Destiny 22, 65-6
Stonehaven 16
stoups 131
Stowe Missal 237
Strathallan 68
Strathallan School 121
Strathclyde Britons 20, 73, 82, 97, 247, 253
Strathearn 11, 15, 17, 19, 24-5, 29, 31-3, *32*, 38, 53, 71, 73, 76, 78, 83, 100-1, 122, 148, 154, 222, 248, **3**, **4**
Strathmartine cross 108
Strathmore 246
Strath Tay 79
string courses 220-1
Stuart, John 104, 157-8, *159*, *160*, 202
succession, royal 21, 65
superstitions 131
Sutherland 68, 167
swords 115, 179-81, 187, 192-3
symbols, symbol stones, Pictish 68, 137, 151-2, 174, 189, 204
symbols, symbolism (see also arch, Forteviot) 104, 108, 130, 135, 151, 156, 166-7, 169-70, 181-2, 184, 188-90, 192, 197, 199, 212, 220, 222, 224-6, 231-4, 236-7, 239-40, 245, 248, 250, 255

'T' (Taylor, Mr) 38-9, 43
Táin Bó Cuailnge 184
Tara 184
tarbhfeis 184
teinds 25, 91
Tempul Mór 194
termonn 130, 197
Terrace Cross, see Tynan Abbey
Terryhoogan 136
Thana, see Chana
thanes, thanages 72-3, *74*, 75, 82
thegns 53
tidal limits 33
tithes, see teinds
Togail Bruidne Dá Derga 184
tombs 97-9, 225
tonsure 94, 177, 236
trackways 79
trade 76, 254
tribute (see also dues) 26, 59-60, 71-2, 76
Trollop, John 60
True Cross 167

Turgéis 250
tympana *171*, 224-5
Tynan Abbey 110

Uí Briúin 98
Uí Dúnlainge 98
Ulaid 98
Ulbster cross-slab 137
Ulster 97-8, 184
Unuist son of Uurguist ('Oengus I'), king 20-1, 203, 207-8
Unuist son of Uurguist ('Oengus II'), king (see also Hungus son of Forso/Ferlon) 20-1, 52, 86-7, 89-90, 96, 99-100, 102, 136, 199, 201, 206-8, 222-3, 230-3, 237-8, 240, 246, 249
urbs 51-2, 59, 77, 79, 81-2, 87
Uen son of Unuist, king 21, 90, 208, 246, 249
Uurad son of Bargoit, king 72, 89

vallum 197, 199
Vatican Library 166
Veremondus 28
Verturiones 17
Vikings 11, 17, 22, 24, 95, 100, 174, 245-50, 253
vill, *villa* 72
violence 115
Violent Death of Diarmait, The 196
Virgin Mary 135, 234
Vitellius Psalter 154, 205

Wales 133
Wales, Prince of 255
warbands 60, 72
war, warfare 95, 184, 207, 248
warriors 113-14, *113*, 122, *123*, 125, 137, 139, *153*, 174, *175*, *176*, 177-9, 181, 185, 221
Wars of Independence, Scottish 255-6
Water of May 33, 36-44, *44*, *45*, 47, 50, 53, 61, 64-5, 73, 76-8, 103-4, 115, 126, 144, 148, 244, 251
Watson, William 36
wealth 26, 76, 85, 98-9, 137, 215, 222, 248-9
weddings 64
Weekly Magazine (Edinburgh) 38
Welton, The 79, *80*
Wertermorum 17
Wessex 17, 87
Wester Cairnie 75-6
West Saxons 56
Whitebridge 68
William I ('the Lion'), king 25-6, 52, 59, 61, 73, 76, 254
Winchester school 203, 205
windows 212, 218-20, 223
Woodrae cross-slab 108, 244
worship, worshippers 38, 40, 64-5, 70, 99, 129, 132, 140, 214, 223, 234, 238-9, 252
Wyntoun, Andrew of 27-8, 88, 256

Yeadon 238
Yeavering 53, *54*, 56, 63, 69, 77, 79
Yetts o'Muckhart 248
York 92, 94